A Clear Perspect[...]
For China-Watching

Sept 3, 1972

THIS BOOK pulls together in skillful fashion the China of a quarter-century ago; the People's Republic of today; the China of the Communist takeover and of retreat to isolation from the West, and the emergence of Ping-ping diplomacy and its new approach to the U. S.

Now assistant managing editor of The New York Times, Seymour Topping has spent more than 25 years actively watching China from within and without.

In 1946 he visited Mao's guerilla headquarters and talked with the men who would become leaders of the Communist state. After three years as correspondent on the war-torn Chinese mainland, he was the first newspaperman to meet the Communist army as it entered Nanking, Chiang Kaishek's capital. He gives a vivid account of the final days of the Nationalist

> ### JOURNEY BETWEEN TWO CHINAS
>
> **By Seymour Topping**
> *Harper & Row. $10*

somewhat wryly publisher Attwood's brilliant remark at the dinner: "Chinese food is so much better in China."

He has been convinced for some time that U. S. diplomatic exchanges with Peking are indispensable—and he welcomes the meetings held by President Nixon with Mao and Chou En-lai.

But he warns that the young people in Communist China have been educated to blame the U. S. for helping Chiang and for defending the Nationalists on Taiwan, as well as for the wars in Korea and Vietnam. He writes that it will not be easy to offset these

BUT NUMBERS are meaningless when you watch one go. So are words. The press site is three miles from the launch pad — the closest you can get and still be safe. It is separated from the pad by an inlet, visited by pelicans and jumping fish.

The first sign of life is a burst of orange flame and black smoke. It explodes into a brick fire trench and spews off to either side. The flame grows more intense. The smoke be-

most put your hand through it. The rocket is, to a large extent, supported by the fuel inside its tank.

It is one of the safest forms of travel we have. The first manned launch was Apollo 8. Since then a total of 27 astronauts have flown on the Saturn 5 without ever having an accident (figuring the actual flight distance of the Saturn 5 on trips. It goes to earth orbit, then the rocket shuts down).

In airline terms that is 35,451 passenger miles without ever down).

JULES ROY

JOURNEY
THROUGH
CHINA

Translated from the French by Francis Price

FABER AND FABER LIMITED
24 RUSSELL SQUARE, LONDON

*First published in England in mcmlxvii
by Faber and Faber Limited
24 Russell Square London Wc1
Printed in Great Britain by
John Dickens and Co Ltd Northampton
All rights reserved*

Contents

influence of the Chinese intelligentsia of the time, the imperfect victory of Dr. Sun Yat-sen and the founding of the Chinese Communist party.

contest between them and in the author's autocritique, and is enabled to evaluate the diplomatic talents of Mr. Tsai and to meditate on the forms of Chinese thought. How the producer of the television film, not realizing that foreigners do not do as they please in China, insists, in a telephone call from Paris, that his crew should rent an automobile and follow out the itinerary of the Long March. Some reflections on the difficulties of being a photographer in China, an account of the insurrection of October 10, 1911, and a visit to the school where Mao Tse-tung formed his peasant cadres in 1917. How the stay in Wuhan ends with another banquet, marked by the reciprocal joy of parting company.

can imperialism, of the atomic bomb and French policy, of the manner in which God has arranged wars and other things, of the considerable progress already made by China and of the forces she represents.

K'i Ying, one of the Chinese plenipotentiaries who had signed the treaties, wrote to the imperial court: "The English barbarians having been pacified, the French and American barbarians also arrived here this year. I treated them in the same manner, designed to put them in a good humor. Born and brought up in foreign countries, these barbarians are incapable of understanding anything about the Empire. I did them the honor of offering them dinner, and I was subsequently invited to their residences. They argued among themselves as to who would offer me food and drink. These barbarians have an enormous affection for their wives, to such an extent that the American barbarian Parker and the French barbarian Lagrené brought their wives with them. When I went to see them, to discuss business matters, these women suddenly appeared to greet me. I was very ill at ease, but they seemed to be delighted. It can be seen from this that it is impossible to expect anything at all in terms of ceremonial from these barbarians, and that it is useless to attempt to enlighten their stupidity."

—René Grousset, *History of China* (*Histoire de la Chine*), cited in connection with the signing of the treaties of Nanking (1842) and Whampoa (1844)

A few more turns of the wheel, and perhaps I shall lose one of my illusions, see the Spain of my dreams vanish, the Spain of the *romancero*, the ballads of Victor Hugo, the stories of Prosper Mérimée, the tales of Alfred de Musset. As I crossed the frontier, I remember what Heinrich Heine said to me at Franz Liszt's concert, his German accent sparkling with kindness, humor and mischief: "How will you be able to talk about Spain after you have been there?"

—Théophile Gautier, *Journey Through Spain* (*Voyage en Espagne*)

A Short *a posteriori* Meditation, Disguised as a Preface

Years ago, no one was very much concerned about these incredible Chinese, relegated to the ends of the earth, and leading a completely mysterious life behind their Great Wall. Everyone was content to savor their tea, admire their porcelain, and laugh at the stories told about this bizarre country.
—E. R. Huc, *Christianity in China, Tartary and Tibet*
(*Le Christianisme en Chine, en Tartarie et au Thibet*),
Preface to Volume I

"Well, so what about the Chinese?"

I have heard that question a hundred times since my return. Are these Chinese, people ask me, as strong as all that, are they ready to blow up the planet? Do they still make that beautiful porcelain? Can you still find art treasures there? Do you still get around in rickshas? Did you really see China? Or did you stay in Peking? Were you invited into those beautiful houses where the wealthy used to live? Are there any mandarins left? Did you get out into the countryside? Has agriculture been mechanized? And what about the younger people—did you see them, could you talk to them?

I said nothing. I had just "done China" like a kind of traveling salesman. Now I was being asked what I had brought back in my suitcase. An exhausted traveler, not yet entirely recovered from my plunge into the socialist world, getting accustomed once again to driving in Paris and feeding the blackbirds of Auteuil on my terrace, complaining about the cold and the noise, and rapidly emptying my checkbook to pay off the mortgage and insurance companies, I no longer knew what to answer.

"The Chinese, well . . ."

I would willingly have repeated General de Gaulle's advice to the diplomat leaving for Peking to become chargé d'affaires: "Don't forget China is a big country full of Chinese. . . ."

When I returned to France, the first thing that struck me was the
solitude: streets almost empty of people, a countryside where I could
walk through the woods or in the fields without meeting anyone, villages
where a few lonely lights flickered in the barns and stables at milking
time. Then there was my freedom to buy tobacco or newspapers from
all over the world, to take the train for any destination I chose, to see
my friends in privacy, to hear the government criticized, to read
pamphlets attacking the head of state. I began to breathe again. Yet
at the same time I secretly felt an uneasiness I was unable to define:
if I fell ill, who would take care of me? Did men live for happiness or
to build together a common destiny? What was more important, the
possibility of contradicting and opposing authority, as precious to me
as bread, or submission to a discipline, which was capable, in the long
run, of changing the course of rivers and the destinies of individuals
and peoples? An insignificant provincial citizen, living on a divided
continent, was I really so sure of being right about the Chinese? Was
I not quite simply a barbarian from beyond the seas, and was China
not, as she claimed to be, the Empire at the Center of the World?

An atom endowed with intelligence and feeling, bound to my own
tastes and loves, I was gradually rediscovering my place in the capitalist
universe, experiencing the joy of treading the earth of my native land
gentle beneath my feet, scenting the familiar odors, running my fingers
through the warm ruff of a dog, seeing the green ponds of a village,
the clouds scudding before a western wind, the rain beating against
the windowpanes, a wood fire in the chimney place, women's lips, the
bindings of books—but on the other side of the globe I still sensed the
presence of 700 million workers and peasants, pulling carts, melting
steel in blast furnaces, and gathering excrement day and night so that
they might spread it greedily across their fields. (Seven hours' difference
by the sun did not change things very much.) While I was having my
breakfast, it was three o'clock in the afternoon in China. When I went
to bed, the sharp whistles of the group leaders were already punctuating
the dawn march of the militia in the streets of Shanghai and Chungking.

Meanwhile each day seventy thousand newborn slant-eyed Chinese
were wailing in the hospitals—the population of a city the size of Troyes.
Seventy thousand children, who would become students in red scarves,
and then militiamen or soldiers clothed in quilted cotton, workers,
peasants or engineers who would have children of their own, until
their substance was exhausted. And they would do it to the tune of a few
verses from the Marxist-Leninist gospel, spiced with the mustard of
Mao Tse-tung, knowing nothing of the outside world except its division
into imperialist and subject nations, rich and poor, oppressors and oppressed. Seven hundred million men and women working for an

average salary of fifty yuans per month—twenty American dollars at the current rate of exchange—lining up for parades twice a year, brandishing their paper flowers before the effigy of their emperor to celebrate the anniversary of the revolution or the visit of some Negro king, satisfied with themselves, proud of their poverty, sure of their cause and ready for anything.

Blindmen? Madmen? Like all true believers, yes. But by what do they measure their faith? What interests a Chinese other than China? What difference does it make to him that other people are happy in other places? He knows that in some places on earth there are others less happy, less independent than he. If he has survived the revolution, he remembers the previous misery and anarchy of his country. If he now pulls a cart, he remembers that once he might have begged and died in the streets, that he was beaten by his landlord, that foreign soldiers guarded the walls of their concessions, that their gunboats plowed the river waters and overturned any native junk that did not get out of the way fast enough.

The China of men in long robes and pigtails, the China of mandarins in jade collars and scarlet silken caps is as dead as the Europe of fortified castles, stagecoaches and barons in feathered hats. Between the A bomb dropped on Hiroshima and the first trials of the H bomb, a world was drowned beneath the tidal wave of the Chinese revolution. The China everyone scoffed at was so long disappearing that we were inclined to complain about it, while secretly hoping that it would always stay the same, an easy prey to the commercial and military expansion of the West. Today socialist China is free, independent and proud. And there is a certain provocation in the pride with which flags are flown and proclamations uttered. China's own atomic bombs exploded in Sinkiang like the first thunderclaps of a storm the world sees rising in the East, a storm which may someday provoke a planetary conflagration. The West has found it difficult to believe the speed with which China has broken her bonds and acquired an emperor dedicated to the achievement of unity and power, and therefore suspects some form of witchcraft. And if that is the case, the cure must lie in exorcising the devil's power.

Shortly before my departure for China, someone in France asked me: "Who is the emperor there now?" If, by any chance, you are still thinking of rickshas, opium dens and women with bound feet, or even if you imagine a simple-minded, peaceful China, you'd better hold tight to the deck rails so you won't be thrown overboard. The simplest way for me to tell this story is to describe my journey just as it was—with utter candor and, above all, without self-deception.

Chapter I

In which the author, in the airplane carrying him to Peking, recounts the events of his stay in Moscow, his first contact with the socialist world, and conducts the reader to Lenin's tomb and the Kremlin. In which Brigitte appears in the author's life and as a traveling companion. In which the author, allowing his disappointment and astonishment with socialist customs to become apparent, leaves Moscow and finds himself in Omsk. In which the reader makes the acquaintance of Simon, and of Siberia, and spends a night in Irkutsk.

> The space that remains before me is not the sea.
> The road I must follow is no road;
> Nothing welcomes me as I return or frees me as I depart.
> This tomorrow is not the day that existed yesterday.
> —PAUL CLAUDEL, *The East I Knew (Connaissance de l'Est)*

I felt an actual hunger, a thirst, for the China now slipping away beneath the wings of the Tupolev, vanishing in the shrill whine of the jets. Ever since I began studying the history and customs of the men who lived here, I had felt a yearning for this land. One of the passengers, who were playing cards, smoking or dozing, suddenly cried: "The Great Wall!"

I left my seat which was right at the front and on the aisle, facing the rear of the plane, and peered out through one of the circular windows. I saw nothing but a chain of blue ridges, wreathed in clouds, and then a chaotic landscape covered with blighted forests. I returned to my seat, vaguely irritated. What more would I have learned, even had I seen this Great Wall that extends for more than two thousand miles, straddling the rivers and hills of the north, barring the entrances to the plains and striding sometimes into the sea? I was preparing to write a chronicle of the revolution, so I could follow the wall for as long and as far as I liked when I went into the province of Shensi, to visit the village of Paoan where Mao Tse-tung established the Red Army after the Long March.

The dark-haired little stewardess was passing out pots of tea and bottles of lemonade, and each time she returned to her serving counter she managed to brush the cheek of her buttocks against my forearm. The Czechoslovakians in the seats in front of mine were yawning. Brigitte had closed her eyes—she had still not completely recovered from our two nights in Aeroflot's concentration camp stopover. Beneath the upswept crown of hair, her eyebrows resembled two tiny birds' wings. I was still in pain from a vertebra broken two months earlier in an automobile accident, and violent migraines occasionally stabbed my head. But I had left on this journey in spite of these, with a protective corset around my back and a tube of optalidon in my pocket. No matter how badly I might feel, at least I was not alone. Brigitte was as eager as I to know China, to photograph it. I was going to write an epic, and help make a film whose producer had joined me in Moscow.

I found an empty seat next to one of the windows and drew the curtains aside. This was no longer the yellow, parched, wrinkled and riddled surface of the Gobi Desert, which had appeared within an hour of our take-off from Irkutsk, like the bloated, dry-lipped face of some old eunuch, but a brown field of earth strewn with little lakes and villages over which there occasionally wandered the black shadow of a cloud. The China of legend, the great Western dream of opium, jade and silk, was coming closer, evoking the heroic symphony of the Long March and the struggles of the revolution. Here beneath my eyes I could already see the 400 million wretches of that earlier time, with no weapons but pitchforks, spears and rifles captured from the enemy, freeing themselves from the foreigner who colonized them and the great and small feudal landlords who oppressed them. What system could have been built on the ruins of capitalism except the stiff-necked, austere and virtuous socialism whose sinister countenance I had already seen in Moscow?

At the thought of Moscow, I frowned. The taxi drivers had cheated and insulted me, like the worst American taxi drivers. I retained a depressing impression of this enormous city and now I knew why. It had nothing feminine about it, but rather a forced masculinity, like those female policemen who stamped our passports. Nothing in it had been built for happiness; people merely worked, thought, slept and ate there. People made children there who might become members of the Central Committee of the party, but they did not make love. Even the Moscow River had been enslaved, for the city had not been built on it, but because of it or in spite of it, and all the bridges which crossed it were purely utilitarian. In order to see the river, you had to go and have lunch on one of the floating restaurants.

Ugly, brutal, stubborn, stuffed with basic truths, dressed like sacks of potatoes, harsh-tongued, seeming hacked out of blocks of stone, clumsy and yet capable of dour persistence in the most formidable tasks, these Moscovites had seemed to me crushed beneath the régime. The Russians could not send cosmonauts to the moon and flood the shops with perfumes, equip squadrons of atomic bombers and at the same time provide the people with an average salary greater than one hundred dollars a month. At first, Brigitte had enjoyed it; she was made conscious of her beauty. Men from the republics of the Black Sea or the Caspian had turned to look at her.

We had stayed in one of the largest hotels in the city, which Intourist had christened a luxury hotel. The shaky elevator got stuck between floors, the faucets leaked, the keys failed to turn in the locks, the lighting was inefficient, the service slow, and the bathtub full of previous travelers' hairs. At first we had been given rooms on a courtyard. I had protested, and the suspicious shrew who presided over the reception desk had finally given us rooms looking out on the big square and the shining white dome of the Bolshoi Theater. The comrade interpreter from the association of journalists, who had been very much upset by our indifference to his guided tour of the residences of military heroes of the Soviet Union, felt that now at last we should be happy. We were being treated like princes, weren't we? I repeated what I had already told him in the VIP waiting room of the airport, where we had looked out at the birches and tamaracks of the forests from which the landing strips had been hacked: that I was leaving for China and simply stopping over in Moscow.

"For a specific length of time?"

"One week."

The comrade interpreter, horrified, had thrown his arms up to the heavens.

In order to get certain information regarding Sino-Soviet relations during the Chinese revolution, it was important that I find someone who would listen and give me answers. But the comrade interpreter, whose name was Constantine, was completely ignorant on the subject. He would look into it at once. The Soviet Embassy in Paris had known about my trip for two months, but had said nothing of its purpose to anyone.

"Our administration," Constantine said, "is a cumbersome machine. Do not hesitate to criticize it. Unfortunately, this is the month of August and many of the comrades are away on vacation."

I gathered from all this that nothing was simple in a socialist country, and that I was going to be forced to hurdle a whole series of obstacles before meeting anyone who would dare discuss the question with me.

"Comrade Khrushchev, perhaps?" I suggested.

The interpreter smiled, but made no reply, letting me know that he was willing to play my game of the capitalist intellectual with little regard for the recognized authorities. Comrade Nikita Khrushchev could no longer bother about Stalin's quarrels with someone named Mao. But Constantine would bring the matter to the attention of the Writers' Association, and I would be given the information I needed before approaching the Chinese themselves. In the meantime, I must relax and enjoy the beauties of Moscow.

The city wearied me. I had expected it to be grandiose; it offered nothing but architectural masses. And everywhere there were muzhiks in short vests and boots, unshaven and flanked by wives in brightly colored skirts, come from every province of the country to marvel at the capital. The buses, the trains and the planes disgorged compact and dismal groups of visitors who rushed straight to Lenin's tomb or were swallowed up in the big shops. Enormous crowds wandered meekly along the sidewalks, walking the length of shopless streets, stumbling against anyone who ventured to slow down. They resembled a vast flock of unmanned machines, bumping into each other, becoming engulfed in underground passages and in the subway, and going enormous distances out of their way to circle the squares one was not permitted to cross. Occasionally, little groups of them would gather in front of an aquarium or around a foreign automobile, thrusting heads and arms inside to feel the upholstery and study the dashboard. At night the city was gloomy; one wanted to get drunk and forget it. A few infrequent automobiles stole down the pitch-black avenues, and lovers already driven from the gardens by the cold took shelter in the stairways of apartment buildings and broke the electric bulbs to make their hiding place more secret. From September to May they took refuge in this manner in every corner of the city except on the steps of Lenin's tomb—though it was kept heated to prevent the dead god from growing too cold.

That tomb was the real heart of Moscow. And on visiting days it was toward this heart that the crowd directed its steps. On such days Red Square was closed to traffic and reserved for the ten thousand faithful who moved across it step by step.

The amiable delegate from the Writers' Association who took me in hand expressed hope that the mausoleum would be closed someday, since she considered it a somewhat morbid attraction and assured me that Lenin himself would certainly have forbidden the rites that take place there if he could have foreseen them. In her company, we visited the Kremlin apartment in which Lenin had lived. We saw the sparsely furnished bedroom with its iron bed, and his office with its hangings of blue cloth, his writing table, his telephone, the straight chair where he sat at work, surrounded by candlesticks, filing cabinets, maps, and porcelain vases and stoves. From the windows in the rotunda of the

Presidium hall, with a red silk flag floating above our heads, we could look down into the kitchen where Lenin ate his solitary supper when he came in late, changing the linen and dishes himself.

This was the holy of holies, the den where great minds gathered to meditate against the background of a flagstone court and a row of cannons left behind by Napoleon. I might have become almost emotional about this little dining room and its Henri II furnishings, these bedrooms so close that their occupants must have heard each other breathing, these canes and the umbrella hanging on the old-fashioned coat rack, the suitcases and the trunks in the entrance hall. In spite of the soldiers, booted and belted in shining leather, posted like monuments before the neighboring doors, one might have thought that Lenin was simply away on a trip. With its golden domes, its finicky, highly colored churches, its clocks, its lawns and paved walks, its massive gates and towers surmounted with the red star, the Kremlin resembled a central European principality whose masters would have given more thought to their amours than to spreading the black wings of revolution across the world, but the illusion vanished the instant one came out into Red Square. Its place in history had magnified the image I had of it, and I was disappointed by its smallness, by the blatant ugliness of the G.U.M. department store which stood directly across from Lenin's tomb, and by the fervor of the Russians taking photographs of each other, standing as close as possible to the guards in poses they thought appropriate to the place.

Brigitte was also taking photographs, but as if she were bored with the whole business. Her confrontation with the socialist world had left her feeling homeless. I watched her with a mixture of anxiety and hope. Could she stand up to the fatigue of the expedition, could she put up with me? For more than a year I had nursed her like a wounded bird. Little by little, she had recovered her strength. But she hadn't recovered from her earlier disappointments. Complicated, invariably drawn into the difficulties even though she dreaded, accustomed to clinging to any rough surface, she slipped and fell on the smooth front I offered her. Everything about me seemed too simple to her: I gave without calculating on any return, I was free, I offered to marry her and to make her a part of everything I did. Unfortunately, I was descending gradually into what it is customary to term life's bitter years, and in just a few days we were going to celebrate her twenty-eighth birthday. If that constituted an obstacle and if I had sometimes suffered because she was taken for my daughter, I got used to it easily enough, preferring it to having her taken for my mother. The difference in age, at least in this respect, was of little importance, and I was ashamed of nothing, least of all of suffering like any other man. There have been plenty of young women enamored of grizzled veterans, and no one has ever been scandalized by it, except for idiots and congenital gossips.

Until now I had always preferred tall, slender women. But at this stage the fashion-model, chorus-girl type no longer meant very much to me. I was more receptive to a gentle, disturbed countenance than to long legs. I could be conquered by sensitivity and intelligence. Brigitte possessed a timid, vulnerable beauty, eyes as gray-green as the throat of a dove. She thought herself incapable of earning her living, her tiny stature disturbed her; I wanted to prove to her that a man could both admire her and be passionately attached to her. It was easy for me to do: I loved her. For six months she had known of my decision to immerse myself in this journey to China, and that I could take her with me. I did not try to persuade her, since our discussions on the subject became more and more difficult. On several occasions, weary of our hard words, I had decided not to persist. And then, as if this was all she had been waiting for, she came over to my side, bringing with her a tender consideration that conquered me once again. Refusing to resign myself to her loss, I wanted to convince myself that I was loved in return.

She convinced herself of the importance of this trip and I was profoundly pleased and grateful. She had a unique vision of the world and the images she photographed revealed a personal and sensitive talent. I had the feeling that if we traveled these roads together I might both save Brigitte and bind her irrevocably to me. It was a humble ambition of which I am not ashamed, since it placed me among those men who work and hope on their own terms; I was prepared for anything that might happen, since I wanted to attain a certain happiness that I had lacked, and also provide roots for a spirit exhausted by the quest for absolutes. During these first days, disoriented by the austerity and harshness of Russian society, agonizing over her assignment and questioning her ability to accomplish it, she drifted indecisively between her fear of failure and a natural resentment toward me for providing her with the challenge. I made every effort to understand this passing mood, took it with a smile and told myself that I would soon hear her laughter again. I helped Brigitte carry the enormous leather case in which she stored her cameras and her reels of film. I tried to give her every reassurance.

In fact, I was worried myself. Some days before our departure a kind of panic had overtaken me, the kind one feels on the eve of an examination. I felt that I really knew nothing about either China or the Chinese, and that I was going to confront one of the great contemporary problems with empty hands and an empty head. I went back to my books, studying feverishly. But at the same time, I asked myself if my system could tolerate a long stay in the Far East when two weeks in North Vietnam two years earlier had resulted in amoebic dysentery, from which I was still not completely recovered. In addition to the headaches I have already mentioned, I was having difficulty with one ear and could not remain standing for very long. If it were not for that obstinacy which compels me to seek out difficulties in spite of my repugnance for them, I would have given up the project. Everyone was going to China, all the newspapers were publishing accounts of it. What original observations could I bring back that ten other writers, more gifted than I, might not have brought back before me? At this distance everything seemed to me useless and futile. Our departure was a nightmare, but once on board the Caravelle leaving Orly with a full load of tourists, I found myself confronted with a *fait accompli,* and I was relieved.

The first Russian obstacles annoyed me. I had been naïve enough to think that people would be eager to answer my questions. I had prepared several. Had not Stalin—and it was possible to speak of him now that he filled the role of scapegoat for Soviet errors—made a mistake about the future of the Chinese Communist party when he haggled over granting it aid? Had he believed in the victory of Chiang Kai-shek, or had he really had the genius to foresee that Russia had nothing to gain from Mao Tse-tung's succession to power? Had he been responsible for the release of Chiang Kai-shek when he was a prisoner at Sian in December, 1936?

The people with whom I talked in Moscow wanted to know why I attached importance to these queries. I was given to understand that it was not possible to judge a policy from so close at hand. My insistence won out. The director of the Institute of Asiatic Studies and his assistant, a specialist on China, were recalled from vacation. I spent two afternoons with them. Another Russian Sinologist also met with me. Seated around the green felt tablecloth common to all libraries, beneath a portrait of Lenin, whose thin-lipped primness reminded me of a constipated schoolmaster, I took notes without enthusiasm.

Our disillusionment was obvious. And yet it was neither Tolstoy's Russia—the nights of princes, silver samovars, sumptuous feasts, an abundance of eager servants, fur-robed rides through gardens in troikas —nor the dark fantasy of Dostoevsky that we had been looking for. We knew that the triumph of the proletariat had swept all that away. But what had it to offer in exchange?

For these few days we missed France badly; French newspapers, with the exception of *l'Humanité,* were not on sale here. We bought it to keep some contact with our country. It dawned on me that both Brigitte and I were poor travelers. Everything was difficult, and even though we were still in the month of August it was already cold. Beneath the first sunless autumnal fogs Moscow took on a certain beauty, which would certainly vanish with the snow. The weight, the heaviness of the city diminished.

Perspectives grew softer, as they did in London, and vanished into an infinite distance. Bravely, Brigitte learned a few words of Russian, which helped us obtain a slice of toast or a glass of lemonade.

It was not that we were preoccupied with any very lofty thoughts, but simply with those of ordinary mortals. Was I going to fail in my attempt to recount the epic of the Chinese revolution? Was I going to win the heart of Brigitte or break my teeth on her as I might on a diamond? Had I made a mistake in not bringing along a large supply of cigarettes? Were the weariness and annoyance of this journey worth putting up with? Not without a certain perverse pleasure, I had had my shoes shined in the lobby of the hotel for twenty kopecks, and I had had lunch at the home of the cultural attaché of the French Embassy, with Yevgeny Yevtushenko, the young star of Soviet literature, a synthesis of Françoise Sagan and Brigitte Bardot. Tall, slender, broad-shouldered, elegant as an aristocrat in a Chekov play, the wind of genius ruffling his blond hair and washing the blue of his eyes, his views on everything were as vast and definitive as those of the Victor Hugo of the *Odes et Ballades*. He was glory personified, complaining of not being able to take a step, either in Europe or America, without being subjected to the flash bulbs of photographers, and since all his books sold in the hundreds of thousands, he found it hard to believe that in France a famous poet might have difficulty living from his writing.

We got up from the table at four o'clock, after he had made twenty telephone calls to cancel other appointments. An hour later, when I stopped by the building of the Writers' Union, I saw him again, this time in a room with antique wood paneling and windows opening on a little garden where pigeons strutted back and forth in the grass. The tables were littered with plates of cold meat and pickles and bottles of that warm, sweet champagne which creates the illusion here of *La Dolce Vita*. All his regular followers were with him, and the group had now been enlarged by a small army of movie starlets, female poets, elderly matrons and nervous critics and novelists.

Brigitte had been buying postcards and sending them to friends at home (of whom I discovered I was jealous), describing all sorts of horrors in an attempt to dissuade them from ever coming to the U.S.S.R. Trying to define the reasons for my dislike of Moscow I decided that it was because of my hatred—which she shared—of Lenin's corpse, which has been made into the heart of the city.

The week passed slowly. We went out each day with two journalists, a husband and wife working for a Western newspaper. With them, we paid a visit to the Cemetery of the Virgins, making a pilgrimage to the tombs of Chekov and Gogol. Cats and pigeons wandered about in the sun and flowers, and seated among the funerary statues, old ladies nibbled at sandwiches and left the crumbs of their meal to the dead. I was eager to leave Moscow and the shrewish guardians who watched over every floor of the hotel, but Brigitte was desolate at the thought of losing these new friends, to whom she had become attached. On the night that we left they accompanied us all the way to the departure area at the international airport.

I was sorry to be flying over Siberia at night, but since we were going toward the east the change in time would bring dawn that much faster. In the black landscape of the sky, three aligned stars glittered like royal lights. It was Orion's belt, very low on the horizon and hanging in its illustrious frame: Betelgeuse, Bellatrix, Rigel and Orion X, just above Sirius. Dawn would come over China—a China gentle and strong as wine. I swallowed a sleeping pill and closed my eyes, trying to forget the stabs of pain in my skull. The Tupolev was still lifting slowly and the sky had almost ceased to move, when a slight variation in the hum of the jets told me that we had reached cruising altitude. Three hours later I was awakened by a shrill note from the engines; the plane was coming down into Omsk. Dawn was here, smothered by clouds.

We learned that there was fog in Irkutsk and that there would be a layover. We were stuffed into buses and taken to an enormous building which circumstances had transformed into a kind of communal sleeping quarters. Hundreds of passengers, already held up here, were slumbering in armchairs and bunks, scattered over every floor of the building, blocking the corridors. At last, on the very top floor, I found an unoccupied cell. I took possession of it and we collapsed on the camp beds. The morning sun came in through the curtainless window. In Moscow it was two o'clock in the morning. Fighter planes and bombers were parked between the neighboring buildings, wing to wing. We could hear the whirring sound of other transport planes, discharging their passengers. How long would we be here? No one told us and I did not dare go out to ask, for fear that someone would steal my bed during my absence. For that matter, how would I recognize our fellow passengers, and in what language would I speak to anyone? Almost against the door of our room lay a couple of aged Russian peasants, their boots off, their arms and legs wrapped around each other. Brigitte was asleep beneath a blanket, with her cameras nearby, her face resembling that of a sad little girl.

We were awakened at six-thirty in the morning. I cut a finger looking for the razor I had taken out of its box and slipped into my briefcase. Terrified at the thought that we might be left behind, we raced downstairs and sought a place in the dining room. Children were crying. Without talking, everyone in the room was greedily swallowing smoked fish, potatoes, jams and jellies, holding their knives and forks as if they might lose them momentarily. Untidy-looking officers with blue insignia on their shoulder boards were eating like pigs. Were table manners a sign of a decadent civilization?

Suddenly, thinking we had seen the group from our plane board a bus, we leaped to our feet. The bus had disappeared by the time we got outside and we started on foot toward the row of Tupolevs. There were a half-dozen of them, standing empty in the gentle wind. How were we to recognize ours? We tried in vain. I remembered having seen in my geography books pictures of this tall grass and these endless horizons studded with factory chimneys and blast furnaces, reddening the Siberian dawn. We entered a vast barracks which served as a canteen, and found ourselves in the midst of a crowd of muzhiks, drinking tea and devouring garlic sausages. The doors blew back and forth in the wind which carried the stink of the nearby barracks' latrines, guarded by policemen with pistols at their hips and helmets with bright red bands.

In Moscow we had met Simon, the deputy producer who had preceded our little television crew. He was to assist me in making a film about the Chinese revolution, utilizing the documents and materials I obtained for my book. He was a boy of thirty, of medium height and frail appearance, so thin that he seemed transparent, and yet he ate with a ferocious appetite. A mass of thick brown hair accentuated the gaunt and dissipated look of his face. I rejoiced at having him with us, since he seemed to know the Russians and he liked the Chinese. He made no attempt to hide his sympathy for a régime which had overthrown the feudal system and built a new and strong state.

Now Simon climbed about among the Tupolevs and identified ours by a cello, which had been left lying in its case across its row of seats. Finally, nine hours after leaving Moscow, we climbed back into the plane and took off between the radar towers that searched the low-hanging sky. Since it was hidden from me by the clouds, I will never know any more of Siberia than the wind I had breathed and the tall grass of Omsk, where I imagined great packs of horses grazing. We were due to arrive in Peking at night. Between Moscow and Peking, I would have no more than a glimpse of lakes, forests, mountains, fields of snow like enormous sheets of blue silk—nothing of what I had expected.

We were moving toward the sun and were thus accelerating the course of the day. Until now I had kept my watch on Moscow time, as a kind of link with the acquaintances we had left, but this would soon have to be abandoned. Dusk was approaching when we set down at Irkutsk, on the south shore of Lake Baikal, after a long descent above forests where the crest of pines sometimes pierced the fog. There was not the slightest doubt in my mind that we would be going on immediately. We had landed with no visibility at all, and take-off was less difficult. The giant silhouettes of other halted Tupolevs, squat little fighter planes, helicopters, cement landing strips and fields of gleaming mud, radar antennae turning against the sky—this was the normal background for the intercontinental air traveler. The only thing that changed was the uniform of the customs men.

To our amazement, we learned that the flight stopped here for the night. All our toilet articles, except for my razor, were in the plane's baggage compartment, and the waiting room was shrill with the tears and complaints of children. Our passports were taken away from us. It was cold and nothing was heated. We looked at each other in silence. Other French tourists on our plane found a group of noisy compatriots, also on their way to Peking but already held up here before our arrival. They moved about a great deal and laughed loudly. Night was falling and the lights were lit. The children continued to howl. An attendant came to lead us to a restaurant reserved for foreigners. The sight of silver tableware and glasses of Bohemian crystal reassured us a little. But we scarcely touched the plates of red caviar. We had no appetites. There was no vodka and the water smelled of cleaning fluid. On our way back to the waiting room, we glimpsed the main dining room of the Soviet airlines, where hundreds of travelers were eating at untidy tables. Outside, the shriek of landing planes tore at the sky. Where did they all come from?

Our escort returned and called the names on the passenger list, as at Omsk. But this time we were conducted to the place where we would sleep. It was scarcely eight o'clock at night in Irkutsk, merely three o'clock in the afternoon in Moscow. Following our guide, we left the airport building, avoiding pools of water that lay everywhere, and walked to a poorly lit overnight lodging which was a luxury hotel compared with that in Omsk. Passengers were slumped in armchairs and on couches, and the corridors were crammed with cots on which shadowy bodies were stretched, some of them holding children in their arms, their eyes wide and staring. Where were we going to find a corner to sleep? Our female guide took a sheet of paper from her pocket and called our names again, adding the numbers of the rooms we had been assigned. I was seized with terror at the thought of being separated from Brigitte since our names were not the same, but Simon intervened, forced our jailer to open a door to which she had the key, thrust aside the people lying in front of it and pushed us inside. A minute toilet and a foul-smelling washbasin adjoined the cell. Curtains at the window would have been a useless luxury. We were beginning to understand that in a socialist country everyone was expected to live in full view of everyone else. The sheets did not seem to have been used before, and we only had to cover them and ourselves with a blanket to be warm again. Simon stopped in to see us, and I had a feeling of relief. Nothing surprised him.

"This is the way it is," he said.

Tupolevs were roaring in the night. Loudspeakers were crackling everywhere.

"There are hundreds of people camping in a station over there," Simon told us.

We wanted to leave the hotel, go out into the streets and have a look around the city, because his uncle, the secretary general of the Rumanian Communist party, had been deported here by Stalin in 1950 and disappeared. Was he dead or was there a possibility that he might be running a shop somewhere? Simon hoped that by mentioning his name at random as he walked through the city, he might obtain some information. An enterprise so foolhardy, so naïve and courageous, seemed to me to belong to the realm of Utopia. My back and head were hurting, so I put out the light and stretched out on my cot.

But where was I to find sleep when the lights of the airport flooded the room and the clamor of planes and loudspeakers shattered the eardrums? From the corridor on the other side of the partition came the constant weeping and wailing of children. Suddenly Brigitte burst into tears. I took her in my arms without knowing what to say to her. I was responsible for this adventure which had begun so badly, but not for the kind of life that existed in a socialist régime, not for this herd of cattle which for centuries had allowed itself to be led about by the seigneurs of the aristocracy or the proletariat. I had made a mistake in not coming alone to confront this world, and our first contacts with it had shattered the laughter which came so easily to Brigitte when she was happy.

When you had a million men of this kind, you called them underdeveloped. But if there were two hundred times a million, submitting to the discipline of a single party and resolved to conquer the world, they became a terrifying force. Their table manners only added to the fear they inspired. And yet these barbarians could lay claim to Tolstoy, Chekov and Gorki, and their scientists were preparing to send to the moon some new Leonov, selected almost by chance from the crowd which marched through the streets of Moscow like an army in the field, staring wide-eyed at the façades of government buildings. Unhappily, the countries where one cared to live were condemned to perish, crushed beneath the mass of men who walked for days to visit the mummy of their liberator.

We were awakened at five o'clock in the morning. Brigitte was smiling. In the restaurant Simon told us about his escapade of the night before: he had found people walking about in the streets, the food stores were open, and the movie theaters changed their programs every two days. But he had found no trace of his uncle.

"Thank you, dear Lord," I said, "for not having caused me to be born in Irkutsk, Siberia."

When the signal for embarkation was given, the passengers made a rush for the plane as a herd of animals which has been shut up in a stable for a long time will press against the barriers of an open field. In this country of order where everyone does as he is told, any form of disorder that cannot be brutally repressed comes as a surprise, to both officials and onlookers. At the foot of the ramp leading up to the plane, a female police officer channeled the flood of passengers into a single file and checked passports and exit permits once again. Since no seats had been assigned, and no one who was already seated wished to change his place, a Czechoslovakian family, separated from each other, refused to leave with the plane. The policewoman had difficulty concealing her fury. A yellow shawl on her head, an evil glint in her eye and a masculine stride, she marched back and forth between the crew's quarters and the area of conflict. It took an hour to straighten out the matter. At last, a tractor towed the Tupolev to the take-off strip and we became airborne.

Chapter 2

An aerial view of the promised land and the first walk on its soil. A feeling of bliss overcomes the author when he is greeted with flowers. How the author describes an avenue and two hotels of Peking, is invited to his first Chinese dinner, and speculates on the idea that the goats beneath his window must have eaten the instructions sent from Paris. In which the reader discovers the capital of China, makes a first acquaintance with the mysteries of its government, the grandeur of its leader, the isolation of this nation and the peculiarities of its administration, and is given an opportunity to compare the society of former times with that of today and to measure the patience which the Chinese have always shown toward foreigners.

You live at such a distance from China that the dispatch of ambassadors on so long a sea voyage should cause you considerable trouble. In addition, your envoys can have no knowledge of ritual Chinese forms. The result would be endless discussions, from which I would derive no pleasure.
> —The Emperor Ch'ien Lung to the King of England, 1793

Here is the Empire at the Center of the World. A land open to the toil of the living. The continent at the middle of the Four Seas. An enclosed life, favoring the just man, happiness and conformity.

Where men rise, bow and greet each other according to their status. Where each brother knows his rank and everything is ordered by the clarifying influence of the sky.
> —Victor Ségalen, *Stelas (Stèles)*

What European nation would permit foreign ships of war to sail its rivers, anchor in its harbors and station police in those harbors? By what right can anyone claim to impose on the Chinese conditions which Europe does not recognize? . . . It must be borne in mind that the right of the strongest is not always either the best or the surest.

In contesting the legitimacy of the claims of English commerce, we are expressing no wish for the maintenance of this old Chinese empire whose haughty and absurd civilization has wearied the world for centuries. We think that China's time is done and that her Great Wall is forever destroyed. With the facility of rapid communications which tend to bring together and mingle all peoples, it is impossible that there should still exist on the surface of the earth an agglomeration of 300 million souls, holding themselves

eternally apart, insisting through stubborn pride on living outside the great
human family. The power of steam having put an end to distances, the
peoples of the East and those of the West can no longer isolate themselves
from each other. Events of importance in Asia can no longer be regarded as
indifferently as they once were; today they are of interest to the whole
civilized world.

—E. R. Huc, *Christianity in China, Tartary and Tibet,*
Volume III, page IX

There it was, the promised land! It was flowing away beneath the wings
of the Tupolev. I waited for the high, piercing note that would warn me
of the plane's descent, and suddenly it sounded. I felt a catch at my
heart, and already it seemed to me that I was breathing more easily.

These fields of grain, these villages framed in clumps of bamboo,
were the Peking plain, surrounded by wooded hills, dotted everywhere
with temples. A vast sky welcomed us. The Czechs put away their cards
and braced themselves in their seats. When the jet engines of the
Tupolev stopped and the doors were opened, it was warm. I was
exultant, and an expression of joy brightened Brigitte's face. She was
tidying her hair. At the Chinese Embassy in Paris I had been told, "You
will be astonished by the manner in which you will be received." I
hoped, of course, that no one had ordered a band or a crowd of people,
but I wondered if some important public figure might not come to
welcome me. In that case I would feel myself bound by gratitude and I
would no longer dare utter the slightest criticism. "You will be astonished . . . " As far as I could see no great preparation had been made
and I felt reassured. I even told myself that perhaps I had been
forgotten. Without a tie, in a rumpled shirt, my hair uncombed, my
jacket over my arm, my eyes prepared to be astonished by everything, I
set foot on the concrete of the airfield.

Someone was looking for us. Among the delegations charged with
receiving passengers, ours was modest but present: a photographer and
a dignified functionary, buttoned up to the collar and holding out a little
bouquet of roses and gladioli which he offered to me. Brigitte and Simon
received theirs from the interpreters. There were two bouquets left over.
We made our apologies; the cameraman and sound engineer would
arrive a week later. Our suitcases were taken away and we were led to
the bar. I was overwhelmed with happiness. After Siberia, this was
Tahiti. I asked to have the names of our friends repeated: Mr. Wen
Peng-chiu was receiving us in the name of the Association of the
Chinese People for Cultural Relations Abroad. He was accompanied by
Mr. Shao Wen-chung, Mr. Chen Tse-chieh and Mr. Li Yuang-chieh, his
associates, and by Madame Yuan and Mr. Shu Chin-yuan, interpreters.
We lifted our glasses of orange soda and clinked them together. We
were offered cigarettes. A pleasant young woman in a uniform of yellow

linen asked for our baggage tickets and told us, with a beaming smile, that the Chinese customs would not look at our suitcases. Mr. Wen added that this little mark of attention was an indication of the importance attached here to the establishment of good relations between our two countries.

"Oh! those Russians," I said.

Mr. Wen pricked up his ears. I explained that it had taken us almost forty-eight hours to come from Moscow and gave him a brief description of the circumstances of our stopovers. Mr. Wen visibly preened himself.

Our companions multiplied their marks of attention. Mr. Wen followed my example and removed his jacket. I sensed that initial timidity and conventions were gradually fading away. We studied each other with affection. Brigitte resembled the crushed roses she held pressed against her heart.

"Madame is a photographer?"

In China there were few women in this profession. Or in France, for that matter. They were wondering if she knew how to use all this equipment or if . . . I reassured them, and they regarded her with admiration. How could one seem so fragile and yet master the art of capturing images on the wing? Then, quite suddenly, we were led away. In a setting of green plants, a monumental white marble bust of a masterful and serene Mao Tse-tung presided over the main hall, the happy father welcoming his children. In white marble? Even though I was prepared to believe everything, I was tempted to go over to the bust and rap my knuckles against it. That day I did not dare.

As we left the air terminal, a flood of warmth swept through me, and abruptly, confronted with the sweep of flowers and fountains spread out before our eyes, the strident song of the cicadas came to me like a memory of happy days. This warm plain, these orchards, these fields of grain waving beneath the wind, these tall vineyards—this was Algeria. Nothing was missing but the perfume of the eucalyptus trees, replaced here by another which I was unable to define and which perhaps existed only in my imagination; something grand and free, calling for me to leave for the villages and mountains—the odor of noon when the wind rises from the desert and beckons one to adventure. I was becoming intoxicated, and in all probability, it was all my imagination. The thing that moved me, stupidly, was the sight of docile little donkeys, harnessed to carts and standing motionless at the side of the road, without even trying to snatch at a leaf or a blade of grass. Later I was to be led across a countryside where I would have liked to stop up my nostrils in order not to breathe the frightful stench exuded by this land. In my mind, I was winking at myself; it was a good thing, once in a while, to be biased and to like without reservation what one wants to like.

The whistling of the cicadas followed us everywhere. It hurled itself at us in waves, left us a moment of respite, then assaulted us again. With constant, imperious blasts of the horn, our drivers made a path between the gleaming backs of the bicycle cart drivers, swaying to the rhythm of their pedals. We arrived in Peking by a triumphal highway whose proportions I admired. The interpreter murmured in my ear: "This is the Avenue of Eternal Peace."

I was not all that anxious to encounter eternal peace, but the Chinese have a taste for hyperbole. They might have said "the long peace," or even more simply "peace." Even in Paris we have a *Café de la Paix*.

Our hotel bore the same name as the highway. The rooms were so narrow that we had difficulty opening our suitcases; the showers were in the corridor. We managed to change our clothes. Our windows looked out on an old section of low houses with roofs of gray tile. A knife grinder pushed his wheelbarrow up the street, swinging a bell, and I thought I could hear him chanting an appeal. I felt that I had returned to the times of Victor Ségalen: "A vendor of cheeses or pastries sometimes passes outside, uttering an extraordinary cry, based on a note of anguish and resolved at the end by an astonishing and triumphant return to the key note." Then eternal China did still exist? I had no time to grow sentimental on the subject; we were being moved to the Hsin Chiao Hotel, where the rooms were less cramped and provided with baths. Was this elevation in rank due to the quantity of our baggage or to the good impression we had made? "You will be astonished . . ." I thought constantly of this phrase of the counselor of the embassy in Paris. Not everything had been precisely foreseen. The machine was adapting itself. We were content.

Before my departure, a friend had advised me not to be sparing in my use of praise. The Chinese had cultivated a high opinion of themselves. They had always occupied the Empire at the Center of the World, an empire one came to admire and which owed nothing to the accomplishment of others. The most shopworn superlatives flattered them hardly at all. They were so convinced of their importance that the slightest reservation annoyed them. Mr. Wen, however, had led me to believe that all was not perfect in China, that all the changes necessary for the happiness of the people were not yet accomplished, and that my criticism would be welcomed with gratitude.

With the cooperation of the Chinese Embassy in Paris, I had arranged a schedule. Even it was too heavy, and a thousand useless visits would be added to it. To escape them, there was only one effective excuse: I must complain of weariness. My white hair would always clinch the argument. All I would have to say was: "The day has been so full, I am so struck with wonder by what you have accomplished that it calls for a period of reflection. This is why I ask you not to be irritated with me if, to my great regret, I cannot attend this meeting tonight." My friend claimed that this would delight them. They would say to each other: "We are making an impression on this barbarian from beyond the seas. But we must not overwhelm him."

After this, my friend had added: "When you are invited out to dinner, don't hesitate to let out a good belch, even if you have to force it. It is supposed to prove your satisfaction." I knew that in the old days belching was a sign of enjoyment of good company, but I wondered if the new régime had not changed that. "Not at all," my friend had said. "In *The Three Principles* Sun Yat-sen wrote that the Chinese were considered savages because they farted at table. That is no longer done. But it is still considered courteous to belch." Brigitte and I had been invited to dine at the home of the counselor of the Paris Embassy, and the cultural attaché had distinguished himself by belching several times.

That same evening we were invited to dinner by Mr. Wen. Actually, at about six o'clock the interpreter came to tell us that Mr. Wen would see us at seven. Where? At the hotel. There was no way to escape the invitation, and there was something touching about this haste to entertain us. In China one dines early, almost immediately after work has finished. Everyone goes home at an early hour and rises early in the morning. At five minutes before seven, the interpreter came looking for us. Our host was waiting for us in the Chinese restaurant of the Hsin Chiao, which also had a European dining room, sheltered from indiscreet onlookers by a tall screen. The friendly informality of the airport had given way to a more official atmosphere, which had an element of stiffness I could not quite define. We were introduced to a new group of acquaintances. After we were seated, Mr. Wen served us himself—dexterously and too generously—from the collection of strange dishes already on the table. "You will be astonished . . ." Since that time I have been a guest at so many Chinese tables and have been so aware of their concern for etiquette and form that the simplicity of this first dinner has given me a clear idea of the estimate that had been made of us.

Since I have little taste for Chinese cuisine, I was able to devote all my attention to listening to what was said to me and observing my hosts. My friend had told me: "Never force yourself to eat anything you do not like. Leave whatever you want on your plate. No one will be offended." I followed this advice, and since I had not come to China for the pleasures of good food I was never disturbed by the fact that I did not like theirs. Everyone has his own tastes in food. Mine generally compelled me to abstinence, and I was the only person to suffer from it.

Almost as soon as dinner had begun, Mr. Wen stood up, holding a tiny glass in his hand, and launched into a speech. Since I did not know whether respect for the old feudal customs might seem out of place now, I was not certain how I should react, but I noticed that I had been seated on my host's right while the formal place of honor was on the left. Finally, I decided to remain seated and simply listen closely to what was being said. I no longer remember the precise words, but I have since heard so many such speeches that I do not think I am mistaken in reporting that my arrival in China was considered an occasion for rejoicing, that I could write of whatever I saw and that in this way I would serve the cause of friendship between the Chinese and French people, to whom Mr. Wen now proposed a toast. We all rose, toasted each other, toasted each other again and sat down.

Rice alcohol would awaken the dead. I had been served a plate of some form of tiny animal of marine origin which resembled nothing so much as a sea slug. I learned later that it was a dish which was considered a particular delicacy in China. Judging that the moment had come to reply to my hosts' courtesy, I picked up the glass, which had been refilled to the brim, and stood up. The interpreter imitated me and followed everything I said with a Chinese version, phrase by phrase, just as he had earlier labored over his French translation. The words I spoke came from the heart, and I had no difficulty in finding them. In my most poetic style, I told of my joy at setting foot on the soil of this country, of devoting myself to an account of its revolution, and of working to transform our old relationship of colonizer and colony into a relationship between friends. We toasted each other again. That night I stubbornly refused to use the knife and fork which had been thoughtfully provided for us, and insisted on a clumsy manipulation of chopsticks.

It was, in fact, quite useless to try to eat properly. Our companions scorned the capitalist theory that a meal should be a ceremony and not just an opportunity to satisfy the appetite. They devoured their food, stabbing at the various dishes and sprinkling the table with a mixture of sauces, bending low over their plates and belching discreetly. When they felt the need to pause for breath, they stood up, spoke a few words to one of us and proposed a toast. The rice alcohol, which I was constantly being urged to drink and dared not refuse, was upsetting my stomach. The succession of meats and the banalities of conversation went on. Had I ever used chopsticks before? Was Chinese cuisine very different from the French? What sort of weather would there be in Paris now?

Brigitte was nibbling at her food and had scarcely moistened her lips with her glass. She seemed intimidated by this society without women, and simply observed it silently, responding to the toasts with a smile. When the waiters at last brought the soup which announced the end of the meal, Mr. Wen, the only one of our hosts who had maintained a polite reserve and some show of table manners, carefully wiped his eyeglasses, replaced them on the bridge of his nose and began to deliver a course of instruction. With his associates listening religiously to his every word, he recalled the condition of China fifteen years earlier, hailed the work undertaken by the Communist party and dwelt on the critical judgment which a friendly partner should express. By the time he finished, his speech had irritated me. Was it possible that they really had so elementary an idea of me? Did they consider me so completely uninformed? Were they going to start from the premise that I knew nothing of my profession and teach me everything anew, as had happened when I went into the RAF at the age of thirty-six? When his last phrase had been spoken, a large smile spread across Mr. Wen's starchy features. He rose to his feet and effusively held out his hand.

We said our good nights and went up to our rooms, feeling somewhat vexed. Simon said, "It's normal procedure. They are like that. You won't change them. They want to test you." For my part, I had decided to be unendingly patient. It was the abrupt change in our normal habits that disturbed me most at the moment. It was not yet nine o'clock at night and it was time to go to bed. In Paris the afternoon had scarcely begun. Brigitte fell asleep at once, but I was wide awake. The heat was oppressive, even at night. The Chinese left the doors to their rooms open to provide some cross ventilation.

"Sea slugs," I murmured disgustedly, thinking of that bizarre food which cracked between your teeth when you bit into it.

There were few automobiles in the streets, but their horns made an enormous racket. Locomotives screamed and whistled in the middle of the night. A railway line that circled the city passed very close to the hotel, paralleling the streets. It was used by freight trains, which announced their presence by long, ear-shattering bursts from their sirens. Above the rooftops of the darkened city, lit only here and there by a few scattered lights, these bellowings as of some apocalyptic beast startled me constantly out of my sleep.

The windows of our rooms looked out on the old gray brick walls of the city. Children were playing in the high grass among little flocks of goats. Goats, in the heart of Peking, beside an ancient gate with pointed roofs! Had they been grazing on the dispatches from the Chinese Embassy in Paris? I had been asked to submit a written list of what I wanted to see, the places I wanted to visit, the personalities I would like to meet and the questions I intended to ask them. From this point on, we were to pay our own expenses at the hotel, and the cost of any trips we might make. I wondered if I were not, perhaps, being put on the same footing as the English Ambassador, Macartney, when he arrived to present his credentials in 1793 and was made to wait for weeks, with a pennant attached to his ship bearing the insulting words "Red barbarian bringing tribute." The difference between Macartney and myself was that I had come here with only one demand, and that of importance only to myself—to know China and the Chinese. I also wondered if the Chinese had not reverted, in my case and in that of all Westerners, to the reply made by the Emperor Chia Ching to his Britannic Majesty George III: "The court does not consider an object (and undoubtedly also an individual) precious simply because it has come from a great distance." I was disappointed—and I admitted it—by the feeling that my frank enthusiasm was being taken with great circumspection, and that they evidently questioned my intentions. Had I not already furnished proof of my devotion to the great human causes? That was evidently not sufficient for me to be received as a friend. They wanted to put their finger on some more tangible proof.

We had a long conference with Mr. Wen's associates, but without him, in one of the reception rooms of the hotel. We were seated in armchairs arranged in the shape of a horseshoe, and the interpreter laboriously translated every detail of my wishes, while the others noted them down. We were served tea without sugar in cups so large they resembled small pots. I was also asked to draw up a summary of the book I planned to write and of the film which was to accompany it. "It's normal," Simon repeated to me in his dry little voice. "In a socialist system, decisions are made from documents. The opinion of an embassy doesn't count. Just yield to these formalities." I resigned myself and sat down at my typewriter. I remained there for days.

Our first trip into Peking, where the cicadas still shrilled their song, resembled a kind of convoy. Compared with the crowds in Moscow, this city in which seven million inhabitants went peacefully about their daily affairs seemed almost empty. It was flat, and scarred with enormous buildings in the Soviet style. Order reigned everywhere. Carts drawn by little mules and donkeys wandered among the cyclists and bicycle rickshas down the majestic avenues which pedestrians seemed to cross whenever and wherever they pleased. On the enormous square opposite the old imperial palace, where a monument to the martyrs of the revolution had been constructed, the children enrolled in the Young Pioneers and the People's Militia were already rehearsing for the parade to be held a month later, on October 1, the national holiday which celebrated the founding of the People's Republic. They were blowing into brass wind instruments, beating drums or brandishing wooden guns, shouting and thrusting their legs out straight in front of them in rehearsal for the goose step of the march. The old people who had brought the youngest children to this rehearsal stood by silently, contemplating this new China which bore so little resemblance to their own, these battalions of young girls clutching the steel of submachine guns to their boyish breasts and staring out at us with an expression as filled with passion as the stone countenances of the Arc de Triomphe. The gentle hands, the tender smile and look, who had changed them?

When we seemed to become too interested in this spectacle and Brigitte began to take photographs, we were hastily removed from the scene and started off again through the streets. Everywhere we went, we saw urchins squatting to relieve themselves—a simple matter, thanks to their divided skirts—watched with a mixture of affection and mischief by goateed elders who were gathering mule dung. The old women, with their gray hair, shining faces and narrow eyes, were quite beautiful. A crowd of young people, standing thigh-deep in the mud of a creek that ran between steep banks bordered with houses, were casting furiously for the fish which floated down the thread of water, already half dead.

Among the orchards and wheat fields, in the air humming with the song of the cicadas, we saw the new buildings of the universities, hotels and ministries. Overwhelmed by the heat, we paused at the far end of the old imperial palace, but our guides insisted that we climb the so-called Hill of Coals constructed from the earth that had been excavated for the moats. From this point, we looked out over the Imperial City, its gardens and rooftops, curling upward at the corners like the horns of a bull or the tail of a dragon. In the heat haze they glittered as sharply as the scales of a fish. In the distance we could see other rooftops rising above the gray level of the city, wreathed in the mist and smoke of factories. In the courtyards beneath us, which once had known only the tiny, precious feet of courtesans, regiments of children scratched at the earth with their fingernails, uprooting the grass that grew between the paving stones. Everything must be completely renovated for the festival, so that the eyes of foreign guests would not be offended by the sight of anything unfinished. Reviewing stands were being built, the gates were being repainted in red lacquer. The people were taking possession of all the symbols of past despotism, stamping them with their own imprint and the formulas approved by the new régime.

The members of my escort, who had doubtless already served on other missions of the same kind, showed me all this with the tranquil pride of men who are perfectly sure of themselves. Mr. Shu, the interpreter, often stumbled over words and shades of meaning. He was a good bureaucrat, experienced and somewhat cynical. As a matter of conscience, he listened attentively when I grumbled something or muttered a remark to Brigitte, who was collapsing under the weight of her equipment cases. Our foreheads were bathed in sweat and we would have liked to relax and breathe a little, sit down on a café terrace and sip an orangeade, as we would have in France. I bought a straw hat, a fan of palm leaves and some light felt slippers. We were spared nothing.

We were even taken to see the tree—strengthened with cement and protected by a railing—on whose lowest branch the last Ming emperor had hanged himself when rebel forces reached the gates of Peking. The defunct dynasty made me think of the new one.

"Where does Chairman Mao Tse-tung live?" I asked.

They glanced at each other in embarrassment, and I realized that my question was considered improper. Mr. Chen replied that they did not know, that the Chairman traveled a great deal in China and that, since he possessed nothing, he had no permanent residence. He was not a capitalist chief of state. I knew that he stayed at three or four secret residences in Peking, and that since the attempt on his life in 1956 great pains had been taken to protect him from whatever adversaries still existed in China and from foreigners who might have desired his overthrow. Scarcely half a century ago, the naval doctor, Victor Ségalen, had anxiously awaited the return of his friend René Leys, who had made his way into the Imperial City disguised as a courtesan. Even in those days the emperor changed his room every night to frustrate the plots against him.

The Forbidden City still existed, bathed in the violet glow of wisteria, girdled with successive walls and gates which once could be passed only with the help of gifts for the eunuchs. No one knew any longer where it began or where it ended; it was everywhere. My companions did their part to expand its limits. Nothing was easier for them; they were ignorant of details and their respect had made them dull. They lowered their eyes when they said "Our Chairman," just as people had once lowered their eyes when they said "Son of Heaven" or "Master of the Ten Thousand Ages," the only names for the emperor that one dared pronounce. I should not have been surprised to see them bow when they passed the busts or statues which reigned over the classrooms, the entrances to schools and factories, the study halls, and the lobbies of stations, hotels and stores. His image and those of the heroes of the revolution could be found even in the cells of the last lamas of the last Buddhist temples. Enlargements of his infallible handwriting were on display in a park museum, and a guard had forbidden Brigitte to photograph them. I asked why. I was told that it was not done. One does not photograph Holy Writ; one worships it. Years ago doctors dared not touch the emperor with their hands, or even with a stethoscope; they simply asked in what part of the precious body the ineffable person was suffering.

"You would be wrong to think that this is a matter of a cult of personality," Mr. Chen told me. "The people venerate the Chairman, and that is all there is to it."

I thought it best to silence the reply that burned my lips: for centuries, so long as he possessed the mandate of heaven, the people also venerated the emperor and called him affectionately "Mother of the Empire."

The rain came down at last, so hard that one would have thought that the heavens had been stopped up since time immemorial, and then it slackened to a drizzle. The fan I had asked for did no more than stir up the stifling heat. T'ien An Men Square was temporarily emptied of its rehearsing militia. I went on typing up my reports and summaries of books I had not written. Brigitte was bored. In the European restaurant of the hotel, we found that we could obtain cold beer and food that was vaguely international. The alcohol served at the bar was undrinkable. I drank it however, and drank it with pleasure after I met the correspondent of France-Presse, Jacques Marcuse, an enormous and lanky blond type, warmhearted and ironic, with a monocle eternally clamped in his eye. He loved China, its cooking and its warm wines, but detested the Chinese Communists. Elegantly dressed, always delayed because he had had to send off a cable, he was a never-ending source of scathing remarks about a régime which appreciated neither his humor nor his courage. His wife sometimes accompanied him, gentle and silent as a pleasant dream.

Other journalists constantly drifted in and out of the bar, as lost as we were ourselves. Their primary complaint was with the rigid compartmentalization in which they were held, and which gave every chance encounter an inestimable value.

Alternating waves of sunlight and rain, marking the end of summer, rolled across Peking. On fair days open-mouthed hordes of children stood about admiring the militia parading across T'ien An Men Square to the sound of march music. Each morning I gave my Chinese contacts a few pages of the program I had been asked to outline or of the questions I wanted to ask public officials. The interpreter translated them, and the text was then studied at the headquarters of the Cultural Commission. The days passed with no sign of reaction, and I sensed that it was futile to hope for any acceleration of the machine which had taken us in charge. On the day after my arrival, a note concerning me appeared in the information bulletin which the soft-slippered hotel bellboys slipped under the doors of the rooms: "Roy, Jules Désiré, French writer, and two other French guests have arrived in Peking for a visit, on the invitation of the Association of the Chinese People for Cultural Relations Abroad. They were met at the airport by Wen Pengchiu, a member of the council of the Association, and other officials."

The tenor of this paragraph said a great deal more than its two short sentences, and the bulletin itself, edited in the style of all bureaucratic writing, constituted the only glimpse left to us of the outside world. We learned from it that Prime Minister Chou En-lai had received a delegation from Tanganyika, or that the President of the Republic Liu Shao-ch'i had seen a representative of the Japanese Communist party. We could read an editorial reprinted from the *Alger Républicain* or the text of the "serious" warning issued to the United States on the occasion of the three hundred and eighteenth violation of Chinese territorial waters by American warships in the Formosa Straits, or even a Cambodian protest against the report of the mission sent to that country by the Security Council of the United Nations. Since no Western newspaper was on sale in Peking, not even *l'Humanité*, we had the impression of being cut off from the world. The Chinese press, if we had been able to read it, would have taught us nothing more, except perhaps for a few edifying stories on the increase in production in the factories or the people's communes. Radio and television blared out the same visits to laboratories and the same acclamations for the chairman of the party.

I had no need to wonder that people in Europe and America knew more about what was happening in China than I did in Peking. I discovered myself light-years removed from all that at home was the foundation of my love for men and life, and a kind of terror began to take possession of me. I was tempted to flee. But to reach even the frontiers, I would have had to cross thousands of miles of plains, mountains and deserts, two of the largest rivers on the globe, dizzying heights of snow, tornadoes, and multitudes of customs men and passport control offices. I held my tongue and waited. Simon begged me not to lose patience. "It always takes a long time to get things going," he kept repeating, "but once started you will not stop again and you will get what you are looking for."

I had prepared for this journey conscientiously. With the help of a Chinese scholar, I had spent six months reading all the principal works that had appeared on China in the past century. I made notes on what seemed to me the most original and interesting observations. I studied history, society, customs, geography, philosophical and religious thought, the imperial régime, the Kuomintang and the Communist party. I made a card file of all the events which had brought on the revolution and established a detailed chronology of the revolution itself. I pored endlessly over the works of Mao Tse-tung, Confucius and Sun Tzǔ. I analyzed the biographies of the more important actors in the drama. I went to classes. Cloistered as a Benedictine monk, my walls hung with maps, my tables littered with specialized books, I immersed myself in Chinese culture, I saw only people capable of expanding my knowledge, I talked of nothing but China. By the time of my departure, the file of my notes measured almost two feet in height. I believed myself equipped to understand the problem.

I did not speak Chinese, even Mandarin Chinese, to say nothing of the ten categories of dialects, and I had deliberately refrained from straying into this field. I have little gift for foreign languages, and had no desire to devote years of my life to this one. I knew that years of dedicated study would have been required simply to write it as well as a simple provincial student. How could I expect to speak and understand this birdlike tongue which includes neither tenses for verbs nor singular and plural for nouns, neither pronouns nor adjectives, and is based on a juxtaposition of monosyllables deriving their true sense from their singing tones? Henri Michaux had warned me that, of the several thousand characters required to read and write, there were not five that could be recognized at first sight and not a hundred that were simple. I would have had to know three thousand to read a newspaper, and five or six thousand to carry on a conversation with an educated man. Pronunciation varies throughout China. People do not really understand one another, except in writing. And in addition to this they employ ellipses, complicated turns of phrase and an order of thought which to us is disorder. In short, I gave up any thought of involving myself, even casually, in this science and art of language. But for that matter, a knowledge of it would doubtless have been of no use to me in learning what I hoped to learn about China, since everyone would have mistrusted me. In Peking I met some French Sinologists employed in the work of translation, and found that they had few outside contacts. They saw their Chinese colleagues only at official gatherings, and their knowledge of the language led to nothing more than the exchange of a few words with a taxi driver or a salesgirl in a shop.

To kill time while our behavior and files were being passed beneath the microscope, we visited the city and its surroundings. We were taken through the old imperial palace at a fast trot, because it was testimony of an abominable and vanished epoch, and as a result we scarcely glimpsed the gold and purple columns and ornate ceilings of the reception and audience halls, council rooms and throne room. A guardian who resembled the mechanical elephants on his timepieces showed us a collection of clocks whose mechanisms seemed the only living thing in this desert of shadows.

At the foot of the western hills, a series of pagodas sheltered gigantic statues of Buddha. We breathed in the secret perfume of ancient China, where the gods held rose petals in their hands. The members of our escort laughed; the revolution had swept away this litter of imbecile legends. China had never been anything more than casual in her belief in the teachings of religion, and now she believed only in the teachings of Marx and Lenin. The temples no longer had worshipers, and the lamas lived on the charity of a government which consented to keep them, like animals from another age installed in gilded cages, as

witnesses to the obscurantism of the past. And when they had done their
duty to their god, they too celebrated the grandeur of the present, with
an ironic bitterness they carefully concealed.

We were eager to learn. We greedily devoured every scrap of information that was fed us. At this writing and at this distance, in the serenity
of the snow-covered fields of Burgundy, I have a better measure of the
hunger we had for China and of the naïveté with which we listened to
everything we were told. And yet how could I not have been struck by
the excesses of the public homage to Mao the liberator, and by the
separation of China into two social classes: the masses and the representatives of the party which controlled the country? The members of
the cultural association who surrounded us belonged to the second
category, and their particular jobs made them privileged characters. To
forestall any objections I might have had, they told me that, like all
party functionaries, they spent a month each year in one of the people's
communes, sharing the life of the peasants, bringing in hay, gathering
the harvest or plowing the fields.

I turned to our interpreter, Mr. Shu. "You, too?" I asked.

Direct questions embarrassed Mr. Shu. He never dared answer them.
A translating machine, he had no right to think since his task consisted
solely of translation. So he translated my question to those who had the
responsibility of leading me about and awaited their answer.

"Yes," he said at last.

"Where?"

He received no authorization to answer that question. I was growing
too curious. And since he slumped exhausted into his seat the minute
we got into the car, I had some difficulty picturing him stripped to the
waist, bent beneath the weight of balancing poles, trotting across the
rice fields.

Brigitte signaled me to drop the subject. I shut up and resigned
myself to listening to the Chinese describe the old society which the
revolution had shattered. But the few things I had seen, the behavior
and language of my companions, led me to believe that what I had
learned from books and the accounts of other travelers had also been
shattered into a thousand pieces.

I learned very rapidly that the average Chinese of today considered
himself proud and free. He was no longer a subject of a handful of
European nations, of Russia or of Japan. He was in command of his
own homeland, and one could see in the devotion to Mao Tse-tung each
citizen's recognition of himself in the man who had found a means of
conquering the foreigners, the war lords and the great landowners.
China possessed an army, a stated policy and a touchy sense of national
honor. Each time I passed T'ien An Men Square, where rehearsals were

still being held for the October 1 parade, I was told: "So long as we are threatened by American imperialism, we will be obliged to prepare for our defense." I replied that we Westerners had revolted whenever we felt that our liberties were being taken away from us, and made little effort to conceal my astonishment that the Chinese had waited so long to take up arms. Since the dawn of time they have been the victims of one of the most terrible climates in the world, of droughts which prevented the rice from growing and destroyed the cattle or of floods in which millions were drowned. At such times famine compelled hordes of people to leave their homes and take to the roads, devouring the bark of trees, bloating their stomachs with earth and straw, and fertilizing the fields and cities with their wasted bodies. Soldiers guarded the homes of the rich, barricaded among their possessions. Foreign concessions closed their gates and took refuge behind the cannon of their warships. Russians, Japanese, Germans, Frenchmen, Belgians, Italians, Hungarians or Portuguese upheld the rule of the landlords for fear that they and that rule might be swept away together by a tidal wave of miserable people transformed into enraged revolutionaries.

After the First World War, while the working masses of Europe were employing the strike as a means of gradually attaining their right to the dignity of poverty, men and women were still dying of hunger in China. They were beaten with clubs when they demanded justice; they were humiliated by the sight of foreign flags floating above their native land, foreign ships docking freely in their ports and sailing their rivers, foreign merchandise flooding their markets, and their national government bowing down before the demands of foreigners. Anarchy had taken the place of the prostrate empire. The First Republic endured only a few months, and then was overwhelmed by the feudal war lords, both small and great. Russia, Japan and the West argued for possession of this old dream that had troubled the sleep of adventurers since the travels of Marco Polo—compounded of opium, rare porcelains, art treasures and coolie labor. The fury of a few free men had captured the Bastille in 1789, but the Chinese waited until more than a century later before revolting, and a century and a half before seeing the triumph of their revolution. This patience astounded me.

Far from admiring, I was indignant about it. Although I personally had played no part in it, I felt ashamed at having participated, even indirectly, in the enslavement of so great a people, and indignant that this same people should have submitted in silence to so much humiliation. In their place, I would have screamed defiance, incited rebellion, raised bands of patriots and scorned the threat of prison. Weakness and misery do not break men who prefer death to the yoke of servitude. Somewhere there was an explanation for this inertia, and I was stubbornly seeking it.

Chapter 3

A bird's-eye view of the dynasties and the emperors, the Empress Tzu Hsi and the attempts at reforms at the beginning of the twentieth century. In which the author discusses the birth of Mao Tse-tung and his childhood, and reports on conditions in the countryside at that time and the nature of the peasant revolts. In which it seems necessary to dwell for a time on Dr. Sun Yat-sen and then return to the adolescent Mao Tse-tung, to appraise the influence of the Chinese Intelligentsia of the time, the imperfect victory of Dr. Sun Yat-sen and the founding of the Chinese Communist party.

We wear chains although the eye does not see them and we are slaves although we are called free men.
—OSCAR WILDE, *A House of Pomegranates*

They have awakened overnight from a sleep of thirty centuries and they will not go to sleep again.
—ANDRÉ MALRAUX, *Man's Fate (La Condition Humaine)*

It is certain that the powers of which we have just been speaking (England, Russia and the United States) are very much concerned about the revolution which has shaken the Chinese Empire to its foundations and which will bring about complications in the policies of Europe more grave than any that have ever existed before.
—E. R. HUC, *Christianity in China, Tartary and Tibet,*
Preface to Volume I

. . . a great people, the most numerous people on earth, a race in which the patient, laborious and industrious capacity of the individual has, for thousands of years, compensated for the collective lack of cohesion and method, and has constructed a very unique and very profound civilization; a vast nation, geographically compact and yet lacking in unity, extending from Asia Minor and the steppes of Europe to the immense shore of the Pacific, from the Siberian ice to the tropical regions of India and Tonkin, a state older than history, always bent on independence, constantly striving toward centralization, instinctively withdrawn into itself and disdainful of foreigners, but aware and proud, unchangeable, perpetual—such is eternal China.
—CHARLES DE GAULLE, Press Conference of January 31, 1964

Who could hope to measure with any degree of precision the scope and
strength of this empire on which the sun never sets, an empire more
than four thousand years old, governed at one moment by myth and at
another by terrible reality? Its princes invented writing and the calendar, designed clothing, bred silkworms, built dams to hold back the
waters and ramparts against the barbarians from the north, taught
music and agriculture, dug the Grand Canal as a means of communication between the two great rivers of China, battled against their own
feudal lords or extended the frontiers of their kingdom by subjecting
their neighbors. Sometimes patrons of literature and science and sometimes burners of books to stop the march of history, peaceful or warlike,
simple or debauched, reformers or tyrants, makers of laws, distributors
of lands, economists, occasionally artists and dreamers, virtuous or
dissolute, zealots or infidels, they used kindness in pacifying the land or
cut off heads by the hundreds of thousands, alternately unifying and
dividing. "A man with a protuberant nose, large eyes, the chest of a bird
of prey, the voice of a shrew, the heart of a tiger"—this portrait of Shih
Huang Ti the unifier, builder of the Great Wall, terror of barons and
scholars alike, might have been that of any one of many princes. They
claimed to have one foot in heaven, and no one reached their presence
without having passed through an endless succession of gates and
legions of soldiers, courtesans and eunuchs.

Sun Kings or Caesars, Sons of Heaven, reigning through terror or
magnanimity, mortal gods sacrificing bulls on the first day of each new
season to obtain the favors of the immortal gods or plowing fields in
golden chariots, traveling across the land dazzling their subjects with
the splendor of their escort, seeking desperately through reform or
violence to establish laws which would permit their country to live, their
dynasties lasted so long as they insured order, then collapsed when
discontent, calamities and restless men, in the name of justice, raised
some soldier or local chieftain to power and made him the new emperor.
Then he, in turn, would attempt to wrest order out of chaos, whip in
hand, imposing his will by poison or the sword and drinking from the
skulls of his enemies.

Sometimes these men were foreigners, but as a rule they were swiftly
conquered by Chinese civilization, customs and sophistication, and their
original hostility toward China would be transformed into a furious
nationalism, prepared to use any means to subdue the opposition.
Whether the dynasty was that of the Chou, the Han, the T'ang, the
Sung, the Ming or the Ch'ing, corsairs, brigands, administrators, generals, philosophers, Mongol horsemen or Manchu princes, idiots or
dilettantes, they were all driven to excesses by the very extent of their
power. When the degradation of customs and the influence of eunuchs
took the place of the wisdom and counsel of mandarins, they wallowed

in blood, but the chief of a new dynasty did not always seek to over-whelm his predecessors or to murder them off. Custom decreed that the memory of the departing emperor should be cherished and that he should continue to reign, in a manner of speaking, over a token empire, so that nothing would be disturbed in the rhythm that existed between heaven and earth, and no phantom would rise up in the night and cry vengeance. In China it was sometimes like that.

In imitation of the Soviet style, the Communists were the first to introduce insults into the vocabulary. Hatred exists everywhere, but its vulgar expression is left to the rabble. The culture and wisdom of men of good taste demand respect for proprieties. Dr. Sun Yat-sen had no fondness for the Manchu dynasty, but when he became President of the Republic he ordered that "magnificent deference and glorious honors" should surround the child Emperor Hsüan T'ung, who had been forced to abdicate, along with his regent. He permitted him to retain his title and his palaces, and he himself rendered the homage of the new cycle at the tombs of the Ming emperors.

He did this because there is a tradition relating to princely succession called *ming*, the mandate of heaven, without which one cannot govern. This supernatural power is compounded of the popular assent accorded worthy men and that divine protection which manifests itself by main-taining the rivers in their beds and regulating the fall of the rain and the light of the sun. Until the revolution, the ruling classes always took care to do nothing, at least outwardly, that would shatter this comfort-able situation, and to this end they maintained the fiction that every-thing continued as it had always been and that the foundation of the state had not been shaken. Thus no insult had occurred to wound the ancestors, sons obeyed their fathers, wives served their husbands and slaves their masters, farmers paid their rents to the landowners, chiefs of clans collaborated with the tax collectors, the mandarins quietly carried out the orders of the provincial governors and the ministers expressed the will of the prince.

Even so, the empire had ended badly. The Taiping rebellion, reaching almost to the walls of the palace, had resulted in the succession to the throne of the child of an emperor dead from poison and debauchery. A concubine, daughter of a Manchu general and mother of the heir apparent, became regent at the age of twenty-six. Beautiful, ambitious, greedy, ignorant yet intelligent, cruel and corrupt, she reigned for half a century, surrounding herself with perverted ministers and hirelings. Having obtained supreme power through intrigue and plotting, she con-sidered the empire her private property. Taxes were used to satisfy her whims, and she subdued revolts with the help of foreigners whom she then repudiated. A eunuch who was in love with her, and was later flogged to death at her order, supplied her bed with lovers recruited from the city slums. They were brought to the palace, blindfolded, in a black carriage with yellow silken tassels at the roof corners, and when the Empress had done with them their throats were cut in the cellars. Occasionally, she stabbed them to death herself before they had left her bed. She poisoned her childless son and proclaimed his five-year-old cousin emperor.

The morality of the woman who was generally referred to as the Old Buddha was on a level with that of the Borgias. Tzu Hsi's foreign policy was a tangled web in which she attempted to trap the diplomats of other countries. A modern army was too expensive and money found its way into too many pockets. During these years, almost unnoticed by the rest of the world, Japan had become the greatest power in the Far East, and in the Sino-Japanese War of 1894–95 China was conquered in nine months, her navy destroyed and her army reduced to fighting with bow and arrow. A sense of utter humiliation swept the country, and the already dying empire began to fall apart completely. Japan demanded Formosa and the Pescadores; Russia, a part of Manchuria; Germany, the province of Shantung; England, Hong Kong, Shanghai and the exploitation of six provinces at the mouth of the Yangtze; France, the island of Hainan and three provinces in the south; the Italians, the port of Ningpo. It was a general sharing of the spoils. Railroads were constructed so that full benefit might be derived from these arrangements, and the contracts were concluded with modest ninety-nine-year leases which disguised annexation as a lifetime rental. For the Chinese, there remained only the heart of China (territory where foreigners dared not venture), the signal honor of working for the aggrandizement of the West and the leisure to meditate on their own misfortunes.

A few Chinese intellectuals were convinced that something must be done to save China, primarily that reforms must be instituted that would enable her to defend herself. They succeeded in convincing the young emperor himself. For a period of a hundred days, reforms followed each other in rapid succession: for the first time, the traditional examinations for the post of mandarin included questions on modern subjects; military schools and a translation service were set up. The Dowager Tzu Hsi quickly put a stop to all this, interned the emperor on an island within the palace, executed most of the liberals, fanned the flames of hatred for the foreigners and secretly aided the revolt of the Boxers. Missionaries and Christians were massacred and churches and legations burned. A new international expedition liberated the besieged foreigners and then pillaged Peking. Tzu Hsi fled in the middle of the night, disguised as a peasant, and did not return to her palace until an uneasy peace was restored a year later. In 1904 Japan attacked Russia, seized Port Arthur, inflicted a disastrous defeat on the Russian fleet and obtained total freedom of action in Korea, bordering on the Manchurian provinces she coveted.

When the dying Tzu Hsi ordered the emperor strangled before her eyes, gave the crown to a three-year-old grandnephew and then died herself, the havoc was total. The whole of China was working simply to pay off the indemnity of one hundred million pounds which had been exacted as reparation for the fires and massacres. Foreign garrisons occupied Peking and controlled the nation's communications system. Before they could rid themselves of the foreigners, it was necessary to liberate China from herself. Mao Tse-tung was fifteen years old.

Mao Tse-tung was born December 26, 1893, just one day after Christmas, in the village of Shaoshan, about sixty miles from Changsha, the capital of Hunan province. At that time it was customary for the local peasants to lead their flocks of ducks from one rice field to another, fattening them up before selling them. Had these men chanced to lean on their long poles and glance up at the sky on that particular night, they must have seen a red star rising above the mountains. And if they had understood the celestial message, they would have returned the ducks to their wickerwork pens and gone themselves to the foot of a limestone cliff which the young men of the village made a sport of climbing on Sundays.

In this spot Mao's father cultivated the twenty *mous* (three and a half acres) of rice field that he possessed. This fact alone made him a rich peasant, since the majority of others owned nothing, not even a roof of their own, and worked as day laborers or farmers for the large land-owners. He was a hard man, whose father may have been an ex-noncommissioned officer in the army of a war lord who had remained in the region after taking part in the suppression of the Taiping rebellion. I have been unable, however, to verify this fact; the Chairman's hagiography feeds on mystery.

His name was Mao Sun-sen and, in this land of misery, he thought of nothing but his property and of the best means of making it thrive. He had three sons, Mao Tse-tung, the eldest, Mao Tse-ming and Mao Tse-tang. Emi Siao, a classmate and admirer of Mao Tse-tung's, describes his comrade as a born revolutionary. Even before he had reached the age of discretion, the young Mao was in rebellion against the tyrannical authority of his father. Mao's mother, a gentle and pious woman, brought up her son in the Buddhist faith. In the vast rural areas of China, woman's work is the hardest there is, and even the livestock receives better care. Women do the cooking and housekeeping, take care of the animals, go to the well for water, raise the children, spin the cotton, mend the clothing and work in the fields, trotting back and forth on the footpaths balancing on their shoulders heavy loads of manure, vegetables or straw. At the age of thirty they are old women. If the man is not happy, he beats them. If he is rich, he installs a young concubine in his bed. Women are put on earth to serve men and they eat in the kitchen, standing up, like servants. At least, this is the way it was.

Mao's father knew what it meant to be a Chinese peasant. Of poor birth, he had for a long time occupied the lowest position in the scale of Chinese society of the nineteenth century: he had been a soldier. Later, as a petty tradesman—he bought rice from farmers even poorer than himself, transported it to the city and resold it there—he managed to buy the strip of land which he worked, and then, through stringent economies, to acquire still another acre. In a world of beggars this made him a rich man.

One day, after having been beaten by his teacher, the young Mao ran away from school and did not dare return home. When he was found, three nights later, even his father showed a certain pride in his action. On another occasion, when he was thirteen, his father treated him as a good-for-nothing in front of guests, and the enraged Mao left the house, pursued by a stream of paternal maledictions. It must be remembered that in the China of that day, where filial piety was the first and most important of duties, a son could not look for pardon if he rebelled against his father, the absolute chief of the family and judge by natural right. He could not hope to get a position or even be a good citizen if he had not first been a good son. If he had struck his father, Mao could have been condemned to death, as was his young friend, P'êng Têh-huai, who came very close to being executed. Under the legal code established by the Emperor Chia Ching (1796–1820), a son whose disobedience caused his father's death in an accident was punished by strangulation. When his father followed him that night, Mao stood at the edge of a pond, threatening to hurl himself into it and refusing to offer more than a halfhearted apology. The father gave in. It was at that moment that Mao realized that revolt pays off better than submission.

During the famines which occurred periodically in those years, the government decapitated agitators and peasants who rose up against the landowners. Mao's father supported this practice when some of his rice convoys were attacked and robbed. Mao himself came under the influence of a teacher who was opposed to the established religion. But the thing that struck his young mind most forcibly was the reading of a brochure on the dismemberment of China; the anonymous author denounced the occupation of Formosa and Korea by Japan and the loss of suzerainty over Indochina, Burma and other areas of China. Many years later, Mao told Edgar Snow: "After reading this, I felt depressed about the future of my country and I began to realize that it was the duty of everyone to save her."

Everywhere in China there were young men who thought as he did. The red-hot iron of shame had pierced their skins and touched their hearts. They knew little of their native land beyond the fact that it extended from the Gobi Desert to the Tropic of Cancer and from Shanghai to the Himalayas, but they knew that in every part of it men lived in servitude. Condemned by the climate to unceasing labor, attempting to extract a meager thirty-six hundredweight of grain a year from each acre of the reluctant, poorly fertilized soil, crushed by the enormous taxes they were forced to pay the landowners, threatened with the most severe punishments if they refused, destined to grow old and die in a situation that was hopeless, they dreamed of overthrowing the régime that enslaved them. How could they have had the normal re-actions of free men, when they had lived for four thousand years under the heel of the rich and the mighty, the burning sun and the flooding rain? Slaves of their fathers, their landlords and the seasons, when hunger drove them to revolt, they pillaged, burned and killed with the savagery of maddened slaves.

These peasant uprisings, set off sometimes by a small group of farmers who had refused to pay their taxes or by a secret society whose leaders had been decapitated, thread the entire history of China with their anarchical lightning, breaking out as swiftly as a summer storm, and setting fire to an entire province as a spark ignites a parched prairie. The people admired those men who lifted up their heads and said no, and at the same time they feared the calamities they caused. The women burned sticks of incense before statues of Buddha and prayed to be spared new misfortunes. Each time the peasants were forced to sell their land to pay their taxes, each time the state confis-cated a portion of the merchants' goods to replenish its empty treasury, there was a threat of revolt. An uprising automatically attracted malcon-tents, and the sorcery of violence deluded the innocent into joining. Armed with pikes and pitchforks, great companies of men besieged the cities, pillaged the ports, burned the palaces of the governors and threatened the poorly defended imperial cities.

No peasant on earth ever lived a harder life. The owners of the fields followed the example of the overseers on the port docks and drove their workers with whips. A landlord, sometimes a prince or even the emperor attached as little importance to his slaves as he did to the grass, and took for himself at least half of the produce of the soil. He accumulated wealth and the farmer accumulated misery. If the latter was forced for some reason to give up, a more unfortunate slave would take his place. The problem of agrarian reform had been studied for years, but it remained insoluble, in spite of the encouragement given small land-owners by the Manchu dynasty: one landowner who had caused the death of a worker was actually punished, and farmers who had culti-vated the same soil for several generations were granted a certain legal right to it. Property was parceled out in smaller and smaller lots at the same time that the rural population was increasing by geometric pro-gression.

A half-century before Mao's father conceived the idea of sending his

son to work for a grain merchant with whom he did business, a famine
had broken out which caused millions of deaths. The Manchu dynasty
had just lost a war against the West and the emperor was dead. In
southern China, in the flooded and poorly controlled provinces of
Kwangsi and Kwangtung, a visionary who had borrowed some Christian
doctrines from a Protestant missionary claimed to be the son of God,
and summoned his followers to revolt. Under the yellow banner of
Taiping, the Heavenly Kingdom of Great Peace, he proclaimed himself
emperor and issued his Holy Writ to the faithful. "The birds turning
toward the dawn are my brothers. . . ." In spite of the government's
efforts to repress them, fifty thousand rebels, their numbers swollen by
three million starving and unemployed, reached the Yangtze, captured
Hangchow and set up a capital in Nanking. For days thereafter, tens of
thousands of bodies of supporters of the Manchus were buried, burned
or thrown into the river. In June of 1853 the Taiping army was preparing to cross the plain that led to the north when the Yellow River rose
from its bed, as it did every few centuries, and flooded the surrounding
country. In October, exhausted, without cavalry, unsupported by the
population and beaten by the imperial army at Tientsin, the Taiping
were forced to retreat.

The Heavenly King set down the basic laws of the new Christian
society: under his authority there were to be kings, and under the kings
an arrangement of people's communes divided into groups that reached
down, at their lowest level, to units of twenty-five families. The land was
to be distributed and cultivated communally, and equality instituted
between man and woman. Alcohol, opium, gambling, debauchery and
adultery were proscribed, and the practice of hobbling the feet of
women was outlawed. All taxes were suppressed. At the age of thirty-
five Karl Marx had not yet written *Dás Kapital* and could hardly have
imagined a more concrete realization of his theory than this first
communist society, in which money no longer served any purpose.

Since, in the Heavenly Kingdom, everyone is a member of but a single
family, that of our Heavenly Father, the possession of private property must
be forbidden and all earthly goods placed in the hands of the supreme sovereign. These our sovereign will distribute equitably, so that every family will
be equally provided for, and each person will be clothed and fed. Such is the
command of God and the will of the true Savior of the world.

The ceremonies accompanying marriage, birth or death were to be paid
for by the public treasury, and the local commune was to furnish the
necessary workmen. The churches were designated as headquarters for
the party.

Because it dared attack Shanghai, the citadel of foreign money and
commerce, the Taiping movement was crushed in 1864 by a Manchu
army combined with mercenary troops commanded by Major Charles

Gordon. The Heavenly King committed suicide, his corpse was slashed to pieces and burned, and a hundred thousand rebels were massacred. The rebellion had caused twenty million deaths and sown despair among the peasants. At the time when Mao Tse-tung was beginning to ponder the misfortunes of his country, there were still old men in the villages of Hunan province who thought back nostalgically to the time of the Taiping. Why had they lost? Sun Yat-sen, whose uncle had been a member of the Taiping, had asked himself the question before Mao and knew that the failure was due to an absence of planning and trained leaders. The insurrection of the slaves took on the proportions of a glorious and savage epic.

During these years of the final collapse of the empire, this little man who had changed his name from Chung Shan, Servant of God, to that of Yat-sen, Spirit of Tranquillity, was studying medicine because he felt that being a doctor would help him penetrate the upper levels of society. He was converted to Protestantism, and after years of study and meditation on the condition of the Chinese people, he departed for Europe and the United States to found revolutionary organizations, write theses on the universality of love and of mankind, and organize militant groups. His countenance was hard, seeming sealed against outside influence; though the bristling little mustache suggested sadness, the eyes were icy cold, implacable—it was impossible not to recognize the intensity of thought behind them. A pedant walled up in a cage of principles, an academician in bearing and spirit, infinitely skillful at disguise and evading the police, living abroad and sowing the terrible seed of revolution at home, captious, niggling over details, an elementary mind with uncomplicated views, he had nonetheless discovered the secret of restoring greatness to China. "It is not action that is difficult," he said, "but understanding."

Concealing a generous heart beneath his impenetrable exterior, avoiding all human warmth that might intrude on the work of the mind, and traveling through the nations of the West to study the systems they had evolved, he constructed an oversimplified philosophy for restoring to China her ancient power. "Japan required only a few decades in the school of the Europeans and Americans to become one of the great powers of the world. China has a population ten times greater and a territory thirty times larger than Japan. If China imitates Japan, she will become as strong as ten great powers." A vaguely Confucian socialism would limit the country's great fortunes and bring about a government of the people, by the people and for the people. In spite of all his reversals, he persevered, with a stubbornness nothing could conquer. Suspicious, nearsighted, magnifying glass in hand, his ears constantly on the alert, always ready to pack up and move on, he visited all the

Chinese colonies of the Far East, spreading his wares before them like the traveling salesman of a revolution supported by a few discontented officers and some bankers of Shanghai and Canton who believed that power should one day belong to them. Constantly repeating his wearisome sermons, he was only the precursor of the messiah. Temporary steward of the cause, but endowed with a strategic vision, he knew how to employ his third-rate brochures and pamphlets to convince his clientele of overseas businessmen, students returning from abroad and the omnipresent secret societies.

Having become an American citizen to escape the police, he was giving lectures and attempting to raise money in Colorado, when he received, almost simultaneously with a request for funds, the news that the eleventh attempt at uprising in Wuhan had succeeded. On his return to Nanking after stopovers in London and Paris, he became the first president of an ungovernable Republic. Forty-five days later, the academician recognized that he was not equipped to lead the struggle against the forces of sedition and stepped aside in favor of a military man with ambitions to found a dynasty of his own. The Father of the Revolution, whose portrait now hangs everywhere between those of Stalin and Karl Marx—wearing an assumed expression of ferocity designed to impress the rabble—married a daughter of one of the greatest fortunes in China, that of the Soong family, and returned to the paths of exile.

Mao had won out over his father and was sent away to school, where he suffered all the humiliations of the sons of the poor when he arrived with his bundle of clothes slung over his shoulder. He cut off the pigtail which was the symbol of subjection to the Manchus and once had served to fasten packages on the head when a man crossed a river by clinging to the tail of his horse. Mao was even a soldier for a few months, at the time of the proclamation of the First Republic. After an uncertain period in which he attempted to learn business, the law and the manufacture of soap, he spent five years at the teachers' training school of Changsha, where his professor of moral philosophy exercised considerable influence over him, perhaps because he had a pretty daughter. He also made his debut in literature, under a pseudonym, with a long study on the benefits of physical education. "If our body is not strong, we will be afraid when we see the enemy soldiers . . . for the principal goal of physical education is military heroism."

In 1918, when Mao suddenly decided to go to Peking to rejoin his professor, he was very probably also thinking of the beautiful eyes of Yang Kai-hui, who later became his wife. This "proud young poplar," as he described her after her death, was a great help to him in his own struggle for maturity. At the University of Peking, which was already alive with revolutionary thought, he obtained a very modest post. "To the majority of people I came in contact with I did not even exist as a human being," he confessed to Edgar Snow. There is a certain rancor in this remark. "They were very busy men. They had no time to listen to an assistant librarian who spoke with a southern dialect." "Assistant librarian" is a rather pompous term for the post, which was actually that of a simple orderly, earning eight yuans a month, living miserably and sharing a room with seven other students. But it is true that in China everything connected with books takes on a certain status. One does not even step on a scrap of paper on which human ideas are written or printed, and Buddhist priests gather them up religiously, to be burned before images of the gods and wise men. Photographs of the time show Mao holding a rolled umbrella in his hand, tall, very thin in his student's robe, his face pale, his eyes dreamily romantic beneath an enormous forehead framed in a cascade of black hair. In later years it would become known that it was at this time that he decided on the organization and objectives of the revolution. In reality, he found it impossible to remain in Peking, went to Shanghai with some comrades who were leaving for France and borrowed money from them to return home. En route he was robbed of his only pair of shoes. It was because of this journey that he missed being present at one of the great events of the revolution.

At Changsha he kept busy and even attempted innovations. It can be stated categorically that he knew how to raise hogs and transplant rice, and that he lectured on the necessity for weeding and hoeing vegetables three times instead of the customary two. But it cannot truthfully be claimed that it was Mao Tse-tung's thinking that brought about the movement of May 4, 1919, in Peking. The teachings of Marxism-Leninism were still only being translated, when the students of the capital were outraged by the Allied decision at Versailles to transfer to Japan the Chinese territories which had been possessed by Germany. Because they had come in contact with the West and Western ideas, they knew that China was wrong in considering herself the Empire at the Center of the World, and the review *La Jeunesse,* published by men Mao Tse-tung had met at the university, advocated a revolution in both ideas and institutions.

In his native province of Hunan, Mao founded a newspaper and a group of secret societies. His editorials conferred on him the authority, somewhat exaggerated, of an intellectual who had studied and talked with the finest minds of the capital. Urged on by the thought that he would see the beautiful Yang Kai-hui again, he departed once more for Peking, where, for the first time, he read the *Communist Manifesto,* Kautsky's *The Class Struggle* and Kirkup's *History of Socialism,* and began to consider himself a disciple of Karl Marx, although his teacher,

Chen Tu-hsiu, the dean of the faculty of letters, did not go along with him. During this period Mao wrote: "Everything that has been accumulating for so long will not be long in bursting forth. . . . Our age of gold, our age of splendor and light is just ahead. . . . This we now know: we have awakened!"

Returning once more to Changsha, bearing the torch of revolution, he obtained a post as professor in the secondary school and director of the attached primary school, and assumed leadership of the Communist movement in the province. Had he foreseen that the age of gold, of splendor and light, would not dawn over China until after the establishment of a Communist system? There was the example of the Russian Revolution. The Czars and the old aristocratic society had been swept away. "For thousands of years, hundreds of millions of Chinese people have led a life of slavery. Only one among them was not enslaved by others: the emperor. And even he was the slave of heaven." To his friend Kai Ho-shen, who was in France at the time, Mao wrote: "Capitalism cannot be overthrown by small pressures restricted to the field of education. . . . If we utilize peaceful means to attain the goal of Communism, when can we hope to succeed?" To his mind, the tragic necessity for armed revolt was already evident. And to him, it was less a matter of putting an end to the exploitation of the proletariat by a capitalist system than it was of restoring her greatness to China and—why not?—of becoming the country's leader, a better leader than Sun Yat-sen.

There was, in fact, nothing of the great leader in the appearance of Sun Yat-sen, this timid little Cantonese, who was terrified by the slightest rattling of a saber. In the long run, he represented an elemental force that was setting China on the path to the future—this tiresome Lenin in a stiff collar, soft hat and bureaucratic air, this scholar whose cold and gloomy analyses never reached the masses of the people. He waited forty-five years to achieve his victory. In 1921 Dr. Sun Yat-sen was named President of the Republic for the second time and, perhaps to impress himself but looking sadder than ever, donned the uniform, sword and plumed cap of a generalissimo. A bourgeois president of the Third Republic would have been ridiculous in such a disguise; Dr. Sun Yat-sen is somehow touching in it.

In June of the same year twelve Chinese intellectuals and a Dutchman, a delegate from the Komintern, founded the Chinese Communist party at Shanghai. It claimed fifty-seven members. Mao Tse-tung took part in the meeting as the delegate from the province of Hunan. He was not yet one of the party luminaries and made no great impression until later. No matter what the official histories may say, the precocity of his genius at the age of twenty-eight was not apparent to anyone else.

Although it had been restored in the south, the Republic was incapable of imposing its authority on the rest of a nation divided into a dozen or more anarchical states. Before dreaming of establishing a nation-wide system, it was going to be necessary to reduce the local feudal powers and build the party around an armed nucleus. One did not have to be a sorcerer to foresee this. To Mao, who had dreamed since childhood of becoming a national hero, the founding of the party was a signal that the hour of glory was approaching. His mother may have hoped simply that he would pass his examinations for the post of professor, but he pictured himself as embodying the salvation of China. And what did that mean if not following in the footsteps of generals and war lords who overthrew dynasties when they faltered and then took the place of the unworthy prince, in their turn wielding the whip that would force the submission of the recalcitrant barons? In China, when a man has blood in his veins, he thinks of himself as a reincarnation of Shih Huang Ti, of the sun king Wu Ti or of Genghis Khan. Years later, Mao would write about this in a famous poem. In this land where nothing is simple and where the logic of history obeys no ordinary laws, the foreign mind reverts to the gaudily colored pictures of childhood books, seeking a key to the mystery. There was nothing petty in the ambition of the young Mao; it had the proportions of the land where fate decreed he should be born.

Chapter 4

Puritanism in China. Visit to a workers' district of Peking and a discussion on art in a socialist country. In which the author speaks of his difficulties with Brigitte and, on the occasion of a cocktail party at the French Embassy, does not conceal his bad humor and reveals a part of his reasons for it to the president of the Association which is his host.

My hairs are white as the mountain snow,
White as the moon between the clouds.
I know that your heart is not completely mine.
—Chinese, second century A.D., anonymous

We visited the parks of Peking and the artificial lakes on which the emperor went boating with his concubines on nights that were too hot for sleep, escorted by gondolas carrying flute players. At the Summer Palace we saw the white marble ship built by the Empress Tzu Hsi after the Sino-Japanese War with funds that had been intended to rebuild the navy. In the pavilion she lived in, set in a paved court planted with lemon trees, the guides pointed out her room, the alcove with the heavy silken curtains, the pink armchairs, the painting that showed her wearing a high golden tiara, with enormously long clawlike nails at the tips of her fingers. They kept repeating: "She had forty-eight ladies in waiting. Each of her meals consisted of one hundred and twenty courses." But they said nothing of her amorous frolics, of the eunuchs who watched over her or of the lovers whose throats she cut. The People's Republic was silent on everything concerning the subject of love, as if it constituted a kind of blemish on human nature. I was told the story of a village leader who was approached by two young people with an announcement of their intention to marry.

"Why?" he asked.

"Because we love each other."

"That is not a good reason. Come back next year."

The Chinese puritans consented readily to marriage, but not to love. It was perfectly clear that nothing intriguing was going to happen to the female soldiers we often saw seated discreetly before a cup of tea in the taverns along the banks of the lakes, and that their conversations with the noncommissioned officer of the Red Army across the table would not have startled a choirboy. The party mistrusted love because love disturbs the emotions and draws off the strength that belongs to the state. Because of love, one can betray the cause, arrive late at work and perform it badly, slowing down production. The deepest thoughts shared by young lovers should be dissertations on the accomplishments of Chairman Mao. But even so, we sometimes saw a boy and girl holding hands or canoeing on one of the lakes. The boy would be rowing conscientiously and the girl sheltering her face from the sun with a lotus leaf. One might have thought that occasionally she glanced at her companion in a manner suggesting love. But no; she was admiring him because he was handsome or because his name had been posted on the factory honor roll.

Simon went to the airport to meet the other members of his team. They had somehow avoided our misfortunes on the journey. The cameraman had just made a great hit with a film about which everyone was talking. He used a palette of pastel colors, knew how to compose his pictures and had an admirable feeling for lighting both faces and landscapes. I told myself that he had been selected because of his ability to capture the strange beauty of China, but I was concerned lest his technical demands and the anxiety he was already revealing might complicate everything. It is true that in Paris it would have been impossible to foresee such difficulties since I had received assurances which offered no possible grounds for objection. "You will be astonished . . . " Of course, they had been right in assigning the photography of the film to this sensitive, introspective artist, even though I was not personally attuned to his ideas or methods. The sound engineer, on the other hand, was a cheerful, uninhibited brute of a man who appealed to me instantly. He was consumed with a desire to get to work. Unfortunately, most of their equipment had been left in Moscow and would not arrive until a later plane, so we could undertake nothing for the moment. We continued our trips around the city. Simon had asked to see the chief of one of the housing units, and his request was granted. One afternoon the three automobiles of our little caravan took us into an old quarter in the Western section of Peking.

We were led into an interior courtyard surrounded by three low houses, each of them occupied by a single family. A pale autumn sunlight picked out the forms of potted laurel, different varieties of thick-leaved plants and sunflowers some of which stood as high as the roofs of rounded gray tiles. Trumpet vines clung to trellises, with here and there a splash of purple from a bunch of ripening grapes. We were

offered tea in the house of the block chief, Madame Hoang Liang, a
woman about fifty, of gentle appearance, who had been elected by the
three hundred neighboring families to represent them with the party.
Just above her in the hierarchy was the district chief, appointed by the
authorities to head twenty thousand families. This was a talkative parrot
of a woman who was so carried away by her devotion to the cause that
she launched instantly into a discourse on the injustices and horrors of
the prerevolutionary years. I had difficulty silencing her so that I might
talk to Madame Hoang Liang.

Madame Liang was of peasant origin. Her father had worked for a
relatively small landowner, and her childhood had been one of great
poverty. At the age of seventeen she had become a servant in the house
of a revolutionary organization. It was there that she had met her
husband, whom she had married almost without knowing him. In the
Hu Tong district, where we now were, she served as intermediary
between the people and the government, passing along the instructions
she was given, busying herself with the children and the state of public
health, and gathering together the delegates of each street and family to
explain the course of events. What she did not tell us and what I did not
know until later was that she was also engaged in a form of police
work: any family that gave shelter to a relative or friend from outside
the district was expected to notify her so that the stranger's identity
could be established. In this way the authorities would know who came
to stay here, for how long and for what reason. The régime was on its
guard.

In defiance of the old traditions, the women ran the affairs of the
households with natural authority, and everything seemed to go along
very well. This knowledge brought us closer. On the walls of the dining
room there were no portraits of government leaders, but simply a color
photograph of a man in a pale green tunic with gold epaulets bearing
two stars and a military cap with gold piping surmounted by the red
star. His features vaguely resembled those of Chu Teh and of Lin Piao. I
asked the name of this marshal I did not recognize. I was told with a
smile that it was Mr. Hoang Liang, formerly a colonel in the Red Army.
Of the masculine empire, this was all that remained. And the men who
had preceded him—his father and his grandfather? Dust. Oblivion. The
cult of ancestors had vanished with the snows of yesteryear. Mr. Chen
was exultant. The cult of ancestors was a thing to be sneered at;
everyone agreed about that.

"What do you think?" I asked Madame Hoang Liang.

"It's the way it should be," she said.

A radio on a sideboard, a table and some chairs, and this glorious
photograph of the master of the house who now seemed a very tired
man. He worked at the Academy of Sciences and rested often because

he suffered from high blood pressure. To welcome me, he had put on a white shirt, loose-fitting trousers of gray cotton that did not quite cover his striped socks, and yellow slippers. During Peking's harsh winters, heat was derived from a single stove, sparingly provided with coal dust compressed into small balls.

We smoked cigarettes made of a blond tobacco which resembled straw, and our conversation was weighed down by a kind of mutual embarrassment. The members of our escort seemed perfectly at ease, slouching in their chairs, listening to everything that was said with a satisfaction that was clearly evident on their faces. Their mere presence was enough to destroy normal discussion. What could anyone say to us other than what they should say, without being reported and severely judged? On occasion, Mr. Chen smiled as he had the night before, when he had taken part in my interview with a gray-haired, gentle-faced intellectual who did not belong to the party. This man had lived in France and spoke our language, and might have been classified as a liberal if the word had existed in the Communist dictionary. He permitted, and even solicited, criticism, but in his eyes the moral and educational value of any form of work was of greater importance than its artistic value. He was skeptical about the theory of art for art's sake and felt that, since the artist always adopted some attitude toward life, it was this attitude that was of primary importance. He might describe immorality so long as he showed how contemptible it was.

Present-day China was not overly concerned with shades of meaning. The times might not glitter with any very brilliant stars in the firmament of arts and letters, but every form of strength and effort must serve the development of the country. In the People's Republic of China, there was no place for the Marquis de Sade, Choderlos de Laclos or even Stendhal. This form of reasoning made me indignant, but it did not prevent him from considering himself a free man. The Marquis de Sade? Well, they would have tried to convert him. And if he refused to be converted? I told myself that he would doubtless have been sent to one of the people's communes to study their problems, to learn about the life and suffering of the masses and how properly to extol it. He would have towed carts, swallowed his rice squatting on his haunches and carried buckets of manure across the fields. And thus de Sade would have been converted to true values. I found all this abominable.

Madame Hoang Liang did not ask herself such questions. In her company, we paid a visit to one of the streets of the district, going into courtyards similar to the one in which she lived. We surprised old women cooking over little charcoal stoves, bands of turbulent children returning from school, the red scarf of the Young Pioneers around their necks, a whole world of humble people, office and factory workers, neatly dressed, eating their fill, sleeping under a decent roof and not worrying too greatly about anything else. The inhabitants stared out at us from behind their doors and windows. Brigitte took photographs of the gray tile roofs, of the low houses and the swarms of wasps at the foot of the vines.

Mr. Hoang Liang followed us, limping. He had enlisted in 1929 in the army commanded by Chang Ko-tao. Mention of this name made me jump. Chang Ko-tao had been Mao's implacable rival, and it was he who had held back a portion of the Red Army, toward the end of the Long March, and not rejoined the bulk of it in Shensi until a year later, along with Chu Teh. Exiled by the present régime, he was now living in Hong Kong. I was on the point of learning something. Mr. Hoang Liang had been with Chang Ko-tao for a long time. He could tell me what kind of man he was, why he had not wanted to follow Mao, what the conditions of life were among the men who took part in the Long March. But no. Suddenly, Mr. Hoang Liang, ex-colonel in the Red Army, no longer remembered anything, even pretended to be ignorant of the fact that the association between Chu Teh and Mao Tse-tung was commonly known as the Chu-Mao, and kept repeating to me that he came from a family of poor peasants and owed everything he had to the revolution.

Mr. Chen inhaled deeply, swelling the powerful muscles of his chest and stomach. There was nothing to do but leave and meet again, on Sunday, among 700 million Chinese strolling nonchalantly through the streets and museums, watched uncritically by old men seated on benches, fanning themselves and smoking their pipes, while the clouds of approaching autumn tumbled across the sky.

Along the streets and sidewalks, miniature cathedrals constructed of scrap iron and empty trunks and cupboards, rolled endlessly by, carried on the bicycles of their sacristans from one ambulatory flea market to another. From time to time, we would pass a stiff-necked, solitary man in a shapeless cap, buttoned up to the chin, in spite of the heat, in a shapeless gray garment, the eyes seeming empty behind the inevitable glasses, separated from the crowd by his dignity and sadness. It was thus that I imagined Mr. Wen going about his daily tasks when an automobile did not come to pick him up, or our interpreter, Mr. Shu, when duty did not call him to accompany some honored guest. I could see both of them, wrapped in their self-satisfaction and weary of mingling with the common horde, burdened with secrets of state which duty commanded them to protect, mandarins of the new régime, dreaming of a higher rank or a newer and better automobile.

Seeking some distraction, we went to the circus that had been built inside the walls of the old Imperial City. The jugglers, acrobats and trained rams were all that still lived in these deserted pavilions, aside from the gilded elephants circling the pendulums of the clocks. Since we could not find a taxi to return to the hotel, we were approached by the drivers of the bicycle rickshas. We had seen the Chinese using them with no apparent sense of shame, but we did not dare. It seemed to us that we would personify all the images of colonialists we had seen in the museums, a big cigar clutched in their mouths and a girl on their knees, being drawn about the city by miserable slaves. In the end, pursued and tormented, we gave in, but not without embarrassment. Whole squadrons of cyclists passed us, and we expected that they would turn to stare at us in disdain. But no one paid the slightest attention to the ex-imperialists we represented, even when our drivers stopped for a red light and then laboriously started up again, standing up on the pedals. There was a fixed tariff for these manually propelled taxis and everyone was supposed to respect it, but I gave the slaves the equivalent of a day's salary and they pocketed it with a happy little grin and no sign of protest.

Returning to my room, stretching out on the bed to calm the stabbing pain in my skull and find a moment's respite from the voice of the interpreter, which constantly compelled me to make mental corrections of his inaccuracies and vagueness—none of this brought me the relief I had hoped for. Brigitte was grappling with her own problems and had no time to devote to mine. Either she did not understand that the whole enterprise depended on me, and that everything would collapse if I gave in, or she did not love me enough to admit it. Like many unstable and restless young women, she refused to identify herself with the eccentricities, manias and fits of melancholy or exultation of a man. She belonged to a generation intoxicated with the importance this century has accorded to the role of woman in society, her person, her appearance and her happiness. The smug, middle-class circle of which she was a product contented itself with sending its sons out into the world armed with a diploma and an automobile, and its daughters with depilatory creams, nylon stockings, brassieres and a few formulas for entertaining properly. The magazines she read taught her nothing beyond the manner in which she must dress or do her hair in order to be certain of conquest. She knew that the destiny of man was to risk his life and the destiny of woman to attach herself to a man and provide him with children and with dreams. But because she feared that she might no longer be her own mistress she could not resign herself to it and was a prey to constant doubt, studying her face in the mirror and forgetting to watch mine for a glimpse of the hope that would help me to go on with the struggle. Could I still have any foolish hope of being loved? Brigitte had changed. Something I had known in her was gone. I had proof of this when I took her to a cocktail party at the French Embassy.

We had scarcely arrived when I realized that Brigitte was no longer following me. At first, I attributed this to her timidity, but then I was

E

forced to recognize that, although she was watching me from the corner of her eye, she was deliberately avoiding accompanying me so that she would not be suspected of being my personal property, and even to show anyone who knew us that she was linked to me only by the circumstances of the journey. I was bored, and did not know whom to turn to or what to say. Instinctively, I returned to Brigitte. She introduced me to an old school friend from Paris who was working at the Institute for Foreign Languages here. Without knowing why, I experienced a sharp and sudden feeling of embarrassment and went off to look for a drink and some self-assurance. It was very hot that day, and I was stifling.

Since I am not a very inviting personality myself, and am often trapped in a timidity no one dreams of attributing to me, I envied Marcuse, the AFP correspondent, who was moving happily from one group to another, drinking and laughing. Abruptly bewildered and seized with anxiety, I wanted to go back to Brigitte. She had disappeared. I found her at last, seated next to her old schoolmate in another room, leaning toward him, looking at him and listening to him with a pleasure that stabbed at my heart. I was jealous of the expression on her face, an expression I had myself rarely succeeded in arousing. But it was a principle with me never to oppose her, and to attempt to guide her with the voice and not with reins, as one would a filly with a very sensitive mouth. So I decided that it would be best if I did not impose my presence on them. I went away.

Unhappily, the president of the Association of the Chinese People for Cultural Relations Abroad had been invited. The ambassador had spoken a few pleasant words about a great French pianist who was present and about myself, and following this the president of the Association read a long speech, larded with all the banalities it is considered good form to employ in official circles, and which serve only to deaden the atmosphere. I had not met him before. He was a slender, fragile old man, wearing a mask of apprehension, and looking as if he might be blown away by a sudden puff of wind. Since he had omitted any reference whatever to me, I made no attempt to approach him. But he had apparently been alerted by one of his colleagues, because he came over to me a few minutes later, holding a glass of champagne in his hand. In the general hubbub of conversation around us, he offered a friendly toast to me, and I forced myself to reply in a similar vein. We touched glasses, and then an unhappy fate decreed that the old president should add, in the same mood of cordiality, that he hoped I was content with my stay and that everything was developing as I had hoped.

Under other circumstances, I would probably have found a courteous formula to express my disappointment. After all, we were in an embassy, and the conversational exchanges which normally took place there had all the solidity of a soap bubble. I might have called an attaché or a secretary to assist me, and asked him to translate into diplomatic language the disillusionment which was assuming greater and greater proportions in my mind. The hurt I had just experienced over Brigitte was like a hair shirt against my flesh, goading me to lash out at the nearest target. And in any case, I was not simply going to say to the Chinese: "I am disturbed because . . . " No one would have understood. Accordingly, I proceeded to hurl at the poor man a series of remarks that were far more sharply barbed than was suitable to the occasion. I was delighted, I told him, to meet at last the director of the Association that had been holding me in leash and causing me to waste my time; he must have been notified of my work schedule months ago, and I was astonished to find myself still in Peking and occupied with nothing more than useless trips. In brief, I was fed up, and since he had asked me to say what I thought, well, this was it.

The little interpreter who accompanied the president was the same girl who had welcomed us at the airport ten days before. She lowered her head, hesitated, then darted a horrified glance at me and translated very rapidly. The glass the president was holding began to tremble, the old man turned pale, nodded briefly to me and walked away, suddenly very stiff and solemn.

I felt a bitter sense of pleasure as I wondered if I had not definitively compromised my position. Basically, it made little difference to me, and my distress at the thought that I was alone in Peking, swallowed up in the futility of an embassy reception, helped me look at the matter objectively. It was not as a docile tourist that I had come to China. It was time I said that I had had enough, even at the risk of causing a complete rupture. I was suddenly tempted to drop everything and return to the hotel, but I was still so tense that I would not even have been able to approach someone and ask for a ride in an automobile. I took a cigarette from my pocket, lit it and took refuge on the terrace,where it was darker and cooler. Someone came up behind me and clapped me on the shoulder. It was Marcuse. The reception rooms were emptying rapidly. He led me away with him.

"You were bored?" he said. "Their whiskey isn't bad though. At least it's a change from the whiskey at the Hsin Chiao; that stuff smells of eau de Cologne."

I followed him. He was shaking hands, saying good-bye. Behind his monocle, his eye glittered with an amused irony.

"I saw Brigitte," he said. "She is more beautiful than ever. A little professor who was with her told me, 'She was my first love.' I said, 'I know what you mean; she was mine, too.' "

He took me by the arm and led me to his car. Brigitte was waiting for me. She seemed in very good humor. It was raining gently. We went to dinner in a Chinese restaurant to which Marcuse invited us. He liked a harsh red wine that was kept warm in porcelain coffeepots and served in cups. It sickened me. Decidedly, I was not impressed with the local cuisine, but I enjoyed the gracefulness and eagerness of the service. There were no photographs of party leaders hanging on the walls.

Marcuse was humming to himself, "*Ma petite chi, ma petite chi, ma petite chinoise . . .*"

We might have been transported a half-century into the past. I was weary. Brigitte was studying her surroundings curiously, and her face seemed to float in front of me in a bizarre, unsettling fashion.

The next day I typed up an article I had contracted to send to *l'Express*. I did not know what to say except that I was suffocating and suffering physically from all the suspicion with which I felt surrounded. China was not at all what I had expected, and nothing of what I wrote would be what they had hoped to receive from me. What concept of the world does one have when one is in Peking? It was this that *l'Express* hoped to have me set down for their readers. America, Europe, the freedom of the world—from here, it was impossible to see any of these things very clearly any longer, because they were buried beneath an accumulation of polemics, insults and hazy terminology. In the lobby of the hotel, in every corridor of every floor, there was a vast display of Chinese political literature, translated into every known language. "*A votre disposition.*" "*A la disposición de Usted.*" I had sampled it. I had long since grown tired of the expositions of the scriptures of Mao Tse-tung, whose own works were piled up everywhere, available to the eager buyer in all kinds of editions. I could imagine the reactions of the French if they were supplied with no other reading matter than the newspapers of the Gaullist party or the *Memoirs* of General de Gaulle.

The goats had disappeared from the field outside our windows. In the interval between the sudden showers of rain, troops of men and women came to cut the tall grass and spread it out to the sun and wind. Once it had dried, it was gathered into bundles and deposited at the foot of the wall, where carts came to pick it up and carry it off to some unknown destination.

That afternoon Brigitte suddenly told me: "Tonight I won't be free." I said nothing. I was helpless. I was sick. It would never have occurred to me to leave her at night when we were traveling away from home. I loved her, and it was this that separated us. In an effort to console myself, I told myself that we were accustomed to doing things without each other, and that it did not matter greatly whether we were in Paris or Peking. Brigitte had a right to get away for a time if she felt the need to do so.

I ought to have been used to it. For a long while I had taken no offense at what Brigitte termed "little nothings"—the wounds she in-flicted, the modicum of attention she managed to spare for me, the indifference in which she wrapped herself. I saw in all these things a reflection of my present condition. After all, I had been as lighthearted with respect to other women as Brigitte now was with me. It was fair enough. But this time I told myself that she was lying to me, and something within me broke. My love for her suddenly became an unbearable burden, and I told myself that the time had come to set it down. How could I hope to light stars of pleasure in her eyes when I was the primary cause of her sadness? I was forced to the conclusion that it was impossible for me to help her.

Elsewhere, perhaps, I might still have gone on trying. Here, confronted with the enormous problems that required my attention and demanded that I devote myself, body and soul, to their resolution, I felt something akin to shame at allowing myself to be distracted, however slightly, by emotions that counted for nothing beside the flowing of rivers or even in the important acts of men. Nothing was left to me any longer except China, and the effort to understand and love it in spite of its present-day mandarins. As was my habit in such moments of crisis, I threw myself into the enterprise with all the energy at my command.

Chapter 5

Visit to a model prison and to a factory. In which the author attempts to get some workmen to tell him what the revolution has meant to them and questions a female worker on her ideas of happiness. In which the reader is taken to the University of Peking and acquires some notion of its teachings and of the privileges enjoyed by its faculty and students. In which a visit to a locomotive factory reveals further details on working conditions before the revolution. In which we return to the young Mao Tse-tung, and Colonel Chiang Kai-shek makes his appearance at the time of the death of Dr. Sun Yat-sen, while Mao Tse-tung is discovering the strength of the peasantry. In which a visit to the Great Wall reminds the author of personal experiences. The Chinese idea of death. The author wonders where his future in this country is being decided.

A civilization becomes transformed when its most oppressed element—the humiliation of the slave, the labor of the modern worker—suddenly becomes a *value*, when the oppressed ceases to try to escape this humiliation and seeks his salvation in it, when the worker ceases to try to escape his work and seeks in it his reason for being. The factory, which is still only a kind of church of the catacombs, must become what the cathedral was, and men must see in it, instead of gods, human power struggling against the Earth.
—ANDRÉ MALRAUX, *Man's Fate*

I no longer remember whether it was Simon or I who asked that we be allowed to visit a prison. I do know that on my own list I had included the archbishop of Peking and the church of Nanchang, some of the participants in the Long March and the military barracks.

The interpreter, Mr. Shu, knocked at my door and came in. He must have been suffering from his liver that morning, because his complexion was even more sallow than usual, but he was wearing a broad smile. On the following day we were to visit the prison. Would a Chinese journalist have been granted the privilege of visiting the prison at Fresnes? I doubted it. It seemed to me a sign that my little speech to the president of the Association was bearing fruit. With an indiscretion that was entirely amiable, Mr. Shu went over to the typewriter and showed obvious astonishment at the number of typed pages lying beside it; I would tire myself out if I went on working at this rate. I replied that I tired far more easily when I was doing nothing, and this too seemed to astonish him. He left then, at his usual shuffling pace, stroking his poorly shaved cheeks in what might have been perplexity.

It was a model prison. It was shown to all the newspapermen and all the television crews because someone had decided it was good propaganda. Eighteen hundred political and common law prisoners were undergoing re-education here. It seemed scarcely closed in at all. Flowers were carefully cultivated in the courtyards, and the library contained the complete works of Karl Marx and Mao Tse-tung. The names of prisoners cited for good conduct were posted on an honor roll. A barber went through every ten days to take care of beards, and every twenty days to cut hair. The prisoners took a hot bath every week. Once each month their families were admitted to see them. Release often occurred before the scheduled date. Some ex-prisoners requested the privilege of continuing to work here for their room and board and a small salary.

Everything was scrubbed, polished, shining. Basketball and volley ball teams were working out on the sports field. A rehearsal was going on in the open-air theater. Loudspeakers blanketed the area with music. The wooden borders of the flower beds were painted, the courtyards were swept, the hospital attendants studiously corrected the position of patients standing before the X-ray machines. There were no bars on the windows, no locks on the cell doors; cabbage soup and a grain porridge were cooking in the pots in the kitchens.

In the workshops the prisoners seemed to be their own guards. They might have been taken for ordinary workmen had they possessed that organ which beats in the breast of men and beasts so long as they have any hope of rescue. Not one of them lifted his eyes to us unless he was reasonably sure that he was unobserved, and the glance they gave us then was one of sadness mingled with despair. Nothing remained of their manhood but an outer shell. Hunched over their looms or machines for molding plastics, their faces closed and withdrawn like a house abandoned for the winter, what were they waiting for? Their liberation? Death? The ruling thought that directed China had not touched them with its light. Yet their resistance manifested itself only through silence. Who knows? If I had asked, one of them might have lectured us on the magnanimity of the government and the healthful atmosphere of the prison. The windows had glass pains, even in the dormitory building, and no one ever broke them to cut his wrists. The possibility of dying was offered freely to those who lived here, and they did not take it. There had been but one attempt at escape; the prisoner had been brought back within the hour.

I left feeling ill at ease. In spite of the sanctimonious air of the assistant director, who was our guide, I was anxious to get back to the automobiles and the Hsin Chiao. The only difference between this prison and the rest of China was that outside of the prison people looked at us and occasionally smiled. People worked everywhere with no more sign of guards than here, but in this enormous chain gang everyone watched everyone else. At six o'clock in the morning I could hear the whistles that regulated the pace of the physical education period of the neighborhood troops of militia. The ricksha men, the peasants and the workers were condemned to peddle their bicycles, spread manure and forge machine parts until the day they died. It was constantly being suggested that I visit a factory. I decided to do so.

A long inscription terminated by an exclamation point had been painted on the wall adjoining the entrance to the factory, and I asked to have it translated: *"Long Live Chairman Mao Tse-tung!"* There were two others on the walls of the administration building: *"Success to the Plan!"* and *"Celebrate the Fifteenth Anniversary of the People's Republic by the Accomplishment of Your Tasks in Every Field!"* Enormous posters, very crudely drawn, depicted a soldier, a peasant and a worker, all three young and masculine, one arm raised in a clenched-fist salute, the other pressing to the heart the works of Mao Tse-tung, the key to the solution of all problems.

In all the factory's shops we were confronted with—and obviously expected to admire—the diligence of slaves who had become the owners of the property of their former masters, caressing their machines and displaying the diligent application of good students, intent on attracting the attention of the teacher-foreman. "Care for your tools as the soldier does for his weapons." The slogans on the walls were framed in paper garlands, the entrance halls and walks were garishly decorated, production statistics were totaled in varicolored chalks. There were many women, wearing jackets and trousers of coarse blue cotton, but their enthusiasm was the only thing that set them apart from the men. Here, as elsewhere, there were only sexless workers, intent on building the new China. Men and women alike fed coal to the ovens, manipulated drills and steam hammers, measured grooves and threads of screws down to the last millimeter. Occasionally, they paused for an instant to applaud us, and we responded by applauding them in return, following the Soviet pattern. We were friends from abroad, here to observe China's industrial effort, and they loved us.

Four of the workers had been singled out to talk with us, and they were waiting in the reception room of the administration building. I wanted to hear something beyond what I was told by my official escorts, and I had hoped that some authentic sound might emerge from this direct contact with the people. But would they be intimidated by the camera and microphones, which had at last arrived, or by the gallery of prophets that surrounded us here, just as their giant portraits now surrounded T'ien An Men Square, in preparation for the parade? Karl Marx, with his flowing beard and lion's mane of hair; Engels, likewise bearded, but at least having visited a barber; Lenin, with his Cossack mustache and pointed goatee—what a collection of hair! Stalin retained only that fat, familiar mustache. From generation to generation, the hair had been pruned and trimmed, and Comrade Mao presided over the group, cleanly shaven at last, resembling a great bear beneath the make-up that beautified even his wart. In spite of his evident fatigue from carrying 700 million Chinese on his shoulders, he was smiling.

I had hoped that some of the workers might be at least middle-aged, to supply me with a basis for comparison. The oldest of them, Mr. Shin, could not have been more than forty. I tried to put him at ease by taking off my jacket and casually stirring the bowl that had been set before me, in which thick tea leaves floated like spinach. There was no hidden trap in the question I asked; I simply wanted to find the key I was looking for: "What has the revolution brought to you?" Mr. Shin need only have uttered a single word. "Liberty," for instance, or "dignity." I would have understood. He might then have added: "Liberty, perhaps not for me, because liberty costs dearly, but for my country. Before the revolution I worked for foreign capitalists, and we were exploited to serve their ends. Today the machines built by Chinese hands serve the Chinese people. It does not matter if we kill ourselves so long as our children profit from it."

He cleared his throat, hesitated. My question floored him. He looked at his bosses, the interpreter, the mandarins of our escort and suddenly launched into an absolute tirade. He told me the history of the proletariat oppressed by feudalism and imperialism. It was an extract from *Das Kapital* or the *Communist Manifesto*. He recited his lesson very well. It was impossible to stop him. I yawned. The camera stopped. He was followed by Mr. Huang, a superintendent with a complexion so glossy it resembled wax. I tried to guide him to more down-to-earth levels, questioning him about his parents and children. In vain. He spoke only one phrase that moved me: "Before, there was never enough to eat." Then he settled himself firmly in the path of his predecessor: "Now, thanks to Chairman Mao and the party, we have conquered feudalism and imperialism and are working for peace." Madame Lio was the superintendent of an assembly shop, with four hundred workers under her. She had two children. "Chairman Mao is the savior of the nation. When Peking was liberated, I felt as if the whole city was celebrating my own liberation." That was rather beautiful—almost too beautiful. Chairman Mao reigned amid celestial splendor. I was not convinced.

The last worker, a lathe operator, was a girl of twenty-five. Her husband worked in the same factory. Her father was a peasant. With her I tried another tack.

"The first time your husband rented a boat at the Summer Palace and took you out on the lake, were you thinking of Chairman Mao and the party, or did you just have a good feeling that might be called happiness?"

The interpreter smiled. The things these Western devils could think of . . . I do not know how he translated my question, but I was forced to repeat it. The girl was baffled.

"In the old society," she answered, "there was a handful of profiteers. Now the working class and the people have the right to relax."

We collected our baggage, feeling depressed and ill-tempered. I know—patience and perseverance were needed to find what I was looking for. We were being shown only the bark on the trees of this forest which I wanted to penetrate to the heart. Once again I tried to explain my feeling of being misled and set forth my real desires: we were not interested in seeing all the things they wanted to show us, so rapidly, with no possibility of doing more than scratching the surface. We preferred wasting time to this program of forced feeding: loitering in one place, talking to people at length, taking in the scene, breathing deeply of the atmosphere and strolling into the underbrush, rather than simply following roads that had been opened to receive us.

We were told that as guests every effort was being made to spare us any kind of difficulty. The word "guest" is never used alone in the Chinese language, any more than the word "tiger." Neither word is ever used without being qualified by another term which gives it its real significance. A tiger is not a tiger, but an old tiger, a *lao hou*. A guest is never simply a guest, but an honored guest. An honored guest must be provided with a screen that will shield them from troublesome people and avoid any possibility of "incidents." Children might stick out their tongues at us, something that was said might offend us. This ancient tradition, which had somehow survived the deluge, did play a part in the attentions with which we were surrounded. I tried to make it clear that we were no lords of the earth; we wanted to approach the people on their own level, to live modestly and share the meals of the laboring masses. That was beyond their understanding; honored guests should recognize the solicitude behind everything that was done for them.

I said to myself: "O.K. I'm paying for my room and meals. I'll be paying—and paying well—for any trips we take by car or plane. I'm obliged to put up with the second-rate mandarins who surround me, but must I also continue to listen to their nonsense and allow myself to be made a fool of?"

"Your way of showing us your respect honors us," I said, "but it is your way. Please don't encumber yourselves with so many precautions. You in China also have a conception of the role of journalist which is not ours. Since you seem so deeply concerned with the need for being agreeable to us, you would succeed most quickly by allowing us to go where we want to go and see the people we want to see."

Mr. Shin frowned and appeared to be considering the matter from every angle. He was not an intellectual but a proletarian; big, standing solidly on his feet and handsome. To him, the problem I had posed assumed the importance of a crisis of conscience.

"Since you are our friends," he answered, "we must do everything we can to assist you."

I began to breathe again.

Except for the fact that it sheltered professors and students, the university resembled no Western university I had ever known. It was a barracks. The comparison had not left my mind since I had paid a visit to a newspaper office, where editors and staff, seated sedately behind their tables, rose to their feet when we came in and hastened to show us their archives. There was nothing lying about anywhere, not so much as a scrap of paper. The corridors, lined with spittoons and washed down to the bare boards, smelled of ammonia. The printing press appeared to be dead.

The University of Peking is the pampered child of the party, and favors were constantly being showered on it. Ten thousand students lived here, in the midst of gardens that stifled all outside sound. In the soft rain that saturated this suburban area, bamboos and willows leaned over the banks of lakes. The eyes of the university's assistant dean held a sleeping fire that flickered to life when he glanced around him, and his thick lips spread into a smile. Heavy-jowled, but with something about him of a supple Oriental cat, he did not remind me of any of the functionaries I had met thus far. Among these stern-looking professors, I was suddenly ashamed of having come here without a tie. It seemed to me that there should be an obvious relationship between university teachers in a socialist country and those in any other; a trifle stiff, perhaps, on the surface, but deeply concerned with the ambiguities and subtleties of human thought. A writer could afford to indulge in the luxury of skepticism, of equivocal references and a sharing of confidences.

These apostles of the new religion had only contempt for the lamas and their sandalwood god; they worshiped a deity to whom any form of affection was as intolerable as doubt itself. The precious, silk-bound books of prayers had been replaced in these temples by the gospels of Marxism-Leninism and the works of Mao Tse-tung. The imperial bust reigned everywhere, even in the rooms where students were crowded in tiers of bunks. There was no indulgence in the looks these men directed at me now. Leaning back in their chairs, their hands resting weightily on the armrests, they were judging me and parceling out the roles they would play. It was the task of the French professor to flatter me, and that of the law professor to celebrate the universal truth of Marxism-Leninism.

That phrase "universal truth" made me smile. I ventured to say that many men who thought they had possessed it had found themselves mistaken, and I was told that this was a matter of a scientific truth, of a law one was forced to accept just as one had to accept the law of gravity. "Among intellectuals, a distinction must be made between revolutionaries and counterrevolutionaries. The former are for the peasants and workers, the latter against." Any difference was quickly obliterated. By a directive of the Central Committee both professors and students were sent into the countryside for one month of every year, not merely to meditate on the situation of the peasant but to work in the fields.

I had been mistaken again; this was not a barracks but a seminary for obtuse Knights Templar where education included training for war to defend the religion of the state, a machine for forming minds while the prisons served to break down any that might resist. Yes, the students had the right to ask questions, and in their first two years it was considered their duty to ask themselves whether they were revolutionaries or, without knowing it, counterrevolutionaries. It was considered a good thing that the will to perfection animated the revolution, not so that it might be destroyed by deviationism, but so that the permanence of revolutionary thought might be sustained and the professors more clearly establish the triumph of universal truth. Marxism-Leninism was therefore taught as a science, along with the history of the revolution. All objections were resolved, consciences sounded, waverers weeded out. Special attention was paid to the small proportion of students who came from the old landowning families and must now find their place among the sons of peasants and workers.

Relations between students and professors were based on the principle of total equality, as they were between soldiers and officers in the army. The capitalist hierarchy that had established barriers between the classes had been shattered. On the other hand, the socialist world had cut the university off from society, though it pretended to have done exactly the reverse. A student did not enter the university because of his intelligence or the brilliance of his secondary studies, but primarily because the directors of the party committees had discerned in him a "Red heart."

The professors also lived within the confines of the university, bachelors in students' rooms, which were not heated until after the fifteenth of November, married men in apartments that were handed out very parsimoniously. With great pride, Professor Hou showed us his five-room apartment on the second floor of a house half hidden by trees. Here he gave his delight in everything free rein. Had he some hidden guilt for which he felt he must atone, or did he think that the assistant dean might doubt a faith which seemed to me closely linked with the availability of food and lodging? In front of the dean, and perhaps to impress us, he indulged in a confession which resembled a session of auto-criticism. Before the liberation, the old society had crushed and blinded him; he had not even aided those who were fighting imperialism and feudalism. An unconscious victim of the past, he had dared take no part in the struggle. When the revolution triumphed, the veil had suddenly been ripped from his eyes. Then, in a dazzling flash of light, he had understood. Without even realizing what was happening to him, and thanks to those who had sacrificed their lives, he had been touched by grace. This was not the phrase he used, but it was the phrase most appropriate to a conversion on Marxism-Leninism. And now, at last, he knew what true happiness was. He earned 250 yuans a month, his rent amounted to only 10 percent of his salary, and his wife also worked. He could, with good reason, consider himself a privileged person.

In his enthusiasm, Professor Hou became suddenly paternal. He brought out his daughter's daughter, a child of little more than a year. She had not been nine months old when she recognized Chairman Mao.

"She said; 'Chairman Mao.' It wasn't until after that that she said, 'Papa.' "

I was annoyed at being forced to listen to this panegyric of the régime from a mediocre man who swept away all objections wtih the enthusiasm which presumably had brought him his present position. He had no intention of protesting, not Professor Hou! No shadow of doubt crossed his mind, even on such contradictions as might exist between the theories of Lenin and the nationalism of Mao Tse-tung.

I asked quietly how one could hold such positive convictions on both national aggrandizement and the principles of international Communism, and how one could put forth claims to ancient Chinese possessions (stolen from whom, how long ago?), north of the Gobi Desert, in Hindu Tibet or in Nepal, and at the same time claim to want only peace. There was a touch of pity and a great deal of pride in the look he gave me. Professor Hou drew himself up to his small height and brushed a hand through his crest of black hair. The tea which no one had touched was getting cold in the glasses. Why had we come here? To admire this smug self-satisfaction, to spread our precious buttocks on his chairs?

"Nothing is difficult for the Chinese," the professor replied.

The welcome we received at the railroad car and locomotive factory pleased me enormously. This seemed to be one place dominated by simple good humor; callused hands shook ours heartily and unaffectedly. People looked us straight in the eyes, laughed and talked with no concern for preset formulas. Men who had witnessed the historic strike of February, 1923, had the wizened countenances of old Barbary apes, released from their cages, decked out in workmen's clothes and waiting for peanuts to appear from our pockets. I liked the noise of the shops, the hot odor of the locomotive bodies these surgeons in steel were sewing and patching. Everything smelled of coal and steam. It reminded me of my childhood in the house of my brother, who was a train engineer and used to return home with his face tattooed with coal dust. I mentioned this, and there was general astonishment that a capitalist writer should have such modest origins. Mr. Shin murmured: "So, then you are one of us?" He had once spent several months in Belgium and could speak a little French when he tried, but he understood it very badly and it was his nature to give everything the worst interpretation. Standing now beneath the enormous portrait of Mao with his wart, he looked at me for the first time with a kind of confidence, wondering perhaps if he had not been mistaken in assuming that nothing good could come from us. A doubt had crossed his mind: it was possible that we might not be so perfidious as he had thought.

It was very warm, so we went out into the sunlight and sat down around a table littered with bottles of soda pop. A snorting locomotive provided appropriate background noise. We asked one of the workmen, who was sixty-four years old, to tell us about the strike of February 7, 1923. He was twenty-three at the time and earned thirty centimes a day, just about enough to buy five or six pounds of grain. With this, his wife could feed him with cakes made of cornmeal mixed with wild grasses and a kind of porridge of millet. There was never meat, and almost never fish. He also had to buy his way into the good graces of the foreman, since men were fired for no reason at all, in which case misery became absolute.

Beneath the blue cap pushed back on his head to reveal a few threads of white silken hair, his face seemed so worn that the skin was transparent, crossed with lines of almost naked veins. His nose was short and pug, his eyebrows eaten away and his eyelids swollen from the constant heat. The wedgelike opening of his mouth disclosed blackened stumps of teeth, and his cheeks, forehead and neck were plowed with uneven furrows. He was not a pretty sight, but his entire person breathed an unexpected dignity.

The strike had been forbidden. Two battalions of troops were stationed outside the shops, but the trains stopped just the same. The railway workers held a mass meeting to demand the liberation of their leaders, who had been arrested the day before. It was then that the soldiers had fired on them. Two men were killed, but the workers had become aware of the fact that they were no longer fighting in a hopeless cause, as they always had before.

Even though his recital was flooded with details which were of no importance to anyone but himself, he did give me some indication of the attitude of the workers at the time when he said: "Our life was worse than that of any animal." I had heard the same thing often in Algeria during the war, and I always experienced the same sense of astonishment. Why had they waited so long before revolting?

In this same period Mao was diligently seeking the means of expression best suited to his genius. He was not yet writing poetry. In later years he would hymn the exaltations of his adolescence with all the romanticism of the old Chinese poets:

> *I opened the window of a solitary tower*
> *And asked: Who, on this enormous planet,*
> *Decides the destiny of human beings?*

In the meantime he had married the daughter of Professor Yang; a son was born in 1922. As secretary general of the unions of Hunan province, Mao followed the example of the Soviet Revolution and organized strikes in the cities, as a means of fighting the military barons who plundered travelers on the roads and turned their ties with foreigners into gold. In the north Marshal Chang Tso-lin, a slender little man garbed in silken robes, sacrificed bulls to Confucius and made a gentlemanly point of personally witnessing the decapitation of traitors. It was not very difficult to hold the old régime responsible for all the evils of today.

Revolt? But how? The Kuomintang, Dr. Sun Yat-sen's party, allied itself with the Chinese Communists to do battle against the common enemy, anarchy, and sent off to Moscow, where Lenin lay dying, a young colonel to whom Dr. Sun had confided command of his personal guard and opened the home of his father-in-law, the banker Charles Jones Soong. Beautiful and ambitious, the three Soong daughters had been educated in the United States. They were courted by every man in the top echelon of political society. Colonel Chiang Kai-shek was thirty-five years old. The uniform was becoming to his slim physique. His face mirrored intelligence and energy. He knew how to command obedience.

An officer who had graduated from the traditional military schools, he had already worked with Dr. Sun in Japan. In Moscow, in spite of a violent antipathy for Communism, he could not help but admire the skill with which the Red Army lived in harmony with the people. On his return to China, he decided to imitate the Russians and founded the military school of Whampoa to form the nucleus for a future army.

The Kuomintang's Russian advisers, Borodin and Blücher, organized a party on the pattern of the Soviet Revolution and Mao Tse-tung was elected to the Central Committee. Did Chiang Kai-shek see in him the man who might drag the party along the paths of the Third International? Did instinct tell him that this was to be his opponent for years of mortal combat? Nothing to date had placed the secretary general from Hunan province in the limelight, and there were other Communists who possessed stronger personalities. Neither Chiang nor Mao has ever referred to their meeting as of critical importance to the future. On the contrary, they have always pretended ignorance of each other, even when Chiang put a price on Mao's head and when Mao held Chiang's life in his hands.

Chiang Kai-shek scented danger. To show his disapproval of collaboration with men whom he accused of greed for power, he suddenly refused command of the military school at Whampoa. In the end, however, he gave in to the insistence of his future brother-in-law, Dr. Sun, and accepted the post. While there, he first came in contact with a twenty-six-year-old political commissar, the grandson of a high official of the imperial court and the son of a professor. Chou En-lai had been sent to prison after the riots of May 4, 1919, in Peking, but now he had just returned from France and was concealing his intrigues behind a personal charm no one could resist. A few hollow formulas enabled Dr. Sun to believe that he could continue to hold the Communists in check. But Chiang Kai-shek was determined to get rid of them. Remembering the time he had spent in the secret societies of Shanghai, he set up a police organization and began to harass them.

Already paralyzed and almost blind, Dr. Sun Yat-sen died of cancer of the liver on March 2, 1925, in Peking, where he had been trying to secure the support of the war lords in the north. Mao had withdrawn to his native village of Shaoshan, and was beginning to discover the importance of the peasant revolutionary forces. Mao has stated that his health at the time made necessary this avoidance of cities. Other informants claim that he was fleeing accusations of collusions with the Kuomintang and collaboration with the bourgeoisie. History will doubtless never provide us with a key to the mystery since Mao's texts of that period are never cited.

Dr. Sun left a letter addressed to Stalin: "In turning their eyes toward you, the millions of men enslaved beneath the yoke of imperialism will

rekindle the flame of hope, and the courage that will sustain them."
Death conferred on him the glory and acclaim that life had denied him.
In all schools and barracks, at every meeting of the party, young and old
bowed before his portrait, and the political testament he had dictated
was read aloud: "The revolution I have dreamed of is not yet accomplished." Idols were torn down and replaced with his image. The people,
to whom he had never known how to talk, now flocked to his banner.
Transformed by death into China's Holy One, he assumed his place in
the nation's history. Four years later, from the temple in the hills west of
Peking which was his first resting place, he was brought back to
Nanking, borne in a ceremonial palanquin on the shoulders of men
wearing the blue and white sun of the Kuomintang. His mausoleum is
one of the most grandiose monuments of the city that had been his
capital.

In later years Mao would say that he had been enormously impressed
by the reaction of the peasants to the Shanghai incident of May 30,
1925, in which foreign police had opened fire on a student demonstra-
tion against "the unequal treaties," and killed twelve students. His
political fortune may have found its turning point in this forced sojourn
at the foot of the red earth cliffs of Hunan. Having found his path, he
threw himself body and soul into revolutionary agitation. Pursued by the
troops of the provincial governor, he took refuge in Canton and set to
work again building up the framework of a future military organization,
using an abandoned, bird-haunted, Confucian temple as his headquarters.

Almost by chance, the supreme truth of the Chinese revolution had
dawned on him at last. What purpose had been served by the fact that
he was born in a region of plodding peasants? His tools had never been
the plow or the hoe, but the pen and the book. The son of the old
peasant who had never allowed himself to be swayed by pity, and who
profited from the famines to sell his rice for its weight in gold, was an
intellectual and, until May, 1925, he had seen a great deal of these
strange animals called peasants but had never understood them. So far
as the Chinese revolution is concerned, Isaac Newton's apple fell on a
clay hillock in the valley of Shaoshan, when Mao discovered that the
true strength of revolutions does not boil up in the cities but in the
hearts of men who long to possess their land. Who owns the land on
which a man lives? And who should profit from it? How did it happen
that Mao had not known the answer sooner: those who fertilize it with
their sweat? Because he was the son of a small landowner who had
become a rich peasant, and because—although he was unaware of it
himself—he had never experienced the feelings of the beggars around
him. He was already a man who owned things, but unlike most men
whose vision is obscured by possessions, he had the ability to surmount

a temporary blindness. Among the rare intellectuals who professed this
new faith, he had the advantage of being the first to practice it. Whether
he was aided by chance or not, this attribute was going to alter the
shape of a nation. Years later, it would alter the shape of the world.

I was in no great rush to pay my respects to the Great Wall, since I
planned on seeing it when I went to Shensi, but I was told that this
project was impossible. The pathways of that province could only be
followed on muleback. And were a few old stones that had played no
part in the revolution worth that much trouble? After all, even Marco
Polo had never mentioned them.

I was beginning to wonder if I would ever leave Peking. Two weeks
had passed since our arrival, and I had made very little progress. It
seemed prudent to resign myself to the loss of this Great Wall that I had
dreamed of seeing ever since reading Father Huc, and to which the
Chinese gave a length of ten thousand lis.* But the figure "ten thousand" never indicates anything precise and merely suggests the infinite:
ten thousand years of happiness, a cavalry charge of ten thousand
horses.

The importance of this immense work has been differently judged by
everyone who has written about China: some have acclaimed it excessively,
and others have made a point of ridiculing it. It is probable that this diver-
gence of opinion stems from the fact that each writer has attempted to judge
the total work by the sample he has seen. Mr. Barrow, who came to China in
1793 with Lord Macartney as historian of the British Embassy, made the
following calculations: he estimates that there are one million eight hundred
thousand houses in England and Scotland. Assessing the masonry in each of
these houses at two thousand square feet, he suggests that they do not contain as much construction material as the Great Wall of China, which, according to him, would be sufficient to build a wall capable of twice circling the
globe.

Father Huc crossed the Wall fifteen times and often found only a simple
ridge of earth, or even a few piled-up stones, in place of the double,
turreted bastion that straddled the peaks.

The Emperor Shih Huang Ti, the Chinese Caesar, decided to build it
in the year 214 A.D., to protect his realm from the Huns. As a matter of
recorded history, however, the building of smaller protective walls had
begun seven centuries earlier. Century after century, princes, generals
and emperors had added to them. Shih Huang Ti sent 300,000 soldiers
and political and common law prisoners to link them together and bring
the entire work to a swift conclusion. To indicate the severity and
diligence he demanded, he ordered the son of the minister of war walled

* The Chinese li is approximately the equivalent of a third of a mile. Ten thousand lis, therefore, would be roughly three thousand miles.

up in the construction, because he judged him too weak for the task at hand. When the poor man's wife learned that she was destined to become a concubine of the emperor, she hurled herself from the highest point of the ramparts. From the sources of the river Wei, in Kansu province, to the shores of the gulf of Chihli, on the frontiers of Manchuria, the Great Wall, secured by strongholds at strategic points and reinforced by secondary lines, strode across the mountains, barred the rivers, descended into the sea, and scaled peaks six thousand feet high. Like the Pyramids of Egypt, it became a part of history and of horror.

After three centuries of futile attempts to surmount this obstacle, the barbarians turned back toward Europe. Of this strategic highway, over which generations of Chinese troops had marched toward the constantly threatened northern frontiers, there now remained only some disconnected blocks of stone, pitted and worn by the hoofs of horses.

In the end, I agreed to go and see that portion of it which was shown to tourists. We left the hotel early on a fine morning which rapidly turned gray. When we arrived at the foot of the mountains north of the city straddled by the Great Wall, it was raining. I suggested that it might have been possible to avoid this mishap by getting a weather forecast before we set out. I was told that we were simply the victims of bad luck. Apparently no one dared suggest that the atomic experiments of the imperialists were the cause of this very unusual weather. Since I was wearing a summer suit, I was tempted not even to get out of the car, but then I thought better of it. Through a gray mist of rain, we could vaguely discern the outlines of the Great Wall, swollen at intervals by great square towers, creeping across the uneven surface of the landscape, descending into valleys and climbing the hills on the other side. With the passage of centuries, the bricks of which it was constructed when stones or boulders were lacking had taken on the color of slate. We noticed one incredible ramification suspended vertically from a rock, and then, as the sky cleared a little, we could see the whole chain of fortifications, reaching out across the hills in either direction, most of it lying in ruins.

In a sense, this visit to the Great Wall was symbolic of my whole adventure in China. I had come to write an epic history, amply equipped with pens and sharpened pencils, with burnished weapons, with fanfares of trumpets, and unforeseen showers had loosened the skin of the drums, wet the powder, rusted the brasses and transformed the flags into sackcloth. Was it my fault if all China, like this little segment of the Great Wall, was being swallowed up by dirt and mud? The Great Wall I was being shown resembled the ramparts of Carcassonne or of Mont Saint-Michel, with hearts and arrows and the names of tourists carved in its stones. The only thing lacking was the souvenir vendors.

I had approached China as I would a medieval legend, and I found myself wandering, bewildered, through a kind of provincial madhouse, complete with excursions to the western lakes, boat trips through fields of lotus blossoms, interviews with carefully rehearsed workers and repentant professors, and tomorrow the museums. This swinging of incense burners and singing of psalms beneath the effigy of Mao should have been left to the accredited turncoats and the acolytes of the propaganda services. The fanaticism whose depths I had barely scratched already filled me with horror, and if the obscurantism of Marxism-Leninism was one day to take possession of the earth, I would rather be dead. It was false to pretend, as Professor Hou did, that justice had not existed in the world before the triumph of the Chinese revolution. Professor Hou knew of Voltaire, but he refused to recognize that he was a courageous man who would have fought with all his strength against a dictatorship that destroyed bodies and souls more ferociously than any society of the eighteenth century. Voltaire was right in scoffing at priests and provoking princes. In Moscow he would have roared with laughter at the line of idiots inviting influenza or sunstroke to bow their heads before a corpse whose stench could be detected along the Great Wall of China. To my way of thinking, universal truth was far more ominous when it limited the future to the crematorium. Suddenly, I had had enough.

Beneath the straw hat that sheltered her from the rain and sharply outlined the contours of her face, Brigitte resembled a young Amazon. I had never seen her look so beautiful. And yet I felt curiously detached from this fragile beauty which once had touched me so deeply. I realized now that everything she had made me endure represented, in her eyes, the price I must pay for loving her, and constituted proof of her own worth. She had seemed disturbed by my recent indifference, wondering why I appeared to be less concerned about her, at the same time questioning herself on her own reasons for holding onto me. In any case, my emotions, from this point on, were of no interest to anyone except myself and I shall spare the reader an account of them. I was like a man recovering from an illness, and the joy of living that flooded through me compelled me to be indulgent.

We walked down through the rain to the tombs of the Ming emperors. The entrance to the subterranean palace built for his mortal remains by the rotund, melancholy Emperor Wan Li, thirteenth of the Ming dynasty, stood in the center of a field of dripping corn. A ray of sunlight came out to warm us just as we reached it. Since there was only sand in the spot selected for the tomb, the earth for the gardens had been brought from many miles away, the stone for the staircases and the marble for the doors from the province of Honan, and the wood for the columns and ceilings from as far away as Canton. The blue tiaras of the empresses, the carved blocks of jade, the coins and services of gold glittered fiercely in the showcases of the museum into which the tomb has been transformed. It was a very modest tomb actually, when one considered the monument Shih Huang Ti had ordered carved in the face of a mountain by seventy thousand slaves; it contained a miniature palace and a representation of China and of the world in which the rivers and the sea were formed out of drops of mercury, and just as the Tartar kings had been buried with the bodies of their young slaves around them, the women and all those who knew the secrets of its construction had been walled up within it, standing eternally upright around the tomb.

The ambition of every Chinese, like that of all the emperors, was to prepare for himself a semicircular tomb far from the cities, somewhere among the hills or fields, as a symbol of his final possession of the depths beneath the land. This people did not fear death. They prepared for it as they would for a festival. Many years in advance, they would buy coffins covered with red and gold brocade and begin the embellishments for the sedan chair in which an image of the deceased would precede his remains. Houses, carriages, furniture, servants, litters and horses, all made of paper, would be burned on the tomb to insure comfort in the hereafter. The revolution had held up these rites to ridicule. No one any longer ruined himself to pay for his funeral, and rightly so. The body of the deceased was sent to the crematorium with a few wreaths of plastic flowers, and all true Marxist-Leninists professed horror at the thought of the wasted masonry and good earth lost to the harvests by cemeteries. And yet even the most humble of the people seemed to cling to this ancient custom. If they had not lived in comfort, they wanted at least to rest in peace in a dry shelter.

"Did you enjoy yourself?" I was asked when we returned to Peking.

I could have lied. If anything, the excursion had tired me. On several occasions I had been forced to halt, exhausted by the pain caused by the changes in temperature and the coughing that seemed to explode in my skull. The autumn had been humid and muggy, like the summer and the spring. Everyone declared that the millions of trees that had grown up since the liberation were changing the climate of China. I answered that I would begin to enjoy myself when I received answers to the questions I had asked about the history of the revolution.

At the Hsin Chiao Marcuse laughed delightedly as he pointed out the Rolls-Royce representative, who never set foot out of the hotel for fear of motor failure on one of the Viscount planes the Chinese had bought. He had been there for a year, living in a state of constant alert, and no one had ever called him. We, too, might wait here for months, drinking beer and wine as sharp as hard cider. I could do nothing to reform China.

Socialist or imperialist, she remained the same, and no decree of the Central Committee would change her thought patterns. The Chinese efficient, precise, logical? Incorruptible, certainly, since money no longer could buy houses or concubines. Withdrawn, padlocked behind the courtesy they offered so freely, insurmountable as all the yawning gates which led nowhere or the canals which crossed the city beneath the earth. Power had deserted the ancient palaces, where the museum guardians now watched over nothing but phantoms and stagnant ditches, and had moved to secret places where sentinels with rifles in their hands had no idea what they were defending.

In which committee was my fate being decided? Which interpreters, forgetting instantly the words they had translated, were betraying my intentions? By what obscure route would the message which seemed to have been dropped into a void arrive at last at the supreme collective authority? Then, if the response was favorable, things would suddenly begin to move. In a country where the unit of time was the double century no one concerned himself very much with a few lost weeks, but a barbarian from across the seas, such as I, would receive the escort that would permit him to move ahead. I had no means of forcing the threshold of the holy of holies and, so long as it was not opened to me freely, the bureaucrats surrounding me would pretend not to understand what I wanted or would answer my questions by saying that the archives had been destroyed. In the Mao dynasty, as in all the others, no one knew anything about anyone.

At night the city rested for a few hours, drowned in a sleep that held the sound of distant trumpets. I twisted and turned in my bed, I felt that I could not breathe, I lit a light and got up. I thought of Brigitte, who was sleeping with her arms folded around her dreams and her anxieties. If I had been able, I would have prayed for her. In other times, the emperors threw up hills around their palaces to protect themselves from evil influences. I did not have this power. I could only question the enormous Forbidden City, stretching out beneath me until it seemed to reach the stars.

Chapter 6

In which the author goes to the bedside of the ill Pierre Nora and then to a Mass in the church of Nanchang. In which the author visits the Museum of the Revolution and identifies himself with the foreign aggressors against China. How the opium which once poured into China from Inda became a passion with the Chinese people. In which the story of the military expeditions of the Western nations leads the reader to understand how the Chinese could be brought to revolt. In which the author, who is not ignorant of the history of China, asks to go through the museum more rapidly and causes a scandal.

To expect to reason and act in China as one would in Europe is either childishness or madness.
—E. R. Huc, *Recollections of a Journey Through Tartary, Tibet and China* (*Souvenirs d'une Voyage dans la Tartarie, le Thibet et la Chine*)

Early one Sunday morning I found a note under my door. Pierre Nora's wife was calling for help.

She and her husband had arrived in Peking a few days earlier. They were traveling through the Far East on a research project, and during their stay in Cambodia the Chinese ambassador had urged them to stop over in Peking on their way to Japan. Who can resist the idea of a trip to China? With a tourist visa duly stamped in their passports, they had arrived at the Hsin Chiao.

I had known of Pierre Nora since the publication, in 1961, of his sound and incisive book, *Les Français d'Algérie,* and our paths had crossed at Rocher Noir, at the time of the cease-fire in Algeria. I liked him at once. His whole personality radiated a bittersweet charm. This student and professor of history was not satisfied with merely acquiring information, analyzing facts and searching out meanings. He wrote with a pen as sharp as a lancet, holding it in a hand which occasionally trembled, and was unable to conceal entirely a natural anxiety and a constant fear of being mistaken. His intellectual honesty had conquered me. Condemned by his own nature to speak out and demand answers, he was nonetheless a gentle man, and the warmth and amusement in his blue-gray eyes were never entirely obliterated by their steely glint. I liked the spirit that had brought him here and the very evident closeness that existed between himself and his pretty wife. I watched them take a joint defensive position when either was teased or questioned, then glance at each other and smile conspiratorially. This kind of exchange between a man and a woman made me nostalgic. Brigitte was touched by the sensitivity and intelligence of Françoise Nora. Being granted the company of friends is always a kind of divine favor. In Peking such a favor was priceless. Suddenly I felt no longer quite so alone.

Pierre Nora was disappointed. The friendly urgings of the ambassador in Phnompenh had found no echo in Peking. Guided by a tourist agency, he had gone like any other tourist to visit the Temple of Heaven and the Great Wall, but he had had no contact with what might naïvely be termed Chinese intellectuals. Marcuse and I tried to help him resign himself to the loss of his expectations.

I dressed hastily that morning and ran down to his room, on the floor below. His wife was waiting for me at the door and brought me up to date on his condition. Three days earlier, he had suffered an attack of nephritis which he had felt coming on for some time. After having searched in vain for an interpreter, his wife had taken him to the emergency infirmary, trying to explain the situation to a doctor who spoke English. That same night the attack had recurred, even more severely, and the infirmary intern on duty had administered a drug which caused Nora to sink into a comatose state. On his return to the hotel, he was immediately put to bed. Possessed with a fear of dying far from home, he holed up in his room, refusing to see anyone, afraid that he might be handed over, defenseless, to unknown doctors who might kill him with their unknown formulas.

I realized it was going to be necessary to force some confidence into him and went over and sat beside his bed. He was lying back against the pillows, his complexion sallow, haggard, almost waxy, his cheeks hollow beneath a lifeless stubble of beard, overwhelmed by a feeling of doom. The room was littered with evidence of panicky disorder, cups of cold tea, tins of pills and open medicine bottles. I had not the slightest apprehension about Chinese doctors and would have confided myself to their care with no qualms whatever. In all the sciences the Chinese had shown themselves to be the equals of the best technicians anywhere; in such an art as medicine their stubborn optimism was capable of prodigies. Pierre Nora agreed with me about this, but he had run afoul of the official regulations which stated that sick people must first of all be taken to the infirmary, and his experience there had thoroughly shaken him. No one was hospitalized unless he had a fever of 104 degrees, and this he did not have. At the thought of returning to the infirmary, he experienced the same horror the political system inspired in me; he was convinced that once he had fallen into this machine he would never be able to extricate himself. He wanted to talk about his illness, but only to someone who might understand him. I went back to my own room and began telephoning every French friend we had in Peking. My own day had been planned for me, and since it was in answer to one of my specific requests I could not very well cancel it now. I was to be taken to the church of Nantang, where I hoped to find some traces of early Christianity.

My escort arrived, and we left the hotel. It was almost cold. The nave of the church, bordered with pillars of fake gray marble, was filled with men and women, many of them young, singing in Chinese the endless litanies which had obsessed me in Vietnam. My mind was on other things. It was very dark in the church and the cameraman was waiting until the Mass had ended. When it had, the old priest came to talk with us in the reception room of the presbytery, accompanied by two curates who were built more like side show wrestlers than men of religion. The room itself was draped in red, with the inevitable picture of Mao enthroned between the Sacred Heart of Jesus and the Immaculate Conception; here he was Pope as well as Emperor. I had asked to see the archbishop, but we were told that he had died two months before. I no longer remember what the priest said to me. We recorded it hastily and started back to the hotel. As we were passing T'ien An Men Square, where the militiamen were engaged in their goose-step rehearsals, Mr. Chen said to me: "We really don't bother about religions, so long as they do not interfere with us. But among the Christians there were many reactionaries who attacked the principles of the revolution. We found weapons in their homes, and we know that Rome is against us." I said nothing, waiting for some more suitable occasion than this.

The wife of one of the counselors of a Western embassy was a doctor, although she did not practice in foreign countries. I was able to reach her by telephone at about noon, and she came by the hotel. She spoke French. With his forehead bathed in sweat and his voice constantly breaking, Pierre Nora gave her an account of his illness and his experience at the infirmary. She listened attentively, only interrupting to ask him an occasional brief question. When he had finished, she went over to the bed, almost dropping to her knees beside him, and pleaded with him to listen to her. She had experienced all the same prejudices with regard to Chinese doctors, and on several occasions had attempted to practice without recourse to them. Then, as she got to know them better, she had come to recognize their ability, their prudence and the accuracy of their judgments. "Today," she said, "if I were ill I would entrust myself to them without hesitation and I would also entrust my children to them." Fortunately, she possessed the gift of persuasion, and promised to use her own influence to have him admitted directly to the hospital. Nora consented, and we all began to breathe again. Sunlight flooded the disordered room.

After the doctor had left, Pierre Nora seemed for a moment as if he might be on the point of becoming delirious again, and then, quite suddenly, regained control of himself. To distract him, I began telling him the story of my tribulations and my present state of bafflement. To my great astonishment, he assured me that this was the best possible frame of mind in which to write a book about China, that the book could be called *Failure of a Journey*, and that there was every prospect that it would be a better book than the one I had planned. At the time, the idea seemed almost grotesque to me and I turned it back to him promptly, hoping to encourage him to take up his pen again. I had always appreciated his corrosive, subtle and precise style, the style of a historian enamored of his times. I urged him strongly to use the title himself, since I felt—at least so far as other writers were concerned—that journeys which are failures often result in books which are not.

The intervention of the French Embassy resulted in a suspension of the rules concerning the emergency infirmary. An ambulance came to pick up Pierre Nora, and Marcuse accompanied him to the hospital, threatening to send off a cable to Paris if Nora did not receive the attention his condition required. In the end, this insistence impressed the Chinese, and Nora was taken directly to what once had been the American hospital.

During the afternoon I went with some friends to see him there. We were forced to search through the deserted hospital corridors for some time before we finally found him. He had been put in a wing reserved for foreigners and already seemed improved. The rooms themselves were pleasant. Although his mind was still not completely at rest, his earlier intense anxiety seemed to be leaving him. We left him feeling greatly reassured. The important thing now was for him to regain the necessary strength to return to Paris as quickly as possible.

The pianist Samson François had given a concert the night before in Shanghai, and this morning had telephoned his manager, who was in Peking, to say that it was ninety-two degrees in his hotel room and he could scarcely breathe.

"What hotel are you in?" he was asked.

He had no idea. No one had told him.

I was reminded of the poet Raymond Roussel, who had come to Peking around 1930. He never left his hotel room, wrote one poem and then fled.

The Museum of the Revolution was one of the places I was most eager to visit in Peking, but both it and the Army Museum had been closed for inventory and renovation for the approaching holidays. Well before the date set for its reopening, however, we were suddenly informed that it had opened again and that we might now visit it. We hastened to take advantage of the offer, guided this time by a new member of Mr. Wen's staff. Mr. Tsai Pao-ling was a dark-haired, easygoing bulldog of a man, slow and stolid in his manner. He seemed wrapped in an unshatterable dignity. Had Mr. Chen been reprimanded for something, perhaps concerning us? In any event, he had been transferred to a lower-ranking post. Mr. Tsai was to be the new director of our escort group, and would make decisions on the program to be followed, after consulting Mr. Chen.

As soon as the cameras and sound equipment could be loaded, our little caravan left the hotel. In the first car Mr. Tsai shared the front seat with the chauffeur, while I was in the back, with the case of cameras and film at my feet, Brigitte on my left, and the interpreter on my right. The second car carried Simon and the cameraman, and the third the sound engineer and his recording equipment; plus, of course, the usual assortment of assistant mandarins and associate interpreters.

The Museum of the Revolution faced the enormous National Assembly Building, across T'ien An Men Square. It was crushed beneath the majesty of a style that was pure twentieth-century Soviet. After the laborious ascent of stairways worthy of a royal palace, we came to a room which smelled of incense—a mark of the importance attached to our visit—and were at last able to set down our equipment. After the customary formalities—tea served in covered pots and speeches to the French people—I began questioning the party-appointed custodian of the sacred relics. He had taken part in the autumn harvest revolt in 1928, been imprisoned in Shanghai and engaged only in underground activity after that. No Long March for him. But had he not at least been present at Mao Tse-tung's entry into Peking in 1949? No. Half reclining on a couch, with a head like that of a sly old jungle cat, he knew no more than any of the others. We were attempting to translate for the West the lessons of this Chinese epic, and thus far I had not succeeded in meeting or talking with a single one of its survivors.

In the main hall of the building, portraits of the principal leaders and marshals of the revolution surrounded a giant statue of Mao, set in sharp relief against the folds of an enormous red flag. Frozen in attitudes of devotion, groups of children were listening to the solemn voice of a professor. This was not a museum but a temple, the largest temple of all.

Fortunately, the origins of the revolution went back only as far as the Opium War, to the entrance of the Imperial Commissioner into Canton, the confiscation and burning of cases of opium unloaded from British ships, and the Western expedition which ended with the humiliation of

China. As I listened to the account of the young woman who was our guide, I was not proud, and I tried to wear my shame without too great an appearance of indignity. It was I who had imported this opium from Bengal, and not some British colonel or vice president of the East India Company who represented the Crown and interests of the gracious Queen of England. I was linked with all the missionaries who became wealthy trying to convert to my religion people who believed in nothing. The American, British and French slave traders who packed the holds of their ships with Chinese laborers lured on board with false contracts for work in the West Indies, the sailors getting drunk in whorehouses ashore and bludgeoning coolies—they were all a part of myself. Without knowing it, I had profited from the twenty million pounds that flowed into the coffers of the City of London in 1836 from the sale of opium alone. Fifteen centuries ago the Chinese were content to drink wine and rice alcohol, and it was I who had forced them into smoking opium. I had done my part to corrupt the soul of China.

The museum bore ample witness to the fury of the nation, at last awakened by the Taiping rebellion. A shield of imitation bronze, supposedly representing the haughty countenance of the Heavenly King himself, was surrounded by his blue and yellow banners, fluttering in the draft through the hall. The pikes, pitchforks and sabers that had been the weapons of the revolt were displayed on racks; the walls were hung with paintings of victorious combats; showcases held the uniforms of British Lancers, the baggy trousers of Zouaves and the instruments of torture employed by foreign armies to break the spirit of the rebels. The history of the uprising was traced in minute detail, from the imperial decrees fixing the rents for farms or appointing governors, to the phrases, etched in gold on a purple background, which Chairman Mao had devoted to the glory of the Taiping movement. It was dignified, impressive, endless, intended to stir the imagination of crowds.

The guide paused before each object or picture, pointed out each uniform button, every flintlock rifle, every fragment of sacred stone. She recited her text in a gentle monotone, and avoided looking at us, as if in that way she might spare us the opprobrium her words attached to the West. The interpreter translated her every phrase. We made our way through the hall step by step, religiously. I took some notes. Occasionally I tried to skip a display, at the same time apologizing with a little gesture of friendly understanding. I knew all this. But no one else moved. The guide continued her lecture, completely unperturbed. I was forced to retrace my steps. My back was hurting me.

When we left the Taiping period, after about an hour, and arrived at the Franco-English occupation of Peking, the burning of the Summer Palace and the Boxer War, I felt I could take no more. This masochism with which China seemed to plunge into past humiliations served only the cause of fostering hatred for imperialism, and it made me highly uncomfortable. Opium was referred to as *yang-tou*—the foreign shit. I knew this, I knew it. My files were cluttered with all that.

I also remembered that, since 1729, imperial edicts had prohibited the smoking of opium under pain of having the upper lip split, prohibited the cultivation of poppies or the maintenance of an opium-smoking establishment under pain of death, and that all this had prevented nothing because the edicts were not enforced, since everyone in China—and the Chinese first of all—derived some sort of profit from the whole deal. The corporation of Chinese merchants in Canton which sold the opium bought its commission for fifty thousand pounds sterling in Peking. The emperor profited from the violation of his own edicts, and the mandarins profited from their complicity with the dealers, the exporters and the Westerners. To become a mandarin in the region of Canton, where cases of opium were unloaded on every pier, was a stroke of good fortune that was not to be passed up. In Europe collections were taken up to feed the starving Chinese infants, children saved the silver paper from their chocolate bars for them or broke into their banks to help the missionaries redeem the Chinese from their national vice. But the rascals had developed a taste for it! They cultivated poppies so that they might dispense with the presence of the British, just as they will someday begin to construct ubiquitous little mechanical bugs if the West succeeds in contaminating them with the urge to roll about on highways in automobiles.

It has been said that opium is a cure for everything. But who said it? The Chinese. The poor demanded it because it helped them forget their condition. The children of women who smoked as they nursed them had bodies and faces covered with boils, but the women continued to smoke. At one time an average of two hundred out of every thousand young recruits were found incapable of military service because of the disastrous effects of the drug. No one thought himself guilty of anything simply because he cultivated poppies. The Taoist monks themselves grew and sold them. For what reasons did the emperor decide to send an honest delegate, Lin Tsê-hsü, to Canton in 1839, to put an end to this degrading commerce? Because his own son had died from abuse of opium, or because he had at last been influenced by the reform factions? When news of this unexpected Chinese action was recieved in London, it caused a few bitter little skirmishes, but the official attitude adopted was one of indignation at a hindrance to trade which affected the interests of British subjects and the dignity of the Crown. After a debate lasting three days, nine majority votes resolved the crisis of conscience.

Where had they been laid to rest, the nine honorable members of the House of Commons whose votes had fed the hatred I could still feel surrounding me? Would the shock of conflict between China and the West have occurred in any case? Perhaps so. But it was not to unload cargoes of cotton goods or wheat that the squadrons of Lord Elgin and Baron Gros bombarded Canton and attacked Tientsin and Peking; it was to enforce free trade in opium. It was hardly an occasion for the display of flags of triumph.

Whether it was based on opium or cotton goods, the important thing about the incident was that it furnished the Western powers—including Russia and the United States—with a pretext for acquiring, at little cost to themselves, the riches described by Marco Polo and guarded by a nation in a state of imminent collapse. To have abandoned opium would have been equivalent to sealing off the source of this wealth. The assassination of a missionary or a brawl between coolies and drunken sailors could only be considered a splendid windfall when it led to the walls of the Summer Palace!

The French went about it quite openly and as an individual enterprise. The English were more methodical, and in no time at all they had organized and regulated a system of pillage. . . . The spectacle resembled nothing so much as an anthill crushed beneath a careless foot, causing the terrified black worker ants to flee in every direction, clutching a grain of sand, a bit of straw, or an unhatched larva between their jaws. . . . Each trooper had his bird, his music box, his monkey, his clock or his rabbit. . . . As soon as the sun was up, the pillaging began again.

General de Montauban's secretary, the Comte d'Hérisson, gives the foregoing description of the entrance of foreign troops into Peking in his *Journal d'un Interprète en Chine,* but he also notes that the inhabitants of the outlying villages took their share of the booty. The fact remains that to the Chinese Westerners were scum, obscene plunderers of tombs, and even after all these years I occasionally saw in Mr. Chen's eyes a flicker of scorn for the barbarians we still were, barbarians who wrote from left to right, began their dinner with soup, danced with half-naked women and not so long ago had rained grapeshot from our howitzers on Tartar horsemen, archers in bronze helmets and soldiers disguised as tigers.

In what respect had we changed through the years, so that he might now be expected to believe in the purity of our intentions? In the period following the Boxer War, the export of opium had gone from 40,000 cases a year to 85,000, and we had demanded and obtained free ports on the southern coast. We had crushed the Taiping rebellion because its troops occupied the valley of the Yangtze and interfered with commerce. We had given to Japan the provinces wrested from Germany after the First World War, and in more recent times we had supported Chiang Kai-shek against Mao Tse-tung. And yet the hurricane brought on by these injustices had awakened the national conscience and forced China to adopt Western techniques. For that at least, Mr. Chen could be grateful to us.

There was certainly cause for revolt. But there was not cause for the creation of a national mania. One of my paternal ancestors was almost unquestionably raped by a Cossack in 1814 in a little village in the Aube occupied by the Russians. No one in my family, certainly including myself, has ever complained of the incident. Our blood was enriched by it. It was the shock of her encounter with the West that forced China into a transformation of herself. Had this shock not occurred, China would still be living in an age of war lords, concubines and infanticide. In 1915 Chen Tu-hsiu, one of the first revolutionary leaders of China and the dean of the faculty of letters with whom the young Mao argued the principles of Marxism, stated that all the misfortunes of China had their roots in her own traditions. The Chinese students who came to Europe found the inspiration for their revolt in the principles enunciated in France in 1789.

We had not yet arrived at the time of the viceroys. Mao had not even been born. Our little group was towed through the rooms of the museum like a boxcar, occasionally being switched to a new guide, much as if we were taking on a new locomotive. I listened to the oily voice of the interpreter, wondering why I had been so interested in the museums of Hanoi two years earlier. It was doubtless because it was I who had been seeking information, asking questions and given answers. The display cases had been filled with documents I could read, because they were written in French. In Peking I was simply being stuffed with useless information. And at the rate we were going, we would be here for a week. I asked Mr. Tsai quietly if it would be possible to go a trifle faster. Mr. Tsai frowned and replied that the only way to learn to know China was to move slowly. I dropped the subject, but declined his suggestion that we pause to rest. At noon we were scheduled to go to lunch. Our cameras and sound equipment had served no purpose. Brigitte was obviously bored, but she at least could leave our group, observe the other visitors and then come back. I was lost.

Mr. Tsai did not accompany us when we returned to the museum in the afternoon. I imagined that he was either having a siesta or had gone to turn in his reports on the morning's activities. We were attached to another new locomotive. At four o'clock we arrived at the events of May 4, 1919, and the guide made a speech in praise of Mao's actions. Everyone knew that Mao had played no part in the student uprising that day; the University of Peking had not awaited the return of its assistant librarian to launch its revolt. I pretended to be very tired, and asked if we might go and rest. We went back to the reception room, and as soon as we had assembled once more around our pots of tea I exploded.

I repeated that I had come to China in the hope of learning something more than what I already knew. I had tried, repeatedly and lengthily, to explain that I had too little time to waste it, and on this particular day I had learned absolutely nothing. To this I added that our primary interest was in seeing the film and photographic archives of the revolution and obtaining statements from its leaders. It was of course necessary to visit the museums to learn facts of which I was ignorant, but I was honest enough to stop of my own accord when I came to a document or display concerning something I did not know. But for more than two weeks now I had been shown things of only minor importance. Not only had I yet to meet a single leader of the government or the revolution, but I was beginning to wonder if I ever would meet them. The tactics employed thus far led me to believe that my guides mistrusted the purpose of my trip. Consequently, I asked to return to the hotel at once.

My speech must have sounded like a clap of thunder in the room, and was greeted by a moment of astonished silence. Then the bewildered interpreter roused himself from his lethargy. He had no difficulty translating my sharp little phrases. Obviously, my anger had come as a surprise to them, and the absence of Mr. Tsai increased their confusion. They pleaded with me to stay, but I was adamant. The other members of my crew agreed with me. In the end I consented to continue the tour, but only on condition that we be permitted to go through the display rooms at our own pace, asking questions when we felt it necessary and not being subjected to interminable lectures.

A scene of desolation surrounded us. We went through the rest of the museum like a funeral procession, a silent and hurried troop, followed now by the guides, holding their usually active wooden pointers dejectedly at their sides. I paused occasionally to inquire about a photograph or a detail of a display. In several instances—notably with regard to the Sian incident of December, 1936—I was confronted with proof that the party had taken it upon itself to create historic truth, to the detriment of the actual events. The museum was a monument not to the history of the revolution but to the glory of Mao, whose every work, and sometimes every phrase, was displayed against a background of red velvet embroidered with gold, the traditional imperial colors. At the end of our day's journey we came at last to Mao's triumphal entry into Peking, standing upright in a jeep, wearing his forage cap and bulky, fur-lined coat. There was no question of returning to the reception room for another round of banalities and another cup of tea. We packed our equipment into the automobiles in silence and returned to the Hsin Chiao, thoroughly disheartened. We parted company with our Chinese companions with no show of regret on either side.

Chapter 7

In which the author relives, in memory, the great moments of the Chinese revolution and invites the reader to take part in the expedition against the war lords of the north. How General Chiang Kai-shek, allied with the powerful Soong family, massacres the Communists, while Mao Tse-tung witnesses the peasant awakening in the province of Hunan, is excluded from the Political Bureau of the Communist party and creates a guerrilla force. In which General Chu Teh joins Mao Tse-tung, founds the Red Army and agrees with him on a strategy inspired by the ancient military experts.

> Notice that the boat in which we are traveling is supported by the water, which can engulf it if the waves become too violent. Remember that the water represents the people, and the boat only the emperor.
>
> —An emperor to his son

In my mind's eye, I could picture the great moments of this revolution more clearly than I had seen them in the museum. I felt that I was reliving them, not as a student listening to an explanation of some geometric principle, but as an impassioned spectator.

After 1925 events began to move with greater speed. On the advice of the Russians, Chiang Kai-shek was made commander in chief of the army, a post left vacant by the death of Sun Yat-sen, and immediately set to work repressing popular agitation, arresting those Communists he considered too greedy and preparing an expedition to unify the provinces to the north of Canton.

To attain this glory he is constantly pursuing, he sometimes endeavors to utilize the masses of the people, the Communist party and even ourselves. His ambition to become the hero of China and his desire to make use of the national revolutionary movement as a means to this end lead him to waver constantly between the Communists and the extreme right. . . . Chiang has a great deal of tenacity and determination. Compared with the average of his compatriots, he is incredibly direct . . . but he can reveal himself to be both mistrustful and jealous. He will not permit discussion of any problem, and neither will he permit anyone else to make a decision for him.

This portrait of Chiang Kai-shek, drawn by one of the Soviet advisers he had expelled, is the picture of a leader. Blücher and Borodin, the only Russians he still tolerated, were compelled to accept his leadership.

Having entered into the peasant world whose strength he had just discovered as if he were entering a monastic order, Mao Tse-tung was analyzing the social classes of the nation, estimating their numbers and judging their explosive potential. Refusing to be diverted by the influence of the bourgeois and capitalist minority, he was counting on determination and numbers:

How many real friends do we have? Three hundred and ninety-five million. How many real enemies? One million. And how many, between these two, who might be either our friends or our enemies? Four million. Even if we add these four million to the total of our enemies, that makes a group of scarcely five million, who would be incapable of resisting so much as a sneeze uttered simultaneously by 395 million men. Three hundred and ninety-five million, unite!

In spite of the Russian theory which held that the revolution could only be won in the cities, he was preparing to exploit the tide of anger that was rising in the countryside. The last harvest had been bad. The peasants no longer feared the police and plundered the silos of the big landowners. As a precursor of the approaching expedition to the north, the chief of propaganda stirred up the emotions of the populace: the struggle to come would not be a simple repetition of the usual internecine struggles among barons, but a profound upheaval which would benefit the common people. Deserters from the armed bands maintained by the war lords and landowners joined the divisions of Chiang Kai-shek by the thousands, and the peasant revolts kindled behind the enemy's back crushed all opposition. Groups of local militia were improvised, unions were founded. There was talk of the Russian Revolution, and proclamations of the suppression of farm rents and cancellation of past debts. The landowners and missionaries fled and their lands were confiscated. When the troops of the Kuomintang arrived on the scene, their officers, who were almost all sons of middle-class families, were horrified by the sight of this peasant rebellion, and accused the Communists of treason.

In six months the major portion of central and southern China was occupied and the cities along the Yangtze were falling one after the other. From the gray hell of Wuhan, the revolutionary movement swept down the river and contaminated the factories. The universities were seething. To everyone's surprise, the Communists seemed always one jump ahead of events. Chiang Kai-shek's promise that foreign property would be respected did not entirely reassure the Western concessionaires. In Shanghai the English raised an army to turn back a tidal wave that recalled the days of the Taiping. At Hankow and Nanking foreigners were molested in the streets and their residences pillaged, and British gunboats opened fire from the river. To the Chinese middle class, the foreigners and the guardians of law and order, the eagerly awaited savior was Chiang Kai-shek.

In the elegant salons of Papa Charlie Soong, the revolution began to take on the aspect of a gilt-edged conspiracy to restore order and install a new dynasty. Sun Yat-sen had been too modest to think of himself and too weak to stand up to the military leaders. Then what about the Soong dynasty? A merchant had never cherished such grandiose ambitions. Merchants were ranked with soldiers on the lowest rungs of the social ladder. But why not a dynasty of the young general who had just led the expedition against the war lords of the north, supported by the Communists, and who now was about to purge Shanghai of Communists? It was said that his future father-in-law, Charlie Soong, had acted as intermediary in arranging an agreement between the general and the banks. Chiang Kai-shek was succeeding in putting the workers back to work in the factories, the servants into the houses of their masters and the runners between the poles of their ricksha. If the foreign armies supported Chiang, the whole affair could be quickly settled, and the inevitable showdown with the Communists would not be long in coming.

Chou En-lai, who had been sent by the Kuomintang to organize a general strike in Shanghai, succeeded in seizing control of the city and duly handed it over to the commander in chief. It was at this point that Chiang Kai-shek suddenly put his cards on the table, ordered the arrest of the Communists and had them massacred. Chou En-lai owed his own escape to a young officer who recognized him from the school at Whampoa and allowed him to slip through the net, as comrades-in-arms sometimes do under such circumstances. Trucks arriving in the city unloaded soldiers and left filled with corpses. One of the founding members of the Communist party, Professor Li Ta-chao, who had had a great influence on Mao in his days at the University of Peking, was strangled by Marshal Chang Tso-lin. Throughout the territory controlled by his forces, Chiang Kai-shek instituted a systematic disarming of the militia and bribed the dregs of the cities and towns to carry out the work of execution. The building of the Soviet Embassy in Shanghai was searched, and compromising documents discovered. Borodin and Blücher fled the country. Chiang Kai-shek established his headquarters in Nanking and assumed dictatorial powers. Terror reigned everywhere. In the rural areas the army officers who had been so horrified by the massacres committed during the peasant uprising now began a systematic massacre of their own, on the pretext of exterminating the Commu-

nist vermin and re-establishing the old order. The landowners returned
to take possession of their fields, and served notice on the peasants that
the announcement of a reduction in rents had been nothing but a
subversive Communist plot. Their frustrated rage led the most determined of the peasants to take refuge in the mountains, armed with
spears, pitchforks and a few old rifles. From this time on, the fury of
revolt was uncontrollable. The Red Army was born.

His office as regional commissar for Hunan during the northern
campaign permitted Mao to escape the butchery around him. Now he
received a directive to curb the excesses which were still taking place.
He spent thirty-two days visiting the districts of this province of violent,
inflexible men. He set down what he saw in a text addressed to the
Central Committee of the Communist party. His conclusions amounted
to heresy. But Marxism, like Leninism, had been smashed to bits by the
hammer of a reality the doctors of philosophy had not foreseen. For the
first time, Mao's own style burst through the conventional forms;
violence and passion lent fire to his pen. His murdered teacher, Li Ta-
chao, had often told him that China was a rural nation and that she
would not be free until the peasants were free; and the peasants had
shown him what must be done before the decaying order could be
destroyed and a new one set up. Although it was still invisible to the
theorists, Mao had seen concrete evidence of this truth and was dazzled
by it.

He wrote his report in Wuhan, in a long, low house with a roof of gray
tiles and a balcony surrounded by wooden columns.

In a short time, we are going to see an uprising of hundreds of millions of
peasants in all the provinces of northern, central and southern China. They
will stand erect, vehement, invincible as a hurricane, and no force will be
able to contain them. They will break their chains and force their way down
the path of liberation. They will dig the graves of all the corrupt imperialists,
militarists and bureaucrats. . . . Should we then place ourselves at their
head and lead them, remain behind and criticize them or take an opposing
stand and fight them? . . . A revolution is not a dinner party among friends;
it is not an occupation as delicate as writing a book, painting a picture or
embroidering a flower. It cannot be accomplished with that kind of refine-
ment, ease and elegance, gentility, calm, respect, modesty and deference. A
revolution is an insurrection, an act of violence by which one class overthrows
the power of another. . . . To call a spade a spade, a brief period of terror
must occur in every village. . . . It must be the peasants themselves who
tear down the idols, break the tablets of ancestral laws, destroy the temples
built in memory of wives who did not wish to survive their husbands and
arches erected to honor chaste wives and despairing widows.

The Central Committee waited a long time before releasing this document. The idea of peasant soviets was originally Lenin's, and had been
taken up again by Stalin. The committee had expected a clarification of
details from Mao. It received a tempest. For once, he made no attempt

at dissimulation and set down only his own instinctive reactions as a revolutionary not yet steeped in Marxism. He was no longer seeking a path; he had found it, without benefit of Marxist speeches or consultation with the Leninist oracle. In a few months the peasants had accomplished what Sun Yat-sen had not managed to do in forty years.

"If we are to grant to each the credit due him," Mao wrote, "then, if the total contribution to the revolution is set at the figure of ten, the contribution of the cities and the army amounts to three and that of the peasantry seven." He knew whereof he spoke. Still stunned, but filled with admiration, he denounced those who considered the rural movement no more than the agitation of a rabble. He had seen landowners held up to ridicule, paraded through the streets with their arms bound behind their backs, forced to wear great coolie caps proclaiming their crimes, and sometimes executed. He had seen images of Buddha turned into firewood, and women shake off the bonds of their traditional chastity. A man at the center of such a storm can become a heretic. The Central Committee rejected Mao's conclusions. After the bloody defeat of Shanghai, the secretary general, Chen Tu-hsiu, was relieved of his office and the Communist party went underground. All the urban movements ended on the same note of disaster.

In August Mao directed the autumn harvest uprising in Changsha. When it failed, he was captured and sentenced to be executed. He first tried to bribe his escort and later succeeded in escaping. A peasant gave him shelter. With the last few coins he had, he bought an umbrella and a pair of shoes to replace those he had lost in his flight. Then he took refuge with a group of rebel militia in the Chingkansan Mountain Range, on the frontier between the provinces of Hunan and Kiangsi, and set to work to organize the first underground resistance groups. Removed from office by the Kuomintang and expelled from the Political Bureau of the party, Mao entrenched himself in villages nestled among rocky hills. Here he began reading the works of Sun Tzŭ the greatest of all Chinese military experts, and discovered that all present tactical and strategic situations had been analyzed thousands of years before. All that was necessary was to profit from the analysis.

Everything was based on intuition. A leader should only make war when peace was impossible, only resort to battle when all compromise had been proved vain and undertake nothing he could not carry to a successful conclusion. The predicament of little bands of men being hunted by the armies of Chiang Kai-shek was very similar to the one that existed in the sixth century B.C. Sun Tzŭ and his disciples of a few centuries later, Szu-Ma Yang-chîn and Wu Tse, offered solutions and set down the conduct to be observed with regard to the enemy, the local populations and one's own soldiers. "Make use of expedients, fool the enemy and wait for the right moment to profit from his confusion." Mao invented nothing. It is all contained in the rules so carefully handed down from Chinese strategists of an age before our history began. His signal merit lay in the fact that he made use of his findings, transcribing them and fitting them into the context of his times. The peasant militia of Hunan had shown him how a revolution was fought away from the cities, and now Sun Tzŭ and his disciples had offered him a bible of military art. The genius of Mao Tse-tung is generally called common sense. In China it is in very sort supply.

At Nanking, in the gardens of the government palace where the Heavenly King of the Taiping had built a tearoom in the form of a ship, Chiang Kai-shek was also reading Sun Tzŭ, who seems to have been very much in fashion that year. Since the Chinese language contains no punctuation marks, a misplaced line or phrase can alter the whole meaning. In the simplest equations a forgotten cipher can lead to a diametrically opposite solution.

In a fit of petulance, the commander in chief had withdrawn to Japan for a few months—just long enough to cause panic in middle-class circles—but now he had returned, with the luster of a brilliantly successful campaign gilding the stars of his uniform. Beneath the military cap, worn at a confident angle, his hair was beginning to thin, but the little mustache gave a masculine air to his face and a heightened energy to his eyes. Having passed his fortieth birthday and acquired a thickening middle and a high position, the man was acquiring confidence. In Shanghai, in Canton, in every foreign concession along the Yangtze, people trembled at the thought of his removal from the scene. To strengthen his position on his path to glory, and provide him with a reliable guide, Mr. Soong had married him to his youngest, and perhaps prettiest, daughter, Mai-ling, a graduate of Wellesley College who yielded nothing to her sisters in intelligence. For spiritual comfort, Chiang Kai-shek had become a Methodist. His alliance with the Soong family contributed to his decision to give priority to economic matters; his position as brother-in-law of Sun Yat-sen brought him the support of the people.

This providential man, supported by provincial professors and many of the poor, came to terms with the financial barons, returned their estates to the rural landowners and put through a series of reassuring laws. He broke diplomatic relations with Soviet Russia. With the Communists crushed, he expressed belief in necessary reforms, but without altering China's social structure. In spite of continuing corruption aggravated by inflation, his prestige was so great that he secured the submission of the northern provinces and entered Peking. Nanking, where there were no foreign concessions, remained the capital. To Chiang went the plains and their farms, the valleys and their cities, a powerful army, the universities and the banks; to Mao, a circle of mountains not much more than a hundred miles in circumference, a thousand or so men and the disapproval of the party.

After a difficult winter, in which the men of Mao's *maquis* had fallen prey to increasing anxiety, it was necessary to re-establish discipline and receive the recruits who were beginning to come in. At last it seemed that fortune had begun to smile on the rebel. Some roving bands who had been scouring the countryside, extracting food and money from the local squires, now rallied to his cause; the fortunes of war sent him General Chu Teh and his little company of regular soldiers, and two months later a brigade of the Kuomintang commanded by General P'êng Têh-huai.

Mao was waiting for them in the mountains, seeming taller because of his excessive thinness, his eyes reddened with conjunctivitis, his clothing in rags. The flags were red and were stamped with the hammer and sickle. Officers and men alike were "comrades." The Red Army existed. It consisted of six regiments, numbered, with an intent to fool the enemy, from 28 to 33. Under the political direction of Mao, military command was given to Chu Teh.

In speaking of Chu Teh, who is never called by anything but his name, the title "General" is inappropriate.

Or perhaps it is necessary to forget everything the title normally evokes: stars, escorts, general staff, bearing and style. He was born in the province of Szechwan, the third son in a family of thirteen children, of whom five were drowned at birth because the father was too poor to support them. His maternal grandparents had been itinerant mountebanks, and his mother was a woman of such humble origin that she had no real name. Like Mao, he knew nothing of his father other than his harshness; he was forbidden to fish in the ponds or eat fruit from the trees of the local landowner. No light was ever lit at night and there was never such a thing as a day of rest, even though Szechwan was one of the most prosperous provinces of China. He was adopted by an uncle with no children of his own, and it was decided that he would study to become a mandarin and thus assist his family. When his passion for the military decided him to enter the military school at Yunnam, everyone thought he had gone mad; soldiers, merchants and itinerant mountebanks were the dregs of the earth. Soldiers were not made from honest men, any more than nails were made from first-rate iron. The word for "soldier" and "bandit" is the same in Chinese. It was at this point that the third son of the Chu family, who until then had been called Tai-chen, "Little Dog," took the name of Chu Teh, "Red Virtue." The misfortunes of China had brought into being a new man. He would live to embody his own name.

Chu Teh had really been a general in the province of Yünnan at the age of twenty-seven. In his own way, he had fought for the First Republic. But he became disgusted with an army that was not an army of the people, refused the money that was offered him by Dr. Sun Yat-sen himself to buy back troops who had deserted, and volunteered his services to the Chinese Communist party. The secretary general of the party, Chen Tu-hsiu, regarded him with suspicion; Chu Teh did not have a good reputation. After having had two wives from middle-class families, he now also had concubines and smoked opium, following the example of the local war lords. Humiliated by this rebuff, Chu vowed to make himself worthy of the cause he wanted to defend. He cured himself of opium, left for France on probation and joined Chou En-lai in Berlin. On his return to China in 1926, he was sent north in advance of the armies of Chiang Kai-shek, with the mission of organizing strikes and fomenting disturbances in the countryside. After the failure of the autumn harvest uprising, he took refuge in the mountains in southern Hunan, and it was there that Mao came to see him with an offer to unite their two forces. Chu Teh accepted without haggling. He joined Mao in May of 1928, at the head of a band of tattered, emaciated slaves, covered with vermin, most of them without shoes, and bearing their sick and wounded on primitive bamboo litters. Along the way, their ranks had been swollen by eight hundred miners from an antimony pit in Shui-kowshan, in worse condition even than Chu's own troop, and bringing with them their children, who had been used to excavate the narrower sections of the tunnels.

Of medium height, standing stiffly erect, legs spread wide and hands on hips, wearing sacklike trousers and a jacket pulled in at the waist by a wide belt, a rumpled cap sewn with a large red star pushed back on his head, a fountain pen clasp and watch chain protruding from his breast pocket, his thick lips drawn back in a malicious grin, his little eyes glittering shrewdly between the flattened nose of a boxer and black tufts of eyebrows, this old soldier seemed ready, at any moment, to disguise himself as a coolie. Once, to escape arrest, he had appeared in the middle of the soldiers sent to pick him up, with a filthy towel draped around his neck, and announced: "I'm the new cook." They believed him. With his slightly husky voice and good-natured clown's face, he resembled anything except a general. Everywhere he went, he carried with him the notes he had made in Leningrad on the tactics of Soviet guerrilla warfare. He had already been touched by legend. It was stated as fact that he advanced toward the enemy wearing an old-fashioned long robe and armed only with a fan, that he could see what was happening behind his back and lift a horse with a single hand, and that the sound of his call could summon the wind and the tempest.

In July, 1928, a brigadier general of the army of Chiang Kai-shek,

P'êng Têh-huai, came directly to the Red Army's mountain retreat instead of encircling it as he had been ordered. Followed by several thousands of volunteers from the rural districts, he joined the rebellion. Born in Mao's own province of Hunan and the son of a family of peasants, like Chu Teh, strong and heavily built, intelligent and courageous, with long sensitive hands bearing the marks of hard work, he brought Mao unexpected relief.

Chiang Kai-shek offered Mao and Chu Teh money and positions of command in his army. Chu Teh gathered together his people. "We could play bridge with the wives of the foreign imperialists, buy concubines, sell opium, ride in automobiles and get drunk with the gangsters of Shanghai. That is what we have been offered. We are your servants; tell us what our answer should be." Chiang's emissaries were sent away, to the accompaniment of jeers.

It was in this period that the fundamental principles of the army's strategy were worked out. Impressed by the famous peasant novel *At the Edge of the Water* and by all the cases in Chinese history in which the weak had conquered the strong, Mao pondered the manner in which the boxing champion Lin Chong began each match by retreating, waiting for his opponent to make the first misstep, and then swiftly attacked. He was also influenced by the prudence of the strategist Ts'ao Kui. When the prince questioned him on his tactics, Ts'ao Kui replied: "I never give the signal to attack until I feel that I have sufficient knowledge of the adversary. War is a matter of courage. The first roll of the drums raises morale; at the second, morale begins to falter; at the third, it collapses. By this time, the enemy had lost his courage, but we were filled with it. That is why we conquered. However, when one is battling a great army it is difficult to be certain of its strength. I suspected an ambush. For this reason, I studied the tracks of the enemy chariots; they were mingled in total confusion. Then I studied their banners and standards; they were no longer held high. It was safe for us to continue with the pursuit." This is the art of deduction, in which Sherlock Holmes comes to the aid of the tactician.

The principles formulated by Mao in 1928 were short and explicit: "If the enemy advances, we withdraw. If the enemy pauses, we harass him. If the enemy is weary, we strike. If the enemy withdraws, we pursue him." Twenty-five centuries earlier Sun Tzŭ had said: "Avoid combat when the enemy is fresh and vigorous. Strike when he has weakened and begins to fall back." Elementary facts of military life. In all the battles that took place during the next six years, the Red Army at first gave way, abandoned terrain and villages that were impossible to defend, vanished into the jungle, and then, moving by obscure paths and tracks, reappeared where it was least expected and struck the enemy in the rear. The same methods have been followed since antiquity. Every conquering general from Alexander and Hannibal to Napoleon, Montgomery, Rommel and Patton has applied the principle, repeated it over and over again to his subordinates, and perhaps imagined that he invented it.

Mao's soldiers, most of whom came from either the Nationalist armies or the bands of brigands that infested the region, conducted themselves as if they were in a conquered country. Some of the local peasants had the audacity to protest. The American writer Agnes Smedley, who shared the life of the Red Army for a time, reported that one day an old weaver spoke out on the subject: "I was a soldier in my youth because my family was poor, and I plundered like everyone else because it was customary. But here is an army that claims to be revolutionary and plunders like all the others. We are told that you are prepared to shoot the guilty men. I do not agree with that. Let only those be shot who directed the plunder. They are the criminals. Let the soldiers repent what they have done and serve the people. Let the man who has dishonored a poor girl pay for his crime, so that the girl need not become an object of shame!"

Wu Tse had said:

After the capture of a city, make a strong effort to win the heart of its inhabitants. Gather together your unit commanders, give firm instructions forbidding robbery and plunder, insist that homes and families be respected, that no domestic animal be killed, no tree cut down, no building destroyed and no shops set on fire. Assign the task of billeting the troops to the most prominent men of the town. Act in such a manner that the conquered will be grateful to have you for conquerors.

Sun Tzŭ had said:

The peasants can be of great use to you and serve you better than your own troops. Make them understand that they must help you in preventing the enemy from seizing their goods and carrying off their fathers, their mothers, their wives and their children. Love your soldiers and obtain for them everything that may lighten their task. When they put up with great fatigue, it is not because they take pleasure in it; when they endure privations, it is not because they are contemptuous of comfort; and when they confront death, it is not because they are disdainful of life. Think about this very seriously.

And Szu Ma Yang-chin said: "A small army should not remain in a fixed place. It should always be on the march and in action. Never do battle on terrain that has the form of a turtle lying on its back; do not camp there for any length of time." And also this phrase, which Mao was to use later, word for word: "Man is the most precious object under the heavens."

Since time immemorial in China, a man had become a soldier to avoid becoming a beggar. Under those circumstances, what respect could soldiers be expected to have for the property of others? They cut down the fruit trees and broke up the furniture for fires to warm themselves, slaughtered the water buffaloes and hogs for food, defiled the houses and polluted the wells, plundered the shops and raped the girls. Wherever they passed, dogs growled, mothers put their hands over their children's eyes, shops were barred and shuttered. Wood that had been eaten by termites was good only to be thrown on the fire, an unruly daughter could only be sold as a whore, a worthless son could only become a soldier.

Mao had the regulatons for both camp and field service drawn up by the soldiers themselves. The punishment of death was promised to traitors, deserters and cowards, to violators of innocent girls and plunderers of the poor. On the march, latrines were to be dug at least a quarter of a mile from any towns or villages, and they were to be filled in before departure. The army must return any vegetables or hay it borrowed, compensate any peasant who had been injured, leave the houses they occupied in order, and never smoke or drink wine.

Mao himself often talked to his companions in this first Chinese soviet on such subjects as the Russian Revolution and the European proletariat. To fight and die for the triumph of the Chinese revolution was also to fight for the revolution of workers throughout the world, under the inspired leadership of Ka Ma-tsu (Karl Marx) and Li Ning (Lenin). A redistribution of the land, based on equal sharing, was put into effect. The companies of the army were organized into cells. Absolute equality existed between officers and soldiers, and the latter controlled their own administration. The officers ate with the other men, and there was no system of insignia of rank or external marks of respect.

This little army, poorly equipped, poorly trained, poorly fed, still largely undisciplined and with no means of communication, was at a great disadvantage when it was forced to fight. Cannon were hollowed out from the trunks of trees, which were then reinforced with bands of iron; the insufficient rifles were augmented with bows and arrows with poisoned tips. Occasionally, weary of burying the dead to the sound of a trumpet and the waving of red flags above the tombs, little groups of men deserted, having lost hope in any possible victory. In the snows of a mountain winter, men shivered and froze in their thin cotton garments. Some committed suicide. Nationalist villages were attacked during the night, simply to procure food. In telling her the story of these years, Chu Teh sometimes said to Agnes Smedley: "That night, we ate." To rid themselves of fleas, their remnants of clothing were boiled whenever it was warm enough. These skeletons of men, with callused hands, clothed in rags, their feet bound in shreds of sandals, their chests crossed with cartridge belts of ragged linen, carrying their ration of hard rice cakes on their backs, were the ancestors of all those who would one day rise in the mountains of Southeast Asia, calling themselves Vietminh or Vietcong. And the foreign armies of occupation would be unable to conquer them, in spite of their tanks and planes. Invisible, unbreakable, always ready to pounce on their prey and then vanish into the brush, these slaves were capable of anything to attain the mirage they saw before them—liberty and an acre of land they could call their own.

In the cities whole cartloads of students suspected of Communist sympathies were being decapitated outside the temples.

In 1931 the Red Army numbered less than sixty thousand men. In 1934 more than 300,000 had been organized into four army corps, with Chu Teh as commander in chief. Five campaigns of encirclement and annihilation were launched against it by Chiang Kai-shek, some of them directed by the German General Hans von Seeckt, and numbering as many as 500,000 men. On the walls of houses in the neighboring countryside, the Nationalist soldiers could read: "Brothers in the White armies, for whom are you fighting and for what? Your pay goes into the pocket of your officers. You are mercenaries of oppressors and imperialists. The poor should not attack the poor!" The chief of staff of one of Chiang's brigades stated: "The Reds have made platoons of our battalions. And of the platoons, there is nothing left but corpses." The soldiers of the Kuomintang, strangers to the region, did not speak the same language or eat the same food as the silent peasants by whom they were surrounded. They heard rumors that the Red soldiers were being given land in payment for their service, but among the Nationalist forces discipline was poor, their equipment mediocre, and their columns frequently returned from an engagement without arms and without officers.

Suddenly, during the fifth attempt at encirclement, directed by General Falkenhausen, chief of the German military mission with the Kuomintang, the Reds found themselves threatened with total blockade. Fortifications barred every path of escape. Little by little, the constant pressure was pushing Mao's men into thickets and gullies where they would be massacred. The specter of famine and death hung over the mountain peaks, where the red flags no longer flew. Mao and Chu Teh were forced to flee, leading an army that resembled a pack of starving wolves, most of them racked with the fevers of malaria, their feet protected against the rocky paths only by strips of linen. Standing in rags, his eyes sunk deep in their sockets, Chu Teh threw a handful of earth on the tomb of Comrade Chang, his wife, killed in battle. Then he and his men turned to face the hills that concealed the pursuing enemy.

He clenched his rifle in his fist and raised his harsh voice in the strains of the "Internationale." In Shanghai his own obituary had just appeared in the newspapers, attributing his death to tuberculosis.

Mao slept little and worked late into the night, sometimes waking his aide-de-camp to ask him for something to eat or drink. His own wife, his "proud young poplar," had also been executed by the Kuomintang. When the army moved, he walked with the rest of the men, carrying slung across his back the gray satchel with nine compartments in which he kept his cards, his books and the archives of the party. A savage pride compelled him not to make use of the horse to which his rank entitled him, but to give it to men who were in worse condition than he.

One day one of these men said to him, "Comrade Mao, I am just a common soldier and my death would be of no importance. But I am on horseback and you on foot. We need you too much to think of ourselves or our condition. Get up."

"No," Mao replied. "You will not die. We will live, we will fight and will think together. It is that that makes us comrades and Communists."

A new revolutionary song had been born and was particularly popular with the women:

> My brother and my love,
> I have sent them off to war. . . .

One day Chu Teh paused in front of a peasant girl of about twenty-five who was humming the song. She had great black eyes, dazzling teeth and a countenance marred by the scars of smallpox. Dressed as a man, with her hair cut short, she was carrying her rifle on her shoulder. Chu Teh asked her if there were many girls like herself in her district.

"Many," she replied, "and the men of the Kuomintang no longer dare touch us, because they know they would be dead within the hour."

The former slave of a local baron who had bought her as an infant, she became the new wife of Chu Teh.

Chapter 8

In which the reader learns that the Long March was decided on by an academic poet, whose portrait is sketched by the author. In which the fleeing Red Army crosses the Yangtze and the Tatu rivers and rejoins the forces of Chang Ko-tao, a rival of Mao Tse-tung. In which a schism takes place in the command group. In which the author compares the Long March to the Anabasis and Mao Tse-tung to Xenophon. How it is considered natural and proper, in China, for a chief of state also to be a poet. In which the author draws some conclusions about the lessons of the Long March.

Men at some time are masters of their fates;
The fault, dear Brutus, is not in our stars,
But in ourselves, that we are underlings.
                    SHAKESPEARE, *Julius Caesar*, Act I, Scene 2

When it became clear that the Red armies were going to be destroyed unless they could find a means of escape, Mao and Chu Teh decided that they must break out. With a price of $250,000 in silver on each of their heads, they could not dream of establishing themselves either in the plains, which were controlled by Chiang Kai-shek, or along the seacoast, where they could again be encircled. Only an enormous evasive movement could provide hope of eventual victory, and this only if it was successful. Counterattack was out of the question; so long as they were surrounded, any direct engagement was unthinkable. Did the Hebrews take Moses seriously when he came down from Mount Sinai and told them he had been commanded to lead them into the land of Canaan? Mao must have been considered a madman when he let it be known that he planned to make for a Communist bastion in the heart of old China, within the great bend of the Yellow River in the province of Shensi. As the crow flies, it was almost a thousand miles. By the mountain and forest paths they must follow to avoid the most serious military obstacles, it could be six thousand—the distance from Edinburgh to the Cape of Good Hope or from Paris to Siam—or, in kilometers, ten thousand, the figure which in China represents infinity.

No one in Europe would have attempted it. In the Empire at the Center of the World, it is admired, but it is not considered astonishing. It is one among hundreds of enormous, everyday enterprises. It pleased old Chu Teh, who concealed a romantic heart beneath his leathery exterior. Everything is possible if only one has the time; after all, the Jews took forty years to cross the desert, and the Greeks required fifteen months to make the circuit of Asia Minor. In China proportions naturally assume those of the land itself, of the rivers, of the catastrophes and wars. Throughout history, and sometimes for a trifling reason, the armies of conquerors or unifiers had crossed the country from north to south or from east to west, on foot or on horseback. What seems folly in the West is part of Chinese logic.

It began October 16, 1934, with the Red Army raiding parties moving out from their bases, followed by long columns of families, of men and animals laden with printing presses, dismantled forges for weapons, sewing machines, scrap iron, tools and camping utensils. A minutely detailed plan called for the raiding parties to force a passage through the blockade, cross the mountains, and then the entire group would move westward, through forest paths that had scarcely existed before that day. On October 16, 1934, the retreat inspired no poems, because it was a defeat. But the Anabasis was also a defeat. When an army strikes camp, it is because death is imminent and no one, except for the enemy, cares much whether you live or die. In later years this retreat would become legend, poets would sound epic trumpets, operas would transform a despairing migration into a grandiose fresco, with choruses and orchestras to impart the thrill of heroism. In later years the Long March would become a victory.

During the first days Mao remained silent—curiously silent, since the smallest feat of arms was generally sufficient to bring out the lyrical pen he kept with his papers in that nine-compartmented satchel. Occasionally, however, he did pause to scribble a verse about the crystal air of the mountain peaks, the flight of wild ducks, the sound of cannon, the banners snapping in the wind, and later, after having answered the directives of the Central Committee, he would recopy them in classic calligraphy. Every private in the army would have done the same thing if he had known how to write. In China even grocers announced the arrival of merchandise in metered verses.

> *Narrow pathways, silent forests, delicate mosses,*
> *Where will our footsteps lead us today?*
> *The red flag unfolds like a sun in the wind. . . .*

Day will be dawning in the east.
Let no one say that we have begun to march too soon.
Man does not grow old walking through greening hills.

If Mao had been nothing more than a poet, his genius would not have disturbed this century. There is nothing here that is any better than the examination paper of a good student. His poems do not benefit from his sharp and personal observation of battles and danger. This man, who as always liked his food highly spiced, writes only in a form that is cool and classic.

When the rain has ended, and the sun is going down,
The mountain is wreathed in mists of aquamarine. . . .

His pen was stopped, his throat constricted by this flight of hunted animals, hoping to escape pursuit by moving silently from one clump of woods to another. He was thinking only of rescuing from the trap the 120,000 men and 35 women who had obeyed his order for retreat. He lived with the fear of death. He, too, could have promised nothing but blood, sweat and tears, but if he did not have the greatness to say it, it was because those who followed him would doubtless not have had the courage to hear it. With every day that passed, he lost men. Some gave up and some deserted, despairing of ever arriving at their goal. It is hard to command the devotion of the masses when one has nothing to offer but cold, fear and an empty belly.

The flight of the Red armies did not go unnoticed. A rear guard of partisans and regular troops, commanded by a former carpetmaker, was left behind to hold back the pursuers, and it was never wiped out. If the fugitives could not be caught, the land could be emptied, the bridges cut, the regions they must cross terrorized. Airplanes were sent to watch over them, garrisons they must confront were reinforced, junks they might have used were sunk, they were followed step by step and traps were laid before their steps. If they did not wish to die, they must someday cross the Yangtze, which barred the gateway to the north. Two and a half months after the march began, Mao entered the wretched hamlet of Tsunyi. A special conference of the Political Bureau of the party, of which he was no longer a member, had been convened here. And it was here, in a rambling, one-storied, brick house that his first triumph was achieved.

As an apprentice in the Leninist school of thought, he was forced to justify his actions, sometimes compromise and occasionally give in, pretending to be submissive and hiding his rebellion in a cloud of smoke. No Chinese ever lacks orthodox clichés when he wants to conceal his thought and disguise his disobedience. Until this time, Mao had evaded the issue.

It would be an enormous error to give up the battle in the cities and lose ourselves in the mentality of peasants. But it would be an equal mistake, if such a thing is possible in the party, to fear the growing strength of the peasantry and believe that it might become more powerful than the workers and thereby become disastrous for the revolution. In a China which is still a semicolonial nation, if the peasant revolt does not benefit from the direction of the workers, it can only end in disaster. But on the other hand, the revolution could not conceivably suffer from a reinforcement of the worker force by the struggle of the peasants.

Mao's strength lies in the fact that he sometimes had the courage to proclaim himself a rebel and disavow the policies of the Central Committee. Four years earlier he had disobeyed an order to hold Changsha, and withdrawn from the city. That had caused a conflict with the leaders of the Political Bureau who were still in Shanghai. Chou En-lai and Liu Shao-ch'i had agreed with him. Even as president of the soviet of Kiangsi, Mao was never more than the leader of a rebel band. All his reversals were attributed to his indiscipline, and no one on the committee had any doubts concerning the ultimate defeat of this deviationist. That Mao should have used the Red Army to establish the revolution in a few provinces seemed a serious fault which could lead to other reversals in the cities. In the minds of Marxist-Leninist theorists, the peasantry could only be an ally of the revolution and not its vanguard.

But the course of events had proved this individualist to be right. At the moment no one else dared assume responsibility for the desperate situation. When it forbade Mao to threaten Nanking and draw the enemy away from the mountains, the Central Committee had put the seal of its responsibility on the failure in Kiangsi. Following this, those who had not believed in the idea of the march had only one desire: to utilize it as a screen for their own flight; a flight so rapid that even the local command was not given a few weeks' respite to organize the retreat. Partnerships dissolved, the appointed leaders were forced to confess their mistakes, and the Komintern delegate himself supported the only man who had demonstrated the ability to extricate the Red Army from disaster. At Tsunyi the authority of Mao Tse-tung was recognized. He was elected president of the party, and from this point on was to be its sole, if not uncontested, leader.

Even at this time Mao's bearing had taken on a heaviness that was a reflection of his responsibilities and his state of mind. The great, round lion's face radiated an assurance he did not perhaps possess. But his pride in having been judged right was gradually becoming more evident, accentuating the strength and serenity which rarely deserted him, when he would be seized with a sudden fit of anger and his mouth would vomit insults and obscenities. The sixty cigarettes he smoked every day

H

yellowed his fingers and blackened his teeth, and the wart at the tip of his chin grew larger. His clumsily barbered mop of black hair would occasionally fall across his forehead, and his hand would automatically come up to push it back, with no sign of impatience. At one time it had almost concealed his enormous ears and brow, but now that he had passed his fortieth birthday it was beginning to thin. From his corner of the enormous boxing ring that was China, he studied the movements of his opponent, Chiang Kai-shek, who had gone personally to the abandoned mountain redoubts in Kiangsi to announce that the rebellion had been crushed. Was the Communist adventure to end in the same manner as the Taiping revolt? Mao's objective was to gain time, and it was this that the Nationalists were striving hardest to deprive him of. "Our long-term strategy must be a fight of one against ten; our immediate tactics must be a fight of ten against one. If we can conquer, we will fight. If not, we will move on." He possessed a formidable capacity for absorbing punishment and a glance that revealed a swift and terrible reaction.

> The winds are violent in the west,
> And against the frozen sky of a morning moon
> The wild duck shrieks his cry.
> The pacing of the horses is like the sound of
>   breaking glass,
> The frozen glass of the morning moon.
> The trumpet begins its lengthy wail,
> This mountain pass is awesome, but do not think that
>   it is made of iron.
> Today, with ever-lengthening steps, we shall cross
>   its peaks. . . .

It was after his political victory in Tsunyi that Mao began again to set down lines of poetry in his florid handwriting. He had rid himself of a major source of anxiety. It had been decided at Tsunyi that he would cross the Yangtze 125 miles upstream from Chungking, and join his forces with those of Chang Ko-tao, which held the northern part of the province of Szechwan. But the Nationalist opposition proved too strong. Once again Mao turned his back on the orders of the party, refused the issue of direct conflict and returned to Tsunyi, planning to move southward from there across the mountains toward the frontier provinces of Indochina and Burma. Illness and desertion had already cost him twenty thousand men. To escape observation from the air, he no longer marched except at night. The men and women who followed him slept in ditches, huddled against each other. They followed a zigzag route and sent out diversionary columns in the hope of fooling the enemy. Three months later, clothed in brightly colored rags, and having survived a guerrilla warfare with half-savage tribes, the Red Army passed to the north of Kunming. On occasion, the fear of its approach emptied villages of their inhabitants and their flocks, even though the army made a practice of liberating slaves, opening prisons, burning government archives and distributing money, salt and sacks of rice. In the whole memory of man, soldiers had never been known to conduct themselves with such dignity.

The Yangtze River raced down the gorges and between the wooded crests of the province of Yünnan. On either side of the flowing mud which came down from Tibet and gave the Yangtze its name of "River of the Golden Sands," the majority of the ferries, rafts and junks had been sunk, and all the bridges had been destroyed. But a ruse proved effective. While the majority of the men pretended to be building a bamboo bridge, a raiding party disguised in Nationalist uniforms fell on a little garrison sixty miles away, and seized a few ferryboats and a strategic crossing point. Within nine days the whole of the Red Army had crossed the river and was beginning its march toward the north. A month later, on May 26, 1935, it reached the Tatu River.

The rocks descended perpendicularly to the river banks, and the river itself was in full flood. The waters could be heard rushing through the mountains long before they were seen. The passage was defended by three elite Nationalist regiments, one stationed at the landing for the village of Ou Chou En Ch'ang and the two others just below. Even though the Red advance guard, commanded by General Lin Piao, had marched forty miles without a halt and arrived at ten o'clock on a night that was black with drizzly rain, the attack was launched immediately. It was in this same spot seventy-three years earlier that the remnants of the Taiping army had been crushed by Manchu troops. Chu Teh has said of that night: "We repeated to ourselves Karl Marx's line that history always repeats itself, once as tragedy and again as comedy." The Nationalist garrison fled without looking back, and within the next sixty hours Lin Piao had transported an entire division across the furiously flooding river on two small ferries. But this small-scale crossing was not enough. A hundred and twenty-five miles to the west, Mao launched his own forces against the town of Lintsing Chou, where there was an old high suspension bridge of which only one platform had been destroyed by bombing. In spite of Nationalist fire which hurled some of them to their death in the racing current, volunteers managed to cling to the still dangling chains of the bridge and reach the opposite bank.

This extraordinary exploit, which the bombardiers of the Kuomintang were powerless to prevent, opened the way to the north and the snowy mountains of Tibet, and it was here that the Red Army lost the great majority of its men and its beasts of burden. Protecting themselves as best they could against the cold and the constantly watching planes, striking bargains with the tribes that held the mountain passes, carving steps for their bloodied feet through the glaciers and cliffs, constantly moving forward to escape death and incapable of caring for their wounded, they arrived exhausted in the area of the Great Plains, and there they were forced to do battle with troops trying to bar their passage. In 1946 Mao Tse-tung told Robert Payne: "We killed our livestock and our horses so that we might eat, and we loaded their flesh on the few animals we had kept to carry the baggage. At the end, we had eaten even these and carried the flesh ourselves. Our most terrible enemies were the native tribes. It was from our contact with them that we learned the most. We have to thank the generalissimo for having driven us into these foreign regions. Without him, we would never have seen them." Chiang Kai-shek had never imagined the Reds could go this far.

On June 20, 1935, Mao accomplished his junction with the Fourth Communist Army, which had come to meet him. Of the 120,000 men who had left Kiangsi, forty thousand remained. A conference was held to decide on the future plan of campaign. Mao has always admitted that this was the most critical moment in the entire history of the revolution. Chang Ko-tao, an enormous man with an eye that flashed lightning, arrived on the scene with his escort, resembling an emperor in an opera or an actor coming on stage. He waited while Mao and Chu Teh walked to meet him, through a beating rain. The schism had taken place. Mao and Chu Teh estimated that it would be impossible to establish a base north of Szechwan where Chiang Kai-shek could be resisted. On the tenth of July, leaving Chu Teh as a hostage with his bitter rival, Chang Ko-tao, Mao departed for the northeast followed by the remnants of his troops.

Harassed at first by Muslim tribes hurling rocks at them from ambush in the mountains, then hacking a passage through the jungle, they arrived at last at the region known as the Great Steppes, a semidesert of grass and water into which the footsteps of men and the hoofs of horses sink without a trace. It is a land above which heavy rain clouds roll, and many of the marchers perished, either from drowning or exhaustion or because they could not be rescued. A few grains of dried corn were sprinkled over the faces of the dead, because the living no longer had the strength to eat them. In the shelters that were thrown up for the night fires would not light. And when they left here, the fugitives arrived in another region where the houses were built of dried mud and the inhabitants had fled. In this area, burned one day by the sun and the next drenched by cloudbursts, they ate rats and sometimes drank their own urine. When they pierced the last enemy lines, entered Kansu province and saw the first Chinese peasants of the north, they ran to them, embraced them and kissed the soil, just as the Greek soldiers of the Anabasis had done when they finally saw the sea.

At the foot of the Great Wall of Shensi on October 20, 1935, only seven thousand men, ghostly and haggard, arrived at their meeting with a few thousand partisan friends. They looked like slaves escaped from the galleys. Mao has said that he no longer possessed anything but his flesh and bones.

There were a few women still alive in this party of escapees, and one of them was the woman Mao had married after the death of Yang Kai-hui. They had nothing in common with the women of Xenophon's army, dragged from bordellos and dropped whenever it was convenient. The trials of this march had left them with marks even deeper than those of the men. They resembled female wolves, wild, sharp-toothed. They had done more than conquer hunger, thirst, cold, weakness, despair and death. They now knew how to read. One by one, a few hundred characters had been taught all the illiterates, which included most of the soldiers, because the women had carried words on their backs. Day after day, mile after mile, step by step, the Chinese characters had been engraved in all their memories. The Red Army did not content itself with freeing slaves. It gave to those slaves the priceless gift which fortune had reserved until now to the masters: knowledge which could open a secret universe. When the survivors paraded through Yenan, behind a fanfare of trumpets and Comrade Lin Piao on horseback, who could have imagined the legendary glory that would crown this band of young people, skeletons covered with the scabs of wounds, bearing on their backs, like beggars, great straw hats, and stamping firmly on the earth, in spite of the torn sandals that covered their feet?

[At Pergamum] Xenophon went to pay homage to the god; the Lacedaemonians, the other leaders of the retreat and the soldiers themselves were in agreement that he should have his choice of the horses, pairs of oxen and the rest of the booty, so that from here on he would be obligated to others. In the meantime Thibron arrived and took command of the army. He incorporated it into the other Hellenic forces and began the war against Tissaphernes and Pharnabazus.

So ends the account of the March of the Ten Thousand, after the remnants of Xenophon's army, abandoning the greater part of its slaves and booty, finally reached the Greek lines.

There is nothing in common here with the Long March. The Greeks, who carried no new message in their baggage, were animated only by fear, the lust for gold and a taste for battle. Underpaid mercenaries who mocked at the cause they served, insolent, vulgar, vain, jealous of each other, vicious and corrupt, they pillaged, raped, massacred or deserted, with no other thought than escaping with their lives, filling their pouches with gold or giving free rein to their depravities. Those among them who succumbed to the snows of the Armenian mountains were abandoned without even a gesture of pity. Mao Tse-tung's men had aroused hope everywhere in the vast stretch of land they had crossed, and left behind them the faith which one day would give these oppressed slaves reason to stand up. Everyone who saw them pass was marked, in one way or another, with the intensity of their belief.

They had survived, but they were little more than skeletons. Chiang Kai-shek need only have followed them into Shensi to have eliminated the military power of the Communists, forcing its remaining elements to die in the Gobi Desert or become captives of the Russians in Siberia. But Chiang Kai-shek believed that he had knocked out his opponent and did nothing. With this piece of strategic negligence, he signed his own defeat and handed victory to the Reds. Everywhere on their passage they had stirred the winds of change which gradually would be transformed into a cyclone. The old forms of property had been destroyed, the land had been shared out among the former slaves, and the weapons had been distributed which would one day set all China aflame. A year later the Reds held the life of Chiang in their hands.

Mao carried with him a few poems, commemorating this immortal march:

> The sky is far, the clouds are pale,
> The wild ducks are vanishing to the south.
> If we do not reach the Great Wall, we are not men. . . .
> Still in the saddle, always in the saddle, I drive my horse.
> And then I turn: surprise!
> I am within three inches of the sky. . . .
>
> The Red Army does not fear the rigors of a forced march,
> To this army, one thousand mountains and ten thousand
> rivers are no more than a gentle walk.
> The peaks of Wumeng are no more than mounds beneath
> our feet,
> And five chains of mountains rise as no more than a swell.
>
> The cliffs are burning, wreathed in clouds,
> Washed by the river of golden sands.
> Icy are the links of the Tatu River chain,
> Soldiers do not fear the ageless snows of Minshan.
> And when the last passage is forced,
> The army will smile.

The Emperor Ch'ien Lung is said to have written forty thousand poems. In the West to be a poet is a sign of weakness; in a leader of men it would be considered the mark of some form of mental derangement. We may admire Napoleon's love letters, scratched out in the same style as his orders of battle, and we may even take vicarious pride in the women he captured as if they were so many cities. But we would never have forgiven him the writing of poems. In China what chief of state, what general would not think of poetry as a symbol of his mastery of all things? When he went to his own rooms after luncheon, Chiang Kai-shek followed the example of all the others and indulged in this secret vice.

> *See how the hill is covered with bamboo!*
> *It gives freshness to summer days.* . . .

Compared with this, Mao's poetry can be considered on the level of Saint-John Perse, but his style is nonetheless amateurish and heavy. On several occasions he had rubbed shoulders with defeat, conquered gigantic obstacles and survived ordeals under which beasts of burden had succumbed. For a time, the rumor of his death was current from Shanghai to Canton. But he himself brought back no account of the Long March; nothing except these few poems. A pastime, an accomplishment of the cultivated man, for the Chinese, poetry should be concerned only with the sublime and contain no personal sentiment. It is for this reason that we shall doubtless never see the full text of the poem he wrote on the death of his first wife. There can be no question that he possesses political genius, acquired from years of studious application and ripened by years of adversity. But he is neither the poet nor the historian of this Anabasis, which had no Xenophon nor even a T. E. Lawrence.

Having assumed command of all the forces that remained behind, Chu Teh, in turn, completed the march. One year after Mao, he arrived at the last station of the railway in the province of Shensi, with forty thousand men and Chang Ko-tao, more resolute than ever in his determination to do away with Mao. Chu Teh was bearded and resembled a ghost. For years he had lived like a wild beast, not even taking off his clothes to sleep. But he, too, wrote poetry.

This defeat, transformed into a legendary triumph whose true heroism can never be properly sung so long as the language of the picture postcard remains its only official literature, was actually more of a manifesto than a national epic, a formidable machine for sowing revolutionary ideas across twelve provinces, eighteen mountain chains, twenty-four rivers and sixty-two cities. It needed only a spark for fire to sweep all China. I had learned that before coming to China. The revolution rested in its museum like an embalmed corpse. It did not stink, but it seemed very dead.

Chapter 9

In which the author describes Mr. Wen, who has been charged with bringing him certain official remonstrances, and in which Mr. Wen announces that the leaders of the State are too occupied with matters of the present to concern themselves with memories of the past. How it is possible to feel alone in the midst of 700 million men and women. In which the author experiences a moment of discouragement, in spite of the amiable assurances of the Chinese, and pays a rapid visit to the Museum of the Army. In which, analyzing his difficulties in following the wandering course of the thinking of those people with whom he has talked, he tells of how the Chinese decided to assume the expenses of his journey. How a general succeeds only in boring the author and his crew.

We were well aware that we were dealing with the Chinese; that is to say with men whose sincerity is always open to question.
— E. R. Huc, *The Chinese Empire* (*L'Empire Chinois*)

A messenger was sent to inform me that Mr. Wen would expect us at eight o'clock in the evening, in one of the public rooms of the hotel. This time there was no possibility of letting it be known that this was our dinner hour. It would be better simply to give in. Since I considered it a serious occasion, I wore a black tie and asked the other members of my crew to make some attempt at formal attire.

In spite of the fact that he was approaching sixty, Mr. Wen was a fine figure of a man. His gift for oratory, the rigidity of his faith in official doctrine, the impassibility of his features and the dignity of his appearance would certainly one day carry him to the presidency of the Association of which at the moment he was only a committee member. Only very rarely, when something was said about the imperialist clique or the bad faith of the Soviet government, did a spark of amusement gleam behind the thick lenses of his glasses. He also occasionally indulged in a malicious little snicker when a Westerner pronounced words such as "freedom of opinion" or "objectivity of judgment." If some trace of kindness had appeared, even fleetingly, on that bland and icy face, it might have been possible to say of Mr. Wen what I had often thought of Dr. Sun Yat-sen—that he resembled a Methodist parson. But he gave no evidence of possessing either kindness or hope. Mr. Wen's heart, and he claimed to have one, and his soul, which he considered a capitalist abstraction, were as tightly buttoned up as his person, without a single rough edge to which any sentiment might cling, and with no color beyond the uniform gray of the tiles and walls of the city. The monotonous inflections of his voice always came to an abrupt end on the razor's edge of universal truth, slicing through imperialist arguments.

The speech he made to us now reeked of sulphur. He started from some far-off point and advanced through thickets of underbrush which made it impossible to tell in what direction he was moving. What he meant by this repetition of the plagues and tyrants China had endured until she was liberated by Chairman Mao Tse-tung was: "You have oppressed us enough in the past; now it is your turn to give in. You have imposed your will on us long enough; now you must comply with ours. We have the future before us, and if you have no interest in it, you might just as well get back to your own affairs." I guessed that I had been judged and condemned. Since everyone on the Chinese side was taking notes on what was said, so that they would have a complete and accurate record, I made a note of one small phrase in his flow of words for myself:

"As for your desire to meet with our leaders and question them about the revolution, we must inform you that those leaders are too busy with the building of China to waste time on an examination of the past."

Mr. Wen was approaching his peroration, and I made no attempt to interrupt him: to anyone approaching it in good faith, the past could be found in the museums, in which there was nothing that had not been thoroughly authenticated.

I glanced around me at the other members of my crew. By this time I had nothing further to lose and could indulge myself in the luxury of a free man's reaction. If I were not to be able to ask Chou En-lai if it was Stalin who had demanded liberation of the captive Chiang Kai-shek; to ask Chu Teh why he had remained with Chang Ko-tao, in 1935, instead of following Mao; to talk with Madame Soong Ch'ing-ling about her dead husband, Sun Yat-sen, and her sister, Madame Chiang Kai-shek; to obtain from Lin Piao an account of the crossing of the Tatu River; and, last but not least, to question the great Mao as to whether he had ever despaired of the future during the Long March; then I might as well abandon any thought of writing a book and making a film about the revolution, return immediately to Europe and turn my attention to something else.

I was about to make my speech to this effect, when Mr. Tsai

interrupted. He was still wearing his cap, as if this emphasized the importance of the moment. He wanted simply to make it clear that he entirely approved of Mr. Wen's statement, so that we should not dismiss it lightly, imagining it the opinion of just a single member of the Association council. He suggested that we read Chairman Mao's 1942 reflections on the problem of literature and art in the service of the people. In Mr. Tsai's opinion, treating the treasures of the Museum of the Revolution lightly was equivalent to siding with the imperialists. Even though it was clothed in a political vocabulary, this declaration cracked as sharply beneath the teeth as one of those sea slugs I had eaten.

I, too, began at the beginning: in China time might be of little importance, but to us who lived among the urgencies of capitalism its price was high and it slipped away too fast. Second, the time for evasive and tentative proposals should have passed; by now they must have come to some conclusion about us, and I would be grateful to learn just what this conclusion permitted us to do. Our ambition was huge, I knew that, but what ambition could not be accomplished if all one's strength was devoted to it? And finally, if we were not allowed to question the leaders about past events, they must understand that the testimony we took back to other Westerners would be worthless. My questions to the leaders would have to do not only with the past. Perhaps they had better tell us clearly, here and now, that there was nothing more for us to see in China.

My reply provoked only a little gust of laughter. Mr. Wen stood up and stretched out a cold hand, which I touched briefly for the sake of form. Discussion was not his strong point. He recited the pages of his breviary, let fly a last arrow and broke off. He was about to vanish into the elevator when Simon caught him by the coat tails.

"Can't we at least see the historical documents in your film archives and be granted the right to reproduce them?"

Mr. Wen seemed surprised.

"We will study this problem and let you have an answer in good time."

Then, with a final admonition to think over seriously what he had said, he disappeared, followed by his little band of colleagues.

In the depths of my distress, I experienced a certain pleasure: the Russians, whom I did not like, were going to shed blood, sweat and tears over these Chinese. In Moscow they had at least answered my questions—not all of them and not always willingly, which had irritated me, but they had answered. Physically upset by the mistrust I was sure I inspired in them and haunted by the thought of the line of people waiting before Lenin's tomb, I told myself that things could be no worse anywhere. I was wrong.

Could it be simply a matter of a change in the clock? The time that flowed by so rapidly in Europe here resembled an enormous river whose muddied, yellow waters barely moved. It possessed a density, a weight I had never observed in it before. The days that fled from me everywhere else here stretched out interminably, mournful, humid and gray.

That night I slept very little. The brittle sound of the rain dripping from the rooftops was drowned out, every now and then, by the roar of the locomotives. After Mr. Wen's departure I had held a meeting with the other members of my crew. No one believed that we could make a decent historical film without documents and without interviews with the principal characters of the revolution. The cameraman talked of abandoning the whole project; he had an aversion to filming any subject that had not been carefully researched and was convinced that his chances here had been ruined by two television crews which had arrived shortly before we did. It seemed now, in fact, that there was nothing to do but to write and film the journey as it developed, but this idea pleased neither Simon nor the cameraman. Only the sound engineer, who was furious at our enforced inaction, agreed with me.

My first thought had been to abandon our historical project and ask to visit Sinkiang, but I rejected this almost immediately; the Chinese might be very relieved to see us concentrating on a contemporary subject, but they were not about to let us visit Sinkiang because it was a forbidden area. It would be better to continue playing the role of offended guest and avoid being ridiculed. Simon urged me to request a hearing at the Ministry of Foreign Affairs, to protest our being denied a meeting with any government leaders. Marcuse agreed to deliver such a message, and I wrote a note which I planned to deliver if the hearing were granted. That afternoon I received a reply from the Ministry, stating that at the moment everyone there was extremely busy but that I might present my problems to the Association of the Chinese people for Cultural Relations Abroad. This was all the proof we needed that the decision about us had been taken on a higher echelon and that the circle was firmly closed.

Pierre Nora was coming back to life. The deathly fear that had clouded his eyes was gone. During his first two days in the hospital, incapable of telling an attendant from a doctor, he had feared that his case was being ignored by anyone with responsibility. Little by little, he had come to realize that it was being studied with enormous care and that the smallest observations were reported to a central service whose function was to analyze and extract from them a sort of electronic synthesis. Three days after his admission, a doctor difficult to distinguish from any other hospital employee came to see him, gave him a detailed diagnosis of his illness and suggested that he could be definitively cured by an operation that was still considered risky in France. He also stated that the Chinese possessed delicate and costly equipment which had only just become available in a few Paris hospitals. This

confirmed my earlier impression that Chinese technicians had no reason
to envy their European colleagues. I also knew that they refused to run
the smallest risk of failure. In this they were following the example of
their military leaders, who decided to do battle only when success was
certain. The political and administrative system of China was perplex-
ing, because it resembled nothing that existed elsewhere, but its
strength and effectiveness were impressive.

The sensation of youth that had pulsed through my veins when we
first arrived was ebbing slowly away. I was unhappy, depressed, and
beginning to think of my trip to China as a shipwreck. At least I had met
a few good friends who would perhaps still be good friends when we
returned home. If I brought back no more than that, the trip would have
been worthwhile.

I left Nora at the hospital and went back to the hotel. Someone was
playing the piano in a neighboring room. Anywhere else I would have
found it intolerable. Here it was like a breath of Western civilization
which I inhaled delightedly; it was a beacon in the night that surrounded me, bringing me security and comfort. But who was sending
me this message I could not decode?

At seven o'clock in the evening, there was a knock at the door and Mr.
Tsai came in, with his cap pulled down so far around his ears that I did
not immediately recognize him. He was accompanied by Mr. Chen and
the interpreter. Even though this visit had not been announced, I
suspected that they had come to ferret out my state of mind after
leaving us to stew in our own juice for a whole day. How was I feeling?
Did I need anything? Mr. Tsai seemed pensive.

We seated ourselves on the little furniture available, while I offered
them cigarettes and attempted to gauge the degree of cordiality I should
display. Suddenly my minor irritations were overridden by the desire to
talk about the one thing that really tormented me: the book on China, to
which I had decided to devote two years of my life, and which now was
foundering. I explained that I must give up any thought of writing an
account of the Chinese revolution. They agreed—to carry out such an
enormous enterprise in such a brief time . . . I shrugged. In the same
length of time I had managed a pretty thorough inquiry into the Battle
of Dienbienphu. But there, it was true, I had been able to see Giap, and
there had been no lack of testimony to the Vietminh story. Mr. Tsai put
his head between his hands.

"Our leaders are very busy," he said. "They must often go out into the
provinces to correct the mistakes that inevitably occur during the
building of a nation." Twenty-five years ago the problems had not been
the same. Then it had been a matter of fighting, and the outcome of the
battle had been in doubt. It was possible to devote time to studying the
problem with foreign journalists. Today . . .

"Your leaders give interviews to visiting basketball teams," I replied.

"The meetings with basketball teams form part of the over-all conferences on economic development. We do not think that you could retrace our history in so short a time, because China is an enormous country, the roots of its revolution go deep and our leaders are not the only protagonists—thousands and thousands of workers performed countless individual exploits. It is on this that we would like to see you concentrate."

As far as film documents were concerned, an effort would be made to show us some. There were not many in existence, but everything possible would be done to help us. We would soon be leaving for the provinces, where we could see firsthand the development of agriculture and industry. In contemporary China more than 90 percent of the once oppressed workers had given themselves body and soul to the building of a new nation; it was this, above all, that should be written and filmed. It was this story that they would like to see over my name. As for the other things—well, I could always come back. What I had not seen this time I could see later.

Mr. Tsai told me this with an intensity that was both serious and mournful. His countenance seemed shrunken, as if he had spent the afternoon standing in the rain. Chen smoked in silence, nodding approval and occasionally betraying a touch of apprehension.

Their promises did not altogether heal my wounds. A few days before, an unknown envoy had suddenly come looking for us. Did we want to see the documentary films on the Long March? We would be taken to see them. We were conducted to a neighborhood movie house, where we took our seats about half an hour before the showing began. The hall filled up, the lights went down, and on the screen appeared a film version of an opera in which actors portraying Mao Tse-tung, Lin Piao and Chu Teh sang of their devotion to the Chinese people, broke the chains of the repressed and waved red flags as they crossed rivers and strode through mountains. Why get upset? I explained that such reconstructions did not interest us, that we were seeking the historic truth and that in the West only unedited documents were considered to be authentic. This astonished the Chinese. Their faith had its roots in legend. They bathed in it as happily as their water buffalo in ponds. Since I refused to be an unconditional believer, we were separated by an abyss.

Mr. Tsai announced that we would soon be leaving Peking, and although I had awaited this news with impatience, it now gave me only vague satisfaction. I replied that I was no longer in any hurry. I would think about it. I let it be understood that I had asked for instructions from Paris. The sharpness of my reactions the previous evening had given the Chinese reason to suspect that I might be better armed than they had supposed to tell the story of their revolution to the West. My indifference to their present proposals robbed them of some of the arrogance they had displayed when they came to acquaint me with the decision of the directing committee. I mentioned in passing that although I recognized that their leaders might not wish to stir up the mud of the past, I could not understand why we were not at least permitted to talk with the official historians of the party.

"Even the Russians," I said, "were not that mistrustful of us. How can I ever know if they lied to me if you remain silent? I can understand your considering certain moments of your history as a family matter, and that you might not want foreigners intruding upon them. But this is a family matter so noisy that it has attracted the attention of the whole world. If you do not want the neighbors to hear your arguments, you should not shout so loud."

I was asked if we might have a full conference the morning of the day after next. I accepted, slightly changing the hour as a matter of principle, and then bade them good night, being very careful to do nothing to dissipate the anxiety with which they seemed suddenly possessed.

That afternoon we were taken to the Museum of the Army, an enormous palace of concrete and marble, surmounted by a Moscow-type tower whose arrow planted a red star in the naked sky. In a reception room with a painted ceiling, tall columns and red tapestry, tea awaited us and sticks of incense had been lit in our honor. But there was only an ordinary lieutenant colonel to greet us—no sign that we had been taken back into favor.

This time, however, Mr. Tsai intervened to spare us the sort of visit we had had to the Museum of the Revolution. We rushed through the main hall like horses on a race track. Everywhere we saw the same photographs, the same gold-encrusted works of Mao Tse-tung, the same statues of the god. By this time I was no longer annoyed or embarrassed. I went up to the statues and discreetly wrapped my knuckles against their bases; they sounded hollow. Their outward appearance of white marble disguised a finely mixed plaster, at which the faithful stared with the same open-mouthed devotion they gave the paintings in which the regime's Winterhalters and Davids represented Mao revealing the truths of Marxism-Leninism, standing in a shaft of heavenly light, like Jesus among his disciples. Mr. Tsai followed us, his face molded into a lard of resignation. Less than two hours after we had left them, we returned to our automobiles.

"You didn't see one-fifth of the museum," Mr. Tsai told me sadly.

The weather was changing. Suddenly, it was almost cold, even though it was only mid-September. Padded vests thickened the silhouettes of the inhabitants of Peking. The old men peddling street carts covered their shoulders with remnants of garments as old as they. The hotel distributed cotton wool coverlets to be attached to the upper sheet, as was the practice in Russia. The lobby of the Hsin Chiao was a vast gulf of icy drafts. The other members of the crew taunted me for having promised them a warm sky throughout the entire journey. And, as a matter of fact, I had foreseen leaving Peking before the arrival of the bad weather, going first to Yenan and then even farther south.

The next day, in a public room of the hotel, rented for eight yuans an hour, we sat about filling pots of tea from steaming thermos jugs and drinking greedily to warm ourselves, although it was eleven o'clock in the morning. Mr. Tsai took off his cap. When his face was not animated by some emotion, it resembled a sail abandoned by the wind. When he was annoyed or upset, his features seemed to become pinched, his eyes grew dark, his cheeks sagged and his slouch cap no longer covered anything more recognizable than a mound of fat. The thick lion's mane of hair that framed his face, however, could give sudden life to the large mouth, short nose, arched brows and powerful cheekbones. At such moments he was almost handsome.

"You were mistaken," he told us in a melancholy tone, "if you thought we attached no importance to your coming here. We will do everything we possibly can to help you, and all our best wishes will go with you. The diplomatic relations our countries have just established make it absolutely imperative that we work for friendship between our two peoples. The most favorable conditions have been authorized for you. After much discussion, the Association of Chinese People for Cultural Relations Abroad has decided to assume all the expenses of your stay."

The interpreter, Mr. Shu, emphasized these words and heightened their meaning with a smile I had not seen on Mr. Tsai's face. I suddenly understood why a boy had come to my room and taken back the hotel bill I had asked for. They thought they had found a simple means of tying my hands. While Mr. Tsai embarked on a new series of lamentations on our behavior, I thought the matter over. A few days before my departure from France, the new management of French national television had gone back on an earlier agreement and refused to lend me the services of a director, on the pretext that what I was doing would only serve as Communist propaganda. Finding myself suddenly deprived of an assistance on which I had been counting, I authorized Simon to ask the Chinese for certain facilities for his crew which, if he obtained them, would put me under no obligation. But now, how could I condemn or even criticize what I might see without warranting an accusation of ingratitude? And, on the other hand, if I should find things to praise, how could they be taken seriously?

"As for the book you want to write and the film you plan to make," Mr. Tsai went on, "it will be up to you to decide on their eventual form.

Fifteen years have already passed since our liberation. How could you possibly retrace all stages of it in so rapid a journey? At one time in China, the people were oppressed and a great many of them smoked opium. You will find no trace of that now. The fortifications built by the Japanese during the war have been torn down. If you look for beggars and houses of gambling or prostitution, you will be looking in vain, but I hope that that fact will not cause any misunderstanding between us. As for the leaders of our government, we have told you that they are very busy and that it would be impossible for you to meet them all. But that is no reason for you to say that you can no longer write your book. The building of a new China is of greater interest to us, but that does not mean that we do not want anyone to look into the past. There are other means by which you can reconstruct the historic truth. We can show you documentary films, find witnesses who will discuss events with you, take you to see the cities that have become the landmarks of the revolution. That is how we feel on the subject. It is up to you to decide what you will do. The president of our Association will be returning to Peking in a few days; he will see you."

Mr. Tsai looked straight at me, his face wreathed in smiles, and insisted that I take a cigarette. Then he waited for my reply. In order to understand what Mr. Tsai was trying to say, I was always forced to make a note of each of his phrases and then tune in on them on my own wavelength. If they were simply added one to another, they revealed no logical link. Then, suddenly, a word would fit in with an idea mentioned earlier and an entire succession of images would come together, making sense, like the pieces of a jigsaw puzzle. Was Mr. Shu translating this complicated language faithfully? I tried to tie together the various parts of this speech, which revealed its true meaning only at the end, much the way the meaning of each phrase only became clear with the last word. In this strange grammar, where the basic thought might suddenly dart off in a completely unpredictable direction at the most unexpected moment, it was always prudent to wait patiently for the end, if one hoped to learn what the elaborate approach was leading up to.

For thousands of years the Chinese had argued among themselves over the meaning of minutize. Neither past nor future existed in their verbs. For them time had begun in the year 2637 B.C., and we were now in the year of the tiger in the seventy-eighth cycle. In the seventeenth century the emperors had been forced to call on Jesuit scholars to bring some order to their calendar and astronomy. The revolution had re-established some degree of agreement with the rest of the world, but it had provided no key to the meaning behind the system. The Chinese had invented gunpowder but not the cannon, and only a few years ago it was still necessary, when a letter arrived, to study it carefully before being certain whether it was a dinner invitation or the telephone bill.

"You surely know the feelings we had when we arrived in China," I
said. "I was perfectly open about the joy and hope I felt. If we have
experienced disillusionment since, it has not been our doing. It is
comparatively easy for me to give up the historic theme I had chosen
and to write another book. But it's not that simple for the technical crew
that came with me and which was organized to do a very specific job.
We don't yet know how to resolve that problem. As for your decision to
assume all our expenses, I thank you for the offer, but I personally
would rather maintain my freedom. One cannot very well write anything critical of a country whose hospitality one has accepted. It is in no
way embarrassing for me to be your occasional guest; that is a sign of
friendship offered and accepted. But I would be embarrassed not to be
able to take care of my own hotel bill. Therefore I ask that you grant me
this favor. I am a free man and would like to remain so, but freedom
must be paid for. I hope you will let me pay for mine in my own way.
You have nothing to fear from this; I am not going to criticize China
because I paid my own hotel bill. But it is important that my judgment
of the country be based on nothing except what I have seen. I think this
is the best proof I could possibly give you of my sincerity."

Mr. Tsai merely made a note of my reply. I did not know whether I
had been understood, but I was relieved. Like anyone else, I could be
seduced, but not this way. I also recognized that my pride might have
wounded theirs because it was based on a bourgeois concept. I reacted
violently to their evident desire to buy me, but at one time, in China,
everyone bartered in everything—a baptism for a machine gun and
even a ceremonial funeral for a miserable life. Honesty had nothing to
do with it. Why, then, should I be so concerned about what I was
saying? At a meeting of the Association's committee, it had been
decided that the Association would assume our expenses. In the eyes of
the Chinese, I was neither more nor less free than I had been on the day
of my arrival, since no one really thought about freedom. They had
simply decided that it should be this way.

A brigadier general in a green uniform with two silver stars on gold
shoulder boards, and three decorations dangling from a plastic bar, one
purple, one yellow and one green, each crossed at the center with a
white or red stripe—this is what they had found to refute my arguments
and explain to us the historic meaning of the revolution. In honor of the
new lunar month, the table was laden with a small mountain of
delicacies which no one dared touch. In my hotel room someone had left
fresh fruit and little round spice cakes stuffed with raisins.

Assisted by a lieutenant colonel and two female translators who were
taking notes, the general had been reading to us for an hour and a half
from a long memorandum on the revolution, and I was not at all sure

but what the memorandum might outlast it. His voice was monotonous, neutral and swift, interrupted only by the hesitations, stammerings and approximations of the interpreter. It was very serious and very tiresome. Mr. Shu, freshly shaven, was as bored as I. Out of the corner of my eye, I watched Mr. Tsai, sitting upright in his high-buttoned blue jacket, resembling a distinguished clergyman. He, too, was studiously taking notes, doubtless thinking he would profit from them. Mr. Chen was taking them with the idea of picking the general's brain.

More than once I came close to falling asleep as we journeyed from the opportunism of the right to the opportunism of the left, with side trips into revisionism and the struggle of Mao Tse-tung's sovereign thought to conquer all. "What is this," I thought, "all of us sitting here goggle-eyed like children in school, listening to the teacher, not daring to utter a word?" Chen Tu-hsiu and his disciples had wanted to take the cities. They were inexperienced Communists and did not think deeply enough. And the Komintern—had it been the Komintern that urged them on in tactics which had succeeded so well in Russia? No. It had been Chen Tu-hsiu, the opportunist of the right, allied with Li Li-san, the opportunist of the left, who refused to follow Mao and stubbornly insisted on arming the proletariat of cities already in the grip of the army instead of calling for an uprising among the peasants.

This general we were listening to as though he were an oracle was a surprise in one way: the round face under the shiny bald skull reflected nothing but my own boredom. I had not asked to see him; his name did not figure in the history of the revolution; and he did not offer to answer any questions. Nonetheless, I ventured to ask one:

"How can you say that the armed struggle was based on the ideas of Mao Tse-tung as early as 1924, when Mao did not become leader of the Chinese Communist party until January, 1935?"

He replied that I was impatient and that he was about to explain everything. If I took the trouble to think about it, I would understand that, between the opportunists of the right and the left, Mao Tse-tung alone had adapted the universal truth of Marxism-Leninism to the Chinese revolution.

The cameraman, Simon and the sound engineer were discouraged. Brigitte had sat down after taking a few photographs. The sun moved across the room; a golden ray touched and abandoned the Soviet beards and goatees of Marxism-Leninism, before blessing the hairless faces of the Chinese. We had not even begun the Long March when an intermission was called. We stood up, breathing a sigh of relief, exchanged impressions and found that we were in complete agreement. Every member of my crew felt that we were wasting our time. I went over to Tsai, complimented him extravagantly on his general and told him that, unfortunately, it would not be possible for us to listen to the rest of his speech because we were expected at the French Embassy, but perhaps later, on our return, well . . . Mr. Tsai seemed wounded—they had inconvenienced a general for us, this general was giving up his valuable time. And already, traitorously and visibly, we were collecting our equipment, peeling an apple, surreptitiously snatching at the mounds of raisins. After a quarter of an hour, during which we listened politely and pretended to record some new statements, we took our leave. I had the feeling that we had behaved badly.

We were scheduled to leave the next day. We packed our suitcases. I had asked for the hotel bill on several occasions, all in vain. From this point on, whenever we went into the dining room I refused to sign the checks and paid in cash. I did the same thing whenever I ordered something sent to my room. I wrote a second article for *l'Express,* in which I mentioned the Emperor Mao, the new popular dynasty and its dream of leadership. I quoted a statement by Marshal Chen Yi which had greatly impressed me—"We will go naked if necessary, but we will have the bomb"—and a story I had been told by Mr. Tsai about the palace of the National Assembly: In 1956 the government had called in foreign architects to consult with them about the construction of a legislative chamber that would contain ten thousand seats and a banquet hall for five thousand. The most optimistic technicians had stated that such an edifice would take three years to build. The Chinese had then set to work on it. The whole project was conceived, undertaken and completed in eight months.

Each night a hundred projectors stationed around the city would suddenly light up, concentrating on the space above T'ien An Men Square, where their beams would cross to form a star. Then they would separate, stand erect as the columns of a temple of light and weave back and forth like the wings of birds before finally going out.

Chapter 10

In which the author leaves Peking, dreams of the English countryside in Chengchow, is welcomed in Wuhan and meditates on the rites of Chinese hospitality. In which a photograph taken on the banks of the Yangtze causes an incident. In which the author invites the reader to explore a gigantic hog slaughterhouse, and then is forced to halt his visit. In which a bridge on the Yangtze claims attention. In which, during a visit to the steel mills, the discipline of the people appears to the author as a symbol of a just pride and the will to a revenge against destiny.

> The traveler, his heart burdened with care,
> Walks alone through a thousand halts.
> The river is dark and the rain will fall;
> The wind rises on the whitened wave.
>
> —Ho Hsüan, fifth century A.D.

The canals that crisscrossed the flat lands before they fell away into the Gulf of Chihli glittered beneath the wings of our Ilyushin. Water courses contained by dikes irrigated the gray flesh of this land, like a network of veins spreading to an infinite horizon. At the altitude at which we were flying, we could see the earthern houses of villages strewn beneath us as thick as hail, but we could not see the men laboring in the fields. By separating me from actual physical contacts and, in a sense, raising me above them, airplanes always gave me a sense of serenity. From the level of the clouds, China became a continent like all the others. It was no longer an object to be feared. The Chinese and ourselves no longer dashed our heads against the walls of our opposing thoughts, our suspicions or our mutually incomprehensible faces. We remained silent.

This flight had transformed Mr. Tsai into a debonair, almost Olympian character. Quite suddenly, he seemed certain that we could not fail to be struck by the truth. A kind of intimacy between us was about to be born, permitting him to dispense the light of his faith and through this to understand me better. Who was I? In what category should I be placed? I had often repeated that I was a free man; I might as well have told them I was a brontosaurus. They had asked me how I lived, how much I earned. It frightened them that I depended on no one but myself, that I undertook only what pleased me and that I had no accounts to render to anyone. I could not tell them: "You have always worked for landowners and feudal lords. For five thousand years you have been afraid of punishment and death. You revolted only because you were dying of hunger. If we are told we cannot read a newspaper, its circulation automatically goes up; if a book is censored by the authorities, its sales increase; and rifles are brought out of hiding places if we are refused the right to hold meetings. That is what a free man is."

I respected the poverty and honesty of China. Money no longer represented a temptation. At one time misery had justified robbery and rape, but now anyone could leave his suitcases open and banknotes in drawers without fear of theft. No one would accept a tip, and if something happened to be lost, it was promptly returned. The thing that united the masses and charged the youth with energy was the fact that China was emerging from a long night, that she was becoming a great power and that 700 million men and women now lived without hunger. The party had succeeded in accomplishing that.

Before landing at Chengchow, we flew very low over the Yellow River, which was streaked with a reddish mud so thick it appeared solid. Junks with heavy sweeps and weather-stained sails moved slowly against the current. It was raining. A car took us to an enormous, sad-looking old building in which proletarians, hunched over their bowls greedily swallowing rice, stared at us as if we were some strange form of animal. Perhaps because of the lowering sky and the damp rows of airplanes outside, I suddenly felt a surge of nostalgia for a hotel in Sussex or Yorkshire where tea would have been served in a silver pot with toast and orange marmalade and a coal fire would be burning cheerfully in the fireplace. In the morning I would have eaten porridge and eggs and bacon.

After luncheon, which it was impossible to pay for, we left again, and the plane stewardess passed out bonbons that tasted like toothpaste and magazines filled with the ecstatic faces of peasants growing food or workers standing beside their machines. The crew wore the same blue cotton uniforms as the stewardess, with no distinction to indicate rank.

We broke through the clouds above a majestic sweep of lakes, canals, rivers, ponds and lotus-filled marshlands, where men and waters fought for possession of the land. The valley of the Yangtze stretched to the mountains that studded the horizon, and then we discovered the river itself, coiling in a series of gigantic loops that sometimes seemed part of the sky, regal, enormous, almost the color of rosewood.

The Association representatives who were there to meet us formed a little group at the foot of the plane ramp, curious to have a look at us: a

vice president, a secretary general, some members of the local committee and a single woman, in honor of Brigitte. I knew that the distaste I
had for this sort of thing was wrong. Throughout her history foreigners
had been received in China with ceremony, and surrounded with
attentions which also provided the means of studying their behavior and
divining their intentions. Father Huc himself, when he and his companion made their two-year journey to Tibet, was welcomed in every city
by the mandarins and conducted to the regional government representative. Our mandarins wore blue suits and the caps of locomotive engineers instead of long robes and skullcaps with brightly colored buttons,
and their caste would be distinguished only by their rank and the quality
of their raincoats.

Had Father Huc ever asked himself if the book he planned to write
would be a service or a disservice to his Chinese hosts? He had had the
good fortune to like Chinese cuisine, but when he remembered the fine
meals he had eaten at the tables of the provincial authorities, had he
ever thought of repressing his criticism? I had something of this feeling
as I climbed into the ancient and colossal Buick and took my place
between Brigitte and the president of the delegation, wondering how
many imperialist posteriors had polished this seat before ours. The first
courteous flow of questions began, and I answered with equal courtesy:
We had been in China for three weeks; we had just left Peking; it was
beginning to get cold there; I planned to write a book on the history of
the Chinese revolution; the French people were delighted that diplomatic relations had been re-established with the People's Republic of
China. I could almost hear the speeches of welcome that had greeted
Father Huc: "Men from the great kingdom of France! We see them so
rarely! . . . Your presence among us cannot fail to bring happiness to
the whole country."

In Wuhan the communal palace was the best hotel. Before reaching it,
we crossed a monumental bridge over the Yangtze, which is over a half-
mile wide at this point, and then drove through the city itself. Standing
on little wooden platforms beneath adjustable umbrellas which protected them from the sun and rain, the policemen halted the traffic of
bicycles and carts and opened the way for us with an imperious sweep
of their arms. In the front seat of the car, beside the driver, our interpreter, Mr. Shu, was yawning openly and ceaselessly. Maliciously, I
made him repeat several phrases which he had massacred with his
mumbling—yes, we wanted to serve the cause of friendship among all
peoples and we were going to return to Peking for the festivities
celebrating the fifteenth anniversary of the liberation. I was urged to feel
completely free to criticize. At that, I laughed heartily, jabbed Brigitte
with my elbow and said that they could count on me, that anyone who
knew me well could tell them that I was incapable of hiding my

thoughts. It was a basic fault of mine that I always said what I thought, and this they would learn, to their regret.

"That," the vice president replied dryly, "is the mark by which one can recognize his true friends."

And then he added: "We thought the Soviets were true friends. And you know how they have treated us."

He was an excitable man, with a weasel face and an anxious air, his blue cap pulled down to the level of his eyes, trying to play the strong, silent type. We did not have time to show our mutual distaste. Our little convoy came to a halt and our suitcases were taken out. The hotel, built by the English, had once been part of the British concession. The rooms were comfortable and spotlessly clean, the bathrooms enormous and abundantly provided with hot water. Through windows that actually had metal mosquito screens, we looked out on the roofs of factories, tall brick chimneys and a little stretch of river that flowed nearby.

Since night was beginning to fall, we could not resist the desire to see it. I took Brigitte's equipment case and we walked down to the river bank. Junks were standing away from the wind, hauling down their sails to cast anchor, deck to deck, in the protected backwaters of the embankment, while others maneuvered their way out for the night's fishing, slowly raising their great stiff wings and bounding forward when they were caught by the wind. Tugboats sped by in both directions, and riding lights were beginning to appear on the ships at dock. There was an odor of brine, sandalwood, *nuoc-mam* and stale river water. On the far bank, the bellowing of the trains was like the long, deep cry of a ship. The fishermen were laughing. A feeble surf washed against the jetties. Some men were hauling in floating tree trunks and loading them into handcarts. The water was dirty, the color of wet earth beneath a leaden sky. A sense of exhilaration swelled through us and we felt our hearts quicken.

Brigitte had taken out her camera and was taking photographs when some fanatic threw himself in front of her, his waving arms blocking her view. He shoved her backward, shouting all the while, calling the nearby workers as his witnesses, pointing to the street and inviting us in no uncertain terms to leave. Without an interpreter, it was impossible to explain what we were doing there. The whole affair embarrassed me, and the brutal behavior of the dock hand made me furious. I forced him to come with us, and he followed along like a great buzzing fly, probably explaining to everyone within earshot that we were spies.

The hotel was not far away. The man, who was almost certainly a militant party member, launched into vehement explanations to the personnel. We finally succeeded in reaching the interpreters, by telephone, then Mr. Tsai, and the vice president of the delegation. Contrary to what I thought would happen, no one was indignant at the way we had been treated. When they arrived, we all gathered in one of the public rooms, and explanations were offered in a quiet voice. So many imperialists had conducted themselves as if they were in a conquered country, so many spies were still trying to uncover the secrets of Chinese power, that the aroused people easily confused friends and enemies.

Every effort was made to calm and reassure the docker, he was congratulated on his vigilance, but no one thought of asking him to apologize. For that matter, they were very careful not to translate his statements for me. He held out his hand with a smile that resembled a deformation of the mouth. I thought to myself that he was very young to have so clear a memory of imperialist humiliations. His attitude was nothing more than a reflection of what he had been taught. But we were going to have to reckon with passionate young men like him. And I was not at all sure that the members of our Wuhan delegation had any broader minds. That evening my crew and I dined alone. There was no invitation elsewhere. There were fragrant little roses on every table in the restaurant.

The program discussed with us was entirely agreeable to me. The complex now known as Wuhan is made up of the three cities of Hanyang, Hankow and Wuchang. It has over two million inhabitants, a university and more than five hundred primary schools. It was here, on October 10, 1911, that the first outbreak against the empire occurred. We were to begin—I don't know why, perhaps to give us a vivid impression of the modernization achieved by the socialist system—by visiting a slaughterhouse for pigs.

The same little greedy, playful, black and white piglets who trailed their paunches into the very heart of town, wandering past garden walls and the steps of houses in search of refuse, were picked up and carried by the junkload to the sheds of this factory, where they were made to fast for twenty-four hours before being prepared for the sacrifice. Their precious excrement was collected, diluted with water and carried to the fields in pails and casks. Before entering the abattoir, we were garbed in surgeon's blouses, boots and caps. A mask of perfumed gauze was fastened over our mouths, to filter the atrocious odor.

Each day six to seven thousand bathed and showered hogs were electrocuted, skinned and cut up. From the top floor of the building, which they reached by ramps or elevators, they gradually descended, assuming different forms en route, until they reached the refrigerated chambers at the bottom. Nothing was wasted, not so much as a hair. The only thing that was useless was the shriek they uttered when the electricity struck through their armor of antiseptic water. Then they fell stiff and dead on the metallic flooring. They were attached by one leg to a lift and carried to another area, where their throats and chests were slit with a knife. In this part of the factory, the floor ran red with blood. The inedible portions of the carcass were used for the manufacture of plastics or for the transparent papers in which caramels were wrapped —which decided us instantly never to touch a caramel again. Bathed, emptied of their blood, scalded, put through mechanical scrapers, rinsed twenty times, reduced to the state of bloodless flesh, cut into pieces with an electric saw, numbered and passed under the microscope, these Chinese pigs had no cause to envy their American cousins in Chicago.

I was forced to call a halt to the visit; I was about to vomit. Pigs or not, there is no other way of saying it: they bore a strong resemblance to men, and the slant eyes of their butchers added something extremely disturbing to the operation. I told myself that in this country where men had once been denounced, imprisoned and flayed alive with delicacy and dispatch, it would require no more than a slight error for my own body to be carried along on this tragic chain, for me to undergo this same fate. And no one would notice it until too late. I looked at Mr. Tsai, shielded behind his mask, and found that he and Chu Teh and Lin Piao, all of whom had greeted us in the reception room under the portrait of Mao, had a definite resemblance to the victims. I was filled with a dreadful nausea. Mr. Tsai was greatly amused by a weakness he did not understand. In their way, these pigs were serving the cause of socialism. Every provincial capital possessed the same kind of model slaughter-house, bringing the people healthful and abundant food.

It was with great pride that they showed us the bridge across the Yangtze. Its construction had required two years, instead of the four that had been estimated. Eight concrete columns, sunk in the river bed, supported a steel platform that carried both a highway and a two-way railroad. Trucks and buses were provided with an easy approach by gently sloping ramps from the hills on either bank of the river, but the masses of humans pushing or pulling handcarts struggled laboriously up the incline and then were forced to brake with their bodies on the descent. It was this bustle and confusion of people hauling carts that struck me most forcibly; this spectacle of children clinging to the hand poles or strapping a harness around their shoulders. I understood now why we had been allowed to photograph the neat-looking carts that rolled through the streets of Peking behind their little horses, donkeys or mules; they represented a form of luxury. Here man generally replaced beasts of burden. There was still only one truck for every seven thousand inhabitants, but the members of the delegation hastened to explain the difference this represented since the liberation. In the days of foreign colonialism, men went everywhere on foot and carried everything on their shoulders, with the help of a bamboo balancing pole. The liberation had reduced human labor. The carts now had rubber tires, and in ten years they would have been replaced by trucks.

I felt a certain shame when we got back into our ramshackle old Buick. But the Chinese who rented bicycle taxis to cross the bridge obviously felt no shame at remaining in their seats while their driver climbed down from his machine and pulled them up the slope by hand. No one seemed in the least scandalized by this social inequity.

The living conditions of one of these members of the proletariat, man or woman, interested me a great deal more than the four 110-foot towers which gave access to the embankments. I would have liked to become acquainted with their miseries and their hopes, see how they ate and learn whether they also had portraits of Mao in their homes. I ventured to suggest such a project. No, I must devote myself to the masses, not to individuals. I must study the work that was being done in common. I was led toward the elevators. The official guardian of the bridge offered us tea in a reception room in one of the towers. I asked if there were other bridges across the Yangtze, and everyone smiled as they told me they did not know. At one time the trains had had to cross the river on a ferry, an operation that had required three hours. Now they raced across, meeting each other with a sound like rumbling thunder above the junks bobbing up and down against the banks. In May of 1956 Chairman Mao Tse-tung, on a visit to the construction site, had plunged into the turbulent current and swum across the river, accompanied by a few of the faithful.

I went down to the embankment, where the water slapped sharply against the stone piers. No plaque had been erected to commemorate Mao's feat. A woman was lifting the two tubs of laundry she had just rinsed. Trains were passing above our heads, announcing their approach with a scream that resembled that of the pigs at the moment of electrocution. Here, too, the river was red with the silt brought down from Szechwan and scattered in pulsing veins by the snub noses of the tugboats.

Our interpreter, Mr. Shu, was wondering what I might be dreaming about on the banks of the Yangtze. That day he had not shaved, and a stubble of black hairs was visible between his warts. He seemed astonished when I asked where it was that Chairman Mao had swum the river. Mention of the sacred name brought him out of his apathy. He pulled himself up very straight and adopted a solemn tone. It was not given to all the peoples of the earth to have a leader like this one.

At dawn the next morning I was awakened by whistle blasts and the barking voices of soldiers directing the morning exercise. I got up and went over to the window. Oustide in the street troops of male and female militia were unenthusiastically going to or returning from their exercise, before proceeding to the day's work. On the boat which took us to the steel works the following morning, the same faces surrounded us, drawn with fatigue. They, as well as we, were trapped by loudspeakers over which a piercing, stubborn woman's voice disseminated the latest bulletins of the Ministry of Culture. As the boat moved away from the pier and maneuvered into the current, the loudspeakers blared the "March of the Red Army." The air was tepid against our faces. Mr. Tsai was laughing, evidently enjoying himself. I had a vague impression of leaving on a cruise. A new morning was washing the river clean of all its debris, shredding the wisps of smoke and fog that lingered along the banks, stirring into motion thousands of men and women gathered on the piers, tugging at carts laden with wooden crates, scrap iron and wearing apparel.

C'était M'sieu Dupont qui v'nait faire la fête. . . .

This idiot jingle from my youth was running through my head, and I could not get rid of it. I dreamed of making a trip down the river, as Father Huc had done a century before. Not, of course, on a filthy junk where the mandarins of his escort smoked opium in the hatchways, but on one of these large ferries where there would be no risk of shipwreck when the wind came up. We were tken up to the captain's bridge, where tea was served. Brigitte resembled a high-spirited bird, darting here and there, plucking images from the light as though they were scraps of food. A kind of happiness flooded through me. Ten years earlier, on the Niger, I had felt much the same thing. It had seemed to me that each time my friends and I piled our provisions and equipment into the canoes or cutters we were setting out to conquer eternity.

In some spots the river was so broad and restless that it resembled the sea. Before coming alongside the landing stage, the pilot turned the boat so that it would be heading upstream as it slowly approached the gangways from which crowds of curious Chinese were watching us. We left them to their junks, sunk to the water line with sand or coal, to their baskets of poultry and their carts. Our automobiles were waiting for us.

A dingy cloud denoting the presence of heavy industry was alrady darkening the sky. Chimneys vomited smoke. The coke-processing plants were wreathed in a yellowish mist, buckets of ore rolled by, gas whistled through the adduction pipes, there was a sound of rushing water. Cities were going up next to the factories, red piles of bricks in which the families of the workers were stacked like bricks. Thirty thousand masons were ceaselessly at work, adding houses to other houses, to service factories whose walls were already built. A few forlorn sparrows who had escaped the great massacre of birds (for a time, the revolution accused them of plundering the harvests) were desperately looking for the hills that had been bulldozed away and the few tufts of grass between the coal piles.

Through a mask of blue-tinted glasses, I watched the steaming and

bubbling of another river, seemingly caught in the winds of some fiery
tempest. This lava filling tubs that were picked up by the hooks of an
endless chain and delivered to the foundries; these waves of fire and
their accompanying spray of sparks; these incandescent ingots being
pressed, lengthened, revolved and transformed into steel beams—this
was the pride of China. Men in asbestos suits watched over the
furnaces, and young girls punched keys on the control boards for cranes
and winches. Before the revolution one old factory made only eight
thousand tons per year of this steel, which is more precious than gold,
and now eight thousand tons are produced daily. Within two years even
more imposing figures will be added to those of the steel mills of
Manchuria and Inner Mongolia, and China will then surpass Great
Britain, the Ruhr and Soviet Russia. With this new scrap iron will be
built new bridges, ships and cannon. There can no longer be a question
of simply maintaining production. Since the power of nations is measured in millions of tons of steel and not in millions of handcarts, the
country must move ahead and surpass all others.

This machinery I was being shown at the same time that my face was
being studied for signs of astonishment, it was this they wanted me to
admire and not the hovels where people lived. But I was thinking of
other machinery which was still kept very secret and which was making
a nuclear weapon in forbidden Sinkiang. It had been discussed a little.
In the West there was a rising chorus of laughter; the Chinese still lived
in the Middle Ages, in an age of rickshas. But I knew that in every
province tens of millions of young men and women sat behind machine
tools, manufactured trucks and tiles, built dams, slaughtered hogs on an
assembly line or tugged the harnesses of carts, in an endless hysteria of
forced labor. Who could doubt that they would explode the bomb? To
misjudge them, one would have to observe them from the viewpoint of a
Westerner devoted to fine living, art films and country houses. No one
gave a damn about art here, and the function of married couples was to
make babies who would conquer the universe. The pride of coming
triumph shone in the eyes of the engineers of Wuhan as they demonstrated their blast furnaces and rolling mills to the caravans of Chinese
who had come from abroad to visit their native land. Little men dressed
in worker's overalls inspected the rolling mills where red-hot ingots
crashed against the buffers; these were the directors, whose salaries
were less than Professor Hou's, who were in no way distinguished from
the other workers, who ate in common dining rooms and, if they were
bachelors, bunked together in dormitories. In this climate animals
sometimes died of the summer heat. In a capitalist country these little
men would have had air-conditioned offices and suburban homes to go
back to.

Under the pretext of avenging their fate, the party was leading this people to a revenge against all the capitalists and feudal barons of the world. Five thousand years of suffering and peasant revolt had brought liberty from one form of tyranny but not from tyranny itself. When the slave rules, he rules in the hard fashion of a slave, who knows he cannot afford to think freely for fear of making a mistake. And when slaves work together as an army, under the command of other slaves who have known punishment and hunger, they will toil and drudge to surpass the work they did for their former masters. Slaves can move mountains and rivers, liberate the atom and blow up the heavens—perhaps better than their masters.

Chapter 11

In which, on the occasion of a visit to a fishing village, a new incident occurs which assumes inordinate proportions and reveals a certain antipathy between the mandarins of Wuhan and the author. In which the reader takes part in the contest between them and in the author's autocritique, and is enabled to evaluate the diplomatic talents of Mr. Tsai and to meditate on the forms of Chinese thought. How the producer of the television film, not realizing that foreigners do not do as they please in China, insists, in a telephone call from Paris, that his crew should rent an automobile and follow out the itinerary of the Long March. Some reflections on the difficulties of being a photographer in China, an account of the insurrection of October 10, 1911, and a visit to the school where Mao Tse-tung formed his peasant cadres in 1917. How the stay in Wuhan ends with another banquet, marked by the reciprocal joy of parting company.

From the lowest coolie to the highest mandarin, it is a matter of not losing face.

> HENRI MICHAUX, *A Barbarian in Asia (Un Barbare en Asie)*

It has been a long time since I reread Voltaire, and I do not know why he treated [the Dutch] as Chinese. Is it because they are nationalists and push logic to the point of rendering it suspect even to themselves . . . because they want to distinguish themselves from all other peoples in the world, or because they are looking for lice in straw?

> GIUSEPPE UNGARETTI, *Desert Beginning (A Partir du Désert)*

The chief of the fishermen's village we visited the next day lived in the poorest hut. He earned no more than the best of his men: two thousand yuans per year, or about four thousand francs at the present rate of exchange. In this country, however, it amounts to a good deal more than that—say, the salary of a minister without an automobile.

When we arrived at the lake, bordered with factories and housing developments for the workers, the morning crews were casting their nets for the third time. Their boats, long and narrow as dug outs, were spread across the water in the shape of an enormous trap into which the "beaters" were driving the fish. Once caught in this trap, the big round-headed carp raced headlong into the nets, occasionally leaping over them and falling into the bottoms of the boats. At this season of the year the catch was eleven thousand pounds a day.

Addressing myself to the village chief, I asked, "Why do you and your men work with such enthusiasm?"

He did not have to search for an answer. "So that the cadres will be better fed," he said.

I remarked that the cadres already seemed very well provided with pigs, ducks and chickens. The chief smiled and launched into an account of his life in the time of the Kuomintang. His sly and weathered face, etched with tiny wrinkles, lit up with his joy in working himself to death for the party. Was it because the members of the commission were listening and that was what he was supposed to say? I could not imagine him returning home at night, exhausted, with other words for his wife: "I'm fed up with killing myself for those bastards." In comparison with what he had known, his life was now a success; the revolution was his revenge against governments that paid a pittance for his fish and cared nothing for their people. He and his people were living. They were eating. Equality had given them a share of the national dignity. No one fished simply for his own gain, and everyone tried in his own way to augment the production figures and the number of points accruing to them when profits were divided. After all, they could not fish from April to August, the tornado season. The chief did not dream of acquiring his own little property, watching his grand-children grow up or cultivating a garden that was his very own in a region where the air was not shattered night and day by the screaming of trains. He dreamed of increasing his production so that he might better serve the building of China.

I understood why there had been so much hesitation about showing me the village when I saw the fishermen's huts, with their litter of cheap furniture and wicker eel traps. Children were playing on the hard-packed ground, among pigs filling their bellies with dust and fighting with the ducks for bits of garbage or a few grains of feed. This biblical, almost hopeless destitution inspires no more pity than the villages of Kabylia, where the basic nourishment is a soup made from nettles. The true wealth of China stretched before us, enormous, threatening: the swarms of happy children who seemed to spring from the earth, went to school and wore the red scarf of the Young Pioneers around their neck. Perhaps these sons of slaves would liberate themselves. The light was dazzling on the mirror surface of the lake, and another crew was making ready for a new catch.

We were late returning to the hotel for lunch, but I wanted to go back to the village to talk with the chief in his own home. I therefore asked the interpreter, twice, at what time we would be returning to work. He did not know. As I left the table, I asked the same question of Mr. Chen, who was just finishing his lunch. He indicated that I should go and rest. I concluded that someone would come after me, as had always been done, and went to stretch out on my bed for a few minutes. We were all eager to go back and film the return of the fishermen at night. Inexplicably, we were simply forgotten.

At a quarter to five someone was sent to tell us that they had been waiting for us a long time, which was obviously false. I would have understood if they had said: "We have thought it over, and we prefer that you do not take photographs of this village. We will show you another one, less archaic, and you can take your film there. Forgive us, but this one would not give an accurate idea of China today." They preferred being crafty; they had not dared disturb us because they thought we were tired.

It was a flagrant lie. When we were late, as we often were, Mr. Shu, the interpreter, immediately began telephoning each of our rooms. That afternoon Mr. Shu had remained silent. He had probably passed on my questions, but had doubtless been ordered not to answer them.

Even so, we set out for the village. In the automobile they explained, in sanctimonious tones, that it had all been a misunderstanding; they had asked us what time we wanted to go back and had gotten no answer. I replied that this kind of conversation would get us nowhere and it seemed useless to continue it; that we had been made to lose a half-day's work at precisely the time we had been warned there was a great deal of rain in the upper Yangtze Valley; and that it would be better to give up the idea of going to Chungking if we didn't want to miss the October 1 celebration in Peking. I added irritably, "So don't take us for idiots," and said nothing more.

We had missed the return of the boats. The fish had been piled into hampers which were being weighed and, obviously, the village chief was no longer inclined to take us to his home. And for that matter, what would we have accomplished? The large crowd that had gathered prevented us from filming the normal life of the fishermen. I was asked then if I had any further questions, I replied that the difficulties we had encountered had so upset me that I no longer felt capable of working. Once again I was told that they had asked what time I wanted to return to work and that I had not answered.

"In that case," I said angrily, "it is because I did not hear. If I did not hear, it is because the question was not translated, since it was certainly one of the questions I was most anxious to answer. Other questions that we have asked have also been left unanswered, so it seems to me there must be something wrong with our translator. Nothing could annoy me more, so as soon as we return to Peking I shall ask for his replacement.

Mr. Shu appeared not to recognize the implication of my words. He acted in accordance with his orders. He went on translating. But his confusion was apparent in the total incoherence of some of his statements. Several times I said, "I don't understand," thereby adding to the general discomfiture. There was nothing to do now but leave, which we did after a few polite formalities. A flock of geese which no one dared disturb blocked the road. Women watched us from the doors of their huts, holding their children in their arms. Hens pecked at the ground, surrounded by grunting hogs. We returned to the hotel in silence. I asked at what time we would meet to plan the next day's program.

"Between seven-thirty and eight."

Anxious to make up the lost time, we were all indignant at the bad faith behind their evasions. To us everything seemed simple, but nothing was for our hosts. Perhaps the members of the Wuhan delegation, who still did not know us, had found themselves in conflict with those who had accompanied us from Peking. What did we want? What were we after? Why did we show so much interest in such a sordid village? Were we going to discredit the work of the revolution by the spectacle of shameful poverty when there was so much new housing for workers built in the very site of the old hovels? We would be satisfied with any conditions at all if only they would permit us to film the life of a family, the work of a man, the hopes of a woman instead of the abstract ideology of the laboring masses.

At the appointed hour we gathered in the customary conference room. The assistant interpreter appeared. Mr. Tsai was tired and had not finished eating.

"We will wait for him."

"To tell you the truth, he hasn't even begun to eat."

The interpreter disappeared and returned a few minutes later. "He is taking a bath and would prefer to see you after dinner."

We went to have something to eat ourselves. In my case, this required very little time. Ever since our visit to the slaughterhouse, the mere sight of pork chops, bacon, ham or a soup that was made from bacon fat had sickened me. At eight-thirty we went back to our meeting room. Mr. Tsai was there, and hurriedly apologized. He had been sleeping and had only just awakened. There was a film being shown downstairs. It would last about fifty minutes, and after that we would talk about tomorrow.

I counted the reels of film lying on the floor beside the projector: there were twelve. We were shown the new people's housing projects, the accomplishments of industry, the celebrations of past Octobers, the dances of minority groups. It was conventional and boring. I refused to pay for mediocrity, so why should I put up with it simply because it was free? Out of courtesy, I had already submitted to an hour of bad film. Courtesy has its limits, and I do not visit people who show me their vacation films and photos of their families when I have not asked to see them. By the time we reached the ninth reel, I could stand no more, so I excused myself and went upstairs to bed. I was almost asleep, exhausted by a migraine and their irritation of the day, when someone rapped insistently on the door. I did not answer. The knocking began again, sharp and continuous. I got up. It was Mr. Fang, the assistant interpreter, looking sheepish and timid.

"Mr. Tsai is waiting for you at the meeting," he stammered.

I was in my pajamas. "I am very tired," I said. "At eleven o'clock at night I expected to be allowed to rest."

I closed my door. I thought of Father Huc and his companions, who, after being questioned one night by the regent of Tibet and the Chinese ambassador, were led to a room of the palace. "We realized at once that we were no longer free to refuse something we had had the credulity to take for simple courtesy. We were, very plainly, prisoners." I reassured myself with the thought that, since diplomatic relations had been established with the Chinese empire in the intervening period, we were in no danger of that kind of misadventure.

To be frank about it, there was no love lost between us and the members of the Wuhan delegation. The vice president no longer appeared except for matters of the utmost importance, and had delegated his powers to the secretary general, a stiff, austere man, so wrapped in dignity that the effort to smile seemed to crack his features. On the other hand, I was beginning actually to like Mr. Tsai. Of course, he took his role very seriously, and he was still asking himself questions about us, but, far from being convinced that we were devils, he seemed to be trying to win us over with a certain degree of humanity. Since we had been in his charge, I had caught fleeting expressions of tolerance and even amusement on his face. Some of our replies to official statements obviously delighted him, although they scandalized our other guides. At such times his expressive face would light up, and he would come over and tap me on the shoulder in a little conspiratorial gesture. He served as a buffer state between ourselves and Chen, who was still petrified with mistrust and watched our every move and caught our every phrase. Had Tsai been judged too indulgent, and was this the reason Chen had been sent along with him? In any case, it was he who made the decisions and these were always in our favor, even when they conflicted with the opinion of Chen. For this I was grateful to Mr. Tsai and wanted to demonstrate that he was right. By accident, the two incidents of the

Museum of the Revolution and the fishermen's village had both taken place in his absence. It seemed likely that they might have been avoided if he had been present.

The following morning there was not the slightest sign of any interest in us. The automobiles were not waiting. I sought out the assistant interpreter, Mr. Fang, and asked him to call a conference in my name. He was a very young man who hid his insecurity beneath a false gaiety. The extremely full cut of the clothing of the mandarins he accompanied accentuated the skimpiness of his short jacket and tight-fitting trousers. He cleared his throat several times over each phrase, to give himself time to think, and made serious mistakes in his translations.

When he took the trouble, which he did occasionally, Mr. Shu was less inaccurate. Although he had been in Paris with the Peking Opera troupe, no one liked Mr. Shu, who seemed resigned to leading a grubby existence in his minor post. Brigitte had asked him to hold his hand in front of his mouth when he yawned. He constantly picked his nose or teeth with no sign of embarrassment, let his socks fall down around his hairy legs and rarely shaved, which gave his pock-marked face the appearance of being always dirty. Often, in translating, he assumed a tone of voice I had not heard in the person I was talking to. Did he think he should not pronounce the word "revolution" or the name of Chairman Mao without giving them an intonation that was indispensable in French? If the discussion involved the American imperialists, his tone was always one of bitter irony. It was undoubtedly his own way of asserting himself. I suspected that when he returned home on his bicycle he took revenge on those around him for the humiliations he had suffered, and I was sure a domestic tyrant was hidden beneath his flaccid manner.

I had thought about him a good deal and frequently been worried about him. Where did he live? Was he happy? Did he suffer from seeing so little of his family, since we monopolized him even on Sundays? When I questioned him on these matters, he answered in monosyllables, undoubtedly because a reflex of permanent self-effacement had been implanted in all interpreters. Incapable of sensing nuances, completely lost when I used the double negatives, he had already provoked some misunderstandings, and as a rule I was careful to use only words I felt were within his reach. Whenever a discussion became lively, however, a precise vocabulary was called for of which Mr. Shu was incapable.

Now a certain dignity I had not suspected him of as I watched him whispering reports of our private conversations to Mr. Chen had brought about his retirement from the scene. Since I had withdrawn my confidence from him, he had become the assistant and the assistant had become the chief. An atmosphere of mourning pervaded the hotel corridors. For my part, I felt in excellent spirits, and I had not even been greatly upset the day before when we were told that our trip to Chungking had been canceled. In fact, the entire crew had accepted this new disappointment with perfect calm, but the Chinese apparently did not consider this worthy of comment. Who knows? Perhaps they really did think we were idiots.

This time the vice president himself presided over our meeting. His expression was stubborn and surly, and a succession of nervous tics gave his face the appearance of being in constant motion. His left leg quivered frantically, he kept glancing at me out of the corner of his eye and then abruptly lowering his head, sputtering with rage. I was forced to recognize that this was one person who was not mincing words— words which Mr. Fang, the assistant interpreter, sometimes had difficulty forcing through his throat.

"We received Mr. Roy and his associates as friends. It is our Association's duty to work for a better understanding between our two peoples. In return, Mr. Roy was arrogant in his treatment of the chief of the fishing village, whom he called aside so that he might question him. He stated that he could not work unless his mind was at peace. Where has he seen any indication that our state is not living in peace? We want only peace. In the automobile Mr. Roy made unfriendly remarks to the secretary general. He accused us of having wasted his time when it was actually we who had been waiting for him, and he added: 'You treat me as if I were an idiot.' Mr. Roy forgets that the Chinese people is a sovereign people. Mr. Roy has expressed suspicion with regard to members of our personnel; this is an attitude we have often come up against in the past but which we can no longer tolerate."

He seemed to have finished, and now the secretary general took over. Why answer? It would be better to let the storm pass, and I could not help feeling a certain jubilation. A discussion of this sort could only lead to a rupture, and then, very calmly, I was going to speak my mind.

"In the automobile," the secretary general said, "Mr. Roy exploded with anger. He claimed that the delay was caused by our negligence. He said: 'I am not an idiot. This wasted time is your fault.' You have been received here as our guests, and we are giving up our own time for you. Why should we wish to waste it?"

These statements, highly abridged here, were not made this simply. They were buried and obscured in extraordinarily intricate language. I tried to untangle their meaning, link them together logically and then reconstruct them. The lips of the speakers trembled with indignation. My companions and I glanced at each other occasionally, wondering whether to be dismayed or amused. It was clear that we were going to be packing our bags. I was inclined to anticipate this with a sense of relief.

But now they were waiting for my reply. I gave it with no display of emotion.

"Everyone heard the words I spoke to the chief of the village. Not only was there no arrogance in them, but I tried to express a genuine feeling of friendship. As for what I said in the automobile, I warned you when I arrived—and your contacts in Peking must certainly have confirmed this—that I have a habit of saying what I think. You knew we wanted to return to the village. You knew it was necessary for us to get there early because of the light. If you ignored these facts, it can only be because you did not know our intentions—which is not the case—or misunderstood them—which would be an indication of incompetence in your personnel. If, through incompetence, mistakes are made in what I say or hear, I think it preferable to change translators and avoid any further misunderstandings. I do not see what crime of *lèse-majesté* I am committing in wanting to make sure I am expressing myself clearly.

"As for your other points, I am not forgetting that you are a sovereign and independent people, but if you are confusing us with the colonialists from whom you suffered in the past, I do not see what we can hope to accomplish by continuing our mission here. I came here only to work toward an understanding of China. We have only a few weeks in which to do this. There is nothing offensive in wanting to make up the time we lost in Peking, and the fact that we are dismayed at losing even more seems to me a sign of our interest. You are confusing the issue, and so long as that remains true, there is no possibility of mutual understanding. Let us give this incident its true proportions and everything will be easier."

It is possible to write an account of this conversation far more rapidly than the words were spoken. There was a pause after every phrase to allow for its translation, and that in turn was interrupted by the fumbling and throat clearing of Mr. Fang. The atmosphere grew more and more tense. On my left, the vice president was fuming. Mr. Tsai and all his group were scribbling notes on their pads. From time to time someone lifted his tea to his lips. Simon glanced at me despairingly. Brigitte was showing signs of exasperation. She no longer hid her indignation, and kept signaling me to break up the meeting. I knew, however, that in every Chinese conversation it was necessary to leave some loophole which would permit the other party to save face. They seemed to be expecting something else from me.

"It is possible," the vice president said, tapping his foot even more violently, "that misunderstandings do exist. But is it necessary because of this to adopt such an arrogant attitude? You are here in China, and this attitude jeopardizes our collaboration."

The secretary general added that he felt it necessary to express his own view. Although my companions had shown evidence of friendliness toward the people, my own attitude indicated that I possessed an imperialist mentality. I had not explained why I had said, "I am not an idiot," and that was certainly an imperialist phrase.

I thought it useless to reply. The cameraman did it for me.

"In a misunderstanding," he said, "no one understands anyone else. You did not understand what was said to you. Why, then, make a mountain out of nothing? The mountain has no more substance than your grievances."

Suddenly Mr. Orthion, our sound engineer, stood up, so tall that his head seemed to touch the ceiling. As I have mentioned before, I had liked him at once because he had both spirit and courage. He was as discouraged as any of us by the mistrust that surrounded us and did not know how we were going to replace our historical film, but he had reacted just as I did and wanted to record everything he came across, in the hope that some meaning might still be extracted from our journey. He dropped his little black cigarillo into an ashtray and waved his arms.

"As far as I am concerned," he said furiously, "I have had enough of these discussions that lead nowhere. I came here to work, not to waste my time like this. I'm leaving. When you are ready to get back to work, let me know."

He strode rapidly out of the room. There was a moment's weighty silence, and then Mr. Tsai stirred slightly in his chair, lit a cigarette and began to speak, in a tired voice.

"I was not there," he said, "at the time of the incident, because I was resting. We are very much concerned about this matter of friendship. In Peking our president charged me with aiding Mr. Roy, and that we have done, even when we were tired. Mr. Roy is certainly aware that he has expressed a great many desires since his arrival in Wuhan and that the majority of these desires have been granted. We were also supposed to go on to Chungking. But Chungking could not guarantee our departure in time to arrive in Peking for the celebrations. Our friends in Wuhan looked after us here, and we would like to express our gratitude toward them. One of the secretaries general has accompanied us every day. As a rule, foreigners do not make trips such as those we have made or will make to the port or the stations. We are also grateful for all the facilities that have been offered us at this hotel and the transportation that has been provided.

"As for yesterday's incident, my interpretation of it is this: we have all been working too hard the last few days. Yesterday, by the time we finished lunch, it was three o'clock. We felt that Mr. Roy's age called for special consideration, and our friends in Wuhan have been equally considerate of us. Personally, I am grateful since I do not dislike resting a while after lunch. This idea of a pause was commendable. Mr. Roy thought it a sign of mistrust. But if we had not wanted to show him this lamentable village, we would not have taken him there. Since he did not understand our consideration for him he became angry, and as a result there have been further misunderstandings and regrettable words."

The admirable, cunning, wily Mr. Tsai! Beneath his feigned weariness, he was gradually growing bolder. While the interpreter translated his last phrases, he sipped thoughtfully at his tea, then stared at the ceiling, tapped his cigarette calmly against the ashtray and began speaking again, quite slowly. We all listened, hypnotized. This time, in spite of the inevitable detours, he was clear and incisive, his words temperate. I understood why he had been chosen to accompany me.

"Mr. Roy is well acquainted with the history of the last century," he went on, "when the Chinese people were exploited by foreign colonizers and even expelled from their homes. Certain sections of our own cities were forbidden to the Chinese and to dogs. It is for our liberty and independence that we have fought and shed so much blood. Now we are our own masters, and we will stand up against anyone who commits the slightest injustice against our people. Our French friends are with us now. They are listening to our words. Let us hope that they hear us clearly! When foreign friends express themselves with bitterness, we are reminded of the past. In the case of Mr. Roy, we find this even more difficult to understand, since we know that he came here to write the history of our revolution. Suppose, simply, that you had been in our place, and then everything will become clear to you. In the present instance, our friends in Wuhan were concerned only with our well-being. There are just two more points."

Mr. Tsai's cautious, gentle homily had already lasted for an hour, and I had admired the art with which he contrived its variations, laid out its curves and approached its more difficult twists and turns. Now that he had brought us almost to the top of this first peak, we could see the pass through which the mountains would be crossed.

"The reactions of peoples are not always the same," he continued. "For example, while we were talking Mr. Orthion left the room. This gesture, which seems unfriendly to us, is perhaps quite normal to you. So let us consider it normal. On the other hand, we could not accept statements or actions which were frankly hostile and arrogant. Since there can be no question of deliberate offense, let us think of our common interests. Let us adopt an attitude of free discussion among friends. In that way we can continue to collaborate. You have come to Wuhan, and you have been accepted here. You are our equals. If we were to act as imperialists toward our friends in a smaller nation, we would be committing an error. The positions of our people and yours are clear. Each of us cherishes his freedom of thought, but in working together he must seek those things which reinforce friendship, in spite of any

conflict of personalities. You have all come to visit China with Mr. Roy.
We consider all of you our friends, on an absolutely equal level, as is the
custom in a Communist country."

It was twenty minutes after twelve. I would have liked to do what one
does in Algeria to express admiration, friendship and complicity: touch
Mr. Tsai's hand with mine and then bring my index finger to my lips
and wink at him. The gesture would probably have been thought incon-
gruous, so I abstained from it, regretfully.

It was finished. Without making too great a show of it, everyone was
exultant. No, we would not pack our bags; we would continue. Mr. Tsai
had saved the faces of both parties to the dispute. I was already closing
my notebook and putting away my pen. Simon's relief was self-evident.
Mr. Chen had relaxed. The left leg of the vice president was continuing
its dance, however, and his eyes were still stubbornly focused on his
knees. The secretary general still wore the icy expression of a grand
inquisitor. The discussions began again, with a series of strange braying
sounds by which the vice president seemed to be saying that this was all
very well, but . . . There still remained the fact that I had offended the
delegation's personnel by demanding the replacement of the chief
interpreter.

Simon looked at me, and I smiled. China was certainly worth a Mass,
and I could put up with anything if I took the trouble to do so. I had, for
instance, put up with Mr. Fang, who was not even as good as Mr. Shu.
Mr. Tsai had provided me with all the help he could. What stupidity it
would be at this point to oblige the Chinese to settle our differences with
a flat yes or no!

Let he who has never found any occasion to make a list of his own
faults cast the first stone. And let he who has never, the morning after,
considered far less important something he considered essential the
night before, cast the second and third. I am not one of these. If my life
or the fate of an important work depended on the firmness of a decision,
I would rather have my skull crushed in than yield, but if it is a matter
of a minor obstacle, I adapt myself to it rather than be broken by it. I
was quite willing to sacrifice all vanity on the altar of China. And in this
particular case I confess that I also experienced a certain perverse
pleasure in showing how Chinese I could be.

"I must first say how conscious I am of the wisdom of Mr. Tsai's
proposals," I told them. "And I would like to provide you with still
further proof that we have been guided by friendship in everything. I
honestly believed that yesterday's mistake was due to the incompetence
of an interpreter. You assure me that this is not so, and that it was due
only to your consideration for us. I beg you, therefore, to disregard my
request concerning Mr. Shu, and to believe me when I say that I will be
happy to find Mr. Shu once again performing the difficult work of

translation. And if I have been guilty of mistaken judgment, well, I regret this mistake and I will be grateful if you do not hold it against me."

Then, returning to the point of departure of our difficulties, I added: "I have only one desire: to go back and see the fishermen, to express my true feelings to the chief of the village and my admiration for the men who work with him."

This time the rites were saved. The vice president looked up from his knees and smiled at me. He had won, and now he held out his hand to me. Yes, I was a difficult man, but it was possible to come to an agreement with me. In China friends of my kind would always be welcome. They were going to prove it to me.

We went to lunch in the hotel restaurant, and by way of restoring our spirits after this display of emotion I ordered a bottle of the tart white wine with its syrupy base. We sought in vain for some flavor that would remind us of a muscadet or sancerre, and we were unable to finish our glasses. The tobacco also disgusted us. Where had I invented my theory that Chinese tobacco reminded me of English tobacco? In the Chinese Embassy in Paris when the offer of a cigarette was part of an offer of friendship? After that I had decided it was useless to burden myself on this trip with cartons of French cigarettes. Now we could no longer inhale this burnt grass and fought among ourselves over a few Gauloises Mr. Orthion had inherited from a crew that preceded us.

Great arrangements were being made. We would not go to Chungking, but we were going to meet some eyewitnesses to the Wuhan insurrection of 1911. It would require a little time to get them together. The afternoon was free. I typed out a cable for *l'Express*. Simon received a cable from the producer, who was annoyed by the difficulties we had encountered in making our historical film and found them hard to imagine in his office on the Champs-Elysées: "Rent car and retrace itinerary Long March." That delighted us. There were no cars to be rented other than those owned by the government, and the government had no desire to see us make a historical film. Moreover, no vehicle of any kind could have traversed the goat paths followed by the remnants of the Red Army when it set out on the Long March. One does not travel in China as one does in America, Europe or even Africa.

Smiles suddenly began to blossom everywhere again. Our Chinese companions busied themselves with our affairs and came to visit us in our rooms, as friends. The weather was gray and sticky. Brigitte wanted to visit some of the antique dealers whose shops we had seen through the automobile windows. Everyone was astonished that we should be collectors of such old-fashioned things. They found it suspicious. It recalled the tyranny of the past, the epoch when the Chinese had worked for colonialists and feudal barons. Now ivories were sculpted by machine, portraits of Mao Tse-tung were woven in factories, a life-size bust of the Chairman cost four hundred yuans in all the major stores, the equivalent of ten months of work for a coolie. Who bought them? Since we were considered enlightened collectors, we were taken to one of the larger stores to see artworks created for the living rooms of professors with middle-class ideas: jades and bronzes turned out by the state factories. On the same floor of the store they sold plastic shoes.

When we returned to the hotel, Mr. Tsai abandoned his jacket and cap, settled himself in the room of the cameraman and Mr. Orthion, and began to talk about Europe and the world. The discussion, translated by Mr. Shu, who was seated on the bed, was interrupted by frequent bursts of laughter. No, we could not share the views of Marxism-Leninism on the future of humanity, and, however strange it might seem here, we lived quite happily beneath the yoke of a capitalist regime. We had our own concerns, and we had no desire to see the state take them over for us.

Everything was going splendidly now. An enormous autumn moon was climbing above the horizon. I had never felt myself more of a stranger, even in New York, or in Moscow when I was forced to write out an address or learn the name of a street by heart in order to get a taxi to take me there. In comparison, Calcutta, where one still heard English spoken, seemed the heart of civilization. In Wuhan it was enough to walk a hundred yards from the hotel without Mr. Tsai or Mr. Shu, to be seized with panic or apprehended by some suspicious militiaman.

The sight of cameras in our hands emptied the streets in front of us. In China no one thought of photographs except in terms of a group, gathered on the threshold of a house, wearing their Sunday clothes and an air of great seriousness. Anything beyond this must conceal some diabolical trick. With her heavy leather sack slung over her shoulder, Brigitte continued stubbornly focusing her lens on faces which quickly turned away, piling up rolls of negatives which must surely yield a few pearls or the miracle of all China reflected in a single image: a worker pouring molten steel, a happy child, a woman clutching a submachine gun to her throat or a sad-looking man coming down the steps of the Temple of Heaven, holding a bowl of goldfish in his hands. When I saw Brigitte like this, my heart still beat faster. At such moments something great bound us together, this young girl who believed that I possessed the truth and I who knew myself to be as lost as she, riddled with fears and constantly tormented by thoughts of my book, which might turn out to be a monster or be stillborn. Each night, convinced that everything was slipping away from her, she bent beneath the weight of another day lost. On my side, I could only wonder where and if I would discover the key to this country and this journey. We were two lost travelers in the Empire at the Center of the World.

We were never taken back to the fishermen's village, and all our many allusions to a return trip were greeted with a deaf ear. To distract our minds from this disappointment, we were conducted on a tour of the lakes in the west. There were a thousand of them in the province. Everyone in China loves lakes. They gorge themselves on them. Everywhere we went we saw families, honest and legitimate families with their offspring, workers after their daily stint in the factory, soldiers on leave, pensioners from the wars and ancestors warming their rheumatic bones. And if, unfortunately, there happened to be a hotel near the water, they spent the day feasting on lemonade and cold cuts of meat. We drank toasts to friendship among all peoples and the strengthening of peace. It was a strain staying both cordial and hungry.

On the day following our meeting with the vice president of the Association, the weather was cool. The room looked out on a park which sloped down to the enchanted shores of a lake, for which, at the moment, I cared absolutely nothing. Two worthy old gentlemen were waiting for us: the director of the teachers' training school, with the round, heavy face of a parish priest, a gray suit and handsome ankle boots of soft leather; and a professor at the Polytechnic Institute, lean and quick, dressed in a simple blue coverall and wearing basketball shoes. Both of them talked to us about the insurrection of 1911.

The revolutionary forces had not yet been coordinated. The various societies which were part of the conspiracy disguised themselves as literary or "progressive" groups. Workshops for the manufacture of weapons had been set up in the French concession, but an accidental explosion had resulted in the arrest and subsequent decapitation of the shops' directors. Anticipating discovery, the army officers in the conspiracy sent out a call for' action during the night of October 10, 1911. The soldiers of an engineering unit responded and a garrison to the south of the city followed suit. The rebels advanced along the walls, effected a junction and occupied the arsenal and the Hill of the Serpent, where they set up a battery of cannon and trained it on the administrative headquarters of the province and the barracks of the Manchu troops. The governor fled and, since the insurrection had no real leader and Dr. Sun Yat-sen was in America, it was decided to bestow command on the only Chinese general who could be found. He was pulled out from beneath his bed, where he had been hiding to escape a responsibility he did not want. Thirty or so British and Japanese warships were anchored in the river, but the workers, dockers, peasants and coolies joined forces with the revolutionary forces and fortified the Hill of the Tortoise. Hankow burned for three days. The little professor at the

Polytechnic Institute had come to Wuhan with friends who were serving in the army; he was studying in an industrial school and also painting red flags whose central gold star bore two small stars on each of its nine points, a symbol of the eighteen provinces. At the time he was seventeen year old.

"When I saw one of the flags I had painted floating above the Hill of the Serpent," he told me, "I understood that the revolution had triumphed. I suddenly felt that I was a free man, and I would have gladly died twice for that."

The Manchus no longer dared attack. Southern and central China followed in the wake of the uprising. On January 1, 1912, in Nanking, Dr. Sun Yat-sen became the first President of the Republic, and the double ten, the tenth day of the tenth month, became a national holiday. Success seemed due to the daring of a few officers, to luck, to the inefficient organization of the imperial forces and to the neutrality of the foreigners, whom the revolutionaries had been careful to reassure. The empire crumbled like a rotted tree, but the social structure remained untouched. The army of slaves and coolies, workers and peasants on the verge of starvation, would search for almost twenty years more before finding the guiding force it needed and the leader capable of guiding it to victory.

We all lunched together—without any excesses. The two eyewitnesses were sparing in their appetites and drank little. Toasts were drunk in honor of a general reconciliation to consecrate the triumph of Mr. Tsai. Lemonade and beer flowed freely. It was Sunday. Since the emotions of the day before had exhausted our friends, we were invited to take a siesta and each of us was given a room. In mine, I waited, with a boredom as vast as the lake, for the recall to work to be sounded. A turtle dove cooed in the motionless air. Brigitte slept. On the lake boating parties threw cake crumbs into the waters in honor of a poet assassinated because he had sung of the misery of the people.

In a garden of poinciana and beech trees we visited the long low house, surrounded by a pillared gallery, where Mao had indoctrinated his cadres in 1927. I was assured that it was here he had written the famous "Report Concerning and Inquiry into the Peasant Movement in the Province of Hunan." There was no washbasin, bed or mess tin used by Mao and religiously preserved; just a chair from which he had given his courses, now set next to a blackboard. No one, at the time, had discerned the halo above his forehead. Of the old school, there still remained the dormitories with the racks for weapons, the refectory tables and benches where meals were eaten in silence, the rope sandals and cotton garments of the pupils.

One might have imagined, however, that the garrulous and impassioned young woman who was our guide had heard the voice of the

Savior, and that she saw him still, with the eyes of faith. When she spoke of him, an aura of love transformed her whole appearance; her voice took on a vibrant tone, her face lit up, her body and soul were offered to the mystical spouse. The flames of the sacred fire she nourished were devouring this Vestal Virgin.

Everyone paid tribute to the interest we had shown with our questions, and, as a crowning gesture, it was announced that the president of the Association had invited us to dinner that night. Two communal meals in the same day—it was almost too much!

Brigitte and I shared a distaste for Chinese cuisine. Our palates could not adapt themselves to these fatty substances and raw vegetables, these thick sauces and peculiar flavors. When we were served what were considered the greatest of delicacies—sharks' fins, swallows' nests or lacquered duck—we barely tasted them. As for the sea slugs, sugared seaweed, ragouts of chicken, steamed biscuits stuffed with pork, and the thousand other delicacies of a refined culinary art, we touched them only when we were forced to for the sake of nourishment. It cannot be explained, and I was the first to suffer from it. In this country where the restaurants' European cuisine possessed nothing European but the name, it would have been far more pleasant for both of us if we had enjoyed Chinese cooking.

If the meals to which we were invited amounted to a form of forced labor for us, the conversation that accompanied them and the toasts to which I was forced to reply transformed them into a virtual Calvary. But the spectacle of our companions at table was worth the trouble. I never sat down without thinking of the dinner Father Huc has described, in a third-rate city on the Yangtze.

> We overwhelmed each other with politeness and courtesy, each inviting the other to take the most honorable place. . . . The banquet was splendid and served with all the formality of Chinese etiquette. On the part of our hosts and the other guests there was nothing to be desired; they evidenced such enormous amiability that we could not doubt for a single instant their sincere and intense desire to see us leave the next day.

Not so much was made of ceremony among the Communist mandarins. The places at the round tables would have been the same in Europe, with the notable difference that these gentlemen never invited ladies, except as servants.

That night, in the private room where we had been invited to relax, the faces of our hosts were bright with good humor. Drinking helped me get through with it, but for Mr. Tsai it was a ritual celebration. His eyes flashed, he shook his great wolf's head, clinked his glass of rice alcohol against mine and, at the command *"Kam-pé,"* bolted its contents in a single swallow. Then he held out the empty glass horizontally, like the transparent corolla of the flower of consummated friendship, and waited until I had followed his example. When I did so, his joy knew no bounds. This was the way it should be. This was good.

The dignity of the vice president gradually dissolved into tenderness. The secretary general became expansive. Everything that had divided us was being swallowed up in the blessed communion of peoples. We were becoming civilized. Brigitte was smiling, but in spite of Mr. Tsai's insistence she stubbornly refused to sear her stomach with this Chinese vitriol. Rising to our feet, one after the other, with recourse to countless banalities, we celebrated frankness, the vital discussions which can only take place among true friends, the victorious proletariat, the strength of the party and the glory of Mao Tse-tung. At this point I bridled. I would not take that hurdle. I tried to say that we did not give our great men the same degree of adulation as the Chinese, that their credit was likely to diminish as they grew older and that we hesitated to attach ourselves to them for life. "With us," I was told, "it is not adoration, as you seem to think, but affection. The Chinese people want to show their gratitude to their Chairman." It occurred to me that slaves might very well experience deeper and more faithful sentiments than ours toward a savior, and that there was something in this of the visceral attachment of a dog to his master.

After these first libations, this great collective embrace, the dinner itself began. I don't remember what we ate. I do remember that the waiters were kept constantly busy filling glasses, bringing on new courses and changing the plates which I left three-quarters full.

"Do you like Chinese cuisine?"

It was the ritual question. I replied politely that it was a very special cuisine and that it required time to accustom oneself to it. Yes, there were many Chinese restaurants in Paris and their cuisine was highly appreciated; it bore little resemblance, however, to the actual Chinese cuisine. Why, I wondered, was I paying so much attention to dissimulation? No one was any longer listening to me. Chen had almost abandoned the conversation and was devouring great mounds of food, whole blocks of *pâté*, which he shoveled into his mouth as if it were the open door of an oven. Between two phrases of translation, Mr. Shu managed to dash to the other end of the table in search of morsels of a particular fish in sauce which he occasionally allowed to fall into his glass of beer. Mr. Tsai spit out the bones of his fish on the tablecloth next to his plate.

This voracity had surprised me at the beginning of our stay in China, but by now I found it oddly moving. Watching them gorge themselves to the point of endangering their bellies, filling their mugs or glasses to the brim and swallowing the contents at a single gulp, in the Russian manner, was a comforting sign of the new abundance. For these men, to whom the mere fact of birth had given the appetite of wild beasts, to eat was to survive, and survival was the ever-present necessity. For thousands of years, when the fear of dying of hunger had forced them to think only of the too rare or too abundant rains, the idea of cultivating the mind had seemed, even to the lower-ranking mandarins who remembered that they were the sons of peasants, a luxury that could become a necessity only after the passage of generations.

The feast moved to its second stage, interrupted by little periods of rest in which everyone stretched out a little in his chair, picked at his teeth and allowed himself a few courteous belches. Then they went back to work, picking up the agile chopsticks, snatching at bits of meat and plunging them into sauces or spices before thrusting them into their mouths. In their fingers these slender pincers had the nimbleness of a magpie's beak, but since we still used them like the barbarians we were they had thoughtfully provided us with forks. And if the truth be told, this trident is a clumsy instrument which can pierce the lips, and even the eyes if one is really greedy.

When the soup that marked the end of the meal arrived at last, I breathed a sigh of relief. At the other table Simon had disappeared. Tsai had forced him to drink, he had given in and he was ill. Mr. Orthion was still lifting his glass with dazed resignation. *Kam-pé!* His great strong-box of a body was capable of absorbing everything. It reminded me of the firemen's banquets I had sometimes attended. At the end, the firemen were always drunk on sausages and coarse red wine. But it was gluttony and the love of wine that motivated them, not this rather mournful drunkenness. Apples peeled for us by waiters, to spare us even this minor trouble, brought the dinner to a close. Since everything had now been said, we stood up and went our separate ways. My head was spinning. I was furious, and staggering with nausea. "Until tomorrow, until tomorrow." I knew how to say "good morning"—*"nin-hao"*— but not "until tomorrow." The next day we were to leave for Peking—by train, since all the planes to the north were already filled. I would gladly have taken a handcart or a bicycle taxi in order to get away from our friends in Wuhan, who were now sleeping, their bellies full, their consciences at peace.

Chapter 12

In which the author, regretting that China has become so completely aseptic, learns that it is forbidden to take photographs in a train and has a meal in a dining car. In which Brigitte, on the return to Peking, is distressed at not returning to the Hsin Chiao. In which the novelist Han Suyin advises the author to think seriously about the achievements of the regime. In which the reader takes part in a great banquet presided over by Mao Tse-tung, and in the parade in celebration of the October First anniversary of the revolution. How the author is impressed by the solemnity of the cult of Mao Tse-tung and by the nocturnal dancing of the crowds.

Throughout the entire day the mandarins of Kienchow were beyond reproach in their behavior toward us; therefore, on the next day, we gave them the satisfaction of seeing us leave.

—E. R. Huc, *The Chinese Empire*

I was worried that the automobiles might not be there in time to load our baggage. Since the train was scheduled to leave at noon and I was tired of the hotel, I said that I would have lunch in the dining car. We had been impatient to leave Peking, and now, at the thought of returning, we were experiencing the same impatience, the same hope of finding what we were looking for. Why had so many travelers who had come to China for a few weeks remained for years? I thought of the diplomat who had said to me: "When I lived in Japan, everything was perfect and I was bored. In China everything smelled of dung and I was perfectly happy." China no longer stank, except occasionally, when one got too close to the tanks of garbage collectors or the washtubs of peasants. The Chinese seemed possessed with a rage to clean, sweep and polish everything in sight. Surely, somewhere in this country there was a China that was the incarnation of a China I could love, a house where I would like to pause, to finish out my days and forget the rest of the world.

The process had already begun. It had been almost a month since we had any news of what was happening in Europe, and we had gorged ourselves on the old newspapers piled up in Marcuse's rooms, on paperback books and the mystery stories in our suitcases. Now we were beginning to shed our Western interests. We cared no more about what was being said on the Champs-Elysées than we did for Soviet foreign policy or the fate of the Common Market. *Peking Informaton,* which I threw in the wastebasket without even looking at it, had disgusted us with the whole idea of reading. On the other hand, when letters arrived after weeks in the baggage compartments of Boeings or Tupolevs, we weighed each word, extracted every drop of meaning. We were shaken by a wind of happiness, as if we had been caught in the backwash of an invisible ship. I asked Brigitte to read me the letters she received from her mother and friends, and she devoured not only my letters but my notebooks.

Hurt and disillusioned by all the obstacles placed between her camera lens and the pictures she sought, she was gradually turning, like me, toward a quest for the China that existed in her heart. She held our guides responsible for the fake sights we had been shown, and reacted by sticking out her tongue at them, as if she were still a schoolgirl.

Even on the thousand lakes of Hupeh, there was no longer a single mosquito. In just a few years the people had destroyed all their hatching places. No longer a flea, no longer a bug of any kind. The cans of DDT Brigitte had brought with her on someone's advice would never serve any purpose. If I happened to see a fly in flight, I followed it affectionately, as if it were the last stag in the forest of Fontainebleau and the guards were about to shoot it down because it represented a danger to the tourists in their automobiles.

My fear of missing the train had been unfounded. It was at the station. The sleeping car in which our compartments were located offered a degree of luxury worthy of such honored guests: a lamp on the table, sliding windows, screens to protest us against any surviving insects and pots of tea. The broad seats had neither backs nor armrests and could be transformed into couches. Our friends in Wuhan were only slightly less happy at our departure than we were, and our demonstrations of mutual affection were brought to a halt only by the departure of the train. We did not know what the future might hold, but we knew what we were leaving. For the moment, that was enough to insure our happiness.

At first, there was music on the loudspeakers in our compartments, but this was soon replaced by interminable speeches of which we understood nothing. When we noticed that it was possible to cut them off, Orthion discreetly brought out his screwdriver and restored us to blessed silence. The chief conductor came to present his compliments. We were like schoolchildren on vacation, taking their first train ride. We pulled back the velvet drapes so that we might look out at the countryside. One by one, villages of mud-walled houses flashed by, groups of laborers plowing the land or beginning to harvest the autumn rice crop, troops of filthy little pigs herded by children with poles to prevent them from getting into the cornfields, caravans of carts pulled by human beasts of burden.

Mr. Tsai had warned us that it was forbidden to photograph anything through the windows, under pain of violating the espionage laws. Only the chief conductor could grant such authorization. When we asked him about it, he took refuge behind the regulations. Only by agreements between governments could journalists or tourists take photographs, and since I had not known this would be necessary, I had never thought of demanding such a permit. More and more, I wondered if they would ever allow us to spend the few days I had requested among the men whose pitchforks had started the revolution. Would we ever see the peasants from anything but a distance?

Gradually now the dusk was reducing them to shadows. The water in the rice fields took on a silvery sheen. Children perched on the backs of water buffalo, bringing them back to their stables. Occasionally, with a great clatter of couplings, the train came to a halt because a cow or a steer was sleeping on the track. We were coming up through the centuries, and were passing through the Middle Ages. How could tractors ever had been used in these diked and terraced rice fields, and what purpose had they served? Several times each day, locomotives and railroad cars manufactured in the new China entered and passed through the destitution that was the heritage of ancient China. Men and women from the villages went to Peking or to the provincial capital, and on their return told stories of having seen avenues, monuments and shops that were heralds of the promised abundance. When the train stopped at a station, crews of men whose homes were shanties where children played with the poultry and hogs in rivulets of mud, dashed out to wash the windows and even the cars.

At one of the halts we were transferred to another car, on the pretext that otherwise we would have had to walk through a baggage car in order to reach the dining car. Our new compartments were more comfortable and paneled in even more expensive woods, but the windows were so narrow that we could see almost nothing through them. Orthion took advantage of the change to move into the compartment with the cameraman and Simon, who was attempting to get rid of Mr. Fang, the assistant interpreter. This brought on still another incident. Although the cameras were stored with the baggage, someone apparently thought we were trying to take clandestine photographs of the landscape, and I was asked to intervene. What would become of the rest of the crew without an interpreter? They might need something, and how could they ask for it? They didn't need a thing, they wanted nothing except to be able to talk freely among themselves. I said that it was impossible for me to force them to do anything, and that this, in fact, was one of the basic premises of our free society. In the end, weary of this renewal of interminable discussions, my crew simply locked themselves in. But there was another incident yet to come.

The dining car bore little resemblance to those of European trains. I had already waited an hour after the train left before I was brought the eggs and beer I .had ordered for lunch. At dinner, since none of the Russian or European dishes listed on the menu actually existed, and since I still could not bear the thought of ham, we settled for a bizarre stew which hunger forced us to chew on. The loudspeaker was fracturing our eardrums, though no one else seemed to be bothered by it. Quite suddenly, the cameraman rose to his feet, stepped onto a chair and cut it off.

"Now," he said as he sat down again, "we'll be able to hear ourselves talk."

In the moment of stunned silence that followed, it seemed certain that lightning was about to strike. Someone was going to demand the intervention of the skinny little policeman in helmet, white jacket and red armband who had been walking ceaselessly from one end of the train to the other, inspecting our tables mournfully as he passed. To my astonishment, and almost to my disappointment, nothing happened. No one made the slightest reference to the cameraman's action.

We settled down for the night. One of the two bulbs in the light above the berths had been cut off, for reasons of economy. The compartment could still be lit, but not sufficiently to read. I felt weighed down by this strange universe, baroque, stifling, vaguely menacing, where everything was regulated without being openly ordered, by this indecipherable language, the padded footsteps of the policeman in the corridor, my revulsion at the flavors and odors and endless succession of pots of tea. I took a sleeping pill, which had almost no effect. As the train rolled north, the temperature dropped, but there was no corresponding expenditure of steam to heat the cars. When the sun rose at six o'clock, the peasants were already in the fields, plowing, reaping and spreading the human excrement they used as fertilizer.

At ten o'clock the train arrived in the Peking station. Our baggage, which was both bulky and heavy, was taken out and loaded onto a cart. The sky was clear and cold. We were all vaguely happy, because we had the vaguest impression of returning home. At the Hsin Chiao we would revert to our old habits, seek out the great lanky frame of Marcuse, find our friends from the embassy and our mail from home. Pierre Nora had promised to write to us from Hong Kong. And now that we had sampled a few others, we decided we loved the restaurant of the Hsin Chiao. Our mouths watered at the thought of what we would find there: red caviar, macaroni with tomato sauce, Russian soups, grilled fillet of fish and finely sliced fried potatoes. The beer would be really cold. The waiters were pleasant, the only taxi stand in Peking was at the door of the hotel, and there was the bar where we could make appointments and meet our friends.

Suddenly, to our consternation, we learned that we were being taken elsewhere. I expressed astonishment and chagrin, and insisted that we return to the Hsin Chiao. I was told that we must make allowances for the changes in plans brought on by the celebration of the fifteenth anniversary of the liberation. Resigned to my fate, I got into the automobile. Brigitte sat down beside me and burst into tears. Suddenly I was furious with the Chinese. I got out of the automobile again and sat down on the sidewalk in the midst of our baggage. I was immediately surrounded.

"I will not budge from here until you take us back to the Hsin Chiao," I said. "Everywhere in the world, I stay at the hotels where I want to stay. I will pay for the rooms or pay for them yourselves if you insist, but for God's sake give me the freedom to decide where I will go!"

There was a hurried consultation. Mr. Tsai and Mr. Chen lifted me to my feet. I promptly sat down again, clutching to my knees the leather briefcase that contained my notes. Passers-by were beginning to stare at us.

"The hotel we are taking you to is more comfortable than the Hsin Chiao," I was told. "It's not far from here. We thought it better suited to your station. We will find out if it is possible to take you back to the Hsin Chiao, but come with us now. You can make up your mind later."

Perhaps I was mistaken after all; they could be telling me the truth. With the thousands of guests from all over the world who were here for the celebrations, it was clear that some degree of regulation must be expected. I was wrong not to adapt myself to customs simply because they were not mine. I gave in.

Not far, this new hotel? Its imposing mass stood several miles from T'ien An Men Square, just across from the Museum of the Army. It had been open only a short while, and the personnel, which must have been recruited hastily, was still inexperienced. We shared a series of enormous, dreary rooms. It was called the Ting-si Hotel, and as yet no one in Peking knew it even existed. I telephoned Marcuse for help, and he arrived almost immediately. A kind of esplanade served as a parking space, but not a taxi was to be found. No one could give us a telephone number where our friends could reach us.

Happily, however, our mail was waiting for us. Since the parade would not take place for another two days and we had nothing to do, we decided to walk around the city. A flowered arch had been built across the Avenue of Eternal Peace, the central artery of the procession. Gigantic portraits of the President of Mali, in his white skullcap and *boubou,* were placed at intervals along the route the official party would follow on his arrival from the airport. The beards and mustaches of Marxism-Leninism stared haughtily across T'ien An Men Square at an imposing head of Mao, which adorned the façade of the official reviewing stand. Masses of children and young people were gathered at every intersection, ready to begin waving their paper flowers. Branches of peach trees, tulips, iris, peonies, narcissus and hyacinth—they were all artificial, and the atmosphere of gaiety reflected this. It seemed ordered for the occasion and cheaply made. An indifferent crowd looked on as the machinery for this picnic was installed, their attitude clearly indicating that they had seen it all before. Long columns of docile bit players, coming in from the nearby countryside, were being led to their camping grounds. For lack of a better subject, Simon wanted at least to make a color film of this regal shindig, but the reels of film he had ordered by cable two weeks earlier had not yet arrived.

That evening we went to dinner with Marcuse. Our appointment was at the Hsin Chiao, and we returned there feeling sick at heart. The hotel seemed no more crowded than usual. I learned that the novelist Han Suyin was staying there temporarily, and it occurred to me at once that I should have an interview with her; half-Chinese by birth, international by educaton, she could perhaps explain the Chinese mystery to me better than anyone else. A friend gave me the number of her room, since the concierge did not know her by the name under which she writes. As a matter of precaution, I slipped a message under her door.

"Today you will rest."

Those were the instructions Mr. Shu left with us, between a smile and a yawn on the morning of September 30. Had we been invited to the banquet that evening, where Mao Tse-tung was to be the host? He did not know. What he did know was that Mr. Tsai wanted to see me, alone, at three o'clock that afternoon. "Just you and him," he told me. I had an appointment with Han Suyin in the bar of the Hsin Chiao.

Sophisticated, beautifully turned out, instinctively making use of all the charms of her sex, Han Suyin did not have Chinese eyes. She spoke French admirably, and I was fascinated by the fact that she had reclaimed her Chinese nationality. She came to Peking regularly, to collect the rents from some houses the government had allowed her to retain. She was lavish in her praise of the present régime and seemed distressed by the disappointments I complained of. A curious intensity smoldered in her eyes, as if about to burst into flame. Perhaps I was expecting too much from her country, and too quickly.

"One must have time to waste here," she told me. "Otherwise one can be very unhappy."

She felt that it must have been a succession of misunderstandings that had spoiled my relationship with the Association.

"You would have to have known this country before," she went on, "in order to judge what it has become and where it is going."

That was one error I was firmly resolved not to commit.

Mr. Shu telephoned me at lunchtime; Mr. Tsai was very busy and would not be able to see me for the next two days. I was intrigued by this abrupt change in plans. Apparently, the report on the incidents of our Wuhan trip was being studied in detail and my behavior was being passed under the microscope. We returned to the Ting-si Hotel, and Mr. Shu brought our invitations for the banquet that night.

Toward the end of the afternoon I received a note from Han Suyin. She excused herself for being unable to grant me a further interview, and urged me to think seriously about the safeguards against famine and misery which the new régime had given the country.

At the Chinese Embassy in Paris I had often been told: "You will certainly meet our Chairman." I had concluded, perhaps a trifle hastily, that I would talk with him, but the phrase could be taken to mean simply that I would meet him. Was being present at a banquet where he presided the equivalent of a meeting? Such imprecision was not a mark of the Han dynasty alone. Euphemisms, litotes and all forms of rhetoric are the jewels of diplomatic language. That evening five thousand other guests could truthfully state that they had met the Chairman.

The scene in the enormous hall of the National Assembly Building resembled a Pontifical Mass at St. Peter's in Rome. The tide of guests overflowed the monumental staircases, broke up into smaller waves and moved on to the numbered places. Generals of the People's Army, gold-braided officers from friendly countries, dancers of national minority groups in colorful costumes, diplomats, smooth-faced mandarins, Africans in *boubous*, sharp-eyed Algerians, solemn Vietnamese, all sat frozen in waiting position, facing the long, empty table of honor which had been set up in front of the stage. Our group was nervous. We had unloaded the cameras, but the cameraman refused to begin work because he had been unable to survey the hall beforehand and the light was poor. He was equipped, however, with a telephoto lens and highly sensitive film especially adapted to use under such conditions. As a matter of fact, we felt that he was upset by the presence of other photographic teams, with whom he did not wish to compete. I under-

stood the annoyance he might feel at not being the only person privileged to film such a ceremonial, but the Chinese had given us freedom
to move about as we wished, and any good artist would know how to
make something individual out of even such a mass meeting. He could
give an idea of the particular décor of the celebration, the arrangement
of the guests, the pageantry of flowers and columns of gold, and the
over-all planning that regulated everything.

There was a moment of silence in which the entire hall seemed to
hold its breath, and then, when all the top leaders had entered, following Mao, a wave of light burst from invisible projectors in the walls and
flooded the room, followed immediately by a stormy ovation, under-
scored by the "Hymn to the Chairman" played by the orchestra.

With the problem of lighting solved, the cameraman leaped onto his
chair, adjusted his camera and began filming the five thousand standing
guests, clapping their hands and singing. From where I sat, I could
scarcely see Mao's gray silhouette as it moved to the center of the table,
answer the applause with applause of his own and then sat down. The
ovation ceased. The orchestra began to play another tune, and the meal
began, to the accompaniment of a joyous clamor. At every table, people
were standing up, clinking their glasses together and drinking toasts.
Other representatives of the Association had taken their places at our
table. Mr. Tsai moved about a great deal, greeting friends everywhere.
Suddenly there was silence, and the President of the Republic, Liu Shao-
ch'i, began reading into the microphones a speech whose text, printed in
every known language, had been given to us earlier. It was an incan-
tatory litany, in turn reassuring and violent, uttered in a sort of guttural
shriek which sometimes resembled a chat. "The Chinese people firmly
support . . ."—with a pause after "Chinese people." *"Chung-kuo ren-
min . . ."* The Chinese people firmly supported all the oppressed peoples of the earth and defied American imperialism. The meal began
again and picked up speed. When dessert had been served, Mao stood
up and climbed the steps to the stage, accompanied by his group of
vassals. The projectors came on and the ovation began again. He held out
his glass toward the hall, made a pretense of shaking the hand of
everyone present and disappeared, trailed by his entire court.

The festival was over, the communion accomplished in the sacred
manner: bread and wine. Our companions were still overwhelmed by
this apparition, as if they had been struck dumb with ecstasy. I had seen
the god for a few minutes, in all his glory, crowned with a halo of light.
He had accorded us the grace of presiding over a banquet, lending
himself to a few good-natured photographs, and then gone as he had
come, snatched up by the cloud from which he sprang. With a great air
of mystery, certain guests were invited to another room where they

might see him more closely and touch his hand. We were hardly judged
worthy to be part of this elite group.

On the morning of October 1, after several long detours, we arrived at
last at the heart of the celebrating city. At each halt on the way, the
actors and spectators massed in the streets had turned to stare at us and
cheer the foreign guests who had come to honor their revolution. T'ien
An Men Square was St. Peter's in Rome again, on Easter Sunday when
the Pope appears on his balcony to give his blessing to the Christian
world. From the reviewing stand where we were placed, to the left of the
imperial pagoda, it was impossible even to estimate the number of
faithful pressed shoulder to shoulder beneath the giant portraits of
Marxism-Leninism. Were they a million? The flat yellow and red boards
they carried on their shoulders were held in such a fashion that they
formed the Chinese characters for the date of this fifteenth anniversary.
A thousand-member band, in white uniforms and gloves, faced us across
the square, beneath a gray and menacing sky. Marching with the jerky
precision of robots, their helmets held in place by a strap beneath their
chins, the Red Guards were detached, one by one, to form a line along
the ceremonial route.

At precisely ten o'clock a sudden tremor seemed to pass through the
whole background of the square as the yellow and red boards were
turned to form a new series of characters. I asked for a translation, and
was told that they spelled out "Long live Chairman Mao." Every head
was turned toward the red and gold tribunal where the gray silhouette of
the god suddenly appeared, without an escort and with no indication of
how he had arrived. The roar of cannon shredded the low-hanging
clouds. The band launched into the triumphal hymn. A wave of accla-
mation rolled out from the crowd and hundreds of balloons were
released, trailing multicolored banners, drifting off to the north like the
smoky flowers of antiaircraft fire. The voice of Comrade Peng Chen,
Mayor of Peking, clattered through the loudspeakers, so loud that it
must have carried to the outer limits of the city, solemnly aggressive
and boring, celebrating the policies of the party and the glory of its
Chairman. Then the parade began.

Women in red skirts were among the first to pass, preceded by a
gigantic statue of Mao, held above the level of the crowd on the shoulders of its bearers, the arm outstretched, the cloak whipped back by the
wind, the face set in a Churchillian mask. The women were formed in
rows of fifty, waving peach blossoms and colored plumes, carrying
banners inscribed with socialist maxims: "Liberate Formosa," "Protect
Leninism-Marxism," "Oppose the Aggression of the United States,"
"Long Live the Great Union of Peoples," "Long Live Chairman Mao."

Standing on the tribunal above his portrait, the living god watched the passage of his statue and the consummation of his triumph.

Another band appeared in the distance, momentarily drowned out the first with the shattering sound of its brasses, became entangled with the rhythms of the first and finally managed to extricate itself. Shouting packs of Young Pioneers constantly repeated a cry that resembled a paternoster and waved wreathes of leaves and flowers; flights of pigeons blotted out the sky for an instant, wheeling above us with a great silky beating of wings. Other bands approached and passed, their giant drums and cymbals first glittering and then vanishing in the distance. Enormous masses of men and women jostled against each other, screaming their faith and pushing or towing pasteboard locomotives and flower-covered floats bearing revolving automobiles and tractors, newly arrived from the factory, polished and gleaming.

Now it seemed that the entire avenue was moving toward us, a frenzied, colossal ocean, an immense cohort of schoolchildren shepherded by their teachers and waiting for their signal to shout the prearranged hurrahs, clinging to their gaily decorated balloons and their branches of flowering trees, offering to the god their cabbages, their fruits, their geese, their giant hogs or their cows with swollen udders. The whole of the Chinese people swept by, in compact, well-regulated armies, representing the workers in all the factories, the peasants in all the communes, the clerks in all branches of government, the conductors of trains and buses, the universities of all the cities, the ethnic minorities, the Buddhist priests with their lotus leaves, the Koreans and Mongols acting out their patriotic joy, their fidelity to the mother country. What were we to film, what could be ignored? Only the Chinese cameramen were in a position to work with any degree of comfort. A location from which they could not move and a limited area of vision resulted in an insufferable monotony for all the others.

After seventy minutes of this carnival, the appearance of a bank of red flags signaled the end of the passage of the masses. There was a pause to lend space and import to what would follow. Then, behind a new and more martial music, the militia moved out, in close-knit battalions, the image of a China that was hard and pure, shoulder to shoulder, heads held high, holding rigidly against their hearts the machine guns, the bazookas and the mortars, and waiting until they were within a few yards of the tribunal to break out in the ostentatious goose step, their heels beating rhythmically on the concrete, underscoring the roar of the cheers. Infantrymen, parachutists, shock troops followed one another in terrifying order, scattering like chaff the boring image of the childlike hordes who had preceded them. This time it was not the chill in the air that made me shiver, but the sight of this youth preparing fiercely for combat, and, far from fearing it, seeming to demand it. Confronted with these faces, we no longer thought of smiling. After the flowers, the weapons. In all China there were some twenty million men and women enrolled in the militia. This army of amateurs, which cost the government nothing but the price of the weapons it held, represented the invisible regular army, mounting guard on the frontiers and training for a Long March that would have no end.

Perhaps to dissipate the uneasiness left behind by this brutal apparition, it was followed by an evocation of literature and art, choirs singing of peace, groups of dancers costumed as sunflowers or harvesters, surrounding another statue of the god Mao, this time in his familiar jacket, standing with his hand behind his back in the gentle and thoughtful attitude of the poet, the universal genius holding the world in his hands and guiding his people of peasants, artists and dancers as they played with their silken ribbons, their fans and their castanets. After the fury of war, the dancers of love, the shimmer and interplay of colors, the supple beauty of Olympic athletes, half-naked swimmers, aviators and mountain climbers.

A square of a thousand red flags closed the procession. The white-gloved band marched across the square to face the tribunal. There was a sudden chattering of firecrackers and the entire square burst into a single roar of sound. The god in the gray overcoat moved closer to the railing, accompanied by a Negro king, held out his hand to his people in a gesture of benediction, waved his cap and disappeared. It was noon. The rain that had begun to fall a little earlier was coming down harder now.

We left the stands in silence, hunting for our automobiles.

"It is not just a Chairman you have," I said to Mr. Tsai.

He simply stared at me, uncomprehending.

"What will you do with him when he dies?" I went on. "Build him a tomb like those of the Ming emperors?"

The aftermath of the procession was sad; the flowers, the smiles and the costumes were crumpled; the skins of the drums were slack beneath the rain.

"The Chairman will doubtless be cremated," Tsai said, "and he will have been replaced even before we know that he is no longer with us."

The statues of the idol were still wandering through the streets of the suburbs, with their escort of musicians and dancers. They still looked out with empty eyes at the people attracted to the spectacle. Where would they halt for the night? In what throne room or pagoda would they be placed for safekeeping until the next triumph? Who would guard them? Would people come to burn sticks of incense before them, as they once had done before the statues of Buddha?

The living god had departed unseen. In a car with drawn curtains, or by one of the subterranean canals that linked the metropolis and the old Forbidden City? Benefactor, father, source of all truth, master of wars, commander of the seasons, of sowings and reapings, it was he who was invoked and blessed for what he gave or did not give, since his alone was the sovereign wisdom. Prophet, messiah, emperor and god, it was a great deal. Suddenly, I was afraid.

My friend Tsai said nothing more, and there was an awkward silence between us. We separated coolly.

The fireworks that night resembled the morning's parade. Their very splendor was fatiguing. The men who had invented gunpowder knew how to use it to light the sky with showers of stars, shimmering rivers of light, sudden conflagerations of purple, emerald and azure, bursts of rockets, flights of comets and nebulae, or explosions of planets which revolved slowly for a moment and then streaked into the night like golden birds. The perfection of each ensemble inevitably produced boredom. One waited for a climax that never came. During the brief intermissions all the giant searchlights stationed around the city suddenly directed their columns of light straight up into the heavens, so that they appeared to be supporting the arch of clouds. Then they would come together at a point above the square, remain linked for a moment like the petals of a giant flower, separate, come together again, and begin to weave across the sky in a dancing pattern. They seemed to be taking part in the gaiety that had taken possession of the crowd around the monument to the martyrs of the revolution and in all of the avenues leading to it.

The bodies of these masses of people moved to the rhythms of orchestras set up on the sidewalks, endlessly repeating the same haunting music, punctuated with the clashing of cymbals and brasses and apparently having neither a beginning nor an end; by the hundreds of thousands, men, women and even children were dancing a slow and chaste ballet whose movements seemed relics of another age. As if possessed by the spirit of a god, they had been circling around each other for hours now, bowing, standing straight again, raising and lowering their arms, indifferent to the cold and the fine drizzle of rain which soaked their cotton garments and caused the flags to hang limp above their heads. It was neither the hysteria of an African dance nor the immodesty of the West, but a strange and delicate charade, rendered somehow fierce and disturbing by the fact that it appeared to be endless. A people spellbound by its liberation, drunk with the idea of it, they did not even see the stars exploding in the sky, and were conscious of the music only to the extent that it guided the movement of their limbs. The night itself lent a strange grandeur to a force that resembled the movement of the sea, the wind sighing through forests and harvest fields, seizing and bending them to its will and drawing a tremor from the depths of the earth. No, this was not a dance of slaves, but a rite that had its origins in dead religions, ruined temples and a civilization that was patient and refined even in its mastery of the air of torture; the civilization of eternal China, riddled with hope and despair, with child-like pleasures and cosmic furies.

Long after I had lost interest in them, the fireworks were stll bursting in the sky, draping the clouds with clusters of golden grapes. This time Mao had not bothered to make an appearance. Only his portrait now dominated the dedicated human tide, celebrating the serene, untroubled day of the revolution with a cold intoxication in which wine and alcohol played no part at all.

Chapter 13

In which Mr. Tsai reproaches the author for what he wrote in his first articles; the author justifies his point of view and is then invited to a cocktail party given by Mr. Kuo Mo-jo and to a performance of the opera The Red Orient. *In which the author leaves by plane for Shanghai.*

Anything that is direct makes the Chinese ill at ease and gives him the painful impression of being false.
—HENRI MICHAUX, *A Barbarian in Asia*

The next morning, which was cold and gray, Mr. Shu came to tell me that Mr. Tsai was waiting for me in one of the hotel's small conference rooms. The Peking climate was again causing me trouble. I was coughing and had an almost continual headache.

From the absent-minded manner in which Mr. Tsai held out his hand and at the same time avoided meeting my eyes, I judged that the matter was going to be serious. We were alone with the two interpreters. Mr. Tsai seemed unhappy, as though he were an executioner simply carrying out his job. Mr. Fang, the assistant interpreter, was seated at a table, prepared to take notes. Mr. Shu was with us, and he too had a notebook. I decided to take out my own.

"Since your arrival," Mr. Tsai began, "we have been exchanging ideas, and I have made up a report for the directors of our Association. Their wish now is that we should have a sincere and frank discussion. On many occasions you have expressed your intention of reinforcing the friendship between our peoples and publicizing the reality of today's China. We, in turn, have provided you with every facility toward this end. We shall continue to do so."

Mr. Tsai paused briefly and sipped at his pot of tea.

"We have come to realize, however, that there is a considerable gap between what you say you want to do and what you are doing. Your first articles have appeared in *l'Express*, and our news agency in Paris, Chine Nouvelle, has transmitted them to us. We have found several misunderstandings in them. We might even claim that, in writing these articles, you have shown no great friendship for us. There are other instances from which we have derived the same impresson, and this is what I have in mind when I suggest that your actions contradict your statements. We have found you to be prejudiced about both the revolution and the socialist system. On certain points we can say that your views are not only inexact but erroneous."

I remained very calm, and carefully noted down each of the phrases Mr. Shu hesitantly translated. For the first time there was no witness to our meeting except for the interpreters. Before this I had liked Mr. Tsai, and I was beginning to like him even more. When he began to speak again, his voice was somber, his head bent over his cup of tea.

"In the articles *l'Express* has published, we could pick out the doubts you have expressed on the break between the old imperial régime and the present one, on China's will toward hegemony in Asia, the nature of the honors shown Chairman Mao, the origin of the victories of the revolution and the liberties that exist in our country today. You also say that you received a cold welcome. We will have to talk about these things.

"It seems to us that your prejudices would make it difficult for you to write an objective book about our country, and in that case the book would surely not please us. You read a great deal before you came here. But to judge our revolution honestly it is necessary to sees its museum, and when you visited it you displayed great impatience and even a certain hostility. In such a frame of mind it is difficult for you to learn. We asked a general officer to give you a résumé that would acquaint you with the spirit of our revolution, but you did not like him. How can we assist you if you have arrived among us with a preconceived idea that prevents you from considering realities? In Wuhan our friends were surprised by the bad temper with which you greeted their cordial welcome.

"You seem to forget that in the past fifteen years China has become a sovereign nation in which the people are the masters. We cannot permit anyone to consider us as a backward nation, and we deal with no one except on a footing of equality. We know very well that there are inadequacies in our organization, but they are also present in your own; your crew is often late, but we continue to grant it the indulgence which is so greatly lacking in you. We respect the masses of the people, while you employ old colonialist habits when you brush the people aside. We have often told you that before her liberation China was a half-feudal, half-colonial country, and that Chiang Kai-shek left us nothing but misery. Our recovery still bears traces of this misery, but they are only traces and you should consider them as such. The same thing is true of our people's gratitude toward Chairman Mao, to whom we are indebted for the work that has been accomplished."

Mr. Tsai had been talking for more than an hour. Several times, I thought I had noticed the outline of a peroration, but then the flow of words began again, muffled, choppy, inexhaustible. Like a cow chewing on its cud, he returned constantly to the same complaints and the same truths, cloaking his thought, as always, in strange twists and turns, tortuous circumlocutions. In China the spray from a fountain does not describe an arc; the spout that launches it waves it through the air, causing it to clash with other sprays, turn on itself and finally come back to its point of origin. In China no one makes a bed or changes a tablecloth as we do in the West. They begin at the center rather than at either end, and move from one half to the other. The result is the same, but the Chinese manner of achieving it is disconcerting. The straight line we cherish as the shortest path from one point to another is to them a barbarian practice. The curve, the circle, the reversion to a point already passed, the sudden forward advance after a geometry of angles and an algebra of mysteries, this is what is bewildering in both the science and the art of China. Time and distance are of no importance when one possesses eternity, and what is an end to us marks a beginning in China. The right is the left, the reverse the face. We find that strange, and our way of moving straight ahead scandalizes them. They are equally upset by our way of thinking, of getting on a horse or of peeling an apple or peach.

Mr. Tsai kept coming back to what he had already said, giving another form to his ideas, refashioning his cloth. So far there had been an hour and forty-five minutes of this discourse, drowned in a note of sorrow. Did he wish to attenuate the harshness of some of his expressions, was he less certain of his truth? Suddenly, after having repeated to me that the leaders of the nation did not have the time to answer my questions and that, in any case, these interviews were not necessary to find what I was looking for, he concluded:

"We hope that you are serving the cause of Franco-Chinese friendship. You certainly have all my best wishes for your success. I have told you, very frankly, the essential points of our thinking."

I thanked him for his frankness, and let him know that I approved of this manner of doing things, but I could not help emphasizing that it had required no great skill to discern faults I had never denied. They revealed my military training, my instinct to go straight to the point, battering my way through obstacles as stubbornly as a ram. Having once begun, I got into my stride.

"I might," I said, "have waited until after my return to the West to publish my articles, as many other journalists have done. On the contrary, I took the deliberate risk of displeasing you while I was still in your country. You might at least recognize that, to this extent, I have displayed a sense of loyalty which you have found lacking in many other writers. My own loyalty is based on saying whatever I think, whether it annoys you or not, whether it hinders me or not, and at the risk of being forced to rectify the mistakes I may make. I set down my basic feeling of disappointment when I wrote that in China there is no means of information outside of official sources, that travel is forbidden in certain provinces and that it is impossible to see the people one would like to meet and talk with. Your leaders' answers to my questions would form the basis of my whole study. This is not your point of view, but it is mine, and as a result, I can only interpret their refusal to see me in my own way. There is one way of reducing my arguments to nothing: by supplying me with the means to write the history of your revolution."

I recognized that I was an impatient and demanding friend. I knew few men who were afflicted with a character as difficult as mine. It was perhaps for this reason that I had, in the course of my life, made decisions that sometimes led me to a break with my own country and to side with the peoples she had oppressed.

"Two years ago," I said, "I went to North Vietnam to make the same sort of study. Logically, I might have expected to encounter more difficulties there than here, because I had once been a member of the French colonial forces. And yet I was received by the highest officials, I was permitted to interview dozens of eyewitnesses, I was taken through the combat zones and to Dienbienphu. Did I deceive the Vietnamese? Did I report them as having said things they had not said? Did they have occasion to regret their confidence in me?

"You are still blaming me for my attitude during my visit to the Museum of the Revolution, but I already knew everything I saw there and I was irritated at discovering nothing more. Actually, I saw less there than I already knew because, as you just intimated, I have read both good and bad books about China. In the West this is our way of getting at the truth, discriminating for ourselves between the true and the false, rather than accepting a rigid set of teachings. Yes, I have asked myself questions and I would like to ask you some more. You can answer if you want to, but when you do not, I cannot help wondering why. As far as my prejudices are concerned, I confess that I came to China with one preconceived and rather naïve idea: the idea of finding myself in a free country. I was mistaken; your form of liberty is not ours. So where does the fault rest? If you prefer servile friends who write nothing but praise and flattery, just say the word—ask me to leave. It is up to you to decide."

Mr. Tsai had noted down all the points of my little speech and seemed moved by it. He shook my hand warmly.

"If you give us a measure of friendship," he told me, "you will receive ten in exchange; a measure of hatred, and you will also receive ten. That is one of our old proverbs."

We arranged to meet again the next day.

That afternoon we were invited to a reception given by the Association. Mr. Kuo Mo-jo presided, with the air of an old bishop granting blessings. Kuo Mo-jo's work was the embodiment of official Chinese literature. His novels and plays were published and produced, his poems were illustrated in the government art workshops and he held the chair of director of the Academy of Sciences. Having become an adherent of the revolution before its triumph, he had been unstinting in his praise of Mao Tse-tung and was now his poet laureate. "Bright sun of the race of men . . ." No matter how much de Gaulle fascinated them, neither Mauriac nor Malraux would ever have dared write that about him.

Kuo Mo-jo was one of those "leaders" who had no time for the past. How much liberty did the artist enjoy in the People's China? Did his duty to his art take precedence over his duty to the people? Were nonsocialist artists and writers allowed to exercise their talents? These were some of the questions I had submitted in writing, in the hope that he would answer them. But it would have required a great deal of audacity on my part to put them to him at this meeting, where he was busily clinking his glass of orangeade with the other guests. Pot-bellied, flabby, tired, so deaf that he had to wear a hearing aid, he scattered handshakes and benevolent smiles indiscriminately, but his eyes were blank and disinterested. What could I say to him?

I knew in advance his answer to anything I might ask; at his conference in Yenan, in May, 1942, Mao had stipulated that intellectuals should live among the proletariat. Art and literature had become the lackeys of government and the forces of production. Literary and artistic workers who came from what once had been the privileged classes must re-educate themselves if they wanted their works to be appreciated by the masses. Sartre on the production line at Citroën, Simone de Beauvoir punching tickets in the Paris subway! Peng Chen, the Mayor of Peking, had issued a proclamation to the effect that the Peking Opera would sing about the workers, peasants and soldiers or it would disappear. The light of socialism was to be the people's only guide. Had Lu Hsün survived the revolution, would he not have been considered counterrevolutionary? Having denounced the Chinese people's enslavement by the old society, the old customs and the prevailing misery, would he have accepted in their place enslavement by the new régime? Would he have accepted the intellectual's fundamental obligation to study the works of Mao Tse-tung, as Prime Minister Chou En-lai had ordered?

M

That night, in the ten-thousand-seat hall of the National Assembly, three thousand singers and musicians put on a production of a musical and choreographic epic entitled *The Red Orient*. The vigorous pace, originality, movement, colors and music of the spectacle were splendid. In fifty naïve tableaux, it retraced the history of the revolution, as it was or as it was now purported to have been: a nation in chains, the rising tide of disasters, the armed revolt, the Long March, the war against the Japanese, the defeat of Chiang Kai-shek, the triumph of Marxism-Leninism, the glory of the peoples in their struggles against American imperialism. Just as the east wind stifled the wind from the West, *The Red Orient* struck down the capitalist Occident. The flags, bugles, heroic soldiers and children brandishing machine guns became an obsession. The militarism of this revolution had not yet reached the age of reason; oppressed for thousands of years, the Chinese were still not fully confident of their strength.

> *Beloved Chairman Mao Tse-tung,*
> *Sun that lights our heart! . . .*
> *With you we have inaugurated the history of a new China,*
> *With you we are marching toward the liberation of humanity.*
> *The thousands of miles you marched are today sown with*
> *flowers;*
> *Your great and ever-triumphant thought shines like the brightest*
> *flame,*
> *You teach us to understand the world, to distinguish the tides*
> *of history,*
> *You teach us to strengthen our position, to increase our will*
> *to combat.*
>
> *Oh, beloved Chairman Mao, our great guide,*
> *Oh, beloved Chairman Mao, our brilliant model!*
> *Following you, we will always advance courageously*
> *So that one day the red flag will float everywhere.*

The thought that the chief of state could comfortably accept so gross a eulogy caused the hairs at the back of my neck to stand on end.

We were going to Shanghai next, to the more temperate climate of the southern seas. Not much was left to me of the illusions I had kindled and cherished, and sometimes I found myself laughing sardonically at what some Paris newspapers had written before my departure: "The Chinese await him with open arms." I felt myself lost at the far end of the world, and there were times when I wavered in my determination to continue. I slept badly, tormented by the little I had accomplished. I had seen nothing I had hoped to see and had no idea of how much or how little I understood.

Pierre Nora, whose illness had led him to the edge of death and into the hospital, knew more about it than I. By now he had returned to the

Boulevard Saint-Michel, the restaurants of Saint-Germain-des-Prés and his friends, who would be expecting him to provide all the answers. I was beginning to suspect that without love one could learn nothing about China, and this love had thus far eluded me. I knew that I liked Tsai, because he was a good man; I liked the ordinary people who pedaled their bicycles in the streets, the women and old men who pushed baby carriages along the sidewalks; but I did not like the escort that accompanied me everywhere nor those higher party officials I had met.

"We have decided," Mr. Tsai told me, "to let you say and write from here all the good or bad things you may think about China. The explanations you gave me yesterday are enough for us. You will have all the freedom you wish."

We left the Ting-si-Hotel, where, along with the Afro-Asiatic delegates who had come to Peking for the celebrations, we had been gorging ourselves on the people's sweat and devouring at every meal the monthly salary of an entire family. At the airport brass bands and brigades of "volunteers" had been stationed to cheer the departing delegations from Cambodia and Algeria. Filled with fresh hope, we boarded the plane for Shanghai.

Chapter 14

In which the author discovers Shanghai and gauges the humiliation to which the West has submitted the Chinese people. In which the author visits the commercial exposition, some new workers' housing developments, a day nursery and a cemetery, and sketches a portrait of Mr. Tsai. In which, after a brief visit to the Grand Monde club, the author seeks out the house where his friend, the poet Louis Braquier, had lived, and questions some witnesses to the events of 1927 and the Japanese occupation. In which the author retraces his steps to the Sian incident of 1936 and lingers for a time over the personality of Chiang Kai-shek, and then over that of Mao Tse-tung.

> He had fought for what, in his time, was charged with the deepest meaning and the greatest hope; he was dying among those with whom he would have wanted to live; he was dying, like each of these men, because he had given a meaning to his life.
>
> —ANDRÉ MALRAUX, *Man's Fate*

The carpeting in the corridors of our immense and half-deserted hotel in Shanghai had been worn thin by millions of British feet. There were two smiling servants before each door, two in each elevator, ten for each table in the almost empty restaurant. The city was drowning in rain and fog. But the people here seemed less suspicious, and they spoke English. With their European clothing and their hard, round faces, full lips, eyes glittering coldly behind glasses, they resembled men who had been cross-bred with the Occident. At least, this is what I imagined until the moment I realized that they, too, wanted to hear from our own mouths who we were and what we wanted. At every turn we were overwhelmed with proof that they had been nourished on the same clichés we had encountered elsewhere.

The air was mild, but almost stifling. At dusk it was filled with the whistles of ships on the Whangpoo. The skyscrapers gave the city the appearance of a half-dead Manhattan. I could not help thinking of these millions of tons of concrete as an enormous gravestone, marking the tomb of colonialism. American elevators raced to the top floors and terraces where the sea wind swept little clouds of gulls into the sky above the white ribbon of beach, far beyond the smoke from the factory chimneys. At one time the streets had been named Broadway, Avenue Joffre, rue du Cardinal Mercier, and the hotels were named the Astoria, the Capitol and, doubtless, the Ritz. I could not believe my eyes. At the end of a row of imposing bank and steamship company buildings, the only flag that still floated as if nothing whatever had happened was the Union Jack of the British commercial attaché, haughty and serene, on the same flagstaff from which it had always hung, in the center of a lawn just a few feet from the Shanghai public gardens, where once a bulletin board had displayed the regulations forbidding entrance to dogs and Chinese.

I would like to know the name of the man who decided one day that the dignity of the West might be threatened if a strolling European happened to meet a Chinese on the embankment where a few trees and a little grass had been carefully preserved. Had he then offered to the governor of the British concession, for his signature, a document containing some of the most infamous words in history? Was he some high official whose wife was shocked at the thought of such miscegenation, or a simple employee of the parks and roads department, or an officer from the Indian Army, scandalized at the idea of such intimate contact with a subject people? The Chinese had forgotten Admiral Courbet and Lord Elgin and the cannon of their ships. Far more humiliating was the shame of having been classed with dogs. Those words "Forbidden to dogs and Chinese" had been repeated to me over and over again since my arrival. They were branded into the consciousness of children, so that they would be marked all their lives with the memory of the humiliation to which their fathers had been subjected. I no longer needed a set of keys to understand China, yet I constantly had to remind myself that this was still a fresh wound that could bleed at the slightest irritation.

At night while the people's houses were lit with candle butts, the great piles of stone that lined the Bund suddenly blazed with light. Strings of naked electric bulbs outlined the silhouettes of the skyscrapers, and at their summit glowed certain words spelled out in lights. I was never sure what they said, but it might have been "Work for the party and the plan" or "Fifteenth anniversary of the liberation" or even "Smoke Bastos cigarettes." I was fascinated by the mystery of a country as poor as this that did not hesitate to burn up millions of kilowatts to advertise its victory over the West.

There was a rumor current among the city's foreign journalists that several thousand Shanghai students had been sent off to Sinkiang, and that some intellectuals and artists, presumbably contaminated by liberal ideas, were resisting the regime. Resisting? It was hard to see who could have done it. Anyone even suspected of a lukewarm attitude toward the party was immediately sent to one of the people's communes for a period of re-education. It seldom required any great length of time, digging in the soil and carrying buckets of excrement, before the recalcitrant no longer thought of anything except returning home and gladly furnished all the required proofs of devotion to the revolution.

How could anyone deny that the country no longer was a prey to famine, that the same degree of poverty was shared by all, that there were no longer any beggars, that a prodigious effort had made available to everyone the education that had once been the privilege of the leisure class, that China possessed all the attributes of self-rule? Not only did the foreigner no longer rule; he now submitted to the will of the Chinese. There were no concentration or slave labor camps, which might have become centers of rebellion and political infection. If there happened to be some few who opposed the regime, they were obliterated by the overwhelming numbers of the faithful. There was nothing left for them but to submit or perish.

On the morning after our arrival we visited the commercial exposition. It was a display of all kinds of machines and manufactured products skillfully copied from other nations: trucks, tractors, devices for scientific measurement and medical control, canned goods, watches, transistor radios and phonographs, shoes and clothing, locomotives and ships. This industrial effort was truly astonishing. Each provincial capital now seemed to possess its own steel mills and its own chemical fertilizer factories. The only thing lacking—in order not to call attention to the war industries—was airplanes, though the Chinese were most certainly manufacturing the latest Soviet models in the factories of some province forbidden to foreigners.

Our guides were anxious to show us the new working-class housing developments, where 300 thousand units had been constructed since the liberation, replacing the hovels that once had stood there. Three hundred thousand units for a population of ten million, who seemed to me to be better off than the people of Wuhan, was perhaps no great thing, but the fact was that a whole middle-class suburb had been constructed on what had once been a swamp. It was not the Avenue des Champs-Elysées, but it was enough to make one suddenly ashamed of the Paris slums.

I went into one of the buildings, and we asked a tenant who was repairing a bicycle in the little courtyard at the foot of the staircase if he would let us see his apartment. He worked in an electro-turbine factory, and occupied an apartment of approximately eighty square feet. There was a little reception-living room, a kitchen and a bathroom; the largest room was the bedroom. It contained heavy twin beds, a mirrored wardrobe, and some laundry had been hung up to dry between the family photographs. No heating had been provided for, though the climate of Shanghai was quite cold for a good two months each year. The man earned 114 yuans per month, and his rent cost him a trifle more than six of these. He did not seem overcome with admiration for the regime, did not belong to the party, and I saw no portrait of Mao in the apartment. He was so gentle and withdrawn that I no longer remember his face. I did not ask his name. There were hundreds of millions just like him. His features were lined with fatigue, but he did not seem unhappy with his lot and compared it favorably with that of his comrades who still lived in prerevolution hovels.

Our guides insisted they would open other apartments for us to see, but my sense of discretion prevailed and we refused. We wandered through the neighborhood and visited the nursery school where the workers' children were kept during the day. They were already being taught the basic characters of Chinese writing, and gathered around the harmonium to sing the party songs and dance.

"When I see these happy children," my friend Tsai told me, "I remember what my childhood was like. An egg and a piece of fish with my bowl of rice, what a holiday that would have been! When my mother found a sweet potato to give me for lunch, my hunger left me for a time and I could think of nothing I wanted more than another potato at night. You cannot imagine what China was like, the extent of its misery, just fifteen years ago. And who worked to give us a country? Chiang Kai-shek? The Americans? The West? Chairman Mao and the party."

It was true. To the credit of the Communist regime, there was this exemplary dignity, this terrifying equality among the workers, this mania for building factories and housing, this obsession with increasing productivity without which the nation would have been condemned to extinction. Tsai had told me that his daughter was studying medicine. And he himself? I had never found out what his work was when the Association did not give him a writer to guide around, or even what he had done during the war. On several occasions, however, I had felt very close to him. Had he served in the Red Army? Was he a political commissar or a company commander? Stubbornly, he always answered no. He was nothing, a man of no importance. He had served his country modestly. I knew only that his father was a poor peasant. At present Mr. Tsai rode in the automobiles that had been provided for us, but in Peking he returned home at night by bus. And when he died . . .

"These tombs," he said, dismissing with a scornful gesture the cemetery I had wanted to see, "all this space made useless for production, that's the sort of thing that brings back the superstitions of other years! I intend to be cremated and my children will keep my ashes."

"A handsome gift," I told him.

Was he, too, without knowing it, attached to the cult of ancestors? He burst out laughing, rested his hand on my shoulder for an instant, and asked me to tell him about my mother and my childhood. I might have said: "We were both born into poor families, you and I, and it is doubtless because of that we are closer to the basic truths of this world than many other people. But there is one difference: I am the son of a free man." I should have had the courage to try to explain to him that in loving both his master and his servitude he was risking the loss of his dignity as a man, and that a real love of independence would not tolerate unconditional submission. But we were not alone, and I did not dare.

"I see nothing that could separate us," he said.

In fact, everything separated us—language, taste, ideas. We left the cemetery and walked back to the automobile through a little drizzle. Tsai shivered and clutched at the collar of his cheap gray raincoat. He smoked a great deal, because Mao smoked a great deal, and if Mao were to decide tomorrow that he would give up smoking, hundreds of millions of Chinese would imitate him. The solid line of Tsai's jaw, the deep black of his eyes, the curling line of his upper lip and the length of his ears made him resemble some rustic Buddha, falling stonelike into the seat of the automobile, occasionally letting out a kind of musical yawn. When he was bored, he knew how to withdraw into himself, to dream or sleep. One day in a confidential mood, he told me the secret of why he had not a single white hair in his thick, black wolf's mane: he ate a walnut every night for a year, just before going to sleep. He also had a secret which prevented colds: he massaged the nostrils and the bridge of his nose thirty times each morning, standing before an open window. He did not particularly like getting up early in the morning, and since the working hours we kept deprived him of his siesta he was often tired. At such times he resembled a bulldog sleeping in front of a fire, his body occasionally twitching with thoughts that came to him in dreams. Then, quite suddenly, if I were to ask him a question, he would shake himself awake, tug at his cap, and his stubborn forehead would show signs of enormous determination. He became a peasant, plowing the land behind his buffalo and dying at the end of the furrow he has traced all his life.

Shanghai, once the paradise of soldiers of fortune, had now become the people's paradise. At one time there had been dancing, drinking and a profusion of beautiful girls in the Grand Monde, the foremost house of pleasure in what was then a vast brothel city; the courtesans on Nanking Road were taken to one's hotel room. The Grand Monde had been converted into a place of respectable amusements, at a price anyone could afford. Sailors no longer came there to drink whiskey and look for girls; they had their own center where they could read the works of Karl Marx and the military discourses of Mao Tse-tung, and then return to get drunk on their own ship, protected by their own flag. At the new, proletarian Grand Monde, plays and socialist operas were put on on four stages at the same time; there was a small rifle range and a gymnasium; visitors stared at themselves in magnifying mirrors, applauded acrobats, bought caramels. They were given their money's worth. I could well understand that the Chinese who had once lived in hovels, while foreigners and Chiang Kai-shek's officers had drunk champagne here with whores disguised as hostesses, might find a kind of revenge in boredom. There was no hatred in it, simply a determination to live in the Grand Monde which once had been ruled by others.

Brigitte had had a fever ever since we arrived in Shanghai, and was forced to stay in bed. A nurse and a young doctor with the ascetic face of a worker-priest had come to see her, applied a stethoscope to her chest and given her some pills and medicine. Tsai had bought her a hot-water bag. I felt myself increasingly overcome by an odd kind of resignation. I rebelled against nothing except stupidity. Here I was, living at the center of a monument to colonialism, the Bund in Shanghai, experiencing the same sadness I had once felt in Algiers, where people were also living in the grave of a defeated West, a West that had lost because it failed to understand that the improvement of the lot of colonized people was more important than the West's business interests.

I walked through the streets of the city, looking for the red brick house in the French concession where my friend, the poet Louis Braquier, had lived when he was an agent here of the Messageries Maritimes. Innocently, I asked about him. And automatically I became suspect again.

"An agent of the Messageries Maritimes, did you say? And he was a poet?"

How could I explain that a man might work for an imperialist shipping line without being a man of greed or blood lust? If I had thought Chinese barbarians more capable of appreciating them than French barbarians, I would gladly have quoted one of his verses to them:

> *Tonight, I am a man living among millions of men,*
> *In a Chinese port where no ship stays. . . .*
> *But I would like to go back and rap at the window,*
> *The unawaited, the drowned man came home,*
> *Who can never speak to them of China. . . .*

My friend Braquier, one of the greatest unrecognized living poets, lived at one time just across from the Cercle Français, at the corner where the rue du Cardinal Mercier met the Avenue Joffre. In Shanghai these street names had disappeared, were covered over with characters written in Chinese, with the dust and oblivion of everything dead. After the typhoon of revolution, how was anyone to find the old addresses, since none of our companions wanted to remember? They consented to point out only those boundaries of the concessions and the imperialist monuments which had now been transformed into socialist monuments.

Among the eyewitnesses who had been gathered to tell us about the events of 1927, there was one woman in whom I was particularly interested. She was seventy-five years old, and everyone called her Mama She. Although her feet did not appear to have been strapped in childhood, she seemed to have difficulty supporting the weight of an imposing torso and the enormous head of an old lioness. The sheer massiveness of this head was surprising: a high, prominent forehead, framed in a gray, short-cut mane of hair; a flat, broad nose; high-boned cheeks; a large and gentle mouth; one ear lobe pierced to hold a golden ring; eyes so puffy that it seemed she could scarcely look out through them; and a parchment-like skin traced with a network of tiny wrinkles.

I decided to begin with her, but she talked as if she did not even hear our questions. There was only one of the events of 1927 of any importance to her, and I quickly gave up any attempt at taking notes, since she bothered little with the fact that her recital had to be translated for me. Little by little, her hesitant voice gathered strength and intensity and took on an odd, metallic accent. She told how, when she had been given the mission of carrying a revolver to the other bank of the Whangpoo, she had taken passage on a small boat disguised as a beggar, carrying a baby and a wicker basket. In the middle of the river, she had realized that the boat would land at a point on the other bank occupied by the soldiers of Chiang Kai-shek, and she was suddenly seized with panic. Should she leap into the water or try to throw away the revolver without being seen? She knew that she would be executed if it was found on her. But when one has worked since the age of eleven, and has always led a miserable life and wants to see the triumph of the revolution of 400 million people, one has no right to give up. She hid her face against the body of the child and watched the soldiers searching the other passengers. When her turn came, she pinched the child to make it cry and, as was the custom when a child cried, got down on her hands and knees pretending to search for some refuse to smear on its face and appease it. In this way she managed to carry out her mission, crawling through the legs of the jeering soldiers.

Ranging through the whole spectrum of emotions, from arrogance to entreaty, she waved her arms in the air, imitated the crying of the child and the insults of the soldiers, alternately murmuring and shouting, and watching us with a mixture of indifference and innocence. A madwoman? In her dotage? She was Mother Courage in person, drunk with self-confidence, dragging a whole people behind her and calling them to arms. We asked her to repeat her account outside on the terrace, where we filmed it against a background of the smoky Bund, interrupted by the whistling of tugboats or the tolling bell of a clock made years ago in London. Understanding what she said was of little importance; the camera was recording every quivering movement of the face of the Chinese revolution.

"On the night of April 12, 1927," Mama She ended, "the soldiers came to the house and arrested my husband. My three sons had been killed within four months."

"What did the revolution bring to you?" I asked.

"I began to learn how to write my name."

We accompanied her back inside with all the consideration due a queen. She whispered in my ear: "For sixty years of my life I suffered, but since our liberation I have known fifteen years of happiness."

One tall, gaunt old man, with eyes set very deep beneath a high forehead, told us: "On April 13, when the workers demonstrated for the release of the men the police had carried off during the night, the soldiers surrounded and fired on them. With my own eyes, I saw more than twenty truckloads of corpses, and since it was raining, rivers of blood ran in the streets."

Chiang Kai-shek had triumphed. Papa Charlie could now go back to directing in peace the financial dynasty of the Soong family. The Communists took refuge in the mountains, resisted the extermination campaigns as best and as long as they could and then made their escape.

Ten years after the Shanghai massacres, at the end of the Long March, Mao Tse-tung founded the capital of his soviets at the other end of China and prepared to continue the long duel with his powerful adversary.

Infuriated by the impertinence of the young Marshal Chang Hsuehliang, who had delayed carrying out his orders, Chiang Kai-shek sent ahead fifteen hundred blue-shirted members of his secret police and, on December 7, 1936, ordered one of the planes of his personal squadron to fly him to Sian. He had had enough of quibbling with undisciplined subordinates who allowed themselves to be duped by the enemy. The Communists were undermining the old society and traditions, fomenting disorder and rebellion, stirring up the peasantry and those idiot intellectuals and students who were always ready to strike a blow at established power. Now they were saying everywhere that the civil war must be brought to an end, so that all the nation's forces could be mustered against Japanese imperialism.

Chiang Kai-shek's technique against the Japanese was to pretend surrender. In case of invasion he would withdraw, abandon the cities and countryside, take refuge in the depths of the country where he could not be attacked, permit the invading forces to disperse and exhaust themselves, then return, when the time was ripe, and drive them out. The Japanese were too deeply hated to ever be allowed to remain in China. In spite of their conquest of Manchuria and of the threat this constituted to the country's safety in the north, the Japanese still represented, in Chiang's eyes, a lesser danger than the Communists. The Japanese were a sickness of the flesh, the Communists a sickness of the heart. In an insolent message, Mao Tse-tung had proposed to Chiang Kai-shek that he would recognize his authority on condition that he end his blockade of the Communists. When their very existence was at stake, the Communists knew how to exploit patriotism to their own advantage, and could display a more chauvinistic attitude than the most extreme nationalists. Chiang Kai-shek did not fall into the trap, but the stupidity of his generals annoyed him. He was incensed at the thought that young Marshal Chang Hsueh-liang, who had inherited from his father command of the army of Manchuria which was now blockading Shensi, and General Yang Hu-chen could allow themselves to be seduced by the sugar-coated sophistry of Chou En-lie. Not so long ago they had been arresting Communists and carting them away trussed up like hogs.

In the ancient city of Sian, whose walls had sheltered the first capital of China and whose surrounding countryside was sown with imperial tombs in the form of pyramids, Chiang dressed down his subordinates in harsh terms. At dawn on December 12, with his headquarters encircled, he had fled into the hills where he was apprehended and arrested. On the thirteenth, the Communists had sent a delegation led by Chou En-lai to Sian to outline a program they wanted Chiang to sign. On the twenty-fifth, a liberated Chiang returned to Nanking, accompanied by his fur-draped wife, who had joined him in Sian, and a sheepish and repentant Marshal Chang Hsueh-liang. He was received with acclaim. He never admitted having promised anything as a ransom for his life. However, all that happened thereafter would seem to indicate that he had given the promise of a united front against Japan.

The words Chiang Kai-shek claimed to have spoken during his imprisonment by Chang were extremely noble: "I am your commander and you are a rebel. According to both military discipline and the laws of our nation, you deserve not simply reprimand but punishment. Do you think that by employing force you could oblige me to give in? You can cut off my head, but I must maintain order and preserve the honor of the Chinese people. Instead of the weapons which you now hold, I have on my side the principles of right and justice. I cannot betray the confidence placed in me by the martyrs of the revolution. If you are courageous, kill me. If not, admit to your faults and let me leave." And later: "Just who are you, young man? My subordinate or my enemy? If you are my subordinate, you must obey me. If you are my enemy, kill me. Choose between those two alternatives, but don't say another word."

As a matter of fact, many long discussions had followed, interrupted by readings from the Bible. The account of the Sian incident, written many years later by Chiang Kai-shek, gives every indication of considerable editing and arrangement, and reeks of lies. But which one of the parties involved has told the truth? Is it true that, with the exception of Chang Ko-tao, the Central Committee of the party had unanimously voted for Chiang's liberation? Possibly, as Mao Tse-tung has subsequently claimed, Chiang Kai-shek's death would not have served the Communist cause, because of the immense prestige the generalissimo still enjoyed. Mao Tse-tung might have feared that Chiang would be replaced by an even stronger man. It is probable that Stalin or Dimitrov, the president of the Komintern, intervened and forced Mao Tse-tung to release Chiang. But why then, if the Soviet decision was in accord with the wishes of the Chinese Communists, did Chou En-lai later say that neither he nor Mao had slept for eight days? Had there been a popular meeting in Yenan that condemned Chiang Kai-shek to death? The Russians had lied to me in Moscow, when they assured me that Dimitrov would never have dared give an order to the Chinese Communist party. Apparently he had done no more than transmit a Soviet agreement to the Chinese proposal to release Chiang.

Against his will or not, Chiang Kai-shek halted the operations against the Communists, freed the political prisoners and agreed to resist the Japanese. He confessed later that this was the greatest mistake of his life. Indecision, the difficulty of turning one's back on power and money, finally led to catastrophe. And the part in all this played by a woman as pretty and clever as Soong Mei-ling, the third daughter of Papa Charlie and wife of Chiang Kai-shek, should not be minimized. She was known as "Madamissima," since her husband was the generalissimo.

At this period Chiang Kai-shek was approaching his fiftieth birthday. He wore his uniform modestly, without elaborate decorations. What decorations would he have needed to add to the luster of his own person? Both his face and his graying mustache had grown thicker. A suspicion of a double chin gave an even greater impression of energy to the strong line of his jaw, and his glance could reveal kindness, irony, cruelty or contempt in turn. He lived simply, wearing the old-fashioned Chinese robe, surrounded by the comforts of the upper middle class. He devoted an hour each day to practicing his calligraphy. He detested the odor of tobacco, drank water, ate little and that rapidly, preferring simple foods. Since his teeth were bad, his meat was always finely chopped.

Han Suyin speaks of this period of his life in terms of genius. His will was as inflexible as the Great Wall, as irresistible as the floods of the rivers of China. Impenetrable, icy, proud, he resembled a Confucian monk who might have manipulated his prayer wheel while reading the Bible. This cold fish, who would doubtless not have had intercourse with his wife until after he had invoked the Lord, affected habits of great austerity. The crafty Madamissima disguised her love of power and wealth beneath a cloak of puritanism. Business was discussed, but surprise parties were banned from the private gatherings of the Kuomintang. Opium was forbidden, and hairdressers were no longer allowed to give permanent waves. To gain admittance to the entourage of the chief of state, one had to lead an exemplary life, eat Chinese food, be married within the church, practice conjugal fidelity, filial piety and respect for authority, and have an adequate stock of flattery for the generalissimo. For his part, he never tired of repeating that if the Chinese were to emerge triumphant from their trials they must imitate the great men of their history, just as he himself claimed to embody the spirit of Tsêng Kuo-fan, the conqueror of the Taiping rebels.

In his pride, he placed himself on a level with the emperors. He never accepted criticism or advice. The emperor listens only to the voices of heaven and is accountable only to heaven. He was animated by a blind faith in the destiny of China, reinforced by an even blinder faith in his own genius. "If we are beaten on the coasts, we will draw back to the plains. If we are beaten in the plains, we will draw back to the mountains; if we are beaten in the mountains, we will draw back into the deserts; and, in ten years, we will return victorious." The Communist puritans in Shensi might have used the same language. They had already proved their capabilities. To win the support of the masses with something other than speeches and flags, Chiang would have had to stamp out the traditional corruption in high circles and that plague from which the people now suffered just as much as they had under the old regime: extortion.

In 1937, after the Sian incident, the Communists of Shense, regathering their energy and strength, moved out of their hovels in Paoan and established themselves in the little city of Yenan, where the river cut between the cliffs of loess. The horses of the Mongol cavalry raced noisily across a maneuver area dominated by gray pagodas. Mao, with great patches at the knees of his trousers and wearing an old cloak that fell to his ankles when the sand-filled wind whistled across the plain, occupied a little office furnished with a narrow bed, a notary clerk's table, a wicker armchair with a sagging back and a kerosene lamp. It was at this time that he was divorced from his second wife, who had been wounded during an attack of Nationalist bombing planes on the Long March.

To some of those around him he gave the impression of a timid student, to others that of a stubborn peasant. His mother had been right: he could have become a brilliant professor. Always ready to pick up and move on, he nonetheless never ceased working on the thesis that was to give him the title of Emperor of China. In it he remodeled the world, conjured up the just war that would permit China and the underdeveloped peoples who followed in her wake to conquer their place in the sun. He took evident pleasure in expounding ideas before pupils who were not too bright. This professor, who had taken to the mountains to escape death and lived for ten years eating whatever he could find and often sleeping on the ground in the dead of winter, explained a Marxist philosophy he had scarcely digested himself. He had a genius for using the simplest language when he was speaking to soldiers and peasants, and the most academic when he was forced to convince more learned listeners. Without knowing it, and in spite of his ironic attitude toward the formalism and dogmatism of the mandarins, he allowed himself to be caught up in the subtle game of thesis and antithesis, although he sometimes departed from it abruptly with a joke, and returned to realities. Yenan became a kind of Spartan university. Students and intellectuals began to arrive to join the ranks of the Communist party. It was the only one in possession of a doctrine suited to the Chinese situation, and beyond that to the whole world.

In exchange for Chiang Kai-shek's submission Mao agreed to suspend the division of lands in the territories he controlled and to place his forces under the authority of Nanking. Two Red armies were thus constituted: the Eight, in the north, under the command of Chu Teh, and the Fourth, which had been guarding the mountain passes of Fukien and Kiangsi since the departure for the Long March and which was saved from extermination by this decision. Under the command of an ex-pupil of the military school of Whampoa, Yeh T'ing, it became the new Fourth Army.

In Europe Hitler had been Chancellor of the Reich for three years. A world war was threatening. Having abandoned the hope of taking possession of China without a fight, no longer counting on Chiang Kai-shek's inertia, the Japanese declared war, occupied Peking and bombarded Shanghai.

Chapter 15

On the occasion of a meeting with some dock workers, the author evokes the atmosphere of Shanghai in 1937, and then visits a club of the Young Pioneers of the party. Why the cameraman leaves the crew and returns to London. In which the author, to his great surprise, confesses to Christ, records a diatribe of the accredited Bishop of Shanghai against the Vatican, then visits an exhibition of painting and a naval construction yard. In which the reader accompanies the author to the home of a Western woman who has lived for more than half a century in Shanghai without ever having had any interest in China.

. . . wherever men labored in pain, in absurdity, in humiliation, they thought of doomed men like these, as believers pray, and in the city they were beginning to love these dying men as though they were already dead.
—ANDRÉ MALRAUX, *Man's Fate*

In the morning we were awakened by the shrilling of whistles and the barking of sergeants, just as we had been in Wuhan. Concealing herself behind a curtain, Brigitte took some photographs of the female militia who were training with submachine guns on the neighboring terraces. In the streets below, the entire city was exercising, going through the movements of open-hand wrestling or posing spectacularly with sabers.

That day we visited the port, which was cluttered with old sailing junks and a few Greek ships unloading British fertilizer and artificial Italian silks. Three dock workers had been picked to meet us, and I questioned them lengthily and with every mark of friendship. They, in turn, asked me to take back to the French dockers, whom they apparently imagined carrying sacks on their backs under the whip of an overseer, their moral support in the struggle against imperialism. I told them that the right to strike had become a powerful weapon in the hands of French dock workers, that our society was less horrible than was thought here, that we had had a revolution to free ourselves from feudal landlords long before theirs and that we did not like any threats to our liberty to think for ourselves. This seemed to astonish them.

The oldest one was forty. He had lived with his family in Shanghai for a long time. Before that, his father had pulled a cart for a capitalist, and he himself had gone to work in the port at the age of eleven, had been constantly beaten and insulted by the foremen. One of the other workmen had a distinctly Mongol countenance, a low forehead, the mustache of a musketeer and an upper lip shaped like a crescent moon drooping at the corners. His clothing was mended and darned and he seemed very poor, but he earned eighty yuans a month and occasional bonuses—not quite forty dollars, but much more than the average worker. It was paradise in comparison with the hell he had known, twenty years earlier, in the chicken coop where his family had taken refuge from the Japanese bombardments.

My memory of what Shanghai must have been like in 1937 was a collection of newspaper photographs of the time: clusters of human insects hanging onto the iron bars of gates, men in winter robes and shapeless felt hats, bare-chested coolies with shaven skulls, carrying on their shoulders the bamboo balancing poles from which dangled the weight of their misery, helmeted guards escorting the automobiles of foreign consuls, carts laden with furniture and clothing, the grim sausages of barbed wire hastily unrolled in front of official buildings, the streets teeming with terrified crowds, the streetcars immobilized on their tracks, skeletons of burned automobiles, the long line of rickshas rolling toward the hope of a ship that might be leaving, roofless walls, the smoke of fires mounting into the gray sky, policemen searching passers-by, families herded together like animals, and those infants in tatters, spared by some miracle, alone and weeping in the midst of ruins.

The Japanese would not dare attack the international concessions, so the Chinese descended upon them in the hundreds of thousands, hoping to escape the coming massacre. The people from the suburbs had taken over the sidewalks of the Bund, staring out at the ships anchored in the Whangpoo, living and sleeping there, bumping against each other, eating from tins or scavenging for food in garbage cans. The dead were piled up in streets sticky with blood; the arms of the dying reached out from piles of debris, appealing for help.

Then the Japanese disembarked. The port was overflowing with their warships. Bayonets at the ready, legs wrapped in gleaming white linen leggings, the marines re-established order. The regular troops, in boots and spurs, wearing high-visored caps, were dispatched throughout the city. The infantry then mopped up each district, smashing down the doors of any houses still standing. Under the eyes of old women in tears, the Japanese decapitated suspects with their Samurai swords, kicked and beat their prisoners, forced them to dig their own graves, then bound them and buried them alive. When the city had become a desert, the Japanese Army paraded behind its flags and its generals on horseback. The coffins and bodies were heaped up on the other side of still standing walls, and the stench became atrocious. Enormous funeral pyres had to be lit to burn the dead.

I asked the workman I was questioning if he remembered anyone who had been kind or helpful to him at the time.

"No one," he said, with a smile that bared his gums. "No one helped anyone."

The Japanese took possession of the factories, forced the Chinese to work under Japanese engineers, and handed over the stores to Japanese shopkeepers. Every Chinese who passed a Japanese sentry was required to bow. Those who did not do so promptly or deeply enough were beaten. Children were forced to remain kneeling in the streets for hours, in the sun or rain. Each morning, to reach their shop or factory, workers had to climb over the corpses of those who had died of cold or hunger during the night and whose bodies were now being eaten by dogs. The girls did not dare leave their homes or even exchange glances, so many of them had been beaten and raped. Then, with Shanghai conquered and occupied, the Japanese moved on, up the valley of the Yangtze, preceded by their squadrons of bombing planes.

The third docker was too young to have known any of this and remembered only the cruelty of the foremen. In order to keep a job, you had to cross their palms with money and, at a time when that money was depreciating in value a little more every day, they sometimes held back an entire week's salary.

In the present, however, there was only one important question: children. The young docker wanted three. The Mongol had five and considered that too many. He thought he had committed what could be translated roughly as "a stupid boner." He added: "I would have been smarter to have had only two. I'm not worried about it any more though; my wife has had an operation."

With the consent of the husband and the approval of the authorities, the government medical services could free women from the servitude of childbirth.

I forgot to ask for the statistics on the tonnage handled by the port. But for the first time, as Mr. Tsai looked on delightedly, a certain confidence had been established between the men I was talking with and myself.

At the palace of the Young Pioneers, things went even better. "Palace" was a grand word that might better have been replaced by "club." Palaces abounded in the People's China. This one, the former villa of a capitalist, resembled a private home in a fashionable suburb of Paris. Beginning at the age of seven, boys and girls were brought here to follow technical and political courses and learn to sing, dance and perform. The party was preparing them for their adult tasks. They celebrated the cult of Chairman Mao, cursed American imperialism, encouraged oppressed peoples to free themselves and applauded foreign friends.

Like each of the honored guests we were, I had a Young Pioneer assigned to me alone. He took hold of my hand to guide me and did not release it for the entire time of our visit. How irritated I was with myself for not being able to love that warm little hand! Instead, there were moments when I wanted desperately to thrust it away. I managed to release myself from it to take notes or greet someone, but it stubbornly regained possession, as if my hand were a form of property, while the youngster lifted his face toward mine and smiled. I like to offer my hand, but I am not fond of having it seized. For some reason, I thought of the comment of a King of France to a Negro ambassador intent on kissing his hand: "Go tell your master that I will never be one of the women in his harem."

As we returned to the hotel, my friend Tsai, who was apparently suffering from liver trouble, since he was grumbling to himself, suddenly burst out: "It is the task of this generation to build China, and it is ours to watch over them. We are going to show the Americans what we are capable of."

This abrupt declaration left me aghast, in much the same way as the mixture of pity and dread I had experienced while watching the children. In Shanghai alone there were more than a million Young Pioneers who were taught the catechism of Marxism-Leninism every day, who would be enrolled in the militia or the army later on, and who would become, everywhere in China, uncountable masses prepared to defy the rest of the world. Who, then, could be so foolish as to believe these naïve and soothing pretensions, this desire for peace which was repeated too stubbornly and too often?

Our indoctrination had been going on now for more than a month, and it never entered anyone's head that the honeyed scent of all these flowers of rhetoric might sicken us in the end. In their eyes, we, too, were Young Pioneers to whom the truth must be repeated over and over. I was obsessed with the endless flow of clichés from the guides in the museums. It was infuriating to be a Western man and be forced to swallow his shame a hundred times a day. For the sake of my conscience, I went so far as to tell my guides that, far from convincing me, their constant repetition of the same things would achieve exactly the reverse result. They looked at each other in silence. My reaction bewildered them.

Brigitte was feeling better and was again accompanying us on our trips, but I sensed that she was as depressed as I was by the funereal

aspect of the city, and I could not shake off another cold which had
made my migraines worse. The cameraman had gone completely to
pieces, and Simon decided to send him home—a new source of astonishment to our Chinese companions. They came to ask me what I
thought about the matter. I could do nothing about it, and I preferred
going on with a Chinese cameraman to continuing to suffer from the
general unhappiness of the crew caused by our man's bad humor. He no
longer felt anything but disgust, a jangling sense of dissatisfaction and
nothing any longer interested him. He refused to leave his room. I had
hoped that he would get over it and that some feeling for China or for
ourselves would keep him with us. But now we were losing him.

The Chinese insisted: one word from me and surely our cameraman
would not leave. He would enter the hospital, and a week later they
would return him to us in good health. I dared not explain to them that
the illness from which he suffered was very different from the one of
which he complained. I myself was so weary of this tomb where ship
sirens shredded the interminable nights that even I was sometimes
tempted to give up.

I had asked to see Bishop Chang Hsia-hsu, although I knew him to be
a servant of the regime. I was told one night that I might attend a Mass
to be held the following morning and that the bishop would see me
afterward. I asked what church we would be going to and was told that
they did not know.

On the questionnaire accompanying the application for my visa,
opposite the question "To what religion do you belong?" I had written
"Catholic." As we were driving across the city, which was awakening to
its morning saber dance, my friend Tsai suddenly asked if I was a
believer. If Simon had asked me the same question, I might have been
embarrassed. I would have answered: "I was brought up in a seminary.
I no longer practice the Catholic religion, but I know what I owe to it. I
do not welsh on my debts. When Christ is attacked, I shall always
defend Him." I would have avoided the direct question, for fear of
giving an answer that might carry me further than I wished to go. I still
wanted to believe in the communion of saints, the Church, the resurrec-
tion of the dead, the word of God, bread and wine transformed into
sacred nourishment, but I did not like pontifical display and liturgical
splendor. The church I carried in my mind was that of the poor and the
persecuted.

To my friend Tsai, a reflex I could not define compelled me to answer
yes without hesitation. Bravado doubtless, or the need to make it clear
that I recognized Christ. To Tsai, all religion was confused with the
superstitions the regime had overcome; it belonged to the obscurantism
of the past, and he was astonished that a mind such as mine might still

be attached to it. I shook off an abrupt desire to proclaim that I was not an atheist and preferred Christ to Karl Marx. I confessed belief in the crucified Christ because the Chinese expected a denial of Him from me. Tsai did not press the point.

"You believe firmly in the universal truth of Marxism-Leninism," I added, "and in the virtues of Mao Tse-tung. Permit me, then, to prefer the gospel you have never read."

On this weekday there were about three hundred of the faithful present for Mass, men and women of all ages. A young priest with very gentle features greeted me and knelt behind me. After Mass we were taken to a sun-flooded room in the bishopric, just next door. The windows looked out on a little rose garden where the spray from a fountain waved back and forth in a strange series of arcs and circles. The bishop came in, wearing a black soutane with a chain and cross of gold, a biretta, violet waistband and stockings, pastoral ring on his finger, and accompanied by the young priest who had greeted me and another one, older, with a cold, suspicious air. Both of these were in lay garments. The bishop's face was sad and dignified. He invited me to sit next to him on a couch dominated by the portrait of Mao, beside a statue of the Virgin.

"I was pleased and enthusiastic when I learned that some French friends were visiting the Catholic Church in China," he told me. "We are prepared to tell the truth to the world."

He asked me to put my questions first, so that he might have time to study them. I wanted to know the situation of Christianity in Shanghai and the reasons for the discord with Rome. The bishop suggested that the young priest, who seemed to me to possess considerable authority, give some relevant details. I was at present in the parish of Zi Ka-wei, which included four thousand of the one hundred thousand faithful of the diocese of Shanghai. More than seventy priests carried out their ministry in twelve churches.

The bishop added that the foreign missionaries in the old days had assured the people that the Communist regime would destroy the Catholic religion. This had been proved untrue.

"We were deceived," he said in a firm voice. "My priests and I will bear witness that the Communists have proved that they respect our faith and have left us total liberty."

The young priest informed me that the parishes lived from the rental of properties ceded to the state and from the offerings of the faithful. In 1956 a typhoon had blown the cross from a church steeple. The government had assisted in replacing it. Priests enjoyed the same rights as all other citizens, many of them had even been elected as delegates. Two Masses were celebrated every day and four on Sundays. Religious life had never been interrupted.

The bishop added that all kinds of false information had been disseminated about the Church in China, that this was the result of a plot between the Vatican and the American imperialists and was fomented by the stories of priests who had taken refuge abroad after having committed crimes against China. As for the separation with Rome, this was a very complicated question. The Vatican recognized the regime of Chiang Kai-shek, prohibited the reading of Communist newspapers and membership in the party. The priest with the long, ill-tempered face asked to be allowed to speak, and then went on to state that the foreign missionaries had fought against both agrarian reform and aid to Korea during the American war of aggression. The superior of the Jesuit Order had recommended nonparticipation in the agrarian reform and had forbidden Catholics to enlist in the army under pain of excommunication. The young priest again took over:

"Many of the expelled foreign bishops retain their apostolic titles in Hong Kong, and are waiting there to return to their diocese. Chinese Catholics cannot help but be indignant with the Vatican when it sanctions such practices and demands that the Bishop of Formosa support the regime of Chiang Kai-shek. Such a course is inadmissible on the part of the Church. Why does the Vatican show such hostility toward us?"

The bishop's hands were writhing, as though he were in pain, and he seemed very tired. Tsai, overcome with boredom, was picking his nose.

"In 1932," the bishop said, "the Vatican recognized Manchukuo even before Germany and fascist Italy. It encouraged the priests to pray for the Emperor of Manchukuo."

To my surprise, I suddenly heard him speaking in French, in a stormy voice.

"In such a case we are made to realize that the Vatican is acting against the spirit of Christ. As men of religion, it is the spirit of Christ that guides us. We cannot accept the oppression of the Vatican."

He never said Rome, and in his mouth the word "Vatican" became a Chinese word, a monstrous imprecation: "Fa Ti-can!"

"The Vatican continues to adopt this attitude with regard to the Church of China. It is not just. If we were to yield, we would become traitors to our country and we would be going against the commandments of God, who orders us to love our country. American imperialism is evident everywhere in the world. Why does the Vatican not condemn it? Where is the justice of the Vatican? Where is its godly spirit and its Catholicism? Everything that we are doing, we do for justice, according to the spirit of the Church and the commandments of God. We have no fear of the future. We have never departed from the spirit of God or of the Church."

He paused, exhausted but victorious, like a fighter who had just felled his opponent. I was left with my mouth astonished, staring at his handsome head still shaken by anger. Then he cleared his throat noisily and spat into a brass container on the floor beside him. I had forgotten completely about taking notes, but I had recorded his statement on Orthion's tape recorder.

I had the audacity then to ask if I might be granted the favor I had requested of meeting the legitimate Bishop of Shanghai, who was being held for espionage. It was the young priest who answered.

"The former bishop is a counterrevolutionary. He betrayed his country. He is no longer the legitimate Bishop of Shanghai. Our legitimate bishop is Monseigneur Chang."

In the automobile Tsai asked me why I had not taken communion with the fifty or so of the faithful who had gone to the altar. More precisely, he said in a joking tone of voice: "Why didn't you take part in the sacred meal?" For once Tsai was beginning to get on my nerves.

"It would take too long to explain," I said. "For communion, it is necessary to be in what we call a state of grace, if you understand what I mean. Something like you when you prepare yourself to hear the word of Mao Tse-tung. I did not feel myself worthy to receive my God."

He let out a great guffaw of laughter.

"I don't know anything about it myself," he said.

It was after noon and we had an appointment with an artist whom I had been told spoke French. I had thought, ingenuously, that we were going to his studio, and once again I was disappointed. In China people do not receive their friends at home. Since plotting is suspected everywhere, intimacy no longer exists. People meet in public rooms, sitting around pots of tea. No one ever talks unless there are witnesses present, so that no one else can cast suspicion on his view, and notes are taken on everything so that there will be visible proof of what was said.

The artist was waiting for us, surrounded by a little group of colleagues, at the exposition of socialist painting in Shanghai. He was a lively little man of about sixty, with a round head, a shaven skull and a handsome, bony face, lit by a pair of glittering, inquisitive eyes. To my great astonishment, he began by apologizing for the fact that he did not speak French and no longer even understood it. He had left France forty years ago.

My disappointment was increased by the fact that I had planned to question him before the sound camera. Three of his paintings hung in the exposition seemed far removed from the general socialist line. While all the other artists portrayed workers in their factories, peasants in their fields or at the controls of their tractors, and landscapes of historic rivers and hills, this one was showing only flowers and birds. At the moment, it did not occur to me that it would probably have been impossible to discuss art with him without in some way compromising him. How could I ask him if traditional Chinese painting was develop-ing along more modern lines, and if socialism was a good or bad thing for art? We had been spoiled by the bishop, and now we could see no interest in filming an interview with a Chinese artist who could not express himself in French. Stupidly enough, we left the exposition hall.

That afternoon we were taken to the naval shipyard. Simon was looking for giant cranes and ships under construction. He got nothing but speeches to the French people, hymns of thanksgiving to the revolu-tion and river dredges. We returned to the hotel, feeling a trifle bitter. Brigitte was better, and since I had been told of a restaurant called La Maison Rouge where one could supposedly dine on real French cuisine, I invited our Chinese companions. The food was revolting and the evening a disaster.

We were supposed to leave that same night for Hangchow, but I asked for a twenty-four-hour delay. I wanted to see a Frenchwoman who had been living in Shanghai for the past fifty years. This puzzled the Chinese. "You didn't come here to see Frenchmen," I was told. "What can they tell you? What trust could you put in their testimony?" I insisted that they respect my wishes in the matter. Then I was told that no one knew where to find this woman. I replied that in that case China was the only nation in the world where a foreigner could live without registering with the police, and that I could only believe that they were simply refusing to allow me to meet a compatriot. At last I won my point. I was told that they had succeeded in uncovering her address and I would be taken to see her the next day.

The following morning, in a working-class district in the southwest-ern part of the city, I felt as if I had stirred up a ghost when I found myself standing in front of a two-story brick house, built in the form of a Norman chalet, with its typical steep-pitched roof, half-timbered walls and a terrace above the entrance door. In an old photograph it re-sembled a suburban villa, in the center of an empty lawn, separated from similar residences by wrought-iron fences. The photo showed a dog kennel at the foot of the steps, clumps of rosebushes and pots of geraniums, bed linen hung out to air on a balcony, curtains at the small-paned windows, air vents beneath the eaves and shrubs that were now giant trees. Little by little, the surrounding country had invaded the suburb and formed a new district of the city. Now buses rumbled in the teeming street, families squatted beneath the porches, separated from each other only by slats from packing cases or simple cotton hangings to hide the beds. The house had lost its form and color. It was as dingy as all the others. A little gravel on the walk, not yet carried away by the rains, bore witness to the splendor of former days. We climbed over children on the stairs. Some of the tenants were living in what had once been bathrooms. Madame Camu lived in one room, on the second story.

Although it was eight-thirty, she was still in bed when we arrived. She opened the door a trifle, allowing us a glimpse of her nightgown. I remember her as a strange and fragile apparition of an old lady with round eyeglasses and thinning, red-tinted hair, whom I surprised in the disorder of early morning. She uttered a few little clucking sounds of pleasure, invited the interpreter and myself to come in, pulled aside a curtain, turned on the electricity, and the light fell across a copper bed, a few chairs, a dressing table with an oval mirror, a cheap wardrobe. There were dozens of framed photographs hanging against the faded wallpaper, piles of newspapers and magazines on the tables, little pots and vases on the mantelpiece. Utter confusion.

"A French journalist, and you almost left without coming to see me?"

I did not tell her of the attempts to dissuade me. I could, of course, have gone to the office of the British commercial attaché and consulted the list of Westerners in Shanghai, but there is no telling what my Chinese guides would have thought of such an act.

"You didn't have my telephone number?"

It was only then that I saw the wall telephone near a door, beneath a list of numbers fastened to the plaster with a thumbtack.

She had gone to see a film at the British consulate the night before, which explained why she was still in bed when we arrived.

"Nowadays, why hurry about anything? The days are all the same, except today because you have come. Some coffee? . . . Boy!"

Since my days in Indochina, I had not heard anyone call a servant in that manner. In China, in the People's Republic, no one seemed to mind. The interpreter smiled. The "boy" arrived. She spoke to him in Chinese and he disappeared. She seated us in front of a table on which there was a bowl of powdered sugar and some cups, as well as a great pile of papers and files. She vanished for a moment into what must have been a bathroom and returned wearing a gray bathrobe. A canary was singing in its cage near the windows and pecking at leaves of lettuce.

"He's eight years old, and he wakes me up every morning. He is a friend."

A black and white cat jumped up on the back of her chair.

"This is Pitou. In Chinese, Pei-to. He's big, for just a year. I watch over him more than I would a child. If he were to stray . . . "

"You have a garden."

"Oh! The garden! If he were so much as to set foot in it . . . Those people eat anything."

She had come to Shanghai in 1917 to join her fiancé, a civil engineer who was serving on a warship and had taken part in the 1900 expedition.

"He told me about everything, do you understand? Marco Polo—all of it. He tempted me to make this trip to China."

The portrait of M. Camu, dignified and mustached, held the place of honor next to the dressing table, beside a bronze statuette of Napoleon. After his death in 1943, Madame Camu had wanted to leave, but then Father Moulis, the bursar of the Lazarist monks in Shanghai, had said to her: "What are you going to do in France? You will never accustom yourself to it again. Stay here." She brought out a photograph of Father Moulis, a genial-looking man with a long and rather skimpy beard, wearing the padded greatcoat of his order.

"He rolled his r's, the way they do in Albi. There was the war in Europe, the occupation. I liked China. I stayed. I was wrong. My husband had put up an office building with his savings. We were doing well. Wait a minute."

She began extracting masses of unsorted photographs from various drawers and brought them over to show to me, in the midst of the coffee cups. I asked if I might smoke. I could do anything I liked, so long as I admired the cousins and the family reunions, recognized Monsieur Camu's noble bearing, nodded briefly to the military men and diplomats, admired the ladies' gowns. She cited one name after another, adding: "Of course you knew . . ."—as if I had myself belonged to the French colony in Shanghai. A ghost from the past indeed. For her appearance on television, she would not consider remaining in that gray bathrobe. She was thinking of her relatives and the friends she still had in Lille.

"What would they think if they saw me in this négligé?"

She opened the wardrobe, where thirty or more dresses hung, and selected one.

"I've lost weight. They are all too loose, but why bother to take them in? What a sad life, monsieur."

Now she was planning to return to France.

"You will be cold," I said.

"That's what Father Moulis told me, when I said that I wasn't afraid of anything that might happen. He kept repeating: 'You say that because you have been living for thirty years in a warm country. You no longer remember.' We lost everything, of course. We sold the building for nothing. Who do you imagine would buy it? Father Moulis wanted me to deed it to the mission. Then the mission was closed. Father Moulis had to leave. So I rent this house, at fifteen dollars a room. That's my price."

"Fifteen dollars?"

"Why? Aren't there dollars any more? Everyone still says dollars."

She disappeared again, to change into the dress. The interpreter and I looked at each other, amused. This was not Mr. Shu, but a Shanghai interpreter who affected a slangy Parisian accent. His eyebrows had gone up noticeably when Madame Camu spoke of fifteen dollars a room. He would certainly make a report about it and I could do nothing to warn her. The hands of the clock had stopped at three minutes after four. A powder box yawned emptily on the dressing table and dust clouded a silver mirror. At the age of seventy-eight Madame Camu was very much alive. She had the lined face of an old Dutch schoolteacher, and eyes—what were her eyes like? I no longer recall those eyes in which M. Camu must sometimes have seen the reflection of his mustaches.

She came back, looking too dignified now, a trifle stiff. In the next room, which had been formed by walling up the old terrace, she showed me the trunks and boxes ready for her departure.

"The French ambassador sends me a hundred dollars a month. If he will pay for my ticket, I'll go back. The Chinese are not very interesting, you know."

All the shelves in the room were strewn with trinkets and knick-knacks. She wanted to give me a porcelain Buddha as a souvenir, but I refused. Except for an occasional visit to the British consulate to see a film, she no longer went out at all.

"Why?"

"The children insult me and throw stones at me. They call me 'old pig, dirty creature.' They think I don't understand. I understand very well. So I stay here with Pitou, and that way there is no trouble. A foreigner, that's all I am now."

The "boy" did her shopping for her. She passed the days knitting, trying to file her correspondence and photographs, writing to Lille. I asked her if she remembered the events of 1927, the general strike that had been called by Chou En-lai, the execution of the Communists by Chiang Kai-shek. No. She had heard about it vaguely. It did not interest her. What the Chinese might do among themselves was of no importance. The concession had closed its gates. People had jammed in there, and then, when things had calmed down, they left again. And the Japanese bombardments of 1938? They hadn't bombarded anything around here, and the only people who had been killed were Chinese. And what about the Japanese during the occupation?

"Ah, those! They were not civilized people. They were rough, but foreigners did not suffer. We knew what was going on, but we did nothing about it. It was no business of the Europeans."

She went back to the photographs, extracting new piles of them from other drawers, showing me consuls' wives, groups of Lazarist fathers, officers of Zouave detachments, little long-haired dogs, a donkey who lived in the garden. The canary sang, the cat leaped up on the unmade bed. She took down some of the portraits from the wall and showed us her aunts, her brothers-in-law. And the church, Mass? Since the Lazarist fathers had left, she no longer went there.

Simon and his crew arrived. The cameraman, who was on the point of taking his flight to London, had come along, since this particular subject intrigued him. He sniffed the atmosphere delightedly, and set to work measuring the intensity of the light with his photoelectric cell. I placed Madame Camu in front of the canary cage, near a window through which sun's rays slipped cautiously into the room. The cat buried itself under the bedclothes. The wires of our equipment were entangled in more than half a century of history, through which Madame Camu had skipped as if by accident. She scarcely knew the revolution had taken place, that the Republic had succeeded the empire, but she had not given up hope of seeing Chiang Kai-shek return someday, accompanied by the Americans. While she waited, she read the magazines given to her by the British consul, which she then passed on to friends, such as the man who happened to come by that day to return a bundle of them. Born of a Chinese mother and French father, he had been a policeman in the French concession, spoke our language admirably, had been imprisoned by the Communists for four years and now lived by giving French lessons. Did people still study French in Shanghai?

"There is no lack of interpreters," he said. "You don't necessarily have the best ones."

He had made no attempt to escape. China was his country. This man's courage made me tremble. He well knew what he was risking.

"Not really very much," he said. "No one has any illusions about what I think, but they have become more liberal in the last few years."

"Do you agree," I asked him, "that Mao Tse-tung has created a unified China, that he has given it a prominent place in the world, and that the Chinese people live better than they did before?"

"I agree," he said. And then he added, "I am proud to be Chinese."

Madame Camu played her role for our cameras simply, although of course she did not dare repeat everything she had said to me. An open umbrella hung from the plumbing fixtures in the bathroom, whose hot-water heater had been out of order for a long time. The odors of Chinese cooking seeped in from the neighboring rooms. The noise of the street, the cries of children, the tinkling of bicycle bells came in through the open window, next to the room where the trunks and cases were piled, waiting expectantly for the hold of a ship that would take them back to Marseille. Where was the Shanghai of Mama She—the factories, the housing developments, the little Christian communities where priests who paid allegiance to the regime gave communion, the fireworks on national holidays, the lights along the Bund, the parades? Madame Camu knew nothing of all this. She wanted us to stay to lunch.

"I will make you some spaghetti. You will have something good to eat."

We left very hurriedly. She kissed us all on the cheek, one after the other. The staircase was very dark when she followed us out, but I was quite sure that she was crying.

Chapter 16

In which the author, in the train from Shanghai to Hangchow, has a conversasation which enlightens him about Chinese apprehensions regarding the Americans and about the measures they are taking to defend themselves. A walk through the parks and a boat trip on the lakes. A portrait of the interpreter, Mr. Shu, and a meeting with Mr. Tsai. In which, after a visit to a textile factory and a banquet, the author leaves Hangchow, passes through Shanghai again, and expresses his indignation regarding the favors heaped on deserters from the Nationalist army.

They invented the strangest tales, they piled lie upon lie to prove to us that it was time to leave.

—E. R. Huc, *The Chinese Empire*

They had all been surprised that I should want to see that artist, since they considered that he had no talent. What had interested me was the fact that the influence of the great Western painters was clearly recognizable in his work. Since I had proof that he did speak French, I thought that he had been ordered to say nothing. Perhaps, however, there had been no need to threaten him and he had decided on his own to adopt this attitude, in the belief that any interest we had in him was not worth the trouble it might cause him. In his place, I might have acted the same way, and this hypothesis seemed even more terrifying to me.

Some of the people we had met in Shanghai came to see us off at the train, but I saw no reason why I should demonstrate any feeling for them that I did not have. I remained silent, and since this was taken as another sign of my indifference, our departure was grim.

Tsai joined me in my compartment, acting as though this were the most natural thing in the world. It was a five-hour trip from Shanghai to Hangchow on the night train. We had a conversation of so general and banal a nature that I did not even take the trouble to note it down. It has, however, remained very clear in my mind. Only later did I fully understand its importance.

Tsai seemed to want to keep me company until we reached Hang-chow, which we were scheduled to do at eleven o'clock. With Mr. Shu beside him, he sat down facing me, pushed his cap back on his head and inquired about my health. In Hangchow we were going to rest. It was a beautiful place. We could go fishing on the lakes. I smiled. I knew that Mao often stayed for long periods in Hangchow, and that he had received the French ambassador there just recently. Since I cared nothing whatever for fishing or the natural beauties of Hangchow, I told myself that they were hiding their real reason for taking us there in order to add to our surprise.

Almost at once, Tsai climbed upon his favorite mare. Several times, when we had had any sort of discussion about the world situation, I had mentioned the fear that existed in the West of a nuclear conflict that would destroy our civilization. I had been repeatedly amazed by the insouciance with which the Chinese envisaged a war with America. Without attaching too much importance to it, I put it down to their ignorance of Western realities and avoided further discussion.

"Why do you make such a point of the military power of the United States?" Tsai demanded.

This time, because I was bored, I answered. "Because it exists."

"It also existed in 1945, and yet we beat Chiang Kai-shek, whose armies were supported by American tanks and planes. We beat the Americans again during the Korean War. So what are you afraid of? The atomic power of the United States does not frighten us."

"You have never been faced with anything more than samples of that power," I said. "I don't deny that in classic and traditional terms you may be stronger, because you are fighting on your own soil, for your own country, and you have known how to imbue your soldiers with a spirit your adversaries do not possess. I simply think that you are in no position to confront an up-to-date nuclear arsenal, because you lack the military and industrial equipment such an arsenal demands."

"What makes you think that we lack it?"

"That's the general opinion. And without the means of retaliating against America if she should attack you, it astonishes me that you go on defying her as you do. To me, your audacity appears to be a failure to recognize the truth. I can understand why you do not like the Americans, even though I do not consider them responsible for all your misfortunes. What amazes me is that you do not understand, or pretend not to understand, that a war between you and the United States would put the entire world in jeopardy and could result in your destruction. Your refusal to accept someone else's hegemony over your continent is understandable to me; I agree with it. But to oppose that hegemony with another hegemony—and that is what you are trying to do, perfectly knowingly, even though you deny it—that I do not approve, because I am among those who will suffer from it in the end."

Tsai seemed to have forgotten the coldness with which he had reproached me when we left Shanghai. He was animated and in good humor. Was it the thought of the Hangchow lakes where he could go fishing, or my gratitude and delight when I would be told that he was taking me to see Mao the day after tomorrow? With every phrase of mine that Mr. Shu translated, his smile became a trifle broader. He tugged at the shapeless visor of his cap, pulling it further down over his eyes, and waved both arms in great, awkward gestures, pretending to chase imaginary flies away from his ears.

"You are making a mistake," he said, tapping his index finger against my chest, "in suspecting us of wanting to found a hegemony directed against the West. The nations of the West have caused us enormous troubles, but we will undertake nothing now to provoke them. We are lifting ourselves up, we are helping oppressed peoples to lift themselves, we are trying to destroy American influence by building up our own power. That is true, and if that is what you mean by hegemony, then we are attempting to establish a hegemony, but you have no right to doubt our desire for peace. We need peace, to build our country and better the life of our people. But we cannot fail to recognize that the Americans think only of beating us down, that they occupy Formosa and part of Southeast Asia, that they may carry the war to North Vietnam, that they send their planes across our territory to spy on us, that their warships violate our territorial waters every day, and that, if they could, they would not hesitate to bring Chiang Kai-shek back to Peking. We are Communists and we have the right to be what we are, whether that pleases the Americans or not. If they should ever send their armies against us and land on our shores, we want to be in a position to exterminate them, and that is why we are training our youth to fight. You say that we do not possess the weapons with which the Americans frighten you and all the rest of the world. What proof have you of that?"

"It would be known if you did," I said. "Experiments and tests are needed to develop nuclear weapons, and you could not keep them secret. We know that you possess Soviet planes capable of dropping bombs on a target three thousand miles from their bases, but they would have no hope of return. And you do not yet have missiles capable of reaching America."

Tsai burst out laughing and looked at me with a gleam of pity in his eyes. To me, it was the reflection of a blind, unreasoning national pride.

"Listen to me," he said. "No matter what weapons the Americans use to attack us, we will answer with the same weapons."

"Do you know that they can destroy all China with fifty or so atomic bombs?" I asked, more for argument's sake than interest. "Turn your country into a desert? Reduce hundreds of millions of your people to dust? And in just a few minutes?"

"We know it," Tsai answered, smiling. "But they will not do it. In the first place, because the Russians would not permit them to."

"The Russians are no longer your friends."

"The Russians have other reasons for opposing the Americans than their onetime friendship for us. And besides, there are many things in Soviet Russia that may change. Khrushchev won't be around much longer. Stalin's picture is still kept in lots of houses. We know it."

To myself, I said; "He is mad."

"There is also the fact," Tsai went on, "that we are less vulnerable than the Americans. You now have some idea of the extent of our country and of its division into regions capable of supporting themselves. Could American bombs destroy forces that had taken refuge in underground galleries?"

"Where are any such galleries?" I demanded. "No one has ever shown them to me."

"So the Americans will not destroy everything," Tsai said, without answering my question, "and we can do a great deal of damage to the Americans."

"With what?" I asked wearily.

"With what we have," he answered, tapping me on the shoulder and raising his eyebrows significantly. "Because we have things you don't seem to know about. The same things as the Americans."

Old Father Tsai was delighted by my naïveté. I was one of those barbarians whose idea of China was simply a reflection of what he had been told, a simple soul who was impressed by American rockets and the aircraft carriers of the Seventh Fleet. After I had seen the parade of October 1, how could I still fail to recognize the power of the masses and their devotion to Chairman Mao? For my part, I was thinking: "How can anyone be so shortsighted about the danger of a modern war? How can anyone conceivably be so simple?" Despairing of convincing him, I shrugged and pretended that I was very tired, to put an end to the conversation.

"We shall see," I said. "Or rather, I hope that both you and I will still be here to decide which one of us was right."

The members of the Association who met us in Hangchow were clearly as anxious to be rid of us as we were to get away from them. Mr.

o

Shu yawned so often during his translation of the welcoming speeches and ritual questions that his words had the sound of a malfunctioning tape recorder. My only consolation was the sight of Orion, very low on the eastern horizon. An endless succession of locomotives bellowed through the night, as if they were chasing great herds of cows. I dreamed that I was an enraged colonialist, driving my fist into the pock-marked face of Mr. Shu, who took his revenge with a flurry of childlike blows to which I silently submitted, overcome with shame.

When I awoke, the birds were singing in the park. It was raining and the famous landscape of West Lake was obscured in the haze. Why had we come here? Suddenly, I was sure I had been mistaken in supposing that at some point, a meeting with Mao would be arranged for me. In the eyes of my Chinese guides, I was certainly not worthy of such distinction. Hangchow was a mournful city, half dead, eking out a dismal existence from the scenery that attracted visitors from every-where. See Hangchow and die. Yes, but of boredom. Groups of tourists wandered through the restaurant and chilly corridors of the hotel. What did I care about the temples and pagodas that our guides proposed to show us?

We had been hustled away from Shanghai in a manner that suggested that we were on the verge of discovering compromising secrets. That city, at least, had character. Before boarding the train the night before, we had walked through its streets for the last time. From a distance, the blaze of light from the illuminations gave the whole town a holiday atmosphere. It was a sober form of merrymaking, for respectable and mirthless families, and we had difficulty imagining the resigned state of people who could become intoxicated on orange pop and slogans and go home early, in order to be properly rested for the next day's campaign for increased production. But no matter how dreary it seemed to us, who else had ever provided such a holiday for the Chinese? Had anyone in the West ever thought of giving them something more than simple charity or labor? The golden shafts of light in Shanghai had a funereal grandeur that was oddly moving, and I sought in vain for anything similar in Hangchow.

Toward the end of the morning we were loaded into three canopied barks, resembling gondolas; but the gondoliers were women, poorly clothed, their countenances etched with the lines of hard work. Our mandarins planted themselves across from us at a bench holding the inevitable pots of tea. It was cold.

"Doesn't it bother you to be paddled about by women on a Sunday?" I asked Mr. Shu.

"They don't get tired," he said.

"Would you like to be in their place?"

Mr. Tsai clapped me on the shoulder and burst out laughing. Sundays were dedicated to the rest and relaxation of the working classes. Women who worked that day were doing their part for the leisure hours of the nation and took their own rest during the week.

The sky gradually became more threatening and the wind came up.

"Monsieur Orthion!" Tsai shouted.

For no reason, simply because he knew that it made us laugh, he would call out the name of our sound engineer. It was the only word of French he spoke, and he pronounced it with an inimitable accent. Simon was aiming his camera. Mr. Shu had stretched out his legs and was already yawning. The round face and quiet dignity of the secretary general of the Hangchow Association who had accompanied us made him look like a well-fed and vaguely unhappy Buddhist priest. We skirted the Isle of the Eleven Moons, and then another one where we tossed out food to masses of greedy goldfish. Mr. Tsai ostentatiously mimed the gestures of fishing in the lake, but I pretended not to see him. I was thinking that I had been wrong in agreeing to come here, that we were wasting our time, but if, by chance, there was an opportunity for a meeting with Mao and I had refused to come, that chance would certainly never present itself again. This soon after the celebration of October 1? Mao was surely still in Peking, receiving the Negro chieftains who had come to applaud powerful and maternal China.

The enormous park surrounding the lake was heavy with the scent of flowering shrubs. People were sleeping everywhere, stretched out on the rocks. At the foot of pagodas there were little markets for caged, exotic birds: sand martins with blue wings, woodpeckers, blue and azure parakeets, honey-colored hummingbirds, purple-hooded tanagers, survivors of Marco Polo's China.

Our guides next proposed a visit to the Shop of Comradeship, where we were told that we could buy art objects and textiles. It was getting late and I refused; I would have plenty of time to buy whatever mementos I might want to take back to my winters in Burgundy. The automobiles returned us to the hotel, and we were told that the guides would pick us up again at two-thirty, to continue the tour. I said three o'clock. By that time, however, it had begun to rain again, and I said that we were too tired to go on that day. Disappointment was visible on our hosts' faces. So many marvels, and we were making no effort to see them? The local delegate who accompanied the secretary general looked at us with positive hatred. We discussed the program for the next day: in the morning a people's commune where tea was cultivated. I said no. In the afternoon a textile factory where official portraits were woven in fabric. I said yes. Again I passed over in silence the one thing which I was really interested in seeing and learning about and which was still stubbornly refused me: the life of one of those gondoliers, a peasant or a worker. Suddenly, I had had enough of this polite insistence, of these guided tours and the voice of Shu. But that, perhaps, was because of my frustration.

Toward the end of the afternoon, Brigitte, Orthion and I went to do some window shopping and take a short walk along the shore of the lake. Orthion's outsized proportions and Brigitte's blond hair provoked curiosity everywhere we went. The day was gray, somber and dull. Families were embarking for the islands we had visited in the morning. We went back to the hotel, and the evening dragged on. I was tormented by the thought of my book.

The night passed and I dreamed again, this time of Albert Camus and his work in the theater. He was in the prime of his strength and young in heart and mind, and when he happened to glance across at me and smile, I felt a glow of pleasure at being his friend. Even now my thoughts were often of him. Was it he who had cast a spell of peace across this night, or was it just that the wind had turned? I did not hear the screaming of the locomotives. In my place, in this country, would Camus have been more just, more open-minded than I, or, would he have handed down a conviction from which there was no appeal? Soon I would be seeing friends again, going to a restaurant with them, laughing at myself and others without fear of being denounced

At dawn a fine rain was dripping from the balcony. I thought of my house in Burgundy and the flocks of birds that would be returning to the linden trees in the spring. I was impatient to hear them again and told myself that when I did my happiness would be complete, even if I were condemned to live alone, like those wild boars for whom solitude is a fact of nature.

Tsai sent for me. Contrary to our habit of always leaving our doors open, he locked his and carried the key with him. While our rooms were always in disorder, his appeared unoccupied. A minor mandarin without attendants, he always carried with him a little overnight kit to be filled with fruits and delicacies which he would take back to his family. His notebook was lying on the table. Was that the repository of his state secrets?

He seated himself in an armchair, sighed, cleared his throat and spat. Things were not going well. Whatever it was he had to tell me was painful to him. He scratched the back of his head and began. We knew each other well now. We could express ourselves without fear of offense. I nodded agreement. Good. Well, then—we had offended our friends in Hangchow by showing so little enthusiasm for the sights of their city, even though it was famous throughout China. They were bending over backward to be agreeable to us and provide us with the leisure we required, at the expense of their own leisure hours. The evening before, Simon had not even come down from his room, and we had gone walking alone, while they were waiting to take us on a tour of the temples and landscapes. The Chinese of today had great respect for each other. The people in Hangchow did not know us, and they were beginning to wonder if we had only contempt for the marvels of China.

"Is that all?" I asked, like a father confessor to his penitent.

Yes, that was all.

"Well," I said, "that's nothing to get so stewed up about."

"Stewed up about?" Mr. Shu repeated, squinting in bewilderment.

"Translate: that's not important. Dear Mr. Tsai, you are here to straighten out these little misunderstandings with our friends from the Association, who do not know us as well as you do. Leisure for us—in China? Take us to Sinkiang and you will see our faces light up with joy."

Tsai's expression relaxed a little. We inquired politely about each other's health. Something in my back had gone haywire again the night before. I had great difficulty standing and was in pain even when I was seated. He was suffering from a hernia, and slept at night with a hot water bottle. Tobacco was yellowing the index finger of his right hand.

"There is no need for you to visit Sinkiang to learn about China or the revolution," he said. "You must read a great many books, and especially those written by the Chinese themselves on the roots of the problem. Chiang Kai-shek commanded hundreds of thousands of well-equipped men, and he was conquered. The Americans put their own officers on his general staffs and it changed nothing. Our soldiers were fighting for the land that was being distributed to them, for houses that would belong to them and against masters who oppressed them. That is the way battles are won, rather than with tanks and dollars. You must also question the men who lived through this period and saw these things. There are no longer very many, but we will find some. Of what use to you was your Madame Camu? And finally, the leaders whom you will see will help you. They led the revolution. They have a broad view of the events."

So I was going to meet some of the leaders? Mao? Not here, since we were leaving for Nanking by train the next day, passing through Shanghai again on the way. I now regretted that I had left that artist so hurriedly, and wanted to see him again and buy one of his canvases. Tsai did not know whether it would be possible to make the necessary arrangements, but he would ask. He told me once more that this artist had no talent and that I could find many others more important. I begged him to allow me my opinions, even if they were only illusions. I said nothing about the fact that they had deceived me when they assured me that the artist did not speak French.

As instinctive as he was, Tsai was not lacking in convincing argument. Its was easy to be caught up by his good nature, to be affected by his changes of humor, his sadnesses, his joys. Modest to the point of constantly effacing himself and cruel to the point of effacing any individual for the sake of the revolutionary masses, he nonetheless existed. He believed. He had his kind of truth. At that moment in his hotel room, I was thinking that we were going to part company in three weeks, and to my astonishment I was grieved by the thought. I wondered how I might prove to him that I was genuinely fond of him. In Europe when men wish to make their feelings apparent, they embrace each other. But was that done in China?

Tsai considered the idea an enormous joke, and his whole frame shook with laughter. No, two men embracing each other would not look well at all. As a rule, only children were embraced or kissed in public. Among men, one simply clasped hands. But there were a thousand ways of doing this, and the important thing was to put all your heart into it. So this would have to be the way in which I took leave of Tsai. I wondered what Tsai would have thought if he had ever seen Camus and myself greeting each other after a period of separation. Some friendships have a quality of almost fiery warmth.

"After you have written your book," Tsai said, "you will take two months' vacation and come back to China, and we will go fishing together."

I smiled. They all said that: "When you come back to China . . ." It was understood that you would have to come back, that even friends must not be shown all of China until after they had been tested, put to the proof. Then, when you knew each other better, everything was easier and you would be taken to places you had not seen before. I replied that it was a very long trip and very expensive.

"You will come back," he repeated.

"And if my book does not please you? If you should find it unjust?"

"That will depend on the way you express yourself. I don't think it will be unjust."

I was already aware that he would be in difficulties if I wrote a frank account of this journey, and that he would be accused of having granted too much freedom to a former imperialist. He no longer listened to Chen, who was constantly telling him to beware of me. He would be held responsible for this book, which would show China as I saw it. He would be relieved of his post, reduced to counting sacks of rice in a people's commune, and Chen would take his place. But who knows where he will be by the time the book appears? If he has risen in the hierarchy of the state, he will be able to prove that my book has done nothing but tear away the mask from the colonialist he had always known me to be. But what would this book have been if Chen had been assigned as the chief of our escort group?

In any case, I never wanted to see Hangchow or its gray velvet lakes again. I no longer had a feeling of suffocation. I no longer felt the lack of the Paris newspapers. I no longer read anything at all. I was becoming more and more Chinese. The world was drawing away from me, glittering fitfully like a star, somewhere below the horizon. Its absence was no longer a weight on my mind. One became accustomed to it. Happily, time seemed to be passing a little more rapidly now. Who knows? I might come to miss China itself, but I would not miss the party mandarins, the Sunday promenades, the welcoming speeches, the visits to the museums or the banquets. Mr. Fang, his mouth already watering, had told us that there was to be one that night.

During the afternoon we went to see the textile factory where portraits of Mao and the other lords of the revolution were woven in silk. And where did they cast the busts? What anointed hands had been given the right to mold and touch the fake marble statues for the railway stations?

The banquet was a curious one. The vice president of the Association, flabby and senile, did no more than stare around him and occasionally emit a little belch. Tsai, completely relaxed and gay, kept moving from one table to another, his glass of vitriol never leaving his hand. A gay dog, our Tsai! The life of the party, straddling a chair as though it were a horse, resting his arms on its back and laughing uproariously. I would gladly have laughed with him had I been able. But we did not have the same idea of friendship.

The expression on the face of the secretary general of the Association in Shanghai was lugubrious. Observing the lack of haste with which our baggage was unloaded and we were led away, I realized I was not going to see my artist. We were simply changing trains, and would be leaving for Nanking in forty minutes. With his feet planted firmly in luxuriant foliage, a plaster Mao strutted through the waiting room which was the destination of our funeral cortege. We must have resembled Father Huc's caravan, en route to Lithang, on the frontier between China and Tibet, carrying three corpses.

"You seem troubled by something," the secretary general said to me.

"I had hoped to buy a painting from an artist whose work I admire a great deal," I replied dryly.

"Ah! The thing is that this artist does not feel that he has anything worthy of your interest. He has nothing at the moment that he would care to sell to you. You know how artists are, how frequently dissatisfied they are with their work. We are all desolate about it, but no one can force a man to sell something, especially an artist. But you will find some of his paintings in Peking. It will be easy for you to buy them there."

I knew very well that the authorities in Peking would do everything in their power to make certain that I found none, even dispersing the

paintings among antique dealers if necessary. This time I was sure that
they were determined to prevent me from contributing, in even the
slightest degree, to the renown of an artist who did not paint factories,
tractors or historic landmarks. I retreated into silence, thereby creating
an awkward tension which Tsai tried vainly to dissipate. I left my place
in the VIP circle where we had been seated, and sought out an armchair
as far from Mr. Shu as possible. When I told Orthion what had happened, he asked whether he should laugh or commiserate with me.

"At this point, it hardly makes much difference," I said.

He shrugged wearily and offered me one of the little black Szechwan
cigars, whose smoke and stench rapidly filled the station.

Our good-byes were rather cursory. I should have been warmer in my
expression of thanks. After all, the Chinese were putting us up and
paying for our trip. I consoled myself with the thought that Father Huc
had had no scruples about forcing the hand of his mandarins when
things did not go according to his wishes, and argued bitterly every time
he was told that a journey was to be made on horseback rather than by
litter. "Our legs had straddled so many horses of all ages, sizes, colors
and qualities, that they would have no more of it; they yearned irresist-
ibly to stretch themselves out in peace in a litter. Thanks to the
perseverance and force of our demands, they were granted this relief."
At the expense of the public treasury, he moved from one place to
another, instructed himself in Chinese customs and history and discreetly taught the Gospels. Even though I had taken great pains to
refrain from any attempt at proselytizing, Father Huc was a master who
had set a very bad example!

Tsai and Chen barricaded themselves in their compartment. What
had happened to the promise they had given me to discuss any problems
that arose between us as soon as they occurred? I waited calmly for
their present consternation to subside. When they came to see me, I
would tell them exactly what was on my mind. After I had thought
about it, however, I told myself that it might be more prudent to remain
silent and listen to what they had to say. It seemed a good idea to hold
back my knowledge of the lie they had told me when they stated that the
artist did not speak French.

Simon was fuming over their refusal to allow us to make the trip from
Shanghai to Nanking by river boat. We had requested this several times,
insistently, but we had always been turned down. They had not dared
tell us that photographing the river was prohibited, and therefore had
invented all kinds of pretexts to dissuade us: the course of the river
made it too long a trip, the waters were rising, we must be back in
Peking on the fifteenth of October. In that case, why had we wasted
those two days in Hangchow? To provide us with some distraction and
give us a chance to rest. The truth of the matter seemed to be that they

did not want us to travel on the Yangtze, even though ten boatloads of other travelers went up and down it every day. What were they hiding there? What secrets could we possibly uncover?

For some time now, I had done no more than glance occasionally at *Peking Information*, but for some reason I was given an article from it to read. I reproduce it here verbatim:

Following the example of Hsiu Ting-tse, who returned to the People's China in June of last year in his American F-86 F jet fighter, Chao Song-li, chief petty officer of Chiang Kai-shek's "Quemoy reconnaissance group," has also returned, bringing with him a mechanized landing craft manufactured in the United States (LCM No. 1279). He was warmly welcomed by the military authorities and the local population on his arrival in a port city of East China, on October 4.

On the following day, Marshal Lin Piao, Minister of National Defense, published an order conferring on him the rank of ensign in the naval forces of the People's Army of liberation and giving him a reward of six hundred gold liangs, in accordance with the regulations governing recompense to personnel of Chiang Kai-shek's navy who return to the side of the people.

On October 7, Chao Song-li was received by Vice Admiral Liu Hao-tien. The Vice Admiral praised his patriotic gesture, and at a welcoming ceremony on the following day conferred on him, in the name of Minister of National Defense Lin Piao, the rank of ensign, and presented him with a certificate for six hundred gold liangs which he can cash at the quartermaster general's office.

After having received his reward, Chao Song-li, wearing his brand-new uniform with the epaulets of an ensign of the People's Navy, stated that this was the greatest moment of his life, and that he was infinitely grateful for the honor his country had done him. He also stated that his compatriots on Taiwan were impatient to see the island liberated as soon as possible, and that those of Chiang Kai-shek's soldiers whose homes were on the continent hoped from one day to the next to know the joy of returning there.

I called Mr. Tsai.

"How," I asked, "do you reconcile the contempt for money that everyone professes to have in socialist China with the rain of gold you shower on Chiang Kai-shek's deserters?"

Where was comrade Chao Song-li going to hide his forty-eight pounds of gold? What was he going to buy? Houses? There were none for sale. Land? The same thing was true. Furs and clothing for the winter? Jewelry?

"If you would admit that it is not soldiers you are buying," I said, "but the equipment they bring back to you so that you can copy it, then I could see a certain morality in this immorality. During the war I changed camps myself, but I would have considered myself dishonored if I had done it for money. No amount of money should be able to buy a soldier from a nation's army, and if he simply puts a certain price on his life he is a mercenary who will fight for any cause whatever. You apparently evaluate your cause at forty-eight pounds of gold, on condition that a man become a traitor and bring you an airplane, a tank or a landing craft."

"This equipment costs a great deal more than that," Mr. Tsai stated frankly.

"No capitalist army would consider giving money to a deserter, even if it benefited from his desertion," I said.

"Chiang Kai-shek's soldiers are not deserting when they rejoin the People's Army."

"Give them a higher rank if you think that is necessary," I said, "but not money. If you do that, how can you pretend to hold money in contempt? And what kind of regulation is it that rewards Chiang Kai-shek's men, while people are killing themselves with work, right here, for next to nothing? I might be able to understand if you did this sort of thing and said nothing about it. But that you should cite this shameful bribe as an example to incite other men to desertion, that I cannot understand at all. Threaten those who do not rejoin the People's Army with death, but don't shower gold on those who do rejoin it."

Mr. Tsai was not in the least shocked. He agreed with me that a soldier should fight for nothing, but he felt that the government was right in using money to tempt the soldiers of an army in which anything could be bought, just as it had been in the old regime.

"In that case," I said, "don't take them into the People's Army and give them a higher rank." It seemed that it was also necessary to honor them.

Decidedly, we could find no mutual terms of understanding.

Chapter 17

In Nanking, the author makes a pilgrimage to the Hill of Martyrs and to the tomb of Sun Yat-sen. Some reflections on the Sino-Japanese War. In the same way in which the author no longer knows where truth lies, Brigitte no longer dares violate China by taking forbidden photographs. In which the Yangtze River appears as an important personage. In which the author, flying from Nanking to Peking, makes an unforeseen stopover at Tsinan and discovers an unsuspected misery. How he chances to see the Yellow River at nightfall and acquires an idea of the spirit of the People's Army.

> You the homeless, you the unfed, all of you! You who have no names, you who are recognized by the sores on your shoulders—the haulers of wood, the towers of boats—and by the sores on your hips and thighs—the laborers in the ports! Listen to those whose grandeur is fed with your blood! Ha! when they say "coolies," these great gentlemen use the same accent I used a little while ago in calling them "dogs"!
> —André Malraux, *The Conquerors* (*Les Conquérants*)

As the train crossed the broad, flat region between Shanghai and Nanking, a pale sun came out to warm and comfort us. Along the horizon, smoke drifted upward from the factory chimneys. Moving along canals that were invisible to us, the high sails of the junks seemed to be cutting through the rice fields themselves. By the time we reached Nanking, the atmosphere of tension had relaxed a little. Night was falling. A little caravan of shiny, well-kept automobiles carried us through the avenues of a city which had been, at several different times, the capital of China. That night there was another banquet in our honor.

The hotel was separated from the city proper by a guarded enclosure, to protect its guests from those undesirable contacts we had been hoping to establish, and like all the hotels we had seen outside of Shanghai and Peking, it was filled with private meeting and dining rooms where one could relax and enjoy himself, secure in the knowledge that he was sheltered from indiscreet observation. I repeated my little speech about what we had come to China to do, I expressed my admiration for the Chinese people, and then there was the usual period of customary banalities. For the first time the food was delicious. Perhaps because they were delighted that we were staying with them for so short a time, or perhaps also because we had been preceded by a reputation for being troublesome, the members of the Association in Nanking were lavish in their attentions. Orthion's appreciation of the niceties of service was clearly evident, and he kept nodding his head in approval of my answers to all of the speeches. *"Kam-pé!"* Even the wine here was of very good quality, and as the round of toasts continued we experienced a degree of warmth and friendship we had not felt in some time. In the restaurant where we breakfasted next morning, the waitresses, in spite of their ugly masculine uniforms, were sublimely beautiful and we stared at them so intently that they blushed.

We began our tour with a visit to the hill where Chiang Kai-shek had massacred the Communists in 1927, as he had also done in Shanghai. At one time the hill had been stripped and naked, but now it was covered with fruit trees. It was known as "the hill of flowering rain" because of the multicolored pebbles to be found everywhere on its slopes. Groups of people from the surrounding countryside made pilgrimages to the museum and left wreaths at the foot of the monument in memory of the martyrs.

On the pine-covered hills beyond the vast wall of Nanking, on the outer limits of the city, a marble walk over half a mile long and a flight of four hundred steps leads to the tomb of Sun Yat-sen. This rustic setting is a favorite spot for family picnics, and the young people climb the steps singing and playing the accordion. At the summit of the mausoleum, crowned with a roof of dark blue tiles, there is an antechamber containing a grandiose seated statue of the little doctor, and beyond this his body lies in a small domed room, beneath an effigy suitable for a Methodist pastor. Engraved in golden characters around the tomb are the words "Love for All" and "The World for All." It was Sun Yat-sen who had first toiled for those words in China, and this was his glory. We talked to an old general with a little mustache and a shiny, bald head. He told us: "He made speeches that went on for hours and hours, but his voice was very moving."

At the government palace we were shown the room where he worked and the conference hall where the Republic was proclaimed in December, 1911. The Heavenly King of the Taipings had once ruled from here, and for a time, at the beginning of the war against Japan, amid the waters and flowers of this park, the seat of Chiang Kai-shek's government could be found here.

What the generalissimo had announced as a victory in that period, when his portrait decorated the streets of the city, was actually more a matter of having yielded to the pressure of public opinion and put up some show of resistance, thereby forcing Japan to commit an army of a million men to reach Nanking. By 1938 the debacle was gradually creeping up the valley of the Yangtze. In their haste to flee, many of Chiang's soldiers simply threw away their weapons, and officers piled into requisitioned automobiles. Freight trains rumbled toward the west, loaded to their roofs with refugees and machinery from the factories along the coast. Long lines of families, carrying whatever they could of their belongings, waited for endless hours on the piers, hoping to find a place on a river boat to Chungking.

Meanwhile, the former Communist armies were being brought into the campaign against the enemy. Resistance units were organized in the hills that border the valley of the Yangtze and in the loess country of the Yellow River. Their staffs had no means of communication and their medical services were totally inadequate, but the villages mobilized, levying a militia force and setting up services for information and supply. There was no pillaging. The wells and the harvests were left untouched. The soldiers' boots were rope sandals, and they lived on grains and vegetables. With the exception of those they judged worthy of being re-educated and then freed, they slaughtered their prisoners, even though they denied it. An ordinary soldier received fifty cents a month. Generals commanding an army were paid three dollars a month, but they never drew it.

In Japan bareheaded soldiers, their field rolls on their backs, prostrated themselves in front of the temples before leaving for the war. Their return was somewhat less ceremonious. When the ships arrived, the first thing unloaded was the booty stolen in China, the pianos, furniture, refrigerators and velvet curtains from the wealthy homes of Shanghai. After this, an officer called out lists of names, and his subordinates distributed to waiting families the little urns containing the ashes of their sons. The bitter struggle of the Chinese Communists was turning into tragedy a campaign everyone had thought would be no more than an honorable excursion.

The carcasses of horses slain in China were not repatriated, but funeral services were held for them. In the streets of the cities the Chinese looked on in astonishment as the occupation troops went through their daily gymnastics. Bearded Catholic missionaries in pith helmets shook the hand of the invaders. In America college girls ripped off their Japanese stockings and burned them symbolically. Sixteen Japanese divisions reached the Great Wall and spread out into the valleys. Many of their officers had abandoned their spurs, but still clung to their boots and plumes. Wherever they went, their sabers were in their hands. And wherever they went, they left a trail of weeping women. Children were herded into the fields to gather vegetables, and Buddhist priests filled sacks of earth to be used as sandbags. The peasants had to be forced at gunpoint to harvest their crops. Along a route sown with ruins and devastated villages, the Japanese Army skirted Nanking and entered Hankow on October 25, 1938. It was raining, and the cadenced step of the dripping infantrymen echoed hollowly in the deserted streets. Behind them, the guerrilla war had begun.

It was obvious that everyone was making an enormous effort to be agreeable to me. Not only was I provided with witnesses to the events of the revolution, but with reams of decaying documents testifying to the credibility of their stories. Since I had said that I was a Catholic, a delegate from the offices of the diocese of Nanking was brought forth to tell me about the crimes of the former bishop. And although I had expressed no desire for anything of the sort, one of the foremost official painters of the regime was summoned and installed at a table on which he placed his pot of brushes, box of inks and saucers. He was an old man with flowing hair and a long, thin beard, eyes as round as the lenses of his glasses and a forehead crossed with a single deep furrow. With a few splashes of color and a few clawlike lines, he sketched willows and bamboos, a river, a house among the trees and a bark on the water. His hands were wonderfully dexterous. Chen was breathless with admiration, and his associates were equally ecstatic. This, then, was genius? Here again I preferred silence to a lie.

Brigitte rejoined us after a trip to the old quarter of the city. In order to supervise her work, a Chinese photographer had accompanied her, taking the same pictures she did: bands of children wandering the streets, artisans at work in their little shops, itinerant dealers in all sorts of wares. Almost ill with disappointment, she told me that her coward-ice had cost her a photograph of a chain of ten men hauling a heavily laden cart. One of them had halted suddenly and cried out, "Bu!"—"No!"

"What would you have done in my place?" she asked me.

"I would have clicked the shutter," I said.

She shook her head. "I didn't dare."

She was like me in that she still hoped to incarnate all China in one sublime image. She was like me in that she felt that this image was not to be found in any evocation of glory. In pride, perhaps, but far more likely in the labor of men and women. This nation was being built with the sweat of the workers and peasants no one would let us see; it was being built with each turn of the wheels of the carts they hauled; it was being built atop a mountain of exhausted, worn-out bodies. Behind the plump silhouettes of our mandarins, through the window of our auto-mobiles, we were beginning to glimpse the 700 million Chinese who were building the China we had been allowed to enter. It was fearful and it was terrifying. "You have to admit," Orthion said, with the common sense that was part of his nature, "that there are two classes in China: those who work and those who work for the party." I no longer knew where my book was or where the truth was, and in this, again, Brigitte was like me. She was constantly afraid of making mistakes in her lens settings or her exposures. I could do nothing for her beyond repeating, without being able to furnish any proof, that she was going to win this battle.

The Yangtze, which derived its name of Blue River from the opal reflections that colored it in the morning light, was more than a mile wide at this point. The gathering dusk enveloped it in mist and smoke. A slanting light filtered through the clouds, catching suddenly at the backwash of a ship and lighting up corners of the somber hills on the opposite bank. My crew had gone out earlier in the day, and as I stood on the pier waiting for the tugboat to bring them back the wind whipped around my shoulders. There was nothing to hinder the wind's course between here and the coast, almost two hundred miles away, and it was still charged with the odor of salt and sandalwood. It filled the tall sails of the junks returning to port, traveling in little groups, like beasts of burden coming home from the fields. Ferryboats from the factories along the river were unloading their cargoes of workmen, carrying loads of wood on their heads, their day finished. Sirens screamed, the propellers of the larger boats churned up the water, the air was filled with warning whistles from pilothouses and the tinkle of bells marking the hour. It was here, in April, 1949, that Lin Piao had commandeered thousands of small boats and crossed the river with his entire army, racing to the south in pursuit of the remnants of Chiang Kai-shek's divisions. At the same time, Chen Yi was taking Shanghai.

It was almost dark when the tugboat finally arrived, and before we went out again the navigating lights were lit. The motors rumbled heavily, sending vibrations through the wooden hull.

"A bridge," Simon cried. "They are building a new bridge on the Yangtze and they hadn't told us about it."

"Where?" I demanded.

"Up there, where you can see the lights. We are going there now."

Tsai smiled. In China one did not talk about bridges until they were finished and tested, until the concrete pillars being driven into the river bed had reached and pierced its heart, until trains rolled across the steel platform as swiftly and surely as they would have crossed dry ground. In all the time that Simon had been asking to be shown some of their great factories and construction projects, they had concealed the existence of this bridge. This, and how many others? Why, for instance, could we not be shown the hydroelectric plant that was being built in the gorges upriver from Ichang, and that was scheduled to supply one hundred billion kilowatt-hours of electricity, one and a half times the total production of France? Moving at full speed now, the tugboat battered its way up the river, whose surface seemed even more restless and angry in the fast-fading light. Some of the supporting pillars of the bridge were already finished. Night crews were working on the floating cranes, by the light of giant arc lamps. The noise of steam hammers, of stone crushers and cement mixers mingled with the rumble of our engines and the thud of waves against the hull.

We took refuge on the boat's bridge with the pilot, protected by glass screens from the clouds of spray. In the blackness that was closing in around us, other boats seemed to be darting in and out of a region of enormous shadows, whistling fiercely and avoiding each other by inches. A long line of junks, lashed together to form a train, moved slowly toward the bridge.

Simon received a telephone call from Paris, asking him to obtain statements about a Chinese atomic explosion which was rumored in the West to be imminent. I, personally had no doubts whatever about it. I even told myself that the Chinese were capable of exploding a bomb without prior experiments. In the automobile that was taking us to the airport next morning, I asked the members of the Nanking delegation about it. They seemed shocked.

"Was it also from Paris that you learned that we were making opium in Yünnan?" they asked dryly. "You are badly informed. Since the revolution, the cultivation of poppies has been prohibited."

"In that case," I said, "why do you forbid us to visit Yünnan?"

"Because of the poor means of communication there."

I sensed a new animosity in these men who at first had been so anxious to please me. Had Tsai said something to them? Had they received new instructions from Peking? I knew that they bitterly resented the fact that I refused to be content with the official information bulletins. I tried to explain that journalists in the West were never satisfied with what they were told and believed only what they saw with their own eyes. I was wasting my time, and the discussion was beginning to grow heated, so I gave up.

We had not remained in Nanking long enough for our friends there to be consumed with delight at losing us, but we parted company coolly. A telegram was brought to us on the plane: one of us had left a package of cigarettes at the airport. It would be returned to us in Peking.

The plane made a stopover at Tsinan, the capital of Shantung province, on the right bank of the Yellow River. Did we want to have lunch there? I had no very fond memories of airport restaurants, and replied that I would rather wait until we got back to the Hsin Chiao. They reminded me that it was a long trip from the Peking airport to the hotel. I didn't care. I preferred Peking.

We were taken into an improvised waiting room, installed in arm-chairs and provided with pots of tea and biscuits. The Tsinan airport was tiny, and thickly populated with flies. Was it possible that no one had noticed this national humiliation? The waiters themselves, who were generally only too eager to wield the fly swatters they carried, did not use them here. A seemingly endless chain of fighter planes was taking off from the landing strip outside. Chen informed me that these planes were manufactured in China and were known as Type 55, a copy of the Russian Mig, and the pilots were simply training in take-offs and landings, without going any distance from the field.

At noon, when no sign of departure was forthcoming, I began to regret having refused lunch. Tsai bought several large pears and put them with the package he was taking back to his family. At one o'clock I agreed to go into the canteen, from which the other passengers were now returning. I wondered if we would have to wait here until the fighter pilots had finished their exercise. The weather was very pleasant and Tsai and Chen went outside to play cards. Simon walked off toward the highway and was promptly brought back, in spite of his protests. I was asked to tell him that entering the area of a military airport was strictly forbidden. I replied that we were not so strict about such things in Europe, and that I could not reprimand Simon since he was only doing his duty as a journalist. Some East Germans were playing basket-ball, and for a time we toyed halfheartedly with a football.

At three o'clock we learned finally that we would spend the night here because the weather was bad in Peking. I was reminded of Omsk. The Chinese claimed that their commercial transport planes flew in any weather, but obviously they did not. "We refuse to take the slightest risk where passengers are concerned," I was told. A few minutes later some automobiles arrived, we were herded into them and departed in the direction of the city.

I could imagine now what an effort they must have made to get us back to Peking and prevent us from seeing what could no longer be hidden. No more than a few hundred yards from the airport, whole families were at work, turning over the earth, breaking up the larger clods with spades, weeding and watering little strips of kitchen gardens. The slender, green stalks of vegetables were visible on either side of us, reaching out to the very shoulders of the road. Brigitte and I looked at each other, not knowing what to say. On my right, Tsai was as silent as we. Brigitte did not dare to bring out her camera, and I did not dare to ask her to. It would have humiliated Tsai out of all proportion to what we would have gained. I was seeing the countryside as it really was for the first time, and quite by accident, but I understood now why they insisted on taking us always to the model people's communes and re-fused to show us the rest.

P

As we approached the city, the increasing density of the ramshackle houses hid the fields from our sight, and the road itself was obstructed by an army of half-naked people, towing carts and wagons of every description. Our automobiles zigzagged in and out among them, the horns blaring imperiously, threatening injury or death at every moment. An ignorant observer such as myself might have thought that the threat of some catastrophe had forced the entire population of the area to gather up its belongings and move, but it seemed that this was nothing more than the normal way of life in Tsinan. Men, women and even children, each attached to some form of wheeled vehicle, tugged or pushed at loads of earth, stones, tiles, cement, coal, bricks, scrap iron, odds and ends of cloth and clothing, anything that could serve for building and any form of refuse that might still find a purchaser. Isolated in the midst of this swarm of emaciated beggars, a few mules and donkeys stood out like symbols of enormous luxury. Beasts of burden had to be fed.

At one particularly crowded grade crossing, we were forced to slow down. Our drivers kept their hands relentlessly on their horns, and as the crowd parted to allow us passage, we caught a glimpse of faces bathed in sweat and deformed by a weariness that was a prefiguration of death. The mandarins of our escort pretended to notice nothing. My back began to hurt and I felt as though my heart had momentarily stopped. The people in the streets through which our automobiles were now moving bore no resemblance to the happy marchers waving their artificial branches of peach trees in front of the reviewing stand in Peking. Was this the real face of China? Was China this world of starvelings, harnessed to piles of stone and earth?

Our caravan made a sharp turn, arrived in an area of quiet streets and abruptly passed through the gates of the enclosure surrounding the hotel. All our rooms had private baths—private baths for the mandarins and honored guests, while the people of Han towed their carts through the streets almost beneath our windows. The shop in the lobby was not overflowing with pyramids of handsome fruit, as it had been in all the other hotels. They had apparently not had time to provide them. The entire crew gathered in my room. Simon had his camera ready, and was intent on going out to film the scenes we had just witnessed. But the interpreters and Chen were standing guard, and he was not permitted beyond the door of the hotel. Simon protested, demanding that he be allowed to do what he had come to China to do, and when I was called into the discussion I, too, demanded that we be allowed to visit the city. I was told that a tour was being organized.

An hour later the automobiles returned and took us out to the shores of a lake where the customary gondola-like barks were waiting. A fine rain had begun to fall. Brigitte sat down on a bench and burst into tears.

When my friend Tsai expressed astonishment at the way she was acting, I said that we had had enough of rowing about on lakes, that we were far more interested in the problems of the Chinese people, and that, if they were afraid of wounding our sensitive natures with this spectacle, they could at least show us the Yellow River. After this there was a long conference among our mandarins and a delegate hastily summoned from the tourist office. Finally, we climbed back into the automobiles and rejoined the horde of people in the streets. Our drivers seemed to pay no attention to them; in a purely reflex action, my foot moved out toward an imaginary brake, I clenched my teeth and clung to the door handle and seat. The tourist office delegate continued to pretend that he saw nothing. In China they were ashamed of something like this, and foreigners were expected to be discreet enough not to notice. When we had left the swarming masses of people behind us and the road was no longer so cluttered, the chauffeur slowed down.

"In Europe," I said, "when the roads are empty we drive fast, and when they are crowded we slow down. How does it happen that you do just the reverse in China?"

Mr. Shu translated my question with a clearly evident contempt. I was not given any reply.

We were driving through an industrial district, dotted with the tall chimneys of factories, belching clouds of smoke. The workers lived in groups of one-story houses decorated with long banners urging them to "Work for the plan and the party!" Each family lived in a single room lighted by a single electric bulb. The women did their cooking outside and emptied their dirty water and refuse into a canal that ran down the street. Everything looked slimy, worm-eaten, leprous. We passed groups of gaunt-looking cyclists, on their way to the factories, which never shut down.

It was almost dark when we reached the banks of the Yellow River. Along the three thousand miles of a course it had altered three hundred times, this river had eighty-three names—Two-Stringed Violin, Strider of Mountains, Gong of Springtime Autumn, Tail of Iron, Head of Bronze, Lord of the Millet Grass. In its last few hundred miles, it had changed course twenty-six times before striking through the hills of Shantung, seeking an entrance to the sea, sometimes to the south and sometimes to the north, finding it once at Tientsin, the port for Peking, and later at a point five hundred miles to the south. Straddling the deposits of its own silt, the heaviest of any river in the world, it rose constantly higher and if its bed was not dredged, the dikes that contained it had to be built constantly higher. There had been times when its turmoil constituted a line of defense. In 1938 Chiang Kai-shek had blown up the dikes in the face of the advancing Japanese. The flood had drowned eleven cities and four thousand villages and plunged twelve million peasants into misery, but the invasion in this area had been halted.

For thousands of years the emperors had given a large share of their attention to containing this monster within its barriers. When the barriers were broken, it was the emperor who was held responsible and he risked being carried away in the flood. The ungovernable dragon, the scourge of the sons of Han, the misfortune of China, had at last been mastered. Socialism had put the bit in its mouth. One by one, the cracks in the dikes had been sealed up, the holes plugged, the bundles of faggots replaced with stone and masonry, new dikes built at every vital point and supported by breakwaters, wharfs and crescent-shaped walls of concrete. Forty-six dams were scheduled for construction, to contain its violence and command its floods—a work on an even greater scale than the digging of the Chinese Grand Canal or the building of the two thousand miles of the Great Wall.

Seen from the spot where we stood, the terrible river of yellowish mud rolled between a line of ramparts that studded the horizon like the walls of a fortress. A new dike was being built along the summit of the existing one, and children were carrying crushed stone to the workmen, walking two by two, each of them supporting on a shoulder one end of the rod from which the pail of stone was suspended. Not far from here, trains were hurtling across a steel bridge. We were not permitted to approach the bridge, but they did not dare prevent us from photographing the dikes. Was it this unforeseen stopover that had made our Chinese companions so nervous? Simon was impatient and angry. He left us abruptly, walking off alone along the dikes toward the bridge, and Chen promptly sent Mr. Fang to follow him.

On the opposite bank, we could see a group of soldiers with their trucks already loaded on a ferry. Suddenly, we heard singing, a chorus of masculine voices reaching us from across the river. Perhaps I was going to see this army at close hand, be permitted at last to observe the flower of the nation's manhood. I had been told repeatedly that the army was never seen, and of course this had intrigued me. A strange sort of army, but the conquerors of Dienbienphu had copied its methods and practices. Since it was impossible to enroll all the young men of this vast continent, the army selected only those with the hardiest physique and whose heart was most surely on the side of the revolution. The officers all wanted to prove themselves worthy of the heroes of the Long March, and for one month of each year they were deprived of their rank and became ordinary soldiers, sharing the life and work of the privates and corporals they normally commanded.

"Even the battalion commanders and the generals?" I asked Tsai.

"Even the generals," he replied. "Even the generals commanding an army corps. On any Sunday the soldiers can go to see him and have tea with him if they want to, but for one month every year the corps commander becomes an ordinary soldier, sleeps in the camp beds with the rest of his soldiers and obeys the corporals. All officers, no matter what their rank, do this each year."

I had an idea that there must be some sort of regimen that favored the generals and spared them the most menial tasks, but I could not be certain. In the Chinese People's Army the leaders made it a point of honor to live exactly like their men and treating them with complete equality. From this fact alone, this enormous revolutionary machine gained a force and flexibility of which no capitalist army was capable.

The ferry left the other bank, was carried by the current far downstream from us, came broadside to the current and finally managed to dock. The falling shadows shrouded the river and the song it had carried. Simon came back, surrounded by children who had also been sent to follow him. We got back into the automobiles. Since I was certain that I would see no more than this, I told Tsai that I hoped we could return to Peking as soon as possible.

"Even by train?" he asked. "I can't guarantee that the plane will leave tomorrow morning."

He was probably lying, but since I was expressing his own wishes he promised to do everything possible so that we might leave Tsinan. That night we were shown a film on the beauties of the hills, the lakes and rivers of Shantung and the village where Confucius was born. We were watching this when someone came to tell us that everything was ready for us to leave. Our baggage was taken away and we were swallowed up by a sleeping car attached to a freight train. It was still raining.

Chapter 18

How the author, on arrival in Peking, learns of an important diplomatic development and of the first Chinese atomic explosion. Why it is difficult to obtain comments from both official circles and from the man in the street. In which the author spends a day of historic importance visiting temples and hills attempting to gauge the importance of the current developments. How Brigitte's love for Peking in particular and China in general might be explained.

> During the reign of the Ch'ing dynasty, Sir Robert Hart asked the emperor's prime minister what he thought of Western influence on China. The prime minister replied: "You are all too concerned with waking us up and setting us off on a new route; you will succeed in doing it, but you will regret it, because once we are awakened and set off, we will go faster and farther than you think, and a great deal more rapidly than you would like."
> —ROBERT PAYNE, *Chinese Journal (Journal de Chine)*

> What is the point of finding out, simply from curiosity, whether it was the Chinese viceroy or the English commodore who was right, whether it was the Sepoy regiments or agents of the Company? . . . The truth is that these are the facts! We are taking part in the beginnings of a struggle which will put all Europe at grips with all Asia. . . .
> —E. R. HUC, *Christianity in China, Tartary and Tibet*, Preface to Volume III

In Peking the festival was over. The portraits and banners that had adorned T'ien An Men Square had been put away. The sky was still dripping with the rain that had blotted out the city the afternoon before. We parted company at the railway station. Tsai got into his automobile, carrying his package of Shantung pears. A minor mandarin of the regime, he was returning to his proper rank, while we returned to the Hsin Chiao. Brigitte was happy. There was mail waiting for us and I telephoned Marcuse. His wife answered, telling me that he was in Hong Kong, and asking me what I thought of the news.

"What news?" I asked.

"Khrushchev has been forced out of office."

I could easily imagine Tsai's jubilation. If I had known how to reach him, I would have telephoned to congratulate him. In Peking, however, no one aside from the Western residents gives out his private telephone number and the only directory is for the government services. When you need someone, you leave a message at his office. The easygoing confidence of the West did not exist here.

To the Chinese, the fall of Khrushchev represented a great victory. They thought that now Russia would become their ally again and America would tremble. Was I expected to write an article about the downfall of the Soviet leader? I am not a political journalist. This was a Friday, the day when *l'Express* went to press. If they had wanted a cable from me, they would certainly have let me know. I sent off a cable, letting them know I was back in Peking and asking for instructions, and then, exhausted by the pain in my back, I took a sleeping pill and went to bed.

It was almost midnight when an insistent rapping on the door forced me to get up. *L'Express* was asking me for an article on reactions in official circles and from the man in the street. I was tempted to do nothing about it; it was already too late for anything that I might send to reach the Paris newspapers in time for that day's edition. A professional reflex forced me to remove the cover from my typewriter, with the thought that this deadline might be held off while they waited for a piece from me. I plunged my head in cold water, to dissipate the fog of the sleeping pill, and sat down to type out my impressions. All my emotions built up inside me and carried me away. I wrote that I had arrived here only this morning, that I had learned of this development at the same time as the foreign embassies in Peking, that is, when the newspapers came out and one day later than foreign ministries in all the rest of the world. This was meant to give some idea of the freedom that reigned in this country. Until the Central Committee of the party had made clear the official position, no one was permitted to discuss the matter or toss around hypotheses.

How was I to obtain official reactions when the authorities kept such things strictly secret? Cabinet ministers in China were not easily reached for interviews and no one knew where they lived. It was impossible to force the door of their assistants, and the Chinese press sat calmly in front of its ticker tapes, waiting for the information that would be sent out by the State agencies. Anyone who wanted to draw a picture of Chinese political thought at this moment would have to have at his disposal an entire network of diplomatic relations, and this was not my case.

I set down in my report the essential facts of my conversation with Tsai about the atomic bomb, which China certainly now possessed. I had seen nothing but tall chimney stacks, factories working night and day, expositions, fishing villages, bridges, locomotives, millions of men and women living in houses without heat and sometimes without even fire, and children carrying stones to the dikes of the Yellow River. The departure of the Soviet engineers had seemed to condemn this people to tug eternally at its carts. How, then, could they hope to possess an atomic bomb? Through the same stubbornness that had made them accept sacrifices that would have seemed intolerable to Westerners. Through the same pride that had made them put up, in a few months, monuments and buildings for which foreign architects had required a period of years. It was merely fifteen years since Mao Tse-tung's armies, equipped only with sabers and rifles captured from the enemy, had put to flight the divisions of Chiang Kai-shek, advised and supplied by the Americans. Now, the successor to Shih Huang Ti and his court of proletarian marshals intended to prove to the nations of the West that China could become just as strong as they.

At one o'clock in the morning, I had finished and corrected my cable. I dressed and went out to look for a taxi. In the deserted corridors of the hotel, I came across a Canadian journalist.

"Two big stories in one day," he said. "That's quite an event."

"I know about Khrushchev," I said. "What's the other story?"

"You don't know?"

He took me into his office. He had learned about Khrushchev's removal earlier in the day, by listening to Australian broadcasts on his radio. But he had learned of the other story in the regular Chinese way. There was never such a thing as a government press conference here. If they had anything to announce, the journalists were sent for and a silent clerk handed out a slip of paper. Although no one had told me about it, the foreign correspondents in Peking had been summoned to the Ministry of Foreign Affairs at five o'clock that afternoon. That appointment had been postponed, however, and the communiqué I now held in my hands had not been published until eleven o'clock that night:

At three o'clock on the afternoon of October 16, 1964, China exploded an atomic bomb and thereby carried out successfully her first nuclear experiment. This represents an important step forward by the Chinese people in their struggle to reinforce their capacity of national defense against the imperialist American policy of blackmail and nuclear threat. . . .

I read no further.

Khrushchev's downfall became a matter of secondary importance. I went directly to the telegraph office and added an urgent message to my cable, announcing this new development. Because of the time difference, which put us seven hours ahead of Paris, I hoped that it would arrive in time for this week's edition. When I returned to the Hsin Chiao, I woke Brigitte and the other members of my crew and we talked for a long time about the consequences of this October thunderbolt. I considered it as important as the day of Hiroshima. Then we went back to bed.

Tsai arrived next morning just as I was finishing the horrible brew they insisted on calling coffee. I offered him my congratulations and told him why I had always believed in a Chinese success of this magnitude. He was purring with delight, and Mr. Shu's smile was so broad it uncovered all his teeth. What could we do that would be suitable to such an historic moment? Simon left, in the hope of obtaining interviews with the man in the street, and Brigitte went with him. Tsai suggested to me that we should visit some of the temples. What a strange idea, on such a day! They knew that I had little interest in temples. I had already had more than I wanted of little Buddhas and great ones, seated and lying down, in gold, in bronze and in wood. And I was annoyed by the sarcasm that inevitably accompanied my guides' remarks. I found it curious that they persisted in showing me ancient idols and stubbornly refused to permit me to see the library where their reigning emperor had worked in his youth. In spite of their constantly professed desire to see me stunned with admiration for modern China, it was obvious that we did not share the same ideas about it. To Tsai and Chen, contemporary China was the museums, the palaces of the people, the factories and the workers' cities. To me, since I felt that I had already had enough of all that, it was the great enterprises of construction that were so rigidly kept secret. As we were leaving the hotel, a cable from *l'Express* informed me that mine had been received in time. I was greatly relieved.

It was quite cold. The city seemed frozen and even more sparsely populated than usual. A few silent and unresponsive passers-by stood in front of the bulletin boards where the newspapers were hung, reading the government statement. I asked Tsai if we could question some of them. He found the idea bizarre, but ordered the chauffeur to stop.

"To us," he said, "today is a day like any other, and we do not feel that the explosion of the bomb has changed anything at all. I told you that in the train. The whole Chinese people was prepared for this development, so it is not surprised. What do you expect them to say?"

"I don't know," I said. "But at home, when something like this happens, we have a habit of asking people what they think about it."

"Very well, go ahead," Tsai said and laughed.

An old man in a jacket and cap of worn cloth answered my questions by reading aloud from the red and black notice that repeated the words of the official communiqué. He pointed out the characters with his index finger as he went along, and Mr. Shu translated: "The success of the effort undertaken by China is an important accomplishment of the Chinese people in reinforcing its national defense and also constitutes a considerable contribution to the cause of maintaining world peace." All the district chiefs would be expected to read these words to the heads of families, gathered together in every neighborhood of every city and village. Quite suddenly, a little group of people had begun to form around us. They seemed to come from nowhere, and just stood there staring at me, open-mouthed. I got back in the car and we left.

I let myself be carted off to the hills west of the city, where we visited the Temple of the Clouds and pagodas crammed with statues of gilded wood. As a matter of professional pride, I questioned another man. Yes, he had heard about it on the radio, and he raised his fist in a thumbs-up gesture like that of the ancient Romans, to show that he was pleased. The leaves of the maple trees were red. A pale sunlight bathed the lotus leaves in the ponds and occasionally glinted on the dark silhouette of a carp. I sat down on a bench. Tsai pulled his cap down over his eyes and pressed his hands into the pockets of his gray raincoat. From time to time, he let out a little rumble of laughter and glanced at me slyly. He talked to me at some length about the bomb, its relative power, the promise China had given to make use of it only in her own defense, her offer of a general disarmament conference, to include all the nations of the world, and finally of the pre-eminence of man in all things. Of itself, the bomb was nothing very important. It was man who would always be the conqueror.

We had lunch in a little lakeside tavern where I succeeding in obtaining some fried eggs, and since the day already seemed lost, I expressed a desire to see the Temple of Heaven. The tiles of the roofs were the deep blue color of the sea. In other times Chinese architects and artists had designed these marble terraces and cupolas so that the emperors might come here and implore the gods to keep the rivers in their beds and grant the people a fine harvest. Today Chinese scientists were erecting the giant tower of an atomic cloud above the mountain ranges of Tibet.

This Saturday afternoon resembled a holiday. Groups of strollers were wandering through the gardens and battalions of students were weeding the flower beds and walks. The heads that turned toward us were marked with an expression of calm and serenity I had never noticed before. "Yes, we are poor, but we have the bomb." I would have liked to know if there had been any similar change in Tsinan. I doubted it. The people there were surely still pulling at their carts, with the same despairing fury. Was it possible that these slave laborers might refuse to move aside for the automobiles of tourists, thinking, "We may be towing carts through the streets, but we have the bomb," or did they care nothing about it at all? Here, an old peasant woman with tiny feet told me that she did not know how to read herself, but all this was for the good of China.

There was no point in searching for a crack in the rock wall of public opinion, and for that matter, what would anyone have dared reply when he was confronted with the frigid dignity of Mr. Shu and the other mandarins who accompanied me? The gratitude of the Chinese people to Mao Tse-tung and the Communist party flowed like the Yellow River racing to the sea, with the same impetus and the same weight of silt.

When we returned to the hotel, I read all the government statements contained in the information bulletin, and as I read I realized that this was exactly what Tsai had told me that afternoon. But when he had been talking to me in the train to Hangchow, about the bombs that China would drop on the Untied States in the event of war, from whom had he obtained his information? Tsai was not a man to let himself be carried away by words or imagination. He said only what he had been authorized to say and never ventured to express a personal opinion. Was it simply a question of the natural boasting of the Chinese, reaching into official circles as it did into all the others? The fact remained that this communiqué read as if Tsai had been its editor.

But if it was not Tsai, who was it? Mao? Mao would certainly not have written: "The atomic bomb is a paper tiger. These celebrated words of Chairman Mao Tse-tung are known to everyone." The secretary general of the party?

The Chinese government is faithful to Marxism-Leninism and to proletarian internationalism. We have confidence in the people. It is man who decides the outcome of a war and not a weapon, no matter what that weapon may be. The destiny of China is decided by the Chinese people, that of the world by the peoples of the entire world, and not by nuclear weapons. China is developing nuclear weapons to defend herself and protect her people against the danger of a nuclear war brought on by the United States.

And, at the end, there was a phrase about man which I could easily believe to have been written by Pierre Jean Jouve or—why not?—the Pope. It was a Christian phrase. Aside from the use of the adjective "nuclear," it might have come from Pascal's *Pensées*. "It is man who creates nuclear weapons. We are certain that it will be man who frees himself from them."

That night the foreign journalists in the hotel gathered in front of the little television screen and Simon focused his camera on it, in the hope of being rewarded with the first pictures of the explosion. The program, which was supposed to be of news, showed us a succession of children and soldiers, anti-imperialist demonstrations in Uruguay, a ping-pong championship and, over and over again, the thickening figure of Mao, the beaming countenance of Mao as an adolescent, and allegories of African peoples freeing themselves from colonialism, sheltered by the protective genius of Mao. Of the atomic explosion, there was nothing. Not even an allusion to it. What would have been inconceivable anywhere else was considered an example of secrecy here. If it can be seen and fixed in a photograph, the greatest event in the world acquires precise dimensions. The reality assumes a specific shape. I had a feeling that this reality would be kept secret as long as might be necessary for it to take on and retain proportions vastly larger than those it actually possessed. The Americans had already announced the news that it was not a very powerful bomb. Later, when the legend had been firmly established, the Chinese might show something which an imagination deprived of any basis of comparison could amplify to a still greater extent. For the moment, the mythology of the government required that the Chinese peeople believe in an explosion of very considerable force.

Days passed, and as the weather grew colder the heavy, padded jackets began to make their appearance in the streets. Khrushchev's removal and the new perspectives it might have opened to the political future of socialism faded into insignificance beside the news of the bomb. We searched everywhere for some technical details, but the Chinese press studiously refrained from giving them and published only the messages of congratulations the government had received. Simon's office telephoned from Paris, demanding that he supply them with a "scoop"—something of a really sensational nature. He had the good fortune to be the only French cameraman in China at the time, so they thought it only natural that he send back film and photographs of the faces of the engineers who had built the bomb, the place where it had been exploded, Mao's expression when he announced the event and the parades that had taken place. When Simon told them that there had been no public demonstrations, no speeches, they were incredulous. But it was true. There had been nothing. This seemed to be a completely blasé people, long accustomed to legend and secure in its faith. What faith? The Chinese people is, by nature, so skeptical that it has never once been torn by the religious wars that are only waged by believers. Was it possible that this same people could attach itself so suddenly to the new dogma without clinging to some secret corner, as a place of refuge in the event that they had once again been deceived? We were forced to recognize that the young generations, brought up in the cult of the revolution, believed firmly in their messiah, and the reading of his works was their confession.

Gathered together in Marcuse's office, we must have resembled a group of ragpickers as we sifted through the rolls of paper from the tickers, seeking some consumable scrap of news. The Japanese had also estimated that the explosion was not of very great force, since the atmospheric vibrations had been slight; they judged it to be a bomb of from twenty-five to fifty pounds, of plutonium or more probably of uranium 235. The cloud of its ashes had passed over their country at a speed of approximately one hundred miles an hour and then was lost over the Pacific. Five minutes after the explosion, however, other vibrations that had not been identified were recorded in India. Had these also been produced by the Chinese bomb or by the earthquake that had taken place at almost the same moment in the north of Japan? Had the bomb been dropped from a plane or had it been exploded on the ground?

Still obsessed by my conversation with Tsai in the train, I suddenly remembered that dummies of a three-stage rocket and a delta-winged plane had figured prominently in the October 1 parade. Could it have been these that Tsai was alluding to when he insisted that China could reply to an American attack? There had been pasteboard models of cabbages and locomotives in the parade, and these certainly existed, so was it not reasonable to assume that models of planes and rockets would not have been shown unless they also existed? What was to prevent the Chinese from possessing both the atomic bomb and the equipment necessary to drop it? The fact that no one knew anything about it? In Tibet and Sinkiang, where no Westerner had set foot since Khrushchev recalled his technicians in 1959, teams of engineers as dedicated as the haulers of carts could have discovered the final solution to the secrets whose beginnings they had been told. China was offering fabulous inducements to foreign scientists and fortunes to any of Chiang Kai-shek's pilots who deserted and brought back a supersonic plane. When it was a matter of serving the cause of socialism, crime no longer existed and money bathed treason in the perfume of supreme loyalty.

The experts of the entire world were already wondering how the Chinese had succeeded, on their first attempt, in manufacturing enriched uranium in place of plutonium. No one had dared advance the hypothesis that they could unhesitatingly undertake expenditures which Europe had renounced. Analysis of the cloud structure had evoked surprise by revealing a highly sophisticated operational system in the bomb, so its performance was no longer questioned, but it was still thought that the great factory required for manufacture of uranium did not exist, since the American U-2 planes, which were capable of photographing an object as small as a milestone, had never brought back any indication of it. A tower in the Sinkiang desert on the bank of Lake Lob Nor, and some nearby construction work, were the only things that had ever been uncovered. I remembered the subterranean galleries Tsai had mentioned to me. Why couldn't this factory or group of factories be underground? What was to prevent the Chinese from assembling millions of laborers and harnessing them to the task of constructing a new Great Wall at the end of a new Long March? I even told myself that, in a discussion concerning the Chinese, the only possible answer to the naïve Western question "Is it possible?" was "It is done." That was Chinese logic.

We put together what information we did obtain as best we could. From Chinese sources, there was nothing but profound silence, as if this were a matter of a eunuch's secret and we had sought to learn the name of the courtesan honored by the emperor the night before or the young man murdered in the bed of the dowager empress. Diplomats attempted to tune in broadcasts from Hong Kong, and tourists arriving from Europe told us that the *New York Times* had provoked great skepticism among specialists by announcing that the first Chinese atomic explosion was a hydrogen bomb. The thesis prevalent in official circles before October 16, 1964, was that China's technical development would permit only an experiment with a rudimentary type of bomb. Such illusions seemed completely shattered now.

I was brought two telegrapms, dispatched from Paris three days earlier, in which *l'Express* had sought to prepare me for the removal of Khrushchev. There was no censorship in China, or at least that is what the government claimed. They simply contented themselves with holding back cables they considered inopportune, and no one could prove that it was the Chinese services that were responsible for the delay in their transmission.

Among our Chinese associates there was a general sense of euphoria. We were scheduled to remain in Peking only for another week and then to go south again to visit Chungking, Changsha and Canton before leaving China at the frontier of Hong Kong. The dwindling time that remained for us to be constantly together made it easier for us to bear each other's presence. A certain relaxation was evident in the bearing of our mandarins. The days passed more rapidly, just as the current of a river accelerates when it approaches a stretch of rapids.

We had begun to feel more at home in Peking and had even acquired little habits of our own. We knew the few words of Chinese that made it possible for us to take a taxi at the door of the Hsin Chiao and journey through the city without our escort, and these brief flights gave us the illusion of possessing a degree of freedom. Brigitte went to see her friends, and they took her with them on their quest of the ancient, buried city. Without realizing it, she was becoming involved in archaeological research. She was in love with the Peking Victor Ségalen and Paul Claudel had known, prepared at any moment to burst into tears at the sight of a family of peasants in rags, carrying their children in their arms, lost in the Avenue of Eternal Peace, but still searching—for what? She was infinitely moved by these people who were condemned to lead the life of worker and soldier ants, and who, without complaining, built canals, walls and underground factories, patiently adding one grain of sand to another.

As a barbarian who had been schooled from one generation to the next in the virtues of forgiveness, the sensitivity of women, the uses of language and the hatred of bloodshed, I was ferociously opposed to this slavelike submission. Brigitte sensed more clearly than I the dignity of that instinct that impelled these masses of slaves along the paths of the only salvation open to them: servitude or death, instead of liberty or death. She saw in this servitude the same impetus that led to the great migrations of people who crossed oceans simply because something deep within them commanded them to do so. She would have liked to be one of them. She loved them for the very drive that frightened me.

The weather became colder and colder, and we were forced to buy some winter clothing. I no longer saw Peking as a smiling city, where the tall, pointed roofs stabbed fitfully through poetic mists. Laid out in the manner of a chessboard, with its enclosing squares, its towers, its kings and queens, its marble lions and warriors, it also possessed a network of underground tunnels which we were not allowed to visit, the once secret preserve of the police, the eunuchs and the concubines, and perhaps the inspiration for the builders of atomic factories. Founded by a prince who planned to set a Mongol stamp on China, this capital had at its heart the palace and its arteries were the temples where the sovereign prayed for divine favors. Everything was artificial. The lakes and canals served for the pleasure and protection of the emperor, the hills thrown up with earth excavated from the lakes and canals sheltered the city from the north winds and evil spirits, the artisans and government servants banded into separate guilds in separate districts of the city.

In the soft light of gray morning, the rooftops of the palaces and the old quarter of Peking seemed to dissolve into an infinite horizon. In a descending line from their peaks, their corners took the form of an arc like that of a Bedouin tent in the desert and then climbed back toward the sky, instead of halting abruptly, like European roofs whose only function is protection from the rain. The art of ornamentation was important here. The cost of such ornamentation had not been considered vain, but among our mandarins I sensed the beginning of contempt for everything that did not provide a ready return. They were already waiting impatiently for the time when blocks of three-story workers' apartments would rise in these districts where the ancient buildings had been swept into oblivion along with the society that lived in them.

Chapter 19

In which the author meets and describes Marshal Chen Yi. In which there is a discussion of the responsibility of the writer, of the liberty enjoyed by everyone in China and of American imperialism, of the atomic bomb and French policy, of the manner in which God has arranged wars and other things, of the considerable progress already made by China and of the forces she represents.

Marxism is not a doctrine, it is a will. For the proletariat and those who belong with them—you—it is the will to know themselves, to feel themselves proletarians and to conquer as such; you must be Marxists not in order to be right but in order to conquer without betraying yourselves. . . .

There is a sense of fatality in Marxism, and an exaltation of the will. Whenever the fatality supersedes the will, I become mistrustful.

—André Malraux, *Man's Fate*

This people simply venerates, without any perplexity. It burns its incense, invokes or repudiates. It awards three or six or nine obeisances. It measures the degree of its respect by the competence, the qualities, the graces that it considers just.

—Victor Ségalen, *Stelas*

On the morning of October 21 Mr. Shu arrived in my room very early and unexpectedly. We were going to meet someone. Who? Mr. Shu could not say and very probably did not know. Someone important? He believed so, and judging by the commotion the news had provoked, I was convinced of it. Mao?

If I were to see Mao and the order of the hierarchy was to be respected, my visit to Mao would only be at the very end of a long series of audiences with others; if I were docile and patient, this visit might crown my two months' stay. To tell the truth, I was beginning to doubt that I would see him. The visitors most highly regarded here were those who sang praises and swallowed indignities. I was not one of these. Sometimes the great man would shake hands of those he could easily impress, sometimes the hero of the Long March would inquire about their health and invite them to his table. Would I have myself resisted if

I had been judged worthy of entering the holy of holies? I often wondered. How can you describe the quirks and weaknesses of so famous a man, or even form an objective judgment of him, when he has shown you marks of friendship and consideration? A politician who could influence the vote of some assembly was important in the political scheme of things. But a writer, an historian, a journalist? The thinly disguised contempt with which the press corps was regarded in China reflected on foreign writers as well.

The automobiles were waiting for us. Tsai was not there. Chen was wearing his high-collared navy blue suit again. After repeated queries, I learned that we were being taken to see the Vice Prime Minister. There were several of these, but this was Chen Yi, the successor to Yeh T'ing as commander of the Fourth Army, the man who had been responsible for the dazzling Shanghai victories in 1949, Marshal of the Red Army and Minister of Foreign Affairs, famous for his animation, impudent language, simplicity and truculence. This was no small fish. Had I misunderstood? Tomorrow, perhaps, we would be seeing the long, sad face of Chou En-lai, and on the day after . . .

With our equipment carefully stowed away, our ties knotted and our shoes shined, we drove away from the hotel. The procession of cars skirted the west wall of the old imperial palace, entered a gate of the Forbidden City and halted. We were expected. Chen Yi appeared, with the president of the Association for Cultural Relations on one side of him and Mr. Wen and Tsai on the other. A cold sun was shining. Rather short and stocky, Chen Yi shook our hands vigorously. We lined up in a row to pose for a photograph and then went into a large, beige reception room with dark woodwork. We were not permitted to make sound recordings, since any statements by Chen Yi could not be considered as commitments of the government. Photographs were permitted. Several stenographers were seated behind us, their ball-point pens held in readiness. Chen and Tsai, looking like eager students, were already leaning over their notebooks, and I placed my own on my knees. The president of the Association and Mr. Wen sat motionless as statues in their chairs, seeming almost in a state of ecstasy. As for Mr. Shu, he was not of a caliber for this meeting and had been forgotten somewhere along the line. The interpreter for the Ministry of Foreign Affairs had a long, sad, thoughtful face, with eyes that glittered behind their glasses.

Within a short time I saw nothing but Chen Yi, his powerful, agile head, modeled by the heavy thumbs of a sculptor, embodying strength. The high forehead, framed by hair cut very short and graying at the temples, dominated the smooth cheeks, the plump neck, the full-lipped mouth and little nose of a well-nourished mandarin. He resembled one of those marble lions guarding the gateways to great residences, with the right paw poised, claws out, on the circumference of the globe.

Q

"Your situation somewhat resembles my own," he began, "with the difference that I was a writer first and a soldier later. When I returned from France, forty years ago, I was also a journalist and worked at making French literature better known in China."

From the three years he had lived in France after the Second World War, he had retained the habit of dropping a few words of French into the conversation: "*Ça va bien?*" or "*C'est comme ça.*" The edge of a scarf protruded above the high collar of his gray jacket. He was in constant movement, first stretching out his short legs and then folding them beneath him, leaning forward in his chair, then throwing himself back or to the side, studying me out of the corner of his eye with a look whose intelligence and guile were not hidden by his dark glasses.

"Well," he said after a booming laugh, "since you are a writer, I am going to begin with a warning to you. Anatole France wrote that literary criticism was an adventure of the mind. If your critics are politically minded, they may expose you to an even greater danger. This book you are planning to write will bear witness to the success or failure of your adventure. Stalin said that the writer is the engineer of the mind. If your book should be malicious, it could only have regrettable consequences. I remember Chairman Mao Tse-tung saying to an old Chinese philosopher that writing could save lives or lose them. So the pen can be mightier than the sword. Certain American writers spend their days heaping insults on China. We are indifferent to them, of course, because their insults are gratuitous. They serve only to deceive the American people. In these last few years Khrushchev's speeches and articles have done a great deal of harm to a great many people, and finally to himself."

"Khrushchev was not a writer," I said.

I put in this word only in an attempt to interrupt him for a moment. He spoke with the speed of a machine gun. Serious at one moment, gentle the next, and then abruptly harsh, his words dominated and submerged everything else. The virtuoso interpreter spoke at the same time as he, his voice keyed an octave lower, underlining the flow of words like the subtitles in a foreign film. Occasionally, to give himself time to catch up with his own thoughts, Chen Yi would cough and utter a vague little clucking sound that resembled mocking laughter.

When he saw that I was taking notes, he said to me: "Don't bother with that. You will have the complete text of our conversation tomorrow." For a time I obeyed his injunction, and then the need for keeping my own record of this monologue overcame me again and I took up my pen. Tomorrow? I was beginning to know the Chinese. I was more pressed for time than they. So I tried to toss a lasso over the shoulders of this galloping marshal. In vain.

In reconstructing the interview, I have placed the thirteen pages of notes I wrote that day side by side with the official text that was supplied to me. I remember very precisely that Chen Yi told me, with a little mocking smile: "Do not be offended if I begin by quoting Mao Tse-tung. As you can see for yourself, there is no portrait of him hanging in here and I did not have it taken away because you were coming. In China everyone is free to have it or not." He had been well informed about me! But I had been struck by the remark itself. It was not included in the official text.

"Khrushchev," he went on, "never ceased spreading lies. We went our own way, without bothering to listen. What we are in favor of is independent thought and reflection. Everyone should be able to analyze facts in his own way. I like the French expression 'laisser faire.' Abstain from intervention and impose yourself on nothing—that is what we believe in. You can see for yourself that China is the freest country there is. Leaving aside the counterrevolutionaries and reactionaries, the Chinese people enjoy the greatest possible liberty. They know what they believe in and respect. If the Chinese people rely on the Communist party and venerate Chairman Mao Tse-tung, they do it of their own free will; no one attempts to impose it on them. To our way of thinking, ideological problems are not resolved by administrative measures. Over a period of many years, Comrade Mao Tse-tung has taught us that such measures would be a mistake that could only result in confusion.

"Now that you are here in China, it is to be hoped that you will seek to know our country as it is and that you will refrain from representing it in too dark a light, which would be no more in accordance with reality than showing it in too favorable a light. We have been working at the building of China for only fifteen years, while the West has had two or three centuries to construct its capitalist industry. The Soviet Union has been building a socialist industry for forty years. Anyone who overestimated the successes China has achieved in this area would be making a mistake. But compared with what existed before, we have certainly achieved great victories, and that is a very important development for our time. However, we will have to work and work hard for thirty, fifty or a hundred years before we can catch up with certain other nations."

At this point Chen Yi said: "We made the Long March. In reality, the Long March was a defeat. We were forced to march because we could no longer stay where we were, but we surmounted those trials." This statement, in the mouth of a Chinese leader, was too remarkable for me to have invented it or to have been mistaken in my hearing of it. Yet it, too, was not included in the official text.

"If, after some success, we are not sufficiently wary of the dangers of presumption and self-satisfaction, it is entirely possible that the next generation will follow the chauvinistic path of other great powers, and that could lead to failure. It is this that Comrade Mao Tse-tung fears, and this is why we instill in our children with their earliest teaching the need of coming to the help of others, and of not infringing on their rights. That is Marxism-Leninism, and it is the thought of Mao Tse-tung."

Driving forward as he now was, at the speed of an express train, I could see no way of halting him.

"President Johnson recently stated, 'We do not want to bury anyone, but neither do we want to be buried.' Fine, but he is lying. The United States buries other people every day. They dare to say that they have only four hundred bases around the world. In reality, they have more than four thousand. The consequence of their determination to bury others is simply that their adversaries are becoming more and more numerous, and they will end by burying themselves."

His mouth open, his expression evoking both American defeat and Chinese victory, he pointed a finger at the red rug, like a Roman emperor demanding the death of a vanquished gladiator.

"The United States claims that the evacuation of their military bases in Southeast Asia would only encourage Chinese aggression. Pure calumny and an even more monstrous lie! China will never be an aggressor nation, but when American imperialism threatens our security we must defend ourselves and help its victims. It was only after the invasion of Korea that we decided that the time had come to resist and send help to Korea. The same thing will be true in Indochina. Neither war nor the atomic bomb will solve these problems."

Here Chen Yi said: "With the atomic bomb, a whole generation may be destroyed, but the second or the third will rise up again to resist and peace will return." This phrase was not included in the official text.

"That is why we proposed the reconvening of the Geneva Conference. Refusing to follow in the footsteps of the United States, General de Gaulle recognized the new China; it was an act of courage that fills me with respect. I have been told that you yourself are opposed to colonialism. I admire such convictions in a French writer and soldier. French policy is wise. To oppose imperialism, it is not sufficient just to resist it yourself. It is also necessary to support smaller neighboring countries, on the condition that such support is disinterested. The yellow peril?" Here his voice struck a note of solemnity. "A lie. But the lies of our enemies are useful to us. We have no complexes. We are proud of our five thousand years of civilization, of the vastness of our country, of its liberation, its industries and its artistic traditions. If we were to indulge in acts of aggression in Southeast Asia, other nations would be right in joining the United States against us. That is not the case, and it will never be the case."

He paused for breath, but only for an instant.

"For forty years Japan repeatedly invaded our country. There is an analogy here with your own situation with Germany. But you possessed a degree of power. We had none. And yet, after the surrender of Japan, we helped that country in its struggle for independence of the United States, and the Japanese were surprised to see that we had no hatred for them. We do not want hatred, because you cannot build a future on it, and it is the future that is important to us. Certainly, we are opposed to the imperialist policy of the United States, but we feel no hatred for the American workers, common people and progressive intellectuals; a traditional friendship has always existed between the peoples of China and the United States.

"What is the basis of your friendship for the United States? They have never treated you as equals. If you believe what they say, they have twice come to your rescue in world wars. But it is your sacrifices and those of others that have permitted them to grow rich. How can anyone dare say that the United States saved France? It is the contrary that is true. It is for this reason that we do not like to hear talk of unilateral aid; all aid is reciprocal. Were Germany and Japan defeated by the United States alone? What a joke! The greatest concentration of wealth in the world is in the hands of the United States. That is where you will find the origin of international tension and war. And that is why we must combat the United States."

This last phrase was not included in the official text, and neither was the comparison between Germany and Japan. His tirade against the United States seemed to release some hidden source of energy in Chen Yi. I listened to him, hypnotized. He waved his arms, his voice rose to a bellow meant to be heard by all the peoples of the world, and then he was abruptly calm again, leaning back in his chair. Brigitte and Simon moved around him, their cameras focusing from every angle.

"As far as the atomic bomb is concerned," he went on, in a voice that was almost muted, "we do not attach too great importance to it. And on this subject, please keep the three following points in mind. We have said it before, we are saying it now, and we will say it again. First, China is determined on her policy of aspiring to peace and the construction of socialism for her 700 million people. For us, it is not simply a matter of possessing nuclear weapons or not possessing them. Next, it is man who manufactures atomic weapons; thus it is man who is capable of eliminating them and not the reverse. Man will always hold first place. He may discover a new and more terrible weapon and the atomic bomb will suddenly become obsolete. Compared with the H bomb, ours is behind the times. You say that we do not attach enough importance to the atomic bombs of others and you consider that a mistake. Well, we prefer man! And finally, the nuclear monopoly must be broken, so that experiments can be halted and stockpiles destroyed. That is why we wanted to possess the atomic bomb. France was right in not signing the tripartite treaty. Its three parties are, in fact, the incarnation of a single country, the United States, which is attempting to assure its nuclear monopoly. Khrushchev was no more than a minor partner, because the United States has never wanted to consider Great Britain and France as equals, let alone China and the U.S.S.R. Khrushchev thought that he could deal with them as an equal. He was mistaken and he lost all his allies."

He stretched out in his chair, stroked his chin and opened his arms wide.

"The policy of President de Gaulle is farsighted, and the United States is becoming more circumspect in its dealings with him. I agree with all his statements. I am a Communist and he is a famous general, and I agree with him. He hopes that all the nations of Latin America will become independent and rid themselves of the influence of the United States—a very reasonable position."

"Is there a possibility that you will invite de Gaulle to come to China?" I asked.

He rested his head on his fist and let out a series of vague "ah's."

"We might perhaps anticipate General de Gaulle and visit him first, and then he would come here later, which would seem to be more in keeping with protocol. That is a personal point of view which I could submit to my government. Although it is true that the French do not know China very well, the reverse is also true."

He had been talking for an hour and a half, and now, quite suddenly, he paused and sighed. I pounced on the opening.

"Now that you have the atomic bomb," I said, "a spark would suffice to bring on a war between you and the United States. Wouldn't you hesitate at the prospect of such a conflict?"

"We will never renounce our right to defend ourselves, and we fear nothing. Thirteen hundred years ago, under the T'ang dynasty, China went through a similar experience. At that time she had a 160 million inhabitants, and after ten years of war she was reduced to forty million. Bah! She recovered. We are opposed to any unjust war, but we will never hesitate before a just war, no matter whether the situation is conventional or nuclear. We shall never retreat from that. But think how far removed we are from atomic techniques and think of the mass of arms stockpiled in other countries. I do not believe in God, but God has arranged things very well, since the atomic weapon is indiscriminate in its manner of distributing death. That is why it is impossible to launch a war with a few bombs. In a nuclear war all adversaries would be eliminated. And the American millionaires are more concerned for their lives than we are. Those who possess the most bombs are the most fearful. I do not think that they will dare bring on a war. On the sixth of August every year, on the anniversary of Hiroshima, they are cursed by all the peoples of the world."

He embarked on a new monologue concerned with Chou En-lai's recent proposal for a conference to discuss the destruction of atomic weapons. He talked to me about the assassination of President Kennedy, about peaceful coexistence and the American Negro. "Why are twenty million Negroes opposed to the policies of the United States? Because they are treated in an inhuman manner. The inquest into Kennedy's assassination was a farce." He leaped from one subject to another, returning periodically to his principal theme, singing the praises of peace, evoking his friends Dean Rusk and Averell Harriman, who could not eat breakfast without insulting China. Finally, he used statistics of the industrial power of the United States as a means of underlining their moral weakness.

"The President of the United States interrupts his vacations for any major development. We are not so nervous; I have just been away for a few days' rest in the country myself. In China we do not get so upset by such developments. As for Johnson, he does not like me and I feel exactly the same way about him, but he will be re-elected."

This time I pounced on the opportunity provided by a momentary burst of laughter to ask him if China was capable of going on with the construction of her nuclear armament, of working for the development of her own country and at the same time assisting the underdeveloped peoples.

"Yes," he said. "We are. We will never sacrifice the betterment of the standard of living of the Chinese people to nuclear armaments, but, thanks to the sacrifices and the unity of the Chinese people, we can attain the summits of science and technology and still continue to help oppressed nations. We were forced to solve the problem of the use of oxygen in the manufacture of steel. That is now accomplished. Our entire industry must be reconverted, and for that we must spend a great deal of money. Some of the French commentaries regarding our atomic explosion seemed reasonable to us. Little by little, we are going to become a great industrial power, but we will need a few decades. A Japanese friend told me that the standard of living of the Chinese people is already higher than that of the Japanese. Such a thing must be judged by the situation and not by wages. We are still living in cramped quarters, but the rents are laughable. Our prices have been stable for fifteen years, and the danger of unemployment does not exist. When I returned to my native country after the liberation, I was no longer recognized by anyone, except by name. And by the same token, I no longer recognized anything; there was electricity in the countryside outside the cities, I saw bicycles, watches, cameras. At one time the landlords themselves could not have owned such things. With the exception of a handful of opponents who are still dreaming of their past wealth and glory, the whole people is behind us. And since that is true, what force is capable of breaking us?"

He was happy, he was gratified by these two hours he had spent with me.

"You will say all that? Then you will have done good work for friendship between China and France. *Ça va?*"

The interpreter drew a deep breath and smiled. He was proud to serve so great a man. Chen Yi burst out laughing. The stenographers raised their heads and wrinkled their noses in amusement. I put away my pen. Glowing with the vigor of his sixty-four years, the marshal cleared his throat and swallowed the contents of his pot of tea. Like Tsai, like Professor Hou and the dock workers of Shanghai, he was no more than an atom in eternal China, one simple human unit among the 700 million men whose master was Mao Tse-tung. When we returned to the hotel, I sat down to type out my cable.

I worked without any feeling of joy, wondering where I was going and what I would be bringing home from this hunt. I was oppressed by a feeling that my book and my study of China had eluded me, that I was missing out on everything. As a sort of finale to our stay in Peking, I decided to invite our mandarins to dine with us at the Canard Laqué, and asked Mr. Shu to make the arrangements with the restaurant. In anything concerning food, he could be trusted. The evening was a great success.

Chapter 20

In which the author arrives in Chungking, recalls his meeting with Marshal Chu Teh and endeavors to establish good relations with his hosts. In which he discovers the misery of this city and refuses to condemn American atrocities because Chiang Kai-shek's responsibility seems greater to him. In which the American General Stilwell is revealed as a true friend of the Chinese people and condemns the vanity and dishonesty of Chiang Kai-shek and of the Soong family. In which the author is taken to a regional spa, so that he will not see the harshness of peasant life. How this gloomy Sunday ends amid the lightning flashes of a stormy banquet.

It is very true that I have no wealth,
But I have always been able to drink my fill,
I am happy that the harvest is ripening
And I bless the work of the All-Powerful.

—WEI YING-WU, ninth century A.D.

At present, the generalissimo is losing the support of China. His orders are not carried out. He has difficulty collecting enough food for his immense army and bureaucracy. From top to bottom, the structure of his government is riddled with open corruption. . . . He knows that he cannot conquer the Communists without foreign aid. Thus he will do everything he can to force us to give him active assistance, which would risk involving us not only in a civil war in China, but also in a conflict with Russia. . . . The Communists will be the dominant power in China in a few years. . . . The destiny of China is in their hands, not in those of Chiang Kai-shek.

—Extract from a report of the advisers to American Ambassador Clarence Gauss in Chungking, dispatched to the State Department, 1942

Ever since our arrival in China, we had been dreaming of Chungking and the province of Szechwan. This, traditionally, was the land of abundance.

The airport was no longer situated in the city itself, between the precipitous cliffs that flanked the Yangtze, but on the other side of this rocky promontory. The autumn harvest was beginning, and through the windows of our automobiles we could see the peasants trotting along pathways through the fields, the poles on their shoulders laden with buckets of sweet potatoes, rice and vegetables, some of them towing cartloads of wood or almost hidden beneath vast bales of straw. They lived in straw-roofed houses scattered over the steep hills along the way. In the ravines water buffaloes plowed the flooded rice fields. Teams of workers with rollers and loads of stone were filling in the holes aong the embankments of the roads that climbed through the hills. Troops of schoolchildren, with packs on their backs and wearing great straw hats that sheltered them from both the sun and rain, were returning from the outlying country where they had camped for several days, planting trees. They marched in companies, with the flag bearers in the lead.

The weather was mild. I would have liked to stop for a while, to see at last at close hand the peasants who had made China into one enormous factory for the manufacture of rice and vegetables. But the idea would have been misinterpreted by our mandarins and those who had come to welcome us, and I did not wish to irritate them further. I consoled myself with the thought that when we came back over this same route I could ask to be allowed to take photographs. The week that still remained of our stay in the People's China might perhaps bring me a revelation of what I had come here to find. I was like the member of a losing team, hoping that the last minutes of play could still bring victory.

Although he had not been judged worthy of being presented to God the Father, our interview with Marshal Chen Yi had covered us with reflected glory, and Marshal Chu Teh had been practically lifted from his deathbed so that he might be shown to us. A broad smile curled the lips of his heavy face. His voice resembled the uncertain murmurings of a child. He had nothing to say to me beyond the customary banalities, and since I had given my word not to ask him questions about the past, there was nothing for me to do but stare at the face of the man who had brought victory to Mao's forces: a full moon of a head with a little uncrowned forehead, a thick rope of eyebrows resembling the paint of a clown, a crushed and flattened nose. Chu Teh was not beautiful, but a certain grandeur emerged from his very ugliness, like the weatherbeaten pride of an old peasant whose years have been spent plowing the land, climbing the hills and observing the sky. In his way, Chu Teh the inflexible was China itself and worthy of every respect. He was also, because of his position in life, his physical makeup, his devotion to the cause of his masters, his determination in battle, his natural taciturnity and his fits of rage, a slave who had resolved to fight to the death. I was well aware of this as I saluted this leader of slaves whose fidelity had carried him to one of the highest posts in the regime.

A time came when there was only silence between us. I looked at Chu

Teh, waiting for some breath of life to pass the motionless lips, still creased with the fixed smile of friendship. He squinted his tiny eyes, so deeply set beneath the arching eyebrows that they were almost invisible, and remained silent. Age? Fatigue? The mandarins who accompanied us kept their own discreet silence. I no longer recall how I managed to extricate myself from this desert of silence, what path I took to put an end to the meeting with this legendary shadow and, as the saying goes, "get myself out of this." But surely I had no cause to complain. I had seen some of the leaders. The promises had been kept.

We had decided, on both sides, to adopt the *modus vivendi* of civilized people for our last days together. Don't bother me and I won't bother you. Show us a few little things and we will deluge you with compliments. I was not going to ask to see the one of five atomic reactors supplied by Russia that was in Chungking, because I would have been refused, but if I visited the erstwhile seat of Chiang Kai-shek's government, if we could pass a morning or an afternoon on a junk on the river, and if I could talk with some of the witnesses to the conference Mao Tse-tung had had here with Chiang Kai-shek in 1945, I would consider myself satisfied.

We were scheduled to leave Chungking two days later, at dawn. If we wanted to see anything at all, we would have to move fast. The hotel was new and sumptuous, adjoining the festival hall, whose green dome dominated the city. By the time we arrived, there was barely an hour of daylight left, so I asked if the automobiles could take Simon and Brigitte to photograph the river and the street scenes while I discussed the schedule for the next day. A false cordiality reigned. The vice president of the Association who had come to meet us at the airport attempted to conceal his mistrust beneath an affected joviality. They did not like to show Chungking to foreigners, except perhaps for visiting members of foreign governments who would be easy to keep on a leash. No Western journalist had set foot in the city for a long time. Things had been carefully arranged so that our stay would be of short duration, but at least we were here, and in my surprise at the effort that was being made to be agreeable to us, I went out of my way to express our pleasure and gratitude. I declined the ritual offer of a visit to the factories, and accepted the proposal of a people's commune for the morning and the old American base for the afternoon of the following day. I did not, however, achieve my goal of living for a few hours with the crew of one of the junks.

Night was falling and I asked if I could be taken to a spot from which I would have a panoramic view of the city. This was perfectly agreeable.

The automobiles raced at full speed through a human torrent that rolled down the streets like the aftermath of a cataclysm. On the steep slopes there was almost nothing in view but handcarts, and only the coolies still used the narrow alleys of the old quarters, tumbling down to the river banks in uneven flights of steps.

Built at the confluence where the furious waters of the Kialing River hurled themselves into the Yangtze in a long curving S, the smoke-shrouded city started on the river banks, then climbed away from them, covered the black hills with a jungle of houses and finally died out at the foot of the mountains that studded the horizon. Four million people live here, in wooden houses built almost on top of each other and all seeming on the point of collapse. The river was thick with motorboats and junks, and when they touched the shore the crowd loaded its baskets, cases and sacks of merchandise on their shoulders and began the climb toward the cliffs above, moving with a kind of feverish intensity that reminded me of Tsinan. Every man and woman coming up from the quays or going down to them was bent beneath the weight of some burden, and their faces bore the stamp of a fatigue to which our mandarins paid no attention. "Before . . ." they told me. Yes, before, it had been worse; a few archaic buses threaded their way through the city, and today there were hundreds of new ones; before, there were no trees and now they were growing everywhere; before, the harvests were always poor.

The shriek of the ships' sirens bounced in echo from cliff to cliff. The junks slipped out into the current, allowed themselves to be carried along for a time, then maneuvered into the main stream with long sweeps, white foam churning in their wake. After plunging down from the mountains of Tibet, through the gorges the Red Army had crossed on the Long March, the river rolled through here like molten copper.

On my return to the hotel, I found Simon and his crew in a state of great agitation. Their escort had tried to prevent them from photograph-ing any evidence of misery in the streets of Chungking, which was the equivalent of a pure and simple prohibition against photographing anything at all. They had continued nonetheless, and the panic that was now evident among our hosts convinced me once again that they mistrusted us.

"You came here to study the history of the revolution," I was told. "Why should you be interested in things that have nothing to do with the history of the revolution?"

"Perhaps no one has told you that the leaders of your revolution refused to answer my questions," I replied, "and that, as a result, we were forced to alter our original plans and concentrate on present-day China. Almost no one in France knows anything about Chungking, so why should you not let us see it?"

"In that case, why did you refuse to visit a modern factory?"

"Because we have already seen them," I said. "We are going with you tomorrow to one of the people's communes. We are also quite prepared to film the dams you are building, your atomic reactors and your airplane factories."

"Those are strategic objectives."

I refused to discuss the subject any further and we parted coolly.

The next morning the atmosphere had not improved. We could not go to the people's commune because the rain that had fallen during the night had made the roads impassable.

"That's just a pretext," Simon said. "The roads are quite good."

"What good does it do to ask me what I want?" I asked. "It would be simpler if you just decided on our program yourselves."

The discussion went on for quite some time. They were torn between the desire to spare us any unpleasantness and the determination to hide anything they did not want us to see. If it was true that the downpour of the night before had flooded the country roads, how could they ask us to walk in the mud without dishonoring themselves and leaving us with something less than a joyous image of China? The simplest solution would have been to say: "To prove that we really want to respect your wishes, we will try to get to the people's commune. You will see for yourself that it is impossible, and that we will have to postpone it until this afternoon." As a substitute for the commune, it was suggested that we go to a museum and a monument to the martyrs. It apparently did not occur to any of our mandarins to say to himself: "Our honored French guests may have already had enough of these. Our martyrs are not theirs, and the sight of too many of our family photographs may become boring to them."

In spite of his promise to discuss any differences between us the instant they arose, my friend Tsai remained silent, taking refuge behind the wall of complications. He had not forgotten what he had promised; it was simply that he did not consider the promise binding in case of crisis. As for the vice president of the Chungking Association, his nervousness was readily apparent from the way his tongue tripped over every other word. In the end I said, "Take us wherever you like."

We got into the automobiles and drove out into the suburbs. Every inch of land was cultivated. The peasants working on the hills were wearing a strange sort of covering, fashioned from palm leaves, which protected them from the weather but also made them look like ostriches. Flocks of children with red scarves at their throats were climbing up to the old American base, carrying flags and funeral wreaths. It was Sunday. My persistent naïveté led me to believe that we were going to be shown what had once been the headquarters of Sino-American cooperation, and that someone would say, "This was General Stilwell's office, and this was General Wedemeyer's." But no. This was the spot where the Americans had tortured the Chinese people and trained the spies they sent into Communist territory. Every one of the buildings was overflowing with damning documents, with weapons and instruments of torture. Our guide stopped in front of the displays, and Mr. Shu, in his most pompous tones, translated the story of the heroism of the resistance and the abominations of imperialism.

I wondered if Mr. Shu had had a bad night. He sweated, stammered, belched, became entangled in his own words and came out at last with the most ridiculous nonsense. The morning was almost gone. Just when we thought we had finished with this, we were led to the other side of the camp, to see the prison. This prison did not resemble the model we had been shown. It had been converted into a wax museum of horrors. One large room contained a "reconstruction" of a whole series of scenes in which blood-splattered American butchers were engaged in breaking limbs, cutting throats, crushing windpipes, tearing out fingernails and peeling the skin from women's breasts. We passed from here into a courtyard and were asked if we would like to see the cells. It was at this point that I realized I could stand no more and insisted on returning to my automobile. The faces of our hosts registered limitless astonishment. What? People came from all over China to admire this display, the youth of the city marched reverently past these masterpieces, and I did not want to pause and mediate in a place that was a monument to courage?

I replied that I had not come to Chungking for that purpose, that I understood their hatred for the Americans but that I did not share it; that we had suffered a great deal from the Germans and had become their allies, that such a development might yet occur with the Chinese and Americans and that I sincerely hoped it would. (At that time the Americans had not begun their bombing raids on North Vietnam.)

"It is precisely because hundreds of thousands of Frenchmen and millions of Jews experienced the horrors of concentration and extermination camps that the sight of such horrors is no longer bearable to me. You seem to delight in it. That is not true of me; I don't have the heart for it. You can look at this with dry eyes, and children come to see it as though it were an exhibition of the most beautiful agricultural products of the province. My reactions are not the same as yours. Perhaps the Americans did commit these crimes against you. Ever since my arrival in China, you have never ceased calling them to my attention, as if you were waiting for me to condemn them. I condemn crime, even when it is my own country that commits it, but I will not condemn the Americans. I can't help it if for that reason you consider me an abominable imperialist. I accept the accusation and, if necessary, would even lay claim to the title.

"To my way of thinking, Chiang Kai-shek, about whom you say nothing, bears a far greater share of responsibility than the Americans.

The Americans would have done nothing without his agreement, but you avoid mentioning that. In my country it is more difficult to obtain a pardon. We execute our traitors. We do not offer them high government posts, as you have done with Chiang Kai-shek. You have reasons which I know nothing about. I have my own reasons for detesting Chiang Kai-shek. My judgment of him, in fact, is less indulgent than yours, but you stick to yours and leave me to mine. As far as I am concerned, that is enough."

Consternation reigned again. The vice president's mouth closed like a trap, and Tsai glared at me sullenly. Decidedly, I was an impossible man.

With Nanking abandoned to the Japanese, Chiang Kai-shek had moved the seat of the Chinese government to Chungking in 1938. Little by little, the ancient city, teeming with flies and reeking with the odors of centuries, began to crack beneath the pressure from the east. And then came the bombs. In the midst of this desolation, the refugees from Shanghai gave lavish dinner parties, bought wives and set about making overnight fortunes. Japanese planes based in Hankow were free to strike wherever they pleased, and soon the entire region was seized with panic. A tubful of water fetched from the river cost five dollars.

Chiang Kai-shek based his hopes of defeating the Japanese on an extension of the war to the rest of the world. On December 7, 1941, the attack on Pearl Harbor brought the United States into the conflict. Two months later the first American planes to navigate the stormy passage "over the hump" landed in Kunming, capital of the province of Yünnan and center of the traffic in opium, weapons, money and supplies for Chiang Kai-shek. The generalissimo was still the uncontested idol of China. The new Fourth Army of the Communists had been almost completely wiped out in an ambush, Yeh T'ing was a prisoner, and Mao remained sealed up in the city of Yenan, blockaded by the armed forces of the Kuomintang. The first American G.I.'s to witness the filth and horror of the war in China drowned their dismay in whiskey and were attacked by syphilis and amoebic dysentery. They baptized the Chinese "slope-headed bastards." General Joseph Warren Stilwell was named Chief of Staff to Chiang Kai-shek, and placed in charge of operations against the Japanese in the north of Burma.

Stilwell was an outspoken soldier, almost blind as a result of a wound in the left eye. He had been stationed in China for thirteen years after the First World War, spoke the mandarin dialect and did not know how to camouflage the truth. In his battered old DC-3, he flew tirelessly back and forth between New Delhi and Chungking, driving and inspiring his weary troops, imposing discipline and zeal, and constantly clashing with the corrupt generals of the Kuomintang, with the generalissimo, whom he nicknamed "Peanuts," and with Madamissima whom he called "Madame the Empress."

The accusation that the Americans had come to China in 1942 to torture and destroy the Communists seemed to me both clumsy and ridiculous. For two years Stilwell demanded that he be allowed to visit Yenan, that the Communists be brought into the Chinese government and that active cooperation be established between his armies and those of the only leaders he admired. The real adversary of the Reds was Chiang Kai-shek. So why were they lying to me now? Pure chauvinism? To place the burden of all the crimes on the shoulder of the foreigner? Or because this thesis reflected the natural resentment of the regime toward an America which continued, stupidly, to support Chiang Kai-shek?

In wartime Chungking, where it was almost impossible for anyone to know his true friends, Stilwell, who was known to his troops as "Vinegar Joe," was forced to wage war against "Peanuts" almost as strenuously as against the Japanese. Chiang Kai-shek lived in awe of him. Sparing no one, himself less than anyone else, sharing the rations of his men, believing in military honor and the dignity of his mission, he denounced the corruption around him in the harshest terms: the Chinese generals insisted that the payroll for their divisions must pass through their hands, they dealt illicitly in gasoline, opium, equipment and even personnel, and lived far from the front lines. Stilwell observed them reviewing their troops, with orderlies leading their horses by a long tether. "Through a series of clever maneuvers," he wrote furiously, "we have been put in the position of supporting this rotting regime and glorifying its representative, the omniscient, the great patriot and soldier: Peanuts! What we should do is to shoot the generalissimo." At a time when country girls were selling themselves for a dozen eggs, when an inflation exploited by his closest associates was destroying the nation's economy, Chiang Kai-shek's ambition was to extract from Roosevelt a billion dollars which would be administered—and digested —by his Soong in-laws.

Gruff, grumbling, indignant at the military incompetence and dishonesty of Chiang Kai-shek, Stilwell wanted to put an end to the blockade of Yenan. Since it was "the Empress" and her sister, the wife of Finance Minister H. H. Kung and the most venal of the Soong sisters, who directed the policies of the government, he thought it prudent to attempt to remain in their good graces. They called him "Uncle Joe" and made a point of presenting him with a cake for his birthday.

Under Stilwell's persistent hammering, the myth of the great man and hero began to collapse. Power had rid Chiang Kai-shek of some of his early luster and laid bare his limitless vanity. Now it was becoming evident that he was no more than the gaunt and shrunken leader of a new dynasty, the dynasty of the Chiangs and the Soongs. His hatred for Mao had its roots in the feelings any tyrant might nurse toward a possible usurper. No one had ever dared speak the everyday language of men to the rulers of China. Like the emperors before him, Chiang Kai-shek found it perfectly normal that his effigy should be displayed everywhere. No one dared venture an opinion, even on so minor a matter as the melon served for luncheon, without first knowing his. Madamissima herself let it be known that she faced enormous problems whenever she had to give him unpleasant news. He was conscious of the corruption that surrounded him, but lacked the courage to root it out.

I found no trace anywhere of the portrait Stilwell had drawn of him, although it is certainly the most savage in existence: bigoted, sterile, of unstable mind, so lacking in self-control that he had been known to throw a teapot at the head of the person he was talking to, an Old Testament Christian ruling by grace of the secret police and refusing to be disturbed at his nightly prayer, a stubborn jackass and God incarnate, possessed of an unbridled passion for glory. I was outraged by the fact that he should still be spared because he was Chinese, and the Americans accused of every imaginable crime because they were foreigners. I remembered that the courageous General Stilwell had succeeded in having his views relayed to the generalissimo by Roosevelt himself, in a long telegram which Stilwell compared to red-hot steel. Less than a month later he was removed from his post. As a gesture of appeasement, Chiang Kai-shek offered him the highest Chinese military decoration and Stilwell replied with an obscenity. I liked General Stilwell. Basically, it was him I was defending more than the Americans.

In deafening silence, we were taken to the buildings on Red Rock where the representatives of the Communist party had lived during periods of cooperation with the Kuomintang. When, after the bombs on Hiroshima and Nagasaki, Japan finally signed an unconditional surrender, the Communists under Chu Teh disregarded Chiang Kai-shek's orders and entered Manchuria to receive the Japanese capitulation. In an attempt to patch things up, Ambassador Patrick Hurley flew to Yenan, where Mao, who was now married to a film actress, kept a portrait of Chiang Kai-shek on his work table. Photographs taken at the Chungking airport, where Mao had been brought to meet Chiang, showed Mao in a colonist's pith helmet, a trifle dumfounded, ironic and polite. Hurley gave a dinner that evening. A meeting such as this could excite the imagination. I hoped that I would be shown the film archives, but I was not judged worthy to see them. The beginning of the civil war dates from the failure of these talks. But at that time no one imagined that the war would result in a Communist victory.

The room occupied by Comrade Mao Tse-tung at Red Rock was built

R

directly against the hill, to insure his safety from any chance burst of gunfire, and still contained the marks of his presence, preserved as though they were holy relics: the little bedside rug on which his naked feet had stood, the table on which he had written his poem, "The Snow," after his first flight in a plane, the cane chair on which he had sat his precious rump, the bed in which he had slept, the round table in the corridor where he took his meals with Chou En-lai, Lin Piao and Tung Pi-wu. The glass for his toothbrush was missing, but not the fan that had stirred up air for the precious lungs. On the heights surrounding the Communist monastery, we were shown the emplacements from which observers and the machine gun crews kept the sanctuary under constant surveillance. At the entrance to the monastery itself, children were seated in a circle, singing "Socialism Is Marvelous" and the hymn to the Chairman.

We drove through the suburban area again, and this time I insisted on stopping to photograph Chungking from a section of the boulevard which looked down on the entire city. They did not dare refuse, but they made the work as difficult as possible, inventing a thousand reasons why we should hurry. I wondered if they thought we were planning to sell the pictures to the CIA. Mr. Chen made no bones of his disapproval, and even went so far as to tell Brigitte that ever since our stay in Nanking he had been aware of the kind of picture she wanted to carry home. He was mistaken, as usual. Brigitte was like all the rest of us. Weary of trying to photograph the streets of a city through the window of a speeding automobile, she was taking her revenge by snapping everything that passed within range of her camera. For my part, so long as I was forced to look at only those things they wanted me to see, I reacted by giving free rein to my critical sense, and each new subterfuge to limit or direct it provided me with a new reason for refusing to conform to their rules.

I looked around, coldly and critically, at this China they described to us as liberal and happy, and saw a vast, miserable segment of humanity working itself to death. Today was Sunday, but just like every other day old men and children were breaking stones in the quarries, other old men and children were carting them away, and new battalions of Young Pioneers were marching off into the countryside, their packs on their backs, to plant new trees. It would have been so simple to say to us: "You are going to see our people at work on Sunday. We will hide nothing from you, because you are friends. You will probably be startled by the effort required of us simply to avoid extinction, and it is true that if we were to stop for a single day life would pass us by. Bear that in mind, but bear in mind also the courage displayed by so many men and women who refuse to allow their country to fall back to the standards of former years. This is still slavery, but it is a slavery we consent to in order to insure our country's freedom. Before, we were oppressed by foreigners and the rich and powerful. Judge for yourselves. Do not forget that, although we are poor, we refuse to wear the yoke of others." But that would have been too simple, and they never spoke to us in such terms. A Chinese word for simplicity—'*chien-tan*'—could be formed, but it does not, in fact, exist.

We crossed the river on a ferry, and after a long drive through a countryside peopled with sweating hordes of workers and farmers, we arrived at a pleasant little watering spot that resembled one of the smaller spas of Europe. This is the China that might have inspired us, but it was our misfortune that our interests lay elsewhere, and that our experience had led us to be wary of everything that delighted our companions.

Our luncheon could not have been more grim if we had been Americans. The Chinese did not even take the trouble to speak to us, and conversed among themselves as if we did not exist. The vice president lifted his glass to me, but did not drink, and Tsai did the same thing, his face rigidly set in an expression of reproval. For a moment I was tempted to get up and leave, but such a display would have been no better understood than my refusal to heap insults on the Americans. On our side of the table, we followed their example and discussed our ideas and plans without bothering to go through the interpreter. It was a one-sided game, however, because Mr. Shu was listening to every word we said. The meal itself was highly spiced and flavored with ginger, and this, at least, pleased me and made me feel somewhat closer to Mao. I shared his taste for pepper and spicy seasonings. The sauces of minced onion and soya and the crusty flesh of the fish had a delightful savor.

We had expected to leave for the people's commune very shortly after lunch, but we realized that our mandarins wanted to linger on and enjoy the pleasures of this spot. Tsai went into a cabin constructed around one of the natural warm springs, and sent word to us that he was planning a siesta. There was nothing left for us but to do the same. The Chinese were only too eager to obtain rooms where we, too, could rest. During the time we were thus walled in, there was no chance that we might see something they did not wish us to see. Since our impatience made sleep impossible and we had to pass the time somehow, Orthion and I bathed in the springs.

When I went back to the lobby of the little hotel, Brigitte was sitting on a bench just outside the door, worried about the waste of time and the waning, unused light she needed for her photographs. Suddenly her face was bathed in tears.

"They are keeping me from doing my work," she said.

"It's their way," I said. "Forgive them."

I envied her for being able to give way to her frustration and unhappiness. At the same time my own, which could not be released in a flow of tears, grew more intense. In an attempt to comfort her, I led her off through the park, where groups of office workers were strolling with their families. Others were paddling about in a swimming pool. We walked down to the river bank, where an old man was washing his basketful of vegetables. The strollers on a little nearby bridge paused to stare at us in astonishment. What was the point in becoming angry? Our nerves and emotions were strained by this inactivity, but we were in the hands of others, who were stronger than we.

Brigitte said, "Why do they pretend to help us and understand us, when it is not true? Why do they avoid showing us the sweat and the tears of the people?" I could only answer, sadly, "Because they are Chinese." No one in our entire crew had come here with the idea of disparaging them. No one of us harbored any evil intent toward them, and yet all their declarations of friendship concealed an indiscriminate and irrational mistrust of the hated Occident of which we were a part.

Mr. Tsai finally reappeared on the scene, and we returned to our automobiles, walking together yet apart, in an oppressive silence. Simon was looking for anything that might form a poetic image on the screen. We came to a pond, formed by an obstruction in the river, where thousands of ducks were gathered, and I asked to stop. But how could we film the ducks without the keeper, who was carefully hidden from us because they had decided that he was too poor? We were told that making films of the keeper would have been an invasion of his privacy. To show how he lived in his hut of plaited straw, how he moved his flock from rice field to rice field, and how his ducks fed on grains of rice, tadpoles and tiny fish would have been to attach too much importance to a profession whose continued existence in China they did not want to admit. We left, as silently and awkwardly as we had arrived. Through the window of the automobile, Brigitte continued to photograph the hod carriers and workers in the field, and Mr. Chen continued to fume.

When we arrived at the people's commune, we were shown the pumping units that carried the water into storage basins from which it was channeled out through enormous fields of vegetables. Twenty-four thousand men and women worked here, in an area of almost four thousand acres, and produced six thousand pounds of vegetables each month, or a total of eighteen tons per acre, an incredible figure; but there were at least three harvests every year, and sometimes five, of potatoes, spinach, lettuce and other greens, eggplant and tomatoes. The rice fields yielded only seven hundred pounds of rice per month, or approximately 260 pounds per acre in two harvests a year. The commune also supported fourteen thousand hogs and 150 cows, each of which produced almost a ton of milk per year.

There is no winter frost in Chungking. Summer is a time of tropical heat, from which one can find protection in the city, but not in the surrounding countryside, where the struggle for life assumes nightmare proportions. In ranks of twenty, fifty or a hundred, the peasants turn each clod of earth, pulverizing it with their pickaxes and fertilizing it with manure and sweat. Everywhere we looked, from the swampy banks of the river to the crest of the hills, sometimes on sixty-degree slopes, there were cultivated fields, divided only by the narrow lines of pathways where women trotted silently, their balancing poles on their shoulders. The hills were dotted with huts with earth walls and straw roofs, better suited to the shelter of cattle than men. In the humidity of the declining day, in this countryside where everything that grew served only to appease hunger and not to give pleasure, where even the vegetables never dared to rest, there was an overpowering sense of determination, of implacable destiny: a man was born here with the knowledge that he would never leave. The children grew up, became beasts of burden, produced new children, labored from dawn to dusk, hoping only that someday they might hang on their walls a certificate of merit from the party, and eventually fertilize the fields with their own bodies.

Mr. Shu had been aware of this well before I had, in all the time he had been guiding foreigners through China and spending his month of vacation in one of the people's communes. Who, in his place, would not have preferred the post of an interpreter, or even, if worst came to worst, of a bootblack or waiter in a restaurant to that of a peasant with a four-toothed hoe and a bucket of manure? In Chungking there were four million people whose lives depended on the rhythm of work in these fields. No one was rich, but no one was any longer forced to beg in order to live. Six hundred million peasants were encompassed in a poverty from which there was no escape except through the loophole offered by the bureaucracy.

I understood why Professor Hou, in the University of Peking, had been so unsparing in his praise of the regime, and why he had taught his granddaughter to say "Long live Chairman Mao" before she had learned "papa." For myself, if I had been born a peasant in the province of Szechwan, I do not know what might have become of the fine conscience instilled in me by my parents and my teachers. Weighed down with balancing poles throughout the year, what conscience could resist the temptation to lie, to conform?

The dinner to which we were invited that night was stormy. We were greeted by another vice president—God knows how many the Association numbers. Beneath his elegant, well-tailored exterior, and his air of a self-assured, vaguely mistrustful pedant, he had a shrewd and supple sense of words. He stood up and proposed a toast, in ten words. I answered him in twenty phrases. I said that, thus far on our journey, we had learned more about museums than about the Chinese people, but from what we had seen today we had learned enough—that our admiration for their courage and endurance was beyond measure, and we would now know how to make the necessary distinction between museums and people in the fields. I added that I found it difficult to touch the feast provided for us when I thought of those workers in the fields. Our fine rooms with their private baths, our splendid meals, all the delicacies with which their friendship surrounded us could not allow us to forget the sacrifices to which the Chinese people consented for the grandeur of the nation as a whole. I raised my glass to the Chinese people.

This little speech produced the expected effect. Tension increased and service quickened. Conversation turned back to the incident that morning at the wax museum. They could not understand our mania for photographing everything in sight, and yet not museum exhibits. I used the words I had used so many times before with my friend Tsai: to Westerners such as ourselves, museums were not a source of great inspiration. We were tired of photographing statues and other photographs. We far preferred what could be seen on the other side of the walls. As for the atrocities of the Americans, what was the point in discussing them again and again? I was here, not to condemn the Americans, but to understand the Chinese. In the discord that separates peoples, the role of an intercessor was occasionally of some use. I repeated my feeling that Chiang Kai-shek, whom they seemed prepared to forgive, was more guilty in my eyes than the Americans.

At one moment, when we were excluded from the conversation, I committed the sin of asking Mr. Shu to translate what the gentlemen were saying, and then made a few ironic comments to Brigitte. I could not but be disappointed at the trouble that had been taken to deprive me of the only favor I had begged for: to talk with the men who had made the revolution, or, if these great men refused to see me, to talk with some of the small fish on whom they fed. I understood why they might not want to show me the places where Chiang Kai-shek had lived, or the eagle's nest Stilwell had termed "Berchtesgaden Huang-han," to which he retired every night. I understood why they had neglected to tell me that he crossed the river on a high-speed cutter, and that sometimes, in a very gentle voice, he sang the old songs of China with Madamissima.

Chungking drew its breath of life from the Yangtze. The thought of meeting and conversing with a family that lived and worked on a junk in that river did not strike me as absurd, but it was refused to us under all sorts of pretexts, as if we risked being attacked by cholera. Was there any reason to lie, the way our hosts lied to us? In the province of Szechwan both men and women bowed down beneath the weight of slavery, their eyes saw nothing but the earth, their bodies were deformed, their shoulders knotted with muscles that provided their only resistance to the weight of the balancing pole or the pressure of the harness. There was grandeur in these breakers of stone, these porters of manure. Now they possessed an atom bomb. My anger centered on those who seemed to be ashamed of them.

We parted company coolly, and my friends and I went back to our rooms, thinking of nothing but our departure. Our suitcases had not even been unpacked. It was clear from the speed with which incidents were piling up that our incompatibility was growing more obvious, and that it would be difficult for us to maintain good relations until the end of the trip.

Chapter 21

In which the author leaves Chungking by plane, sees the mandarins of Wuhan again for a few hours, receives a stern bit of advice from his ex-friend Tsai and arrives in Changsha on the train. How the entire group pays a pious visit to the village of Shaoshan, the house where Mao Tse-tung was born and the museum dedicated to the glory of the chairman. In which a difference of opinion arises regarding the relations between the young Mao Tse-tung and his father. How, after the return to Changsha, the author goes to the school where Mao Tse-tung spent nine years, attends still another banquet before his departure for Canton and no longer has the heart for anything. In which the author visits more museums and rummages through the antique shops. How he is taken to visit a people's commune in the region outside Canton.

They began again, from zero.
—VICTOR SÉGALEN, *Stelas*

When we left the hotel for the airport, it was still dark and rain was falling. Even at this hour the lights of the city outlined the forms of men with baskets on their heads and carts at their backs. Doors stood open, revealing sleeping rooms with rows of mosquito nets, lit by naked electric bulbs. Columns of soldiers were running along the road beside us.

We were very quiet, each of us for his own reasons, haunted by the thought that the weather might prevent us from leaving. The summit of the hill we had to cross was wreathed in fog, and our automobiles were forced to slow down. Clouds lay low on the opposite slope. I had imagined that Tsai was my friend, but this morning his face suggested that he did not know what expression to assume. He wandered back and forth in the waiting room, carrying his little package of delicacies for his children and family, occasionally dropping into an armchair with an air of resignation, as if destiny had consigned him to us.

Ignoring the poor visibility, our pilot took off, and when we broke through the clouds at ten thousand feet we found ourselves in an archipelago of golden islands, washed by the gentle blue of the sky. I had at last accepted the fact that I would never see the places where the revolution had taken place, the Tatu River and the gorges of the upper Yangtze where the men of the Long March had crossed. It had been suggested that we might visit the mountains of Kiangsi, where Chu Teh had come to join Mao Tse-tung, but after considering it we had not taken up the offer. In their eagerness to sing the praises of their master, so many official artists had already described these mountains that they themselves no longer seemed worth the trip.

The plane was flying over a vast expanse of silvery, inundated fields. The Yangtze twisted and turned between a succession of lakes, over which banks of low-hanging clouds floated like islands. The smoky haze of Wuhan appeared on the horizon, and shortly thereafter we landed, in an area of lotus-filled ponds, dotted here and there with fishing boats. The same Association vice president who had greeted us when we first arrived here was waiting at the foot of the ramp. So many later clashes and misunderstandings now separated us from him that it was difficult to believe that we had once been so concerned about his feelings. Curiously enough, we felt no particular dislike for Wuhan, although none of us, remembering our earlier disappointment, had wanted to see it again.

I thought I detected a certain warmth in the vice president, and wondered if he might have come to the conclusion that our frankness with him and the others was not without merit. Or had he simply been impressed by the newspaper photographs of our meetings with Chen Yi and Chu Teh? He asked me what I thought about the removal of Khrushchev. I told him that if Khrushchev's policies were continued there was no likelihood of any significant change so far as China was concerned and that the explosion of the atomic bomb seemed to me more important. He then asked about the interview with Chen Yi, and I told him of my intense interest in what the marshal had said.

"For that matter," I added, "the gist of our conversation is being published today in Paris."

"Already?" he said.

The air in Wuhan still smelled of burning fat and the nearby river. Our train was not scheduled to leave for three hours, and our hosts were thoughtful enough to take us back to the same rooms in the hotel we had occupied during our earlier stay. By this time we were familiar with the protocol for our railroad departures. We went into our compartments, deposited our hand luggage and immediately returned to the platform to exchange the customary banalities.

"We will hope to see you for a third time," the vice president said.

"I shall hope so, too," I said, and added a string of phrases of gratitude.

I no longer remember much about the trip, beyond the fact that we crossed the great iron bridge on the Yangtze. We saw nothing of the lakes, even of Lake Tungting, which is as large as an inland sea. Night had fallen when my former friend Tsai suddenly arrived in my compartment, accompanied by Mr. Shu.

"I have a message to convey to you," he said flatly. "You would be wrong in treating lightly the statements made to you by Marshal Chen Yi. His remarks were extremely important. You were promised that you would soon have a copy of the text. I can tell you now that it will be delivered to you within two or three days. Do not consider this warning as coming from me; it comes from Peking."

"This is the first time that I have ever had to be warned to take things seriously," I replied, uncomfortably aware that I was losing my temper. "Unfortunately for me, I have never been thought to have a very good sense of humor."

"I am not giving you advice," he said, with a sharpness that revealed only too clearly the collapse of our friendship. "I noted down everything Marshal Chen Yi said to you, without omitting a single phrase."

"And I did the same thing," I replied. "So, if there are errors or omissions, they must be the fault of the interpreter."

Since the discussion was beginning to grow heated, I broke it off by asking about our schedule for the next day. He departed without answering, but I had not been taken entirely by surprise. The vice president in Wuhan had told him that my interview with Chen Yi was appearing in *l'Express*. Tsai himself had doubtless not believed me when he saw me typing out the text in my room at the Hsin Chiao. I had shown him how long it was, but it had probably never occurred to him that I would have the audacity to cable it to Paris so soon. Now he was probably afraid he would be blamed for having forgotten to inform his superiors.

I had learned by this time that the best way to put an end to a discussion that was leading nowhere was to ask what we would be doing next. Even though they might know very well that nothing had been planned, it was a rare occasion when our guides said to us, "Tomorrow, you will be free." By the same token, they invariably concealed until the last possible moment the name of anyone we might be going to meet. That was the way it was.

This altercation with Tsai hung like a cloud over our arrival in Changsha, the capital of the province of Hunan. It was here that Mao Tse-tung had first studied, but this fact had not caused the mosquitoes to disappear, and this was the first hotel we stayed in where there were mosquito nets above the beds. In spite of the lateness of the hour, we

had time to discuss the schedule. Next day we were to be taken to
Shaoshan where Mao Tse-tung was born.

Tombs had been carved into the flanks of the red hills, and the rivers,
running almost dry through their pebbly courses, reminded me of
Algeria. Young people were walking along the roads, with sacks slung
across their shoulders; children were returning from school, carrying
their abacuses and notebooks.

A tiny valley wound through the mountains, clinging to the foothills
and climbing up toward the terraced rice fields and pine-covered ridges.
Clouds jostled each other, tossed by the wind, and birds sang. In spite of
the cold, peasants wearing great round straw hats were walking barefoot
through the fields, moving with that quick, sharp step which the
intellectual Mao had never had, even though he, too, was born in this
country. Dogs that might have been destined for the stewpot in some
other part of the country were unconcernedly sniffing at the trunks of
trees and dashing off on some unknown scent.

Down below, at a point where the narrow ravine opened out to form
part of the valley, a house roofed partially with round gray tiles and
partially with thatch had at one time sheltered the Mao family, a
separate little tribe among the six hundred families of the village. The
house had been burned in 1929, but the party had later restored it,
mingling authentic relics with counterfeit fetishes. It stood just above
two lotus-filled ponds, where children still paddled about among the
ducks on summer days, just as the young Mao and his brothers had once
done. A little kitchen garden extended right up to the walls of the house
itself. On the other side of the valley, scarcely a stone's throw away,
there was another farm. A wisp of smoke rose from its chimney, and we
could hear the clucking of chickens.

The Mao family home had been transformed into a museum which
attracted pilgrims from all over the country. Here they could reach out
stealthily and touch the alcove where the god had been conceived,
observe the rows of buckets, the caldron where mash had been prepared
for the hogs, the long earthen stove and kitchen utensils, the benches,
tables, and cupboards, the cask where rice was stored, the heavily
spiked shoes for rainy days and the rice pestles used by the women.

"He put his feet in these clogs," said our guide, ecstatically. "He used
this comb to groom the buffalo."

Most of it was probably fake. We had been told, "All these things were
located in the homes of neighbors." A framed photograph of the parents
dominated the main room: a father with a mustache and goatee, the
skull concealed beneath a close-fitting little cap, a long nose, bushy
eyebrows and a cold, hard expression. From the gentle, handsome face
of his mother, Mao Tse-tung had inherited the oval shape, eyes, sensual

lips and broad structure of the jaw. Some swallows had built a nest in one of the beams of the dining room ceiling. A wheelbarrow, a harrow, a plow, and some wooden yokes and hoes had been stored in a little shed just next to the house. The guest room opened out into the pig sty, which now was clean and empty. Could it be true that guests had once been expected to stay in the midst of the noise and stench of hogs? In the room in which "our Chairman" had lived, an oil lamp stood on a little table beside the bed and a mosquito net still hung from the ceiling. The only thing lacking was the books he had read in those years: *The Romance of the Three Kingdom*s and the Chinese translations, prepared by early missionaries, of Adam Smith's *The Wealth of Nations* and Rousseau's *Social Contract*.

Our mandarins seemed to have been touched by a kind of grace, but the members of the Association from Changsha were as blasé as sacristans for whom daily contact with the divine has removed its power to stir the emotions. The intensity of his meditation clothed Chen in a quite unusual mood of indulgence. Only Mr. Shu sought in vain to imbibe this sacred atmosphere, and continued to trail his boredom behind him as heavily as his thick-soled shoes. Tsai was hoping that some ray of light would stab me and that I would be forced to give in. As far as he was concerned, everything had begun here, at this window where the young Mao had dreamed that he would continue the work of Shih Huang Ti. I surmised that he was tempted to get down on his knees and kiss this earth. Far from bearing any grudge against me, he was quietly pitying this poor skeptic who would soon be returning to the dark capitalist world. I was once again encompassed by the warmth of his friendship. He thought perhaps that he might still be able to convert me.

"Did the Chairman get along well with his father?" I asked innocently.

"Very well."

The disagreement between father and son was notorious. I was indignant that they should still be lying to me.

"Why do you bother with all that?" they said irritably. "To understand it thoroughly, you would have to understand everything about the old feudal society. It is of secondary importance, and you do not have the time to go into secondary matters."

I was persistent. "So," I said, "you claim that the relationship between the Chairman and his father was a good one?"

"What source of information do you have that would make you think anything else?"

"Mr. Edgar Snow, who was told about it by your Chairman himself."

In 1938, under conditions that permitted no doubt as to the accuracy of the facts, Mao had given a detailed account of his youth to Edgar

Snow. Snow had been perfectly right in attaching considerable importance to this meeting, and when Mao Tse-tung subsequently became one
of the most important of the world's leaders, confidences of this nature,
because of their very scarcity, took on even greater value. Fortune,
served by great courage and a rare understanding of the journalist's
function, had smiled on Edgar Snow, who became and remains today
the only authorized biographer of Mao and the only Westerner who has
found favor in his eyes. In those days the members of the Central
Committee were still willing to speak. Today their own interests compel
them to remain silent. If certain of Snow's information seemed in
contradiction with the doctrine expounded in the museums, the party
had simply rearranged history. As a minor example, Mao's mother's
name was listed in the museum of Shaoshan as Wen Tsu, although Mao
told Edgar Snow that she was named Wen Ki-mei.

At the mention of Edgar Snow's name, my companions grimaced. It
was always easy for a foreigner, they said, to pretend that the Chairman
had told him the story of some part of his life. The only documents on
which I could rely were right here in Shaoshan. They had been gathered
in the course of a survey that was years in the making and had required
the help of all the peasants of the village and nearby towns. Anything
else was of no value.

"Even the Chairman's statements to Edgar Snow?" I asked.

"We see no reason why Mr. Edgar Snow should be considered an
exception."

The house of his birth had not been sufficient for the cult of Mao Tse-
tung. Shaoshan also possessed a very large museum, where every detail
and incident of his life could be studied. Everything in the museum
reflected the glory of Mao: Mao as an adolescent, garbed in a student's
robe, standing with his hands on his hips and talking to his classmates;
Mao traveling through the surrounding villages, holding a child in his
arms and listened to in wonderment by the old men and women; Mao in
Peking; Mao founding a secret society for study of the Soviet revolution,
in Changsha; Mao teaching the peasants of Hunan; Mao outlining the
plans for strikes and directing the union organizations; Mao resisting
the opportunists of both the right and the left; Mao discovering revolutionary doctrine in the mountains of Kiangsi; Mao revealing the truth to
a dazzled China; Mao in fake marble, surrounded by green foliage; Mao
depicted by the brushes of the second-rate Davids and Géricaults of the
regime, wearing the halo of the revelations of Marxism-Leninism; Mao
in a blue robe, clasping the hands held out to him and blessing the
mothers; Mao heroically etched against the red flags atop the mountain
peaks and snows; Mao and his thought lighting the world . . . We
paused before every relic, every photograph, every painting, every new
display of any kind. "Thanks to the direction of Chairman Mao . . ."

Our progress through the museum seemed an interminable Calvary to me; I was crushed beneath the weight of so much glory. Sacrilegiously, I rested by leaning against the statues of the god, and envied the goldfish in a pond in the interior courtyard. They were not forced to listen. Tsai, his raincoat slung across his shoulders, leaned over the display cases as intently as if he were drinking from a life-giving source. I said that I was very tired and did not feel well, and the words were close to the truth. The trip back to Changsha was long. I felt that we must leave.

On the far side of the road, some keepers of ducks were guiding their flocks to a new feeding ground, prodding them with a long pole. We stopped for a moment to photograph a man plowing his field.

This pilgrimage to Shaoshan re-established a form of peace between us and our mandarins. The next day we visited the secondary school where Mao had studied, and where he taught in the period from 1913 to 1922. The party had transformed the school into a seminary of Marxism-Leninism, and the life of the students was no longer regulated by the sound of a bugle, as it had been in Mao's day, but by the chimes of a clock. I wondered if there was a single one of the students we glimpsed that day who had not secretly dreamed of resembling this pale-faced boy with the long, thick hair, parted at the center and falling almost to the high collar of the white robe which gave him the air of a Roman seminarian. Zero in English, very poor in mathematics, but formidably gifted in composition and debate. "Zero in English" was a fact that was not taught in Changsha. Chairman Mao must shine in everything and be possessed of all the virtues. If he chanced to look at one of the pretty girls who also attended the school, it was with the cool eyes of a budding Marxist-Leninist, and not with those of any other young man.

We were informed that it was in Changsha that he had first revealed his genius and founded three militant groups: one to remain in China and direct the revolution, another sent into Southeast Asia to obtain the financial support of Chinese expatriates there, and the third sent to France to study the methods that would be required for victory. The books whose margins he had covered with notes were on display, and the manual of philosophy alone was said to contain twelve thousand minutely calligraphed characters of his comments. When he was shown this volume in 1949, he had said, "What I wrote here is not entirely correct, but at that time it had some relevance." To him, the failure of the 1911 revolution was due to the fact that the masses had not felt themselves sufficiently involved and the intellectuals were still living in their ivory towers. He made use of his vacations to study the real China, by traveling through the countryside with a friend.

Mao's great awakening had come with the discovery that it was the peasants, rather than the workers in the cities, who held the real power of insurrection, and that their strength, properly organized and unified, could shorten the nation's path to Communism. He was considerably helped by the circumstances of the time, but he did not allow himself to be misled by the mirage of any false Utopia. A native instinct drew him back to the earth that had produced him, to the tough-mindedness of his father and the futile anger of the poor his father had exploited, to the brutal repression of the Changsha revolts by the imperial troops. It became apparent to him that both the regime and the structure of society on which it depended must be destroyed before a system of true social justice could be established. What rendered his thought unique was his realization that it was the countryside beyond the cities that held the key to the future. There can be no doubt that he recognized this fact well before any of his companions, but it did not come to him with the blinding clarity that was now claimed.

Our luncheon fairly bubbled with cordiality. We drank a great deal, lifting our glasses in toasts to everything imaginable. Mr. Tsai's eyes sparkled delightedly beneath the furry, black cap of his hair. He seemed suddenly to have forgotten all our misadventures, and showered me with boyish compliments. His joy at having seen these holy places was evident in his every movement and in the laughter with which he greeted the most trivial remark. It was when he laughed, and revealed the decaying roots of his teeth, that his age, which was normally concealed by the youthfulness of his skin and the thickness of his hair, became abruptly apparent.

"Monsieur Orthion!" he cried.

Orthion unfolded his great frame, stood up and walked over from the other table, glass in hand. Tsai stood up to greet him, laughing at the length of hair that almost concealed the back of Orthion's neck.

"Kam-pé!"

Tsai liked the way Orthion managed to swallow glass after glass of both the white alcohol and the sweetish red wine without ever showing signs of collapse. I required somewhat more urging, but even I found it difficult to resist Tsai when he glanced at me in that innocent manner which seemed to say that friendship should be drunk like wine. Toast followed toast, and we were very gay. Mr. Shu translated, without ever removing his eyes from his plate or halting the movement of food to his mouth. The bare skull of our newest vice president glistened with the warmth of the atmosphere, and his round, honest face was wreathed in smiles. We drank to the Chinese people, to the French people, to each one of us, to a happy end to our journey, to the book I was going to write, to the film we would make, to the city of Changsha. Even Brigitte, who normally rebelled at such exuberance, proposed a toast to the women of China, and there was a spark of tenderness in the pale green of her eyes. We were all wearing jackets with high-buttoned collars, and it occurred to me that we must resemble a congregation of priests celebrating their dean's anniversary. Mr. Chen, normally the most reserved of all our mandarins, filled and refilled his glass. He ate in a manner that made it seem as if he were attempting to compensate for a hundred generations of Chinese who had never had enough to eat. And on that day—who knows?—he may have believed in the existence of goodwill among peoples and in the sincerity of our intentions.

Our plane was a trifle late leaving, and Brigitte took advantage of the delay to send off some postcards. Freedom was very close, and the scent of it was good. The plane ascended through the low-hanging clouds and emerged into the clear sky above. To the east, I could see the range of mountains where Mao, in 1928, had written the poem of the first revolutionary base:

> High in the mountains, our flags are streaming in the wind,
> Our trumpets beckon from hill to hill. . . .
> At Hwang-yang-ki our cannons thunder,
> Announcing that the enemy has fled.

We were flying through a realm of dusty gold, approaching the fertile plain of Canton, a pale yellow expanse of rice fields, ready for the harvest. I thought I could see the distant sea and peaceful islands. We were separated from the rock of Hong Kong only by the thin line of a frontier. Tsai leaned over and said, "I will take you that far. I would even go with you if I didn't have to be careful about English secret agents." I said nothing, but I knew very well that, once I was in British territory, secret agents would be the last thing in the world with which I was concerned!

As soon as we arrived at the hotel, I wanted to go out again, to bathe in the eighty-degree temperature that greeted us. The annual fair was in progress, and there was considerable excitement in the streets, since many of the visitors to the city had been provided with automobiles. It was suggested that we pay a visit to the palace of culture, but I had had my fill of these. I refused to look at any more statues of Mao the protector of the people. Where could we go without our mandarins? Here it was possible to get along by jabbering in English, but taxis did not exist and I still did not have the courage to ride about in one of the tricycle cabs. Simon went off on foot, hoping that fate would toss something of interest in his path. The hotel was surrounded by green lawns, brightly colored flowerbeds and palm trees. The walls of the lobby were plastered with notices of welcome printed in every major language, and the tables were piled high with official news bulletins and propaganda leaflets. We no longer had much heart for anything, and even the zest for discovery had deserted us, leaving us restless and uneasy.

We went to dinner in the big, garishly lit restaurant of the hotel, where it was said that a thousand meals could be served at one time. I no longer remember whether we had a meeting that night to discuss the program for our last three days in China. I wanted to see the military academy at Whampoa, founded by Chiang-Kai-shek in 1923 with Chou En-lai as its political commissar, and also one of the people's communes of the rich province of Kwangtung. Beyond this, I was quite sure that I would be shown some museums and some beds in which Mao had slept.

In a sense, however, we were already on the other side of the world. Crickets were singing. Orthion extracted a few Gauloises from the depths of his suitcase. When I opened the window of my hotel room, I could see nothing but gardens and the pleasant activity of a provincial town preparing for an agricultural fair. Canton had once been known as the City of the Five Goats, in commemoration of an ancient legend to the effect that five saints had come down to the city from heaven, each riding a goat that held a blade of rice in its mouth. Our rooms were spacious and sunny. Some drunken Negroes were making a commotion in the corridors. Our suitcases were so full that we had trouble finding a place for the trays of gilded wood which had been presented to us by the Association on the night before our departure from Peking.

The next morning our caravan consisted of fine new Japanese automobiles. The rear seats were equipped with a row of push buttons that controlled the car radio. I could not be sure whether it was because of the sunlight, the softness of the air, the summer clothing we had unpacked again or the idlers in the streets, but Canton seemed almost prosperous. There was a certain abundance in the shops, and a certain friendliness—perhaps due to the warmth of the sky—in the behavior of the people. Along the banks of the Chu Chiang—the River of Pearls— the buildings of the old colonial concessions resembled the Thames embankment in London. It was from these concessions, granted by the imperial government, that the representatives of the Western nations conducted their traffic in Bengal opium in the eighteenth and nineteenth centuries. In Canton today the local hero was still the Imperial Commissioner, Lin Tsê-hsü. He was a welcome relief from Mao. I admired the courage and impartiality of this little man with the heavy mustache and goatee who had ordered the seizure and destruction of the twenty thousand cases of opium he found in the city's warehouses when he arrived there in 1839. The museum was filled to bursting with evidence of the abominations of the West, and every display was surrounded by a swarm of noisy children, being duly instructed in the horrors from which the revolution had freed them.

The imposing mass of its Gothic cathedral, looming over the huddle

s

of the surrounding houses, gave Canton some resemblance to Cologne.
We took advantage of a free afternoon to visit some of the antique shops
and spend the money the hotels refused to take from me. We wanted to
offer some parting gifts to our mandarins. They would have preferred
transistor radios, so that they might listen to the voice of Mao. What
about the complete works of Mao, bound in simulated leather? They
already owned them. We picked out some old porcelains and drawings.
Brigitte discovered a still life she liked: some anemones in a glass, with
a few pieces of fruit and a spray of furze that might have been painted
by Rouault, and signed with a Western hieroglyphic. She was intrigued
by it, and questioned Mr. Shu about it. After he, in turn, had spoken to
the dealer, he smiled.

"It was done by the painter you liked in Shanghai," he said. "It's
nothing very much, as you can see."

The price was one hundred yuans. For an artist without talent, as he
was officially defined, that was no paltry sum in China. Two months of
work for a factory hand. Mr. Shu apparently thought that he had made a
stupid mistake and would be rebuked for it. He intimated that he had
been joking.

"A joke like that is out of character for you," Brigitte said. "Now
please tell me truthfully if it was done by the artist in Shanghai."

"Yes, it was," Mr. Shu said resignedly.

We left early next morning to visit the people's commune of Sing
Tang. The road passed by Whampoa, and I asked when I might see the
military academy. They were terribly sorry. They had asked about it, but
the academy was one of the places that could not be shown.

"Because it is occupied by the army?"

"We don't know."

I shrugged. "Well, at least show me approximately where it is when
we pass."

They were very careful to say nothing more about it.

Sing Tang was a miserable village built around a pond which served
as a sewer and drainage canal. Many of the houses, flimsily constructed
of board or light masonry, had been built over the water and were
supported on piles. Half-naked men were standing in the water up to
their waists, dredging the mire from the bottom of the pond, using a
kind of hollowed-out wooden scoop. They dumped it into little, flat-
bottomed boats, and it was then towed to the banks of the pond and left
to dry to become fertilizer. Other men were swimming in this cesspool,
gathering the periwinkles which attached themselves to the rough
surfaces of the docks and pilings.

An unfriendly little man of about thirty directed the work of fourteen
thousand families, cultivating an area of almost fifteen thousand acres.

Since I was invited to say what I would like to see, I asked if we could be shown some examples of the extent to which the work had been mechanized. I was told that this was not possible. Some of the tractors were being repaired, and the others were too far away. I asked then if we could visit one of the families of the village. That was not possible either. We must not interrupt the work, but I could stop wherever I liked, talk to the people and even go into one of the houses. The autumn harvest of rice was not yet being gathered and the new plowing had not begun. In 1957 an agricultural worker earned 111 yuans per year; today his salary had almost tripled. In addition to this, each member of the family was allocated forty-five pounds of rice a year. We were again asked what we would like to see. It would be shown to us.

"A family," I repeated.

Ah! Yes, of course, a family. But the families were busy. The families were working to raise the level of production.

We resigned ourselves to a tour of the village. The streets were teeming with children, poultry and hogs. We saw men and women cutting sandals out of old tires, weaving ropes and baskets, repairing small boats and bicycles. Some peasants from neighboring villages were selling sugar cane. We were surrounded by an impoverished Middle Age of handicrafts, of naïveté and mistrust, yet my friend Tsai wandered through it admiringly; as Marshal Chen Yi had told us, this Middle Age possessed bicycles, wristwatches, newspapers and bottles of soda pop.

"You would have to live here for several months to see and know everything," Mr. Tsai explained. "Then you could form a judgment without risk of being mistaken. But even an entire day spent with a family would teach you nothing."

Mr. Tsai was right and I had not claimed to understand everything. I felt, quite simply, that they did not want me to consider this problem too deeply. Several months? They were disguising their refusal beneath an offer they knew perfectly well could not be realized. In that way they could attribute the errors certain to appear in my book to deliberate prejudice, and accuse me of bad faith. This oversimplified Machiavellism amused me. We went back to the commune's administrative headquarters for lunch. The fruit was excellent. After this, it was suggested that we go visit one of the rice production brigades, and I accepted.

We went by boat down the River of Pearls, which passed not far from here on its southward course to the sea. The pale light of the sky was reflected, almost unbroken, in the surface of the waters. A few fishermen were setting out their traps, and we passed some junks with patched and mended sails hanging slack in the listless wind. At the village of three hundred families where we docked, we were expected and there were officials to greet us. Loudspeakers were blasting sound across the square and in the streets, and I thought that it was in our honor. I was wrong. It was always like this. Throughout the day, the news bulletins of the state radio and patriotic music were broadcast everywhere in the village. I, in fact, was the only one who seemed surprised or deafened by it. No one else paid the slightest attention, just as someone who has grown accustomed to the sound of a waterfall or trains no longer seems to hear it.

The brigade was apparently resting. Some young people were playing basketball, men were calking barks and leveling the earthen paths, mothers were nursing their children. Families were gathered in their open doorways for a breath of air, surrounded by troops of obese hogs and sows. Water buffalo were bathing voluptuously in the river, only their nostrils and horns visible above the surface. A few old peasants were returning from their fields, their tools over their shoulders, their forms as gaunt as tree trunks, their weather-beaten faces sheltered beneath great, round straw hats.

The rice paddies and sugar cane fields began at the very edge of the last houses of the village. Women were turning over the hard, dry earth, and then breaking up the clods with the sharp ends of their picks. Beasts of burden were carefully tended, but the women's work ended only with death. Almost from the day of marriage, their faces began to wither, their bodies thickened, their shoulders stooped, their feet and hands became rough and callused. Even among those who retained some beauty, the youthful sparkle was clouded with a veil of resignation. Only the older men showed some sign of friendship toward us. The younger ones flaunted their toughness and their limitless pride. We were that day's attraction, although I surmised that they were not unaccustomed to the sight of foreign journalists. Aside from Chungking, what surprise had we ever happened on? We had seen only what others had seen before us, and those who came after us would see nothing more.

It was very warm. Brigitte had been carrying her heavy photographic equipment since early morning, and I had not been able to help her very much. Occasionally I had tried, but had only succeeded in irritating her, since I was never where I should have been when she needed something. Stubbornly, then, she would take the sack away from me and replace the strap on her slender shoulder. In any case, she preferred to follow as far as possible behind us, in the hope of avoiding the confusion that accompanied our passage.

Toward the end of the afternoon I could see that she was on the point of collapse. I was weary myself, and made no attempt to refuse the chairs that were offered us. It was not until later that the thought occurred to me that they had not been brought out by chance from a house that we were passing by chance. A woman wearing a jacket and trousers of black cotton hastily cleared away a bench and ran to get cups and make tea for us. She was thirty-eight years old. The gold fillings in her teeth sparkled when she smiled. A blue-violet ribbon was plaited into the braids of her hair. All her movements and gestures had a distinctive charm. We sat down next to her, and she took her youngest son on her knees. When she began talking to us, telling us about the abundance of the present, a second interpreter had to be called in, to translate what she said into mandarin so that Mr. Shu would understand. In the year just passed, her family had earned more than two thousand yuans and had been allocated three thousand pounds of rice, which she used to feed the animals and to sell in the marketplaces. She had four pigs. I asked how she could recognize them among all the others. She ran out to the street, uttered a long, wailing sound, punctuated with sharp little cries, and the pigs replied with a noisy honking. She laughed delightedly, and we all joined in.

Khrushchev and the atomic bomb? She knew all about that from the loudspeakers. Her husband worked in the brick-making plant. She owed all this great happiness to the government, to the party and to Chairman Mao. She did not weep with emotion as she said this; she shouted it in the face of the world, on a note of victorious joy. At present she herself owned a trifle more than a *mou*, or about nine hundred square yards, of sugar cane, garden vegetables and banana trees laden with fruit. And there were thousands of other slaves like herself, who had once owned nothing but their nakedness and the marks of the bamboo switches on their backs, and who today knew the glory of having children who could read and write and always had enough to eat. Under such circumstances, the women cared little about losing their youth and beauty, and gladly rolled their trouser legs up to their thighs and carried basketloads of earth and stones to strengthen the dikes which prevented the rivers from flooding. With every step they took, with every drop of sweat they shed, China was raising higher above the world the red silk flag which announced the end of Western rule and held out the promise that the atomic bombs of Sinkiang would someday rain down on America.

As they listened to the woman's words, the frozen faces of the brigade leaders were transformed by that arrogance and hatred we had already noticed so often. Mr. Tsai closed his eyes slowly, sanctimoniously, like a great sleeping cat. The sight of Brigitte and Simon photographing the symbols of this peace and labor no longer caused anguish to Mr. Chen. There was no combat exercise that afternoon; it had been canceled so that we would not be alarmed by it. The thousands of young men and women who formed the local militia had been sent back to carting sacks of rice or building walls of mud, and we did not see them hurling themselves on imaginary enemies, brandishing bayonets and submachine guns, as the twenty million militia men and women from the fields and factories normally did each day.

On the river bank where we said good-bye to the rice production brigade, the representatives of the People's China sent their best wishes to the people of France, and offered us oranges. As our tugboat pulled away and the distance between us lengthened, we waved back at the little group that had gathered to salute our departure. Canton no longer resembled the calm city it had been just the day before. New platoons of children were returning from visits to the tombs of the martyrs, marching, as always, with the flag bearers in the lead. The crowd in the streets was so dense that it seemed that the walls must burst beneath the pressure. It overflowed into the gardens and onto the docks, thronged across the bridges and piled helter-skelter into the boats. Our little caravan of automobiles had difficulty forcing a passage through this vast and frightening human tidal wave.

At ten o'clock that evening Mr. Shu knocked at the door of my room. Mr. Tsai wanted to see me to discuss some documents he had received from Peking.

"Tomorrow morning, please," I said.

"The secretary general who accompanied you has said nothing about this matter?" Mr. Shu asked.

"You know very well that he didn't," I said, "since you were our interpreter. I haven't yet had time to learn your language, so that I could speak directly with him."

Mr. Shu deigned to smile. When he left, I went back to jotting down some notes, feeling heavyhearted, my thoughts muddled by an uneasiness for which I could find no certain reason: the sound of a flute in the night outside my window, the memory of villages where hogs moved freely in and out of houses, the thought of so many men who were too weary at the day's end to lift their hand and place it gently against a woman's thigh, the thought of the futility of this journey. I did not know what bound me to this China I had so much wanted to love and which was already slipping out of my grasp, like a boat that has broken its moorings. I knew that I was unhappy. I knew also that it was time for me to return to the shark-infested world of capitalism, because I felt the need of my normal surroundings, of the scent of warm bread and good red wine.

I began to type up an article the Chinese had asked me to write for a Peking newspaper, certain in my own mind that they would never publish it and that the request was a subterfuge to find out what I really thought.

Chapter 22

In which the author experiences a certain emotion in leaving the People's China and the mandarins who have escorted him. How the spectacle of the other China, under the rule of the British, has the contradictory effect of evoking in the author's mind a picture of the seizure of power here by the Communists. Why the feeling of rediscovered liberty is accompanied by a certain disappointment with the spectacle presented by Hong Kong at the dinner celebrating the return to a capitalist country. How the author, abandoning the idea of going to Formosa, explores the refugee shantytowns with a young Chinese he meets in Hong Kong and talks with a director of the Communist press and then with some Nationalist intellectuals. In which the author decides that he must go to Macao to question some of the refugees there from People's China, but comes to no conclusion about what he hears.

> When we parted company with these worthy Tibetans, we could not stop ourselves from shedding a few tears. Gradually, and almost without our knowing it, bonds had been formed between us that were extremely painful to break.
> —E. R. HUC, *Recollections of a Journey Through Tartary, Tibet and China*

In the train that was carrying us toward the frontier, we had difficulty disguising our emotions. I was still making corrections in the text of the article I had written on the key points which might permit Westerners and Chinese to understand each other. The time had already come when we addressed ourselves to our Chinese friends as one equal to another. But now we were returning home. We resembled children who had been told that they must behave very carefully until they reached a certain point.

What was left to me of China? The obsession with cleanliness, the absence of flies, the politely sorrowful expression on the faces of the train conductors, a few old drawings, a pair of felt sandals, the memory of an ancient temple filled with birds, the warm scent of flowering magnolias in the spot where Mao Tse-tung had formed his peasant cadres, our last sight of the University of Canton, where the female students had been practicing the handling of weapons. In Canton there were restaurants where the silence of family dinners in other cities was replaced by a hubbub of voices.

A kind of melancholy had clouded everything we had had to say to each other since the day before our departure. At first, our mandarins had refused to accept our gifts and we had threatened to become irritated. Documents arrived from Peking that evening containing the text of the interview with Chen Yi, as it had been set down by Mr. Tsai. I had not immediately reread it, but I was assured that it was complete in every detail. I had a week to make use of it for my own purposes, and after that it would be published in the Chinese press. We had a very hurried luncheon at the frontier station. The chief customs officer announced that our baggage would not be inspected, because of the friendship of the Chinese people for the French people.

"Friendship," I said to Tsai, "is primarily a matter of not deceiving one another. Why did you tell me that the artist in Shanghai did not speak French, when I know that he does?"

"It was he who said he didn't," Mr Tsai replied, "and why should we have doubted his word? As for you, you offended him by changing your mind about making the film showing him at work. He had made preparations for it, and you left without even an apology. After that, are you still surprised that he did not wish to sell you a canvas?"

Perhaps it was true. Perhaps they had not lied. But someone had. Was it the artist because he was afraid? Anyone has the right to defend himself, even by lying, from a regime that annihilates conscience. One escapes as best one can. Had we, without realizing it, really offended him? But if that were true, why had they not told me? Why had they constantly failed to keep their promise to tell me, perfectly frankly, about anything I did that might cause misunderstandings between us? Because they were Chinese, and in China the idea of being perfectly frank has no meaning. They were now even ready to leave me in doubt as to whether I was not, in fact, really the guilty party.

A policeman suddenly appeared, looking for us, and Tsai stood up. We had had neither the time nor the heart to propose any toasts. I had eaten nothing. Nothing had happened. And now it was time to leave. We gathered together our hand baggage. "Don't worry about the other things," Mr. Tsai said. "They will be in the baggage car. You will find everything in Hong Kong."

Our passports were returned to us on the platform. Mr. Tsai pointed out a tower on a hill overlooking the station.

"The English are up there, defying us, threatening us. Their flag floats right there."

It annoyed him that there should be British flags on hills as naked as the hills of the People's China once had been, marked only by ancient tombs built in the form of an upside-down U. At the other end of the platform, I could now see policemen in military caps and khaki shorts, with cross belts and leg guards of gleaming leather. They were Chinese, too, but from the other side, and in their presence our companions cut a shabby figure. I do not know why, but these starched and polished Chinese warmed my heart.

"A photograph, Mr. Tsai," Orthion said.

A photograph in a railway station? We were on the frontier, we were already crossing the Rubicon that flowed down from the hills of Hong Kong; we could photograph whatever we liked.

"All right," Tsai said, and held out his hand to me. "Good-bye."

I thought of the time when I had wondered how I might demonstrate my friendship for him, and whether I would dare embrace him. He had told me that this was not done in China, but I realized now that I no longer had the slightest desire to do it. What, after all, was Tsai? An honest, second-string mandarin, the only one whose lies and evasions I had managed to tolerate until the end, because he was a man of basic integrity and sound heart.

"Au revoir, Monsieur Tsai," I said. "I . . ."

He was paying no attention to what I wanted to say to him. With his cap pulled down almost to his eyes, he no longer even saw me, and seemed to be gazing off to some distant point above my head. He began giving me advice about the book I was going to write. Above everything, I must protect the friendship that existed between France and China. I was more concerned with writing the truth and I listened no further. After we had parted, we both turned around for an instant and I would have liked to make some sort of gesture, but the suitcases in my hands prevented it. I set them down, took out my handkerchief and waved it, and then we went into the office of the British police. When we came out, I turned again and glanced down the length of the platform. The spot where our escort had left us was empty.

"They have gone," Orthion said.

It seemed strange to be alone in a railway station, surrounded by disinterested Chinese. We had a momentary feeling of confusion. There was no longer anyone to look after our little group of orphans.

"They have gone," I repeated, as if I were trying to convince myself.

What secret corner of my being still held back the delight I had expected of this moment? When would the joy of liberation first reveal itself? The instant we entered our train car, we were conscious of the pleasurable relaxation of capitalism. The fans that were only turned on at intervals in socialist trains, in order to prolong their life, were whirring softly and constantly. There was Scotch whiskey for sale, and American cigarettes. Simon was anxious about the transfer of our baggage, and an inspector calmly reassured him.

I leaned back in my seat, listening to the unfamiliar chatter of voices around me. I lit my first American cigarette and inhaled greedily, seeking to fill my lungs with this fondly remembered aroma. But I was forcing myself; it no longer had the same taste. Only the whiskey brought with it the same pleasure it always had. We found that the windows could be lowered, and when the train began to move we learned out, offering our faces to the warm breeze, holding glasses in our hands, like the capitalist pleasure-seekers we were. Tsai, in his closed compartment, would now be moving in the opposite direction, crossing the fertile rice fields of the Canton plain, but not seeing them. The rice fields on this side were barren-looking, poorly irrigated and an ugly greenish-yellow; the villages were poor and dirty. In a few months the discipline of socialism would have changed all that, just as it had in 1949 when the armies of Chiang Kai-shek had broken and the Reds had swept over China.

After the decisive battles in the north, and particularly the crucial one of Soochow which lasted for sixty-five days and in which Chiang Kai-shek lost 600 thousand men, the whole of the country between Siberia and the Yangtze was conquered. In Peking the microphones had amplified the sudden break in Mao's voice when he proclaimed the People's Republic and the red flag was raised for the first time over T'ien An Men Square. Chiang Kai-shek still had an army of a million and a half men, an enormous supply of armaments and a thousand or more generals. He still attempted to issue orders and still promised final victory, but no one any longer obeyed. The generals issued statements saying that they would make a new Stalingrad of every city they had been ordered to defend, but when the time came to make good on their words they either went over to the other side or loaded their wives and furniture onto planes and fled.

In April the final big push was launched and resistance broke down everywhere. With the silence, swiftness and implacability of a rising tide, the Communists rolled through the countryside and cities of the Yangtze and into the far corners of the northwest provinces. General Yen Hsi-shan, the governor of Shansi province, claimed that two hundred Flying Tigers and 200 thousand Japanese mercenaries would have been sufficient to halt the Communists, but was this true? A flood cannot be halted when the dikes have burst. The will of an entire people cannot be denied when it sweeps across a continent and accompanies with dancing and applause the burial of one dynasty and the rise of another.

China had never before witnessed the spectacle of ardent young warriors who sang as they marched, who respected the daughters and property of others, slept in the streets and explained to the peasants and townspeople that they represented justice and the people. Were these men bandits? For years they had been trained to respect the masses of the poor, to which they belonged, and to identify themselves with the dreams and the blood of the downtrodden. These were no longer the undisciplined hordes of the Kiangsi mountains and the Long March, armed with picks and staves. They were known now as "combatants," rather than by the detested name of "soldiers." Their faded uniforms were in sharp contrast to the shining newness of the American supplies, tanks and trucks left behind by the fleeing divisions of Chiang Kai-shek. The soldiers of the Kuomintang were treated like cattle by their officers, and abandoned to their fate whenever these officers felt the time had come to seize an ambulance or plane and get out.

The astonished city populations that once would have been subjected to rape and pillage found themselves, instead, confronted with an army that set up theaters in the streets and enacted allegories of tyrants vanquished, misery overcome, virtue rewarded and China assuming her proper place among the great nations of the world. Children spoke out against traitors, even if they were members of their own family, the authority of the father passed into the hands of the political commissar, and well-trained instructors laid the foundations for the new regime. Order succeeded complacency and discipline took the place of bribery.

In May the lower valley of the Yangtze was conquered. In August the Red Armies were halfway to Canton; by the end of the year they had occupied all China, and there was nothing left to Chiang Kai-shek but the island of Formosa, where he and his followers set up a miniature empire which Mao Tse-tung derisively allowed him to keep. The Communist consolidation of power was greeted with frenzied tears of joy and relief. Nothing could have been worse than the government of the Kuomintang. Those who still resisted were mercilessly put out of the way, through brainwashing or simple execution. Were there twenty million dead, or "scarcely more than 700,000," as Mao claimed? The screams and moans of the victims of the Great Wall were buried beneath the dust of twenty centuries, and no one had ever numbered them. If Hong Kong were to fall to the People's China, here, too, everything would change within a matter of months.

At the other end of the seat, Brigitte was looking out on the other China, where everything seemed miserable, abandoned, dispirited. She was taking no part in our delight. The train stopped at local stations. It was Sunday, and people were waiting all along the platforms. There were laughing young men and women with their arms around each other. Lines of English automobiles filled with Chinese waited for the barriers to rise at the grade crossings.

Was Tsai talking about us? Were he and Chen summing up our journey, savoring the slightly bitter satisfaction of duty accomplished?

The station in Hong Kong resembled nothing we had seen. We had crossed the frontier between two worlds. People pushed and shoved and laughed, Western newspapers were on sale, we were offered every imaginable service, including women. I had wired ahead to the hotel to send someone to meet us. There was no one waiting. No delegation came forward to greet us. Without quite knowing why, I had hoped that Tsai would have someone there to guide us to the ferryboats that crossed the bay. Simon found an agency that agreed to take our baggage across to our hotel, the Mandarin.

The bay was crowded with motorized junks, threading a perilous passage between the bigger ships. Brigitte stared wide-eyed, as the richest rock of the West drew nearer, crowned with its imposing blocks of concrete and teeming with its turbulent crowds. A scabrous film of shantytowns disfigured the steep rise of hills.

We had selected the largest hotel in Hong Kong, where the doors were opened by Hindus in turbans, gilt-adorned red capes and polished boots. Bellboys, disguised as the lackeys of an emperor, weighed our tips in the palms of their hands and bowed, somewhat scornfully. We had lost the habit. Our rooms, which looked out on the sea, cost more per day than a cart hauler's monthly salary. We had left the universe of the poor, and almost instantly we found ourselves hating this universe of millionaires, finding it more than offensive, without dignity. Tsai was right. I could imagine his bewildered, socialist confusion among the dinner-jacketed boys and the carefree girls who gave us our keys and took care of our mail. A few more years and Tsai would make of this rock what he had made of Shanghai: a tomb for the living, where these palatial hotels would be used for the people's culture and as the residence of visiting Negro kings.

From our terraces, we could look out on the oceangoing ships anchored in the blue waters of the port, the busy scurrying of the ferryboats with their escort of gulls, the mountains behind the pale mist of Kowloon. Vultures floated high against the sun, allowing themselves to be lifted lazily by the wind, then diving suddenly toward an invisible prey, which was probably no more than a reflection in the water. The city was swept with waves of sound from the bay, the imperious blasting of ship horns, the insistent murmur of motors and propellers, and when, for an instant, it stopped, there was a breathless silence. I suddenly understood why Shanghai had so indelibly marked those Westerners who had found in it, a city built to the image of Manhattan and London, an open door to China and its scent of sandalwood, slime and incense.

We went out into the streets, immersing ourselves in their fury of life and traffic, hoping to find some French newspapers. Our mail had been waiting for two weeks, and had lost its initial urgency. "Winter has begun very early. When I think of the world that is opening up before you . . ." We had seen nothing of that world. China had remained sealed up behind its Great Wall. Here in Hong Kong streetcars clattered, automobiles clamored impatiently and double-deck buses whisked by each other in a tumult of steel and rubber.

Even before night had fallen, the sky was suddenly lit with the brightly colored lights of Chinese letters, resembling mystic signs in the heavens, the handwriting of a secret music, the wings of birds and the traces of their feet in the sand or snow. For an instant, they would hang like this and then hurl themselves elsewhere in columns and tabernacles of gold and purple, hieroglyphs for royal tombs that I wanted, for the first time, to decipher, because I knew they would not say, "Work for the party and the program."

I liked the China that I saw around me here. I would have liked to know these people, whose faces resembled ours because they expressed something more than just fatigue and sorrow. But were these free men, living under the protection of the British flag and of the aircraft carriers whose riding lights winked across the bay? I was dreaming. Tsai, whom I had reproached with being a slave among 700 million other slaves, possessed the sure knowledge that he belonged to a sovereign nation, a member of an army in constant readiness for a new Long March. "As your ambassador can see for himself, we possess everything." I was haunted by the Emperor Ch'ien Lung's arrogant reply to a message from the King of England in 1793. At this very moment Tsai would be getting into the train for Peking, his raincoat over his shoulder, his eyelids drooping with fatigue, yet his mind and body weighed down with the knowledge of a certain truth while I still sought for mine.

We devoted our first evening in Hong Kong to drinking to the full this luxury provided by capitalist society. We pretended we were allowing ourselves to be seduced by it. I smoked a great deal, but some gift had apparently abandoned me; I could not reaccustom my lungs to the taste to American tobacco. To establish some esential link with our country, we were determined to have a good French meal. There was no need even to set foot outside the Mandarin, which had the best restaurant in the city. We ordered a bottle of burgundy, and Orthion and I drank it delightedly and greedily. The renewal of our acquaintance with the good things of life had the added savor of something forbidden. We would have been happy to have Tsai at the table with us, but he would no more have appreciated our *steaks au poivre* than we had appreciated his sharks' fins and soya cheeses. As for the wine, we took a solemn oath that if he should come to Paris, as he sometimes dreamed of doing, we would drown him in toasts of good Beaujolais and Bordeaux, served in proper glasses.

"Not like these and not like theirs," I said.

"Proper glasses," Orthion said.

As though in a deliberate attempt to complete the shamelessness of our surroundings, the wine had been served to us in great balloon snifters. I wondered about the wages of the waiters in white jackets and gloves and the cooks in the tall white caps who presided over the dining room and grill. My appetite would not have been nearly so good if I had known then, as I learned later, that they never tasted the delicacies they served, even the leftovers, and more often than not went without eating altogether, because the director of the hotel charged them full price for their meals. They seemed to find it perfectly natural that they should carry the silver trays from the kitchens to the tables until the day came when they would be sitting there themselves. There was nothing extraordinary about this, in a city where hard work, shrewdness and luck could make a millionaire of a coolie. We were even told of a dozen or so enormously wealthy Chinese who had been granted titles by the Queen.

Brigitte's expression was animated, but curiously remote. Since I felt the same way myself, I could understand the stab at her heart when she thought of the women of the people's communes who would carry baskets of mire up the hills to the dikes and wade knee-deep in the water of the rice fields until the day of their death. Here the people who lived in the shantytowns in the hills searched for food in the trash cans of the rich. Two years earlier sixty thousand refugees had fled Communist China and several hundred still arrived each month, adding to the crush of the half-million men whose only shelter was a strip of corrugated iron, a doorway or the corner of a staircase.

We had not had such a party in a long time, and at its end, satiated, a bit high, vaguely unhappy with ourselves, we reached into our pockets for the dollars to pay the check and found little bundles of money from across the frontier, which would not have been sufficient here to buy a glass of mineral water. We went upstairs to our rooms, landlords who fattened on the sweat of the people—that was what we still were. The peasants of Tsinan hauled their carts through the fields so that we might drink wine that had traveled halfway around the world. I had a guilty conscience. Brigitte remained silent. We could, of course, have asked permission to remain there, to swell the ranks of the little band of hirelings who sang the praises of the new China. In some old quarter of Peking where sunflowers grew on the roofs, we might have had a house with a flagstone courtyard, a trellis, some vines and servants supplied by the party. We could have exchanged greetings with Anna Louise Strong, and listened as she denounced her native land for not appreciating the genius of Mao Tse-tung. Very little was required to assure oneself of the friendship of the leaders of the most numerous people on earth; burning a stick of incense at their shrine was quite sufficient. But it was not our way of doing things.

Seen from the terrace of my room, the harbor sparkled with lights. Brightly lit ferries moved across the bay like links in an endless chain, vanishing at last into the purple mist that was Kowloon. The sky swarmed with stars. Françoise and Pierre Nora had given us the address of a tailor in Kowloon, and said that we must go there and look at his cashmere suits. Our journey was over and the promise it once had held was gone, leaving us with a feeling of emptiness. We would not even be able to film a Hong Kong typhoon that would empty the harbor and the streets as if the city were awaiting the fallout from an atomic cloud. The last typhoon of the season had swept through a few weeks before, and people still talked of it as they might of some powerful, bad-tempered uncle, whose visits always had unforeseen results. This time it had ripped off a few roofs, tossed a few boulders around and killed a few people, but it had also left a great deal of water in the reservoirs.

We were relaxing. It was all very well for me to repeat that we could find the key to this whole Chinese adventure here in Hong Kong, but if I expected the others to believe it I would have had to believe it myself. The fact is that none of us expected Hong Kong to be anything more than a paradise for adventurers as Shanghai had once been. Ever since our first days in Peking I had kept repeating, to the others as well as to myself: "At the end of this Long March, there will be Hong Kong."

The Mandarin Hotel, where we would be staying, was itself a subject of legend. In Hong Kong we would find everything: information that had been concealed from us, secret agents. We could even, if we wished, get on a plane and go to Formosa to interview Chiang Kai-shek and his Madamissima. Had Mr. Tsai ever suspected that I might be so frustrated by my experience in the People's China that I would go to pay my respects to the Emperor of Formosa? He had asked me if I wanted him to arrange for our reservations on the plane to Paris. I had replied that I would decide on our departure after our arrival in Hong Kong.

No one was enthusiastic about the idea of visiting Chiang Kai-shek and his 600,000 men, constantly training for a landing they would never make. On Formosa a man became a soldier as naturally as a Corsican became a customs agent or a smuggler; the army was the country's industry. Why would they imprudently invade mainland China when the source of American dollars was still unexhausted? Chiang Kai-shek's old veterans had married and settled down, and the new soldiers were all natives of Formosa. What could they expect from an expedition to the continent? Nationalist propaganda put out a steady stream of leaflets showing tractors working the rice fields, factories making steel

and chemical fertilizers, and crowds acclaiming the gold-braided figure
of the marshal. The young girls no longer worked in brothels, as they
once had for the Japanese and the officials of the Kuomintang. Bribery
and embezzlement were said to have disappeared, and the marshal's
government was supposed to have rid itself of the corruption that was
the cause of its downfall.

I investigated the possibilities of a visit. No one could guarantee that
the President would see me. I would go to Formosa, make a tour of the
island, be shown what the government had done, outline my ideas and
plans and perhaps then . . . It was a discouraging prospect, and I had
little desire to drink more tea in the company of Nationalist mandarins.
For that matter, I was quite sure that Chiang Kai-shek, pink and well
scrubbed and playing the role of the venerable father, no longer granted
interviews.

Even here in Hong Kong no one talked very openly. So long as they
remained ignorant of the intentions of Communist China, no one
wanted to compromise himself. Would they occupy Hong Kong on June
30, 1997, the terminal date of the English lease? Would they break the
agreement before that date or would they extend it? For the moment,
Peking contented itself with keeping speculation alive by sending greetings to its Communist brothers in Hong Kong and discreet warnings to
the imperialists.

I could not help smiling when I remembered the sorrowful indignation of my friend Tsai as he pointed out the towers on the hills overlooking the frontier. A battalion of infantry and a squadron of tanks to
defend the entire territory—what a mockery! The governor was careful
never to show himself outside his official residence, and entertained
with discreet opulence. He was English and bore a marked resemblance
to a colonel at the time of the British Raj in India, but it was easy
enough to foresee a day when some Sir Wang or Sir Li would be offering
tea to his guests from the same fine London silver and supervising the
interests of the Crown with the same dignity and smiling firmness. The
police and civil administrators of the territory were Chinese. Individual
liberties and the rights of the trades unions were respected. The People's
China had its own bank and its own press in Hong Kong, as well as
several large stores and a permanent exposition hall. Perhaps the Peking
government felt that this Hong Kong Communism, whose newspapers
increased their circulation by publishing the results of horse races and
waged a token war against capitalism, was not yet ripe for the doctrine
of permanent revolution and people's communes. Peking could, undoubtedly, have speeded up the process, but they may have felt that
there was some danger of creating a deviationist schism by lodging in
Mao Tse-tung's bosom this bastard born of a shameful marriage between a Communist male and a capitalist female.

The customs adopted by the Chinese in their encounters with the West were known by a name that was never pronounced in the party's Central Committee without a shudder of horror: liberalism. No matter what was done to stamp it out, something always remained. When I had innocently mentioned the subject to the members of the Association with whom I talked in Shanghai, their chorus of laughter was too exaggerated to be altogether real. Liberal tendencies in Marxist-Leninist doctrine? I would be given the opportunity to judge for myself. I had, in fact, seen for myself that many small tradesmen had managed to retain their shops, and that there still existed, wherever a man still owned something, the embryo of a middle class.

The Chinese in Hong Kong did not share the crusader's wrath of my friend Tsai, and appeared to be suffering very little from the British presence. Those who were not Communists trembled at the thought of the red flag with its golden star replacing the Union Jack on the flagstaff of her Gracious Majesty's governor. A French-speaking student whom I met by chance told me, with that freedom of speech a person sometimes adopts with strangers he knows he will never see again: "The Communists of the People's China will never come here. They would make a desert of Hong Kong and they prefer to keep it as it is."

"What would you do if they should come anyway?" I asked.

His expression became abruptly very serious. "I don't know where I would go," he said, "but I would leave. I am too weak to fight the Communists and I know it, so I would leave."

"But the Communists have made your country into a powerful nation."

"I know that," he replied. "Not so long ago, right here, my father was insulted and beaten by the British, and it is the Communists who are really responsible for whatever rights we now have. I am proud of the Chinese atomic bomb."

He thought for a moment, and then came out with the expression that has been used in China for centuries to indicate that pride could be shown. He said: "We regained face with the bomb."

"The Chinese," he went on, "are no longer nothing, the way they were once. No one spits on us any more, and that is what counts. They have even begun to scare the rest of the world. Yet it's only in the West that I can breathe."

"I have just come from the People's China," I said. "There are no shantytowns over there like the ones in those hills."

"Would you like to see them?" he demanded. "I can take you there."

He wanted to practice his French a little, and I hastened to make an appointment for the next day. He left me very quickly then, and I watched as he vanished into the crowd. He was twenty-five years old.

In the windows of the Hong Kong headquarters for Communist

propaganda, there were two photographs of the atomic explosion, showing the ball of fire and the great, long-stemmed mushroom cloud, lanced
by the rays of the sun. Those Chinese who lived beyond the frontiers
and were accustomed to seeing the products of the West had to be
shown what China could produce.

The next morning I waited for my unknown acquaintance at the
corner of a street just below the hotel. The hour of our appointment had
passed, and I was beginning to think that he would not come when
suddenly he appeared. I had rented an automobile. The little port of
Aberdeen was completely filled with junks, moored side by side, forming
a floating city with a population of 120,000 people. They reached out
beyond the bay itself, into the shallow waters between the steep hills,
and then climbed to the dry ground itself, their keels lying on the rocks
like stranded fish, rotting in the sun. Little by little, necessity was
forcing families to leave their boats. This mountain had once been
hollowed out for cemeteries, but now the living disputed its slopes with
the dead. On either side of the roads used by handsome cars from the
residential districts, stretched a vast expanse of cabins and shelters
made from slabs of board and strips of corrugated iron. Hordes of
children wandered loose, ready to pounce with their hands outstretched,
their eyes wide and pleading. Down below, in the city of junks, there
were chapels where young American missionaries preached the gospel.
But there were also quarters that belonged entirely to thieves, where
even the police dared not venture.

My unknown acquaintance questioned me about the China I had just
visited. He gave me his name—Lu—and told me that he worked in a
Chinese restaurant patronized by a great many foreigners in search of
what they thought was exotic. One of his cousins lived at the other end
of Hong Kong, in the hills where bulldozers were constantly gnawing at
the earth. Whole blocks of new housing had been put up in the valley,
and they were already crammed with children and decked with washing. The urban housing offices were now completing a new block every
ten days. At this rate it was hoped that within the next ten years the pus
and scum could be drained away from the agglomeration of shacks that
now clung to the mountainside.

The section of this vast shantytown we were going to visit was built
along one slope of a line that followed the lowest part of the valley.
Cement staircases bordered by sewers had been cut into the side of the
hill, and each day the tangle of boards and scrap metal crept a trifle
closer to the ridge. Children were playing in little rivers of mud, and
racing up and down the stairs, holding the strings of paper kites which
darted through the sky like sparrow hawks before being caught in a
sudden gust of wind and dashed abruptly to earth. Dogs were sniffing at
the refuse that lay everywhere. Women were busy over cooking pots or

assembling the petals, leaves and stems of plastic flowers. Added to the money brought in by the men, the fifteen cents a gross they were paid for the flowers helped in the struggle for survival. Fifteen cents was enough to buy a little rice.

"Obviously," Mr. Lu said, "no one pays rent here."

Compared with destitution such as this, the villages of the People's China were positively abundant, but I had never seen there the smiling faces that I saw everywhere here. The air swarmed with mosquitoes, these shacks were certainly flooded with every rainfall and their roofs torn off by every passing typhoon, but I sensed that hope existed, the hope of moving elsewhere, of living better, of someday owning something that would make all this worthwhile. They lived in misery, but they did not seem to be destroyed by it.

In the corrugated-iron hut of Mr. Lu's cousins, sleeping bunks were ranged from floor to roof. Towels had been set out to dry on packing cases, and there was a lithograph of the Holy Family on one wall. A carefully tended hibiscus seemed to be thriving. The children went to school, where they were taught both Chinese and English. With Mr. Lu translating, I asked if they did not want to return to the People's China. I was answered by a burst of laughter. Along the far horizon, beyond the crests of hills and cemeteries, the sea glittered with a fiery light like the Mediterranean. Islands, mountains, light—it was these things that held out to us the mirage of happiness. But these people had turned away from them and were looking toward the machines which, even now, were biting into the hills. The road which would lead to the new city was already staked out between high palisades of bamboo shafts. In a little while we would be going back to the automatic elevators, the bathrooms, the orchestras and the whiskey of the Hotel Mandarin. Some of its servants probably lived right here. In their place, I think I would have hated the white man. They did not, or at least, they did not seem to.

"If the Nationalists decide to talk to you, we will be delighted to hear whatever nonsense they tell you. As for us, we will say nothing. Our revolution is not finished, nothing is definitely set yet. So why talk about it?"

"To say that much, at least."

"We see no useful purpose in it."

I was tempted to tell this wily character who had consented to receive me that the "we" he used seemed to me a symbol of enormous vanity, since his opinion was doubtless of very little importance when he made his periodic trips to Peking to get his orders. In Hong Kong, perhaps, at the meetings of the committee he directed with a geniality that concealed dictatorial authority, he might pretend to make his own decisions. Later, however, he would have to justify those decisions and wait

like a dog at the feet of his master for the word of approval that would
set his tail to wagging or the reproach that would send him cringing into
a corner. What did he hope for? A post as secretary general when the
regime took over Hong Kong? Or simply a certificate to hang on his
wall?

He was a very busy man, and very well protected. Access to the room
where we now sat was thoroughly screened by a succession of pass-
words and guards. In addition to his native tongue and English, he also
spoke French, quite easily and with a slightly slangy accent. Almost his
first words to me had been "Cher ami . . ." Dear friend? I was no dear
friend of his. The colleague who had introduced me had a cordial
working relationship with him, but no more than that. It was hardly a
basis for endearments.

But this was of no importance, since I was here, I had been in the
People's China and I wrote articles for newspapers; that was quite
enough to warrant his affection. No matter how small it might be, it was
possible that I might add one stone to the building of socialism. That
alone made me worthy of favorable treatment. I had been disappointed
by my experiences? Ah, well! There must have been some misunderstanding on their part of what I had wanted. Too bad! If he had known,
he might have put in a word with the proper authorities on his last visit
to Peking. Mistakes of judgment were sometimes made with Westerners
of goodwill who visited China. This, in fact, was where he played his
own role. But none of it was really important. A little whiskey? No?
Well, then, a cup of the traditional tea from Canton. This man's
cheerful loquacity reminded me of the fishwives and shopkeepers of
Marseille.

"You say nothing," I managed to put in, "because you do not know
what to say. Of course your revolution is not finished, and you do not
know where it will lead you in the future, but you also do not know what
you are going to do about Hong Kong. You are tempted to take it over,
but that would mean losing what it now brings you: 200 million American dollars for the merchandise you sell here; 200 million more sent to
their relatives in China, through your bank here, by the Chinese who live
in other countries; a million pounds sterling for fifteen billion gallons of
drinking water brought from the frontier by three pipelines. A gold mine
like that is not given up without thinking twice. But what is China's
basic interest? That is the real question."

He tapped me on the shoulder. This kind of talk pleased him. It was
the language of friends, and one did not always hear it in Peking. The
Communists here talked the same way. What I did not understand,
however, was their primary concern in keeping the revolution moving in
the right direction and not letting it be sidetracked. Had I been told that
every member of the administration spent one month every year in a

people's commune or factory, leading the life of the people and taking part in their work, so that he would not lose contact with them? Yes, I knew that. I also knew that all army officers, even generals, lost their rank and became private soldiers for one month of every year. That I admired.

"What you do not know perhaps," he said, "is that the Central Committee has carried this procedure even further. It is no longer for one month each year that officials will live with the masses, but one year in every three."

The colleague who had accompanied me sat up straight in his chair. Suddenly, this interview had become a scoop. This was news. A third of the entire administration at a time, everyone above the rank of office supervisor and below the age of fifty-five, was to be sent out into the industrial cities and the countryside. The measure, which was already in force, could include government ministers and the highest party officials themselves. There was already an expression for it. A man said he was going "to squat in the provinces." I suggested that "to retire" might be a better phrase. No; to squat, to sit back on one's heels, as many peasants did to eat. This signified that one could stand up again very quickly when there was another task to be undertaken.

Under this system, no one could possibly lose sight of the great revolution. The true aspirations of the people would always be present in one's mind, and mistakes would be avoided. It was because of this that some well-known officials had already disappeared from the scene. Without anyone being told, they had gone off for hundreds or thousands of miles, to squat on their heels and meditate. For a year? Perhaps even longer. Some of them might not return at all, if they were judged not to have gotten the message. And no one should be surprised if this happened; for it was in the basic interest of China. What other interest should be considered in directing a nation and a revolution?

I had hoped to be able to meet Chang Ko-tao, who lived in a villa at the southernmost extremity of Hong Kong, and question him about his reasons for holding Chu Teh and a part of the army of the Long March in northern Szechwan in 1935, and also about Mao, whom he had once described as a hero of the steppes, a peasant Robin Hood carved from solid stone and clothed in dreams of glory. I was forced to give up the idea. He was old, suffering from a cardiac condition and almost blind, and he had been so upset by the publicity given an earlier interview that he now refused to say anything more.

I spent an entire day with a group of Nationalist intellectuals. They avoided talking about Chiang Kai-shek. They retained little hope of ever taking part in a reconquest of the mainland, and blamed the Americans for the fact that there had never been even an attempt. "Why must they always interfere?" one professor demanded. "Why have they always prevented us from returning to the continent?" These Nationalists even went so far as to accuse the Americans of collusion with Mao Tse-tung in hopes of an agreement with him on sharing spheres of influence in the world.

It was apparent that many Nationalists still lived in a world of illusions. On the basis of information dating back several years, they had constructed a theory about the weakness of Mao Tse-tung's regime: a Nationalist reconnaissance plane shot down near Shanghai, and not over Peking, proved that the defensive installations were not reliable; a discreet inquiry, conducted among the members of the "imperial guard," had revealed that 60, out of a total of 240 men, had ideological doubts. I shrugged. The U-2's shot down from an altitude of fifty thousand feet proved that the Chinese possessed powerful and accurate weapons. The cadres and men of their army constituted a protective armor in which there was no flaw.

The most serious argument advanced by these Nationalists concerned the opposition to the Mao regime by a certain segment of his early associates who had been disillusioned by the elimination of P'êng Têh-huai. Apparently the removal of P'êng Têh-huai, who was born in Mao's own province of Hunan and once had been second only to Chu Teh, was due to his opposition to the people's communes and his sympathetic attitude toward Khrushchev. He had disappeared, along with ten other members of the Central Committee, in 1959. Even Lin Piao, who had succeeded him, was seldom seen.

"Why should a man like P'êng Têh-huai be the only one who disagreed?" I was asked. "The reasons that led him to oppose Mao Tse-tung still exist. We are certain that the regime is weaker than it would like to appear and really rests on a core of only five or six million fanatics."

The thing that impressed me most about these men was their frankness in manner and speech, and it led me to wonder whether they could belong to the same race as the mandarins of Communist China. They actually dared express a thought which was not in line with official thinking. They argued among themselves, and were not in the least hesitant about voicing disagreement. These were not the familiar monologues to which I had learned to listen as I might to a boring sermon. Here, in Hong Kong, people talked. The corner of China that was open to the wind from the West was no longer that enormous college of docile students and dogmatic professors, of slaves parading, applauding, working and resting at the command of their masters, who might be squatting in their midst. In the restaurant where we had lunch, there was a clamor of voices and laughter. We were the only foreigners there, and, looking around me, I recognized for the first time in China a kind of happiness that resembled our own. Would Tsai have seen a prostitute in each of the women and a banker or landlord in each of the men? No one stood up to propose toasts and no one needed to get drunk in order to be gay. There had been no attempt to organize an artificial atmosphere just for us. I had the feeling at last of being in a country where I would have been willing to live.

Brigitte was simply dragging along without any interest. We took the ferry to Kowloon, to try on the cashmere jackets we had ordered. She could not make up her mind about the cut of the lapels, and asked my advice. I consented to leaf through the style catalogues. She bought some Japanese transistor radios the size of match boxes, as gifts for friends. But this kind of activity did not really amuse her. Her curiosity was no longer stimulated by adversity and disappointment. She had been as unhappy and frustrated as I on the other side of the frontier, but her heart had remained there. Simon was worn out, and thought only of leaving.

One evening a friend took us on a night tour of Kowloon. For the first time, we saw the gambling dens of old China, with intense mah-jong players tossing their "tiles" noisily on the tables. In the street fortune-tellers kept birds in cages, and when a customer stopped, a bird was released to pluck a paper strip of horoscope from the handful offered to it. The music of flutes and accordions punctuated the more strident rhythms of this all-night fair, where people ate seated in the street and where everything imaginable was for sale, from candied fruits to clothing, watches and odd-looking toys. Filipino pickpockets roamed the bars in search of prey. The musty odor of turpentine and resin hung in the air, and the sirens of ships anchored in the harbor periodically shattered the night. Drunken sailors wandered up and down in search of girls. In a corner of the port that was a floating city of junks, prostitutes waited for their clients in sampans transformed into tearooms, and turned their eyes modestly away when we passed. Beacon lights winked on the hills above. Airplanes of every nationality, destined for every city on earth, took off and vanished into the blackness like shooting stars.

Brigitte was bored with all this, and kept complaining that we had not gone to Mongolia instead. "You might have seen a few Mongols," I said, "for a moment or two, through the window of an automobile." She insisted on clinging to the myth she had created in her mind. She did not share my pleasure at being with Chinese who did not worship at the shrine of Mao. She was already forgetting the many disappointments she had felt in Chungking.

The hydrofoil ferry hugged the banks of the islands, but even so the yellowish sea waters slammed against its hull, like the wind beneath the wings of a plane flying at low altitude in bad weather. I had a vague feeling of nausea, and tried to ignore the violent shudder that ran through the vessel whenever it hit a crest. Sometimes, trying to avoid the deeper troughs, the pilot cut the throttle sharply and then almost immediately shoved it forward again, causing an abrupt acceleration that flattened us against the back of our seats. Then we came into the shelter of the line of breakwaters and the sea became calm again. We could see a cluster of whitewashed houses against the dark background of the hill of Macao.

We rented an automobile and drove through the city, which seemed immersed in an unshakable lethargy. At some of the street corners stood little statues of Zouaves, one outstretched arm pointing to the location of shabby hotels. The day was gray and windy. When we reached the cobblestone square in front of the church and the Portuguese Jesuit mission house, a crowd of refugees was gathered for the daily distribution of spaghetti and noodles, and the air was filled with the wailing of children. Cats wandered over the corrugated-steel roof of the mission. The central courtyard was littered with piles of bricks and empty gasoline cans; a portion of one wall had been whitewashed, to form a screen for the showing of films. We saw a small chapel and some classrooms with worn and battered benches, each with its crucifix, ornamented with a withered bit of palm. The white-robed fathers went about their business with a tolerant good humor. In the midst of these utilitarian surroundings, the packages of food, the mounds of blankets and clothing seemed almost like an index file of charity.

I had been told: "In Macao you will see the real refugees from the People's China and they will talk to you." What sort of man fled from the Communist paradise? In the first ten days of that month, 175 of them had reached Macao, either by swimming or in sampans. I had a picture of the ordeals of the Long March in reverse. In reality, all that was necessary was to avoid the guards on some moonless night, get to the foot of the hills on the opposite shore and from there to the protection of the Portuguese gunboats that patrolled the demarcation line in the middle of the river between the two territories. In 1962, at the time of the famine that ravaged Communist China, almost eleven thousand refugees had poured into Macao; in 1963, almost four thousand; in 1964, more than two thousand. The situation inside China was improving, and the frontier was better guarded. But in spite of risks, people still came.

I would have liked to ask my friend Tsai about the fate of those who were arrested. Of the 159 people living near the frontier who had fled their homeland in October, 1964, there were 92 peasants, 14 unskilled laborers, 7 fishermen, some electricians, a miner, a maker of incense, a butcher, 2 carpenters, a bricklayer, a mason and 28 children. More than half of them were between the ages of eighteen and thirty. The old people were apparently resigned to dying in their own homes; but the young, in whom I had thought I saw the solid foundation of the regime—were they thinking of deserting it? What gradually took possession of them, seeped through their minds and into the marrow of their bones and gave them the courage to break the tie with their country? The illusion that, when they had reached the other side, they would be on the shore of a river of gold?

In the camp where they were kept for a month, supposedly the time required to find them work, families were crowded together, doing their cooking in the open on little portable stoves. Children and adults alike wandered through the barracks-like shelters, distraught with anxiety and the lack of occupation. The liberty they had attained was no longer of any use. They looked like people whose pockets were filled with a currency no one would accept. In the dining hall some were devouring the rice served them in heaping ladles. They sat hunched over their bowls, swallowing greedily, and when they looked up their eyes were sad.

I talked to one boy of eighteen, with a full, round face, and another of twenty-one, with a mass of rebellious hair, prominent cheekbones and the look of a lost dog. It was certainly not hunger that had forced them to escape. This, at least, was what I thought, but they both told me that they had been employed in production brigades where the average salary was forty yuans a month per family, and that they could not have lived without the money sent to them from Hong Kong by relatives. One of the boys' families numbered seven; the other, eight. But I had seen hogs and poultry in families of this size everywhere I went. In the villages they came from, there was nothing to feed to animals. I had been shown only the richer countryside.

I asked them if they had been afraid during their escape.

"Yes," the older one said. "For a moment I was afraid the Portuguese police were going to hand me over to the Communists."

His parents had died of hunger in 1959. Things had been going a little better since that time, but 90 percent of the people were dissatisfied with the regime. In that case, why did they not revolt?

"Because we have no weapons. Because anyone who shows his discontent is arrested. Because there are only twenty-five pounds of rice each month for each worker, and even this is held back if they are not sure of your loyalty. How could we revolt under conditions like that?"

Any escape had to be planned with the greatest care and in the greatest secrecy. One woman had taken her four children with her when she left Canton, but she had had to plan for months to be sure that she would find a family that would help her somewhere near the frontier. For someone living in Canton, it was possible to evade the police and district leaders and cover a distance of sixty miles on foot. But not thousands of miles. For people in Shanghai or Chungking, liberation came only with death.

"In that case," I said, "what would happen if the West had territories such as Hong Kong and Macao on all of the frontiers of China?"

The interpreter burst out laughing. He translated my question. His laughter swept through the dining hall, becoming a piercing yelp that shattered my eardrums. At last the guide answered me. "There would be no more Chinese in China," he said.

I was not convinced. I went back to the younger boy, thinking again that he resembled a stray dog who has found a house where he can lie down for a moment without fear of being chased away. He was picking his teeth methodically with a little splinter of wood and his eyes were gloomy. "You may find it difficult living here," I said. "Someday you will have had enough of shantytowns and social injustices. Over there they will be happy to welcome you back and show you off as an example. So you will go back."

He made the interpreter repeat what I had said, and then looked up at me. The expression in his eyes had changed. It was dark and stormy now.

"Never," he said loudly, shaking his head.

Again I regretted that Tsai was not with me. Then I asked myself if the Chinese might not be deceiving me again, even here. Even when I feared the things they might do, I admired the Communists, but I did not admire these men, I did not even like them. How then could I be sure of their good faith, their patriotism and the unselfishness of their motives? I might have been duped by the men of one side, but if I listened too complacently to the men of the other, could I avoid falling into their trap?

Chapter 23
Reflections on the Chinese phenomenon and the difficulty of penetrating it. The author meditates on the realities of the yellow peril and on the reasons that the Empire at the Center of the World is separated from the rest of the world. Why the official text of the interview with Marshal Chen Yi has been deprived of its force and originality. Reflections on what it is that separates Chinese truth from pure truth and Chinese liberty from pure liberty.

> We realize that all this must seem fantastic to our readers—this vast army, this avalanche of men descending from the high plateaus of Asia, as they did in the times of Genghis Khan, these numberless Chinese ships crossing all the oceans of the world and casting anchor in our ports. We ourselves are sometimes inclined to think that these things will never occur, and yet when one knows China well . . .
>
> —E. R. Huc, *The Chinese Empire*

Casting about for a means of approaching this continent, watching it draw near in all its majesty, the navigator is left with a feeling of helplessness. Everywhere he looks, the cliffs drop sheer into the sea, the mountains are covered with forests. "Beyond a hundred rivers, beyond a thousand mountains . . ." But there are a hundred other rivers, a thousand other mountains, and no end in sight. The urge to set foot on the soil of this empire and unravel its mystery gives way to the despairing realization that it will never be solved. The plains themselves reach to infinity. All the villages are built of the same mud and clay, all the rice fields blossom at the same time, all the herds of swine devour the same roots, all the men are weighed down by the same burden of labor. Who could hope to create order out of this chaos? Which explorer, knowing his time to be too short, would not be tempted to abandon the thought of ever understanding what centuries have wrought behind these all but impassable mountains, deserts and typhoon-racked seas.

Nothing in China is built to that human scale which makes it possible to separate lies from truths and reason from madness. In order to survive in the eternal struggle, man must sacrifice his own life for the survival of his children, conquer not only the injustice of other men but the sun and the waters, famine and plague. The Chinese revolution, which is the refusal to serve any longer the century-old masters, was born of a flame kindled in the hearts of untold millions, stamped out, rekindled, stamped out again and finally bursting free. Oceans, rivers, catastrophes, rebellions, all of man's accomplishments—whatever words one uses to speak of China take on the legendary weight of centuries.

It is not at all unusual for a Chinese scholar at the age of eighty, to be still taking examinations, studying the pronunciation of thousands of new words and practicing each day the tonal differences which alter their meaning. A lifetime of study may just barely permit a Westerner to move through this world without making too many mistakes. Under such circumstances one is tempted to leave the study of China to those lofty professors. They spend their entire careers arguing among themselves, deciphering poetic texts, studying customs, and when an outsider ventures to ask their advice he is given the feeling that he has interrupted some private meditation.

I had labored for six months and had accumulated twenty pounds of notes before leaving for China, yet I had known nothing. I know very little more today. My library overflowed with novels, essays, volumes of statistics and philosophy. All those who have taken China's pulse have arrived at the same fatal and unalterable diagnosis: there is a rhythm of order and disorder, alternating every second century, which condemns the country to an endless cycle of grandeur and misery. The reading of even a fraction of what had been written on the subject was a dizzying enterprise, but a single look at China itself was worth more than the contents of all these books.

Yet I had only gone from hotel to hotel and from city to city, always escorted by my little group of mandarins. I would have been happy to tell the great story of the crossing of the Tatu River, or to fly by military plane across the snowy mountain ranges that once had been the only shelter of the remnants of Mao Tse-tung's and Chu Teh's armies. Is it my fault that I was instructed to put no questions about the past to any of those government figures I did meet? Is it my fault that the bulk of our conversations concerned nothing but commonplaces, that the mere thought of friendship between our two peoples was expected to bring tears to my eyes, and that our guides were happy only when they knew we were safely in our rooms or in the sleeping compartment of a train, with our cameras stowed away for the night?

I would have understood some initial mistrust, but the truth is that they continued to act more and more fearful that we might discover something. My reputation as a man of the left (whose origins are, to say the least, dubious) had been useful in our dealings with the Chinese Embassy in Paris, but before reaching Peking a reputation must survive a journey not just of ten thousand miles but of ten thousand light-years. China has never devoted much time to the study of Western ideas, and for the past fifteen years Karl Marx has taken the place of literature in the universities. Possibly Bernard Shaw, Thomas Mann and André Gide may be known to them by the year 2000. The imperialist William Faulkner will certainly still be unknown. In the Empire at the Center of the World, the matter of what the West may think is of no concern to anyone, and it was only after a series of shocking disasters that they decided there might be some point in copying its methods of production. The works of Mao Tse-tung surround the libraries like a new Great Wall, and one of the most intelligent peoples on earth is on the way to becoming one of the most stupid. A socialist stupidity, content with itself, its statistics and its own system of self-criticism, which employs the humiliation of the individual as a means of glorifying the regime.

As for me, I was only a writer. To the Chinese, whose acquaintance with writers is limited to those approved by the government, this meant that I was no more than a paid scribe. That I should have the temerity or naïveté to undertake to write the story of the Chinese revolution was simply one more preposterous idea of these barbarians from beyond the seas. The emperors and their court archivists and scholars had arranged history to their own liking. Mao Tse-tung, Chiang Kai-shek and their disciples see no reason to change the pattern. They are supremely indifferent to the fact that books about them may be published in London or Berlin. They will never be read in China, and if it seems necessary they will fabricate their own versions.

What Chinese does not believe that he both possesses and serves the cause of truth? But it is an elliptical form of truth which has nothing in common with ours. How could I claim that I intended to write the history of the revolution when I ignored the display cases in the museums? What insight into the future could I have when I seemed so badly informed about the past? Confucius, who still occasionally cited as a reference, had used the history of vanished dynasties to foretell the actions of future ones. What dark intrigue was concealed behind my passion for dates? Of what use were all these details about individuals when history belonged to the past and what was important now was not to alter its course but to dam it up, just as all the rivers of China had been dammed, to prevent them from ever again overflowing their banks? If necessary, new texts were written or old ones modified, as often as might be necessary to align the past with the present. The same thing had been done for Mao Tse-tung, so that the prophet of the revolution should not appear less great than its theorist.

This tinkering with documents annoyed no one but me. In the eyes of the Chinese it was a matter of small consequence to adjust the truth when reality descended on it like a river flowing into the sea. Once all these waters had mingled, no one was disturbed by the thought that their original course might have been altered by men. But I could still see the layers of mud and silt that dirtied the estuary. I was not far enough away from the shore.

"The Chinese know nothing of liberty." That confession was made by Dr. Sun Yat-sen, the Father of the Revolution, who noted that the very word "liberty" was of recent importation and added that the Chinese actually possessed too much liberty. His ghostly shade can rejoice. There is no more liberty. Is an eel free to leave the migrating horde when it assembles off the coasts of Europe for the journey to the spawning ground in the Caribbean? The notion of liberty has no more meaning for the Chinese than it has for the migrating eel. Slaves by vocation, they want to choose their own master, and once this master has been crowned no one complains of his harshness, especially when he provides food and a sense of dignity the slaves have not known before. The fact that no one has the right to receive his own mother in his house without notifying the district leader is simply one of the rules to which everyone willingly submits, to assure the security of the state. And it would never enter anyone's head to protest because a neighbor suspected of a lack of enthusiasm was sent off to a people's commune for a period of re-education.

What foundations are there that might support a demand for greater freedom, when no one knows anything of the West except the example of Stalinist Russia and the specter of American imperialism? And who could rid the Chinese of their illusions? They know about events in the outside world only through their radio and their newspapers. They ask no questions of the few foreigners they see, and when I asked questions of them, what could they reply, surrounded by the mandarins of my escort? At the University of Peking I tried to learn what the students of French knew of America and Europe: nothing but the stupidities that were endlessly repeated to them. Nothing but a sense of profound pity for our obscurantism and despotism. In China our working class is thought to be crushed beneath the whiplash of capitalist landlords and merchants.

In this country where everyone has acquaintances who are always ready to denounce him and no one has friends, I asked myself if a student would ever dare to confide the doubts that might cross his mind to a comrade. In private, certainly not. In public, self-criticism is one of the sacraments of education. Once this time of forbearance has passed, one does not relapse in one's faith without inviting the accusation of deviationism. In this enormous barracks where everyone else lives in a similar compartment, no two people are ever really alone. There are no confessionals in China, but there are tribunals, and if one has occasion to repent, it is here that one goes to confess.

In former times there was a practice, by no means always practiced, that anyone who was oppressed could strike on the great gong that stood in the inner courtyard of the tribunal and the mandarin would come out, at noon or at midnight, to listen to his complaint. Now no one, not even a government minister, is entirely safe from false accusations which one cannot appeal.

Chapter 24

In which the author, dwelling on the person of the Emperor of China and on that of Mao Tse-tung, attempts to describe the leader of China and the basis of his strength and greatness. How a terrible weakness might cause the destruction of the Chinese colossus if it dares provoke the American giant. Why the Americans are tempted to attack China and put a final ending to all of their previous mistakes, and how the West conducted itself in sending its missionaries, its traders and its soldiers to the Empire at the Center of the World. In which the question arises of the possibility of another Dienbienphu in the event of war with China. Why the West will witness still further surprises. In which the author concludes his journey with a melancholy report.

. . . when one knows China well, this empire of 300 million inhabitants, when one knows its resources in population and in the soil of these rich and fertile provinces, one wonders what would be required for this people to shake the earth and exercise a great influence in human affairs. What is lacking, perhaps, is a man; that is all—but a man of vast genius, a truly great man, capable of bringing together all the power and life in this nation, more populous than all Europe and with a heritage of more than thirty centuries of civilization. If there should arise an emperor endowed with a broad view of the world and a will of steel, a reformer, determined to break with the old traditions and initiate his people in the progressive achievements of the West, we believe this task of regeneration would move forward swiftly and that a time would come when these Chinese who are today considered so ridiculous might be taken very seriously, and even awaken mortal anxiety in those who lust so greedily for the spoils of the old nations of Asia.

—E. R. Huc, *The Chinese Empire*

The adversary is now familiar with our habits, but he can neither prevent our victory nor avoid our blows, since he does not know when or where we will strike. That we keep to ourselves.

—Mao Tse-tung, *Strategic Problems*

More than a century ago, after having narrowly escaped shipwreck on the Yangtze, only to find himself in the midst of an armed conflict between Chinese and Manchus, Father Huc noted down some of his

286

thoughts on the destiny of China. In the first half of this century, the emperor he dreamed of arose and took his place on the throne, acclaimed as the father and the mother of the people, served by a court of new noblemen and guarded by extremely efficient police. No one ever knew where this emperor was, where he might be going or where he had come from, nor even if he would be present at public ceremonies. Did he travel in an automobile with drawn curtains or in some invisible machine, using the underground passages with which Peking is honeycombed? Just as the emperors once had confined their movements to the sheltering darkness of night, there was nothing now to signal his arrival or departure. Suddenly, there would be a stir of voices, rising to a storm when he appeared, to the accompaniment of a fanfare of music and the glow of a hundred beams of light focused on his person.

Since no ornaments had ever been worthy of their majesty, the emperor habitually wore only a long robe of brown silk and a cap of black velvet with a single pearl. Mao went them one better. Garbed in a gray sack in which holes had been cut for his arms and legs, weighed down with glory and years, smiling at the ovation and replying to it with his own applause, in the socialist manner, he moved across the platform as heavily as though he were returning from the Long March. Occasionally, he would cover his nakedly gleaming forehead with a shapeless cap which he waved at the crowd, in a gesture reminiscent of a farewell from the door of a train. There was nothing very imperial in the wave of a cap, but it never failed to unleash new ovations. To each prince, his own formula. If the flick of a cap was all that was required to release torrents of love from the masses, the Mao dynasty saw no reason for employing grander methods. A word of command sent out to the district leaders would call forth the million or so men, women and children who were always ready, day or night, to display their devotion in an orderly and dignified manner.

This apparent simplicity conceals an organization which is both as flexible and as rigid as any in existence. No one has ever seen Mao surrounded by guards. To what purpose, since every member of the party is also a member of his guard and no one knows the location of his palace? From experience of the early clandestine struggles and the trials of the Long March, the Mao dynasty has retained its policy of keeping strictly secret the actual seat of government and the minutes of the meetings of the Central Committee. If there is dissension, it is never known until the excommunications have been revealed and the instigators of trouble eliminated. The deepest and widest moats defending the regime are still those of ideology.

Since the day Mao became uncontested master of the empire, his bust, his statue and his portrait have occupied the place reserved for the leader of a new dynasty. When he is gone, could anyone ascend the throne by repudiating him? When the time comes, the strongest of many possible successors will undoubtedly prevail. One or another of them is occasionally given his chance to be seen and heard, and each is prudent enough to identify himself with the reigning emperor, whose shadow covers all China and whose power and glory will follow him into the tomb. For it has taken thousands of years for China to produce Mao and he has been long awaited. If his only victory had been a retreat, there would have been many names in history greater than his. But even Napoleon did no more than alter for a time the balance of a continent, while Mao Tse-tung has upset the balance of the globe by throwing into the scales the lives of 700 million poor men.

In seeking for comparisons, it is necessary to go back to the founders of empires and religions. He is a more important figure than Alexander the Great, but until very few years ago the world was undisturbed by any suspicion of his military strength. Like Peter the Great, he has realized that his backward country must imitate the West if it is to attain its full effectiveness. Like Christ and Mohammed, he has sown across the globe the seed of a new mystique whose harvest is still uncertain. Lenin, Karl Marx, Stalin? There is not a philosopher or statesman to whose words or actions he refers who has not been surpassed, swallowed up, digested and made as Chinese as Mao himself. Sheh Huang Ti, the unifier of the empire, is a child compared with the leader of the Long March.

Until the beginning of the twentieth century, how many Westerners had set foot on the soil of China at Shanghai or Canton without knowing, consciously or unconsciously, that they were there to oppress and exploit? The treasures stolen by our soldiers in Peking are still on sale in the antique shops of France and England. The bas-reliefs, the great carved gateways and the enormous monochrome vases which could not be carried off were smashed with the butts of rifles, and coffins were broken open in search of jewels.

Like the Manchus before us, we thought of nothing but filling our own pockets. Cheap labor and human fodder for the mines and plantations of the tropics where no white man could work—this was what we wanted, and if the Chinese resisted, the artillery opened fire. Our armies left behind them some missionaries who distributed Bibles translated into Chinese and attempted to dethrone Confucius and replace him with Christ. When the good Father Huc urged Napoleon III to undertake a crusade for the conversion of China, he envisaged it as being Biblically meek and humble, and he was highly indignant when he realized that it was serving only as a pretext for the opium traffic.

Bearing this in mind, I do not blame the Chinese for being nationalists. In their place, I would probably be as nationalist as they, simply through hatred of my former masters. What I blame them for is pretending that they are not. In essence, therefore, I blame the Chinese for lying.

History is an endless series of beginnings. It never stops repeating the same formulas, the same violences and the same contradictions. Looking back on the events of the last century, one is amazed at the stubbornness with which men whose ideas are rooted in the past have refused to understand that the past is as dead as those who lived in it. Had they learned the lesson of revolutions and global wars, they might have understood the triumph of the "underprivileged." But they did and do not. Years ago, a Chinese doctor returning to his native land with a European diploma was treated with contempt by his Western colleagues, in spite of the fact that most of them were men who had failed in their chosen profession at home. They did everything possible to create difficulties for their upstart rivals, and until 1927 if a Chinese citizen attempted to bring such a matter into court, he was judged, in his own country, by a foreign tribunal.

Yet if the West did not take more than it did, is it because it could not? The sins of the West must be weighed on the scale of history. The Nazi crimes would be considered less important if they had only exterminated fifty thousand Jews. If we use the same ratio, the West did not deport fifty million Chinese but 500,000, and it could be said that this was no more than the number of victims of one rather minor famine. We are guilty, but a good deal less guilty than the Communist party, and not to the extent of deserving the death penalty. If one just man could atone for our sins, that man exists. He was Flemish and his name was Frédéric Lebbe. A Lazarist missionary, like Father Huc, he lived as the Chinese did and embraced all their sentiments and causes. When his European brothers refused to condone this behavior, he was forced to leave the order. He cried out to the West, "You are making a mistake. We are not your servants." To the Chinese he said, "Do not look at my nose or my eyes. Look into my heart: I am Chinese."

The first Chinese atomic bomb caused no major astonishment. It had been expected in the capitals of the West, and was greeted without too much apprehension. Until now, it has required a period of years before such a mechanism could be made transportable, or, in the terms used by military men, "operational." Some of the journalists who were in Peking in October, 1964, reassured themselves by resorting to such obsolete formulas. Of what use was a bomb that could not be strategically employed?

It was naïve to think that the Chinese, who had invented both gunpowder and the compass, could not manufacture an airplane capable of carrying the bomb. They were already manufacturing Mig fighter planes and Ferguson tractors, by the simple expedient of copying them. I remembered that there must still be in China at least 250 of the 400 Ilyushin 28's the Russians had given them, and that these planes had an effective range of almost two thousand miles. Obviously, one would need to at least double this if the pilots were not to be deliberately sacrificed. But until such time as the Chinese possess missiles capable of threatening the American continent itself, such a plane is quite sufficient to reach all American bases in Southeast Asia. Nothing and no one can completely halt a wave of two hundred bombers.

The formula the Central Committee of the party came up with to dispel the shadow of the Chinese atomic cloud did not rid me of my fears. Too many secrets and too many unspoken ambitions lurked behind this benevolent façade. Everyone in China lied too much and too well. When the Western press published reports of an imminent Chinese atomic explosion a week before it actually took place, government officials had categorically denied them. They had even denounced the reports as just another proof of neurotic American suspicions. Reality proved that, in this instance at least, the Americans were not mistaken. Analysis of the cloud, however, dumfounded Western experts: with her first explosion, China had shown evidence of a technique superior to that of the British and French tests which had been going on for several years. China was progressing more rapidly than anyone had thought possible.

The second explosion, just seven months later, demonstrated that the mysterious factory where the bombs were produced really did exist. And, in fact, American U-2's photographed it at just about that time, near Lanchow, on the banks of the Yellow River. Moreover, it would now have to be accepted as fact that the bomb had become a genuinely strategic weapon and could be carried in a plane or fixed in the nose cone of a missile. If this explosion had not taken place, the experts would have concluded that unexpected difficulties had arisen. I would have said that the Chinese had simply by-passed further experiments, but that the weapon was ready. Some accounts caused even further consternation among Western technicians by claiming that the bomb was contained in the nose cone of a missile and had been exploded while the missile was in flight.

I suspected, at the time, that there very probably had been some dissimulation of the actual facts. Prime Minister Chou En-lai is so thoroughly convinced that the West's judgment of China is erroneous that he did not even bother to conceal this from Edgar Snow. The Americans consider themselves to be extremely well informed, but they are repeating the same mistake committed by the French high command in Indochina, and estimating their opponent to be less powerful than he is. The endless chain of fighter planes I chanced to see in Tsinan, taking off and landing without the slightest pause, in defiance of all the rules of usage for jet planes, proved that China was turning out pilots on an assembly line, giving them only the elementary reflexes they absolutely needed. Kamikaze pilots do not have to be trained to sit at the controls of a deluxe airliner, and the equipment they are given lasts only the length of time required for a single suicide mission. It is not, therefore, imprudent to foresee a time in the very near future when the Chinese will be capable of bringing down American bombers or of striking with weapons which their own denials, naïvely accepted, have led us to believe they do not yet possess. During those October days in Peking I told myself that the first Chinese atomic bomb was like the bridges we had seen, whose existence is denied until they have been built and tested and are in use. The bomb would be exploded only because it was no longer possible to go further without one test. Other bombs might be ready, but there would be no need for testing them, since they would have learned from one test what they had to know for all.

At Dienbienphu, on a smaller scale, one of Mao Tse-tung's pupils, General Vo nguyen Giap, had employed tactical and strategic surprise to bring about one of the most far-reaching defeats in recent Western history. No one believed in the existence of Vietminh artillery until it opened fire on the French citadel. Experts in such matters had been brought in from Korea and had reassured the French commander, General de Castries, on the excellence of his defensive system. Just three months before the attack on the fortified camp, French technicians wrote: "It is highly unlikely that the enemy would fire on even our outermost positions at any time when the weather permits good observation. He would draw an immediate response." No one at Dienbienphu had observed the arrival of a single enemy cannon. They had been brought there, however, towed behind trucks over roads through the mountains no one had seen being built. No shred of information ever indicated that they were being put in place. Yet they were there, sheltered beneath layers of rock in casemates no one had seen being dug. In order to conform with the ideas held by the French general staff, such cannon, if they really did exist, would have been set up on the reverse slopes of the ridges surrounding the camp. The Vietminh chose to ignore the finer points of Western military strategy and placed them in hollows or on the forward slopes, where they could fire at point-blank range and from direct observation. The French strategists were scandalized; such things were not taught in their war colleges.

If their pupil Giap, with an army drawn from a region of only ten million inhabitants, could achieve such a victory against a powerful Western enemy, is it unreasonable to think that the Chinese marshals envisage victory on a scale fifty times greater? Dams in China are built with wheelbarrows and little baskets, not with bulldozers as they are in America. "Attack only when you are sure of victory." Giap had learned this principle from the military writings of Mao Tse-tung, who had himself adapted it from the rules of Sun Tzŭ. And Sun Tzŭ had also written: "At one time, those who were experienced in combat never engaged in wars which they foresaw might end with their dishonor. Before undertaking them, they were sure of success. If the circumstances did not seem propitious, they awaited a more favorable opportunity. According to them, one was vanquished through his own fault and victorious through the fault of his enemies." Why should the master cease to practice the teaching he has passed on to his disciples?

After my return to France, when I read the Chinese statement meant to reassure the rest of the world about their atomic explosion, I could not help but smile: "We have no desire whatever to utilize nuclear weapons as a means of augmenting our national prestige and acquiring a greater influence in international affairs. . . ." If the event itself had come as a surprise to those experts who are always ready to explain everything after it has happened, why should anyone assume that no other surprises would follow? It had required a century to build the Great Wall, ten years to dig the Grand Canal, one year to complete the Long March. The bombs will be turned out at a rate that will change all the initial forecasts.

For some time, I debated with myself as to whether the account of this journey was really worth setting down. It bears so little resemblance to what people in the West expect to hear about China, and even less to the fairy tales the sycophants and the blind have brought back. Like myself, they have been wined and dined at the expense of the Chinese people, and they will at least have shown their gratitude. Yet it would never occur to them to go to live there.

I was certain that China's generosity was a mockery, China's innocence a swindle, China's love for peace a lie. I knew that the Emperor Mao Tse-tung, founder of the new people's dynasty, and his whole silent and mournful court of hirelings dreamed of nothing but revenge. But I was a man like other men, and I had not left Europe with empty hands and a listless heart. I became the subject matter of my book because the Chinese had not wanted me to write about them.

When I wrote this book, the stars and the moon in the night sky over Burgundy seemed frozen. Silence walled me in. I was suddenly aware of being alone again, withdrawn from the world and face to face with an enterprise that had begun badly. As I began this book and once again stepped across the frontier of the People's China, it was not only to Tsai that I had returned, but toward everything that had formed the sum of my life and being. For a while everything had disappeared, almost by chance, like the lights of a ship seen across a night-dark sea. Oddly, I felt a surge of contentment at the thought that I was going to bury myself in the winter and force this book into life. I may perhaps never see the blossoming of the rosebushes, the clematis and honeysuckle I planted last autumn, because a new war may have carried me away, but others, for whom I worked without knowing it, will see them in my place and all will be well. The tide of despair I had felt filled me with a kind of savage happiness.

China was at the other end of the earth.

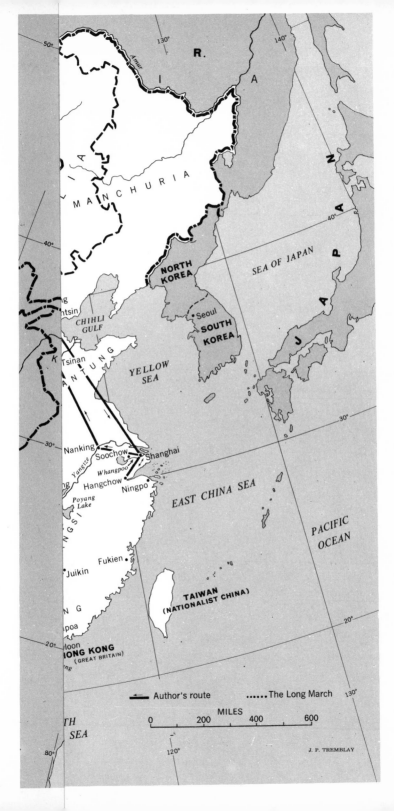

R.

Amur

MANCHURIA

NORTH
KOREA

SEA OF JAPAN

J A P A N

CHIHLI
GULF

Seoul

SOUTH
KOREA

Tsinan

ANTUNG

YELLOW
SEA

Nanking

Soochow

Shanghai

Yangtze

Whangpoo

Hangchow

Ningpo

*Poyang
Lake*

EAST CHINA SEA

PACIFIC
OCEAN

Fukien

Juikin

TAIWAN
(NATIONALIST CHINA)

poa

loon

HONG KONG
(GREAT BRITAIN)

━━► Author's route ⋯⋯ The Long March

MILES

0   200   400   600

TH

SEA

J. P. TREMBLAY

Index